French-Speaking Africa
Since Independence

PRAEGER LIBRARY OF AFRICAN AFFAIRS

The Praeger Library of African Affairs is intended to provide clear, authoritative, and objective information about the historical, political, cultural, and economic background of modern Africa. Individual countries and groupings of countries will be dealt with as will general themes affecting the whole continent and its relations with the rest of the world. The library appears under the general editorship of Colin Legum, with Philippe Decraene as consultant editor.

Already Published

French-Speaking Africa Since Independence

GUY DE LUSIGNAN

FREDERICK A. PRAEGER, *Publishers*

New York · Washington · London

FREDERICK A. PRAEGER, Publishers
111 Fourth Avenue, New York, N.Y. 10003, U.S.A.
5 Cromwell Place, London S.W.7, England

Published in the United States of America in 1969
by Frederick A. Praeger, Inc., Publishers

© 1969 in London, England, by Guy de Lusignan

All rights reserved

Library of Congress Catalog Card Number: 76–76091

Printed in Great Britain

To my wife Suzanne

1. Africa

Contents

Contents

Acknowledgements

UNLIKE many books on Africa which have been published as a result of one- or two-year surveys requested and financed by research agencies, foundations or universities, this book results from a long stay in Africa which took me, with my family, first to Brazzaville from 1959 to 1961, then to Lagos from 1961 to 1963 and finally to Algiers from 1963 to 1964. Thanks to my professional assignments, I was lucky enough to spend about six years of my life on the African continent and to travel extensively in what is called 'Black Africa' and also, during the latter part of my stay, in the Algerian Sahara. The idea of writing this book arose from a series of lectures on the development of African countries under colonisation which I gave to a very receptive group of students from Congo-Brazzaville, Gabon and the Central African Republic at the Centre d'Etudes Supérieures (now the University) of Brazzaville. However, I had to wait until I was in Algeria to conceive and start this work. Since this occupation was strictly extra-curricular and since there are only twenty-four hours in a day, it was impossible to complete it until now. In fact, I would not have been able to finish it without the most efficient and understanding co-operation of my wife, a former correspondent of *Le Monde* in Brazzaville, who played a major role in preparing the first draft of the English text, the whole book having been thought out and written in French. We also worked together taking notes on various books, newspapers, reviews, periodicals, etc. It is because this book is a joint effort and venture that I have dedicated it to her.

I should also like to express my warmest thanks to Nadine Fendley for the excellent job she made of revising the translation, to my secretary Monica Baker for her efficiency and conscientiousness in typing the final version of the manuscript, and to Madeleine Moraillon who typed some parts of the drafts. I should also like to express my gratitude to Pierre Terver, Mamoudou Touré,

ix

French-Speaking Africa Since Independence

Françoise Biro, Arslan Humbaraci, Robin Bishop, Colin Legum, Derick Mirfin and Ross Pye for their suggestions and encouragement.

The opinions and comments expressed in this book are my own and do not reflect the official views of any institution with which I have been or am today connected.

Preface

THIS WORK is divided into three parts. The first part, "French-Speaking Africa becomes Independent, or de Gaulle's Africa", and the third part, "Final Clarifications and Conclusions", embrace a series of chapters, as brief as possible, on themes relating to the French-speaking African world as a whole, concerned chiefly with its political evolution and, incidentally, with its economic development. The economic data presented in this book support the political data. The description of the political evolution covers the whole period up to late 1968. The economic data, is based on the most recent information—i.e., generally not beyond the years 1965–66—because there is a certain lack of statistics in Africa and also because a clear-cut reference year seemed desirable. An attempt has been made to give the main resources of the countries, and to give some facts related to their budgetary and trade balances; but it has not been possible, unfortunately, to give precise information on balances of payments. These are established on a global basis for each of the components of the French franc area: the West Africa monetary union, the Central Africa monetary union (former Equatorial Africa), and Madagascar. However, some countries do try to figure out their own balances. The objective in the chapters of Part II is to treat each country individually, as factually and as concisely as possible; the chapters of the first and last parts aim at highlighting the overall problems.

General de Gaulle has left his mark on Africa. The first chapter tries to explain why and to show how French policy was pushed towards decolonisation. African events forced de Gaulle to change his decisions quicker than he had initially expected. During the war years, 1940–45, he used the French overseas territories as a stepping stone to strengthen his power and to ensure the legitimacy of the French Republic and the French nation. To express his gratitude and that of the French people, he reaffirmed the need to integrate and 'assimilate' overseas peoples with the French people within the French Union, the new form of the French Empire. During his years in the wilderness between 1946 and 1958, he witnessed the deterioration of the French Union as a result of the irresponsibility and incapability of the parties then in power. When he came back to office he gave assurances to the African peoples and granted them, first of all self-government within the French Community, and then, under the pressure of a series of events, independence. The French colonial administration and French private interests were thus obliged to change their attitude completely. Instead of colonising, they had to 'co-operate'. However, in spite of independence, France maintains even to this day an undercover and cryptic political influence which is difficult to analyse. Maybe in a few years' time we shall be able to reveal the *real* history of neo-colonialism in French-speaking Africa.

Chapter 2 focuses on African problems as seen from Africa. It tries not only to explain how and on what basis the French overseas territories became independent, but to bring to light the fundamental contradictions that the Africans are facing after independence.

The last two chapters of the book show that the new Africa has to grapple with various very serious dangers. Africa is divided. While my wife and I were in Africa, we recognised the desire of our African friends to proclaim at all costs the need for African unity. We tried to believe that Africa could be considered as a whole— geographically, socially, politically. But this is not true. One must be reasonable and use one's judgment; one must have the courage to say that the countries of East Africa are different from those of West Africa, that the countries to the north of the Sahara are profoundly different from those to the south. We, in Europe, know how stirring and stimulating is the idea of unity. We can believe in a united Europe and we can appreciate that Africans would like to believe in a united Africa. However, regional structures, which can be achieved in Africa in the same way as in the Europe of the Six, may perhaps be more viable and more suited to Africa. French-speaking Africa can be divided into three major communities: former Equatorial Africa, including Cameroun; the countries of the Entente Sahel-Bénin (Ivory Coast, Dahomey, Togo, Niger, Upper Volta); and finally, the neighbouring countries of the river Senegal basin (Mauritania, Mali, Senegal, Guinea) which have now established a formal organisation. However, these regional gatherings cannot develop unless Guinea revises its economic and financial policies as Mali has, and unless the rich countries of the coast assist as much as they can the land-locked countries of the savannah belt. Last but not least, these regional communities will be able to survive provided there are no series of pronunciamentos and provided also that they stick together.

In this respect the signature in early April 1968 of the Charter of the United States of Central Africa by Congo-Kinshasa, Chad and the Central African Republic seemed most unfortunate. In the first place, when this new grouping was proposed, it was not received with much enthusiasm by Gabon, Cameroun and Congo-Brazzaville, members with Chad and the Central African Republic of the Union Douanière et Economique d'Afrique Centrale (UDEAC). The new agreement caused the virtual collapse of this very important and successful customs union. Secondly, what advantages would Chad and the Central African Republic gain from a union with such a large country as Congo-Kinshasa? The economies of Chad and the Central African Republic have always been tied to and dependent on transport via the Congo river down to Brazzaville and then via the Brazzaville–Pointe Noire railroad. Would this have changed? Thirdly, the Transcamerounais, a railroad which will cross the whole of Cameroun from Yaoundé to Fort Lamy, will, when completed, become the normal transport route of Chad. In a sense, from the point of view of a united Africa or of the regionalisation of Africa, it was a pity that such a new grouping could not assemble all the members of UDEAC, particularly since Congo-Kinshasa belongs to the Organisation Commune Africaine et Malgache (OCAM). Just as this book went to press (in December 1968), it was learned that this new union had collapsed, as a result of deterioration in relations between the Central African Republic and Congo-Kinshasa. The UDEAC is likely to revive, with its original members (except for Chad, for the time being).

But what of the relationship between French-speaking and English-speaking Africa? Some international organisations—for instance, the Commission for Technical Co-operation in Africa— have tried to urge French-speaking and English-speaking African states to discuss their problems jointly. Can there be a real dialogue between English-speaking and French-speaking Africans, whether, for instance, within the Economic Commission for Africa or the Organisation for United Africa? Is it possible for an Economic Community of West Africa, for example, to establish itself not only on paper but in reality? Is it possible to contemplate regionalisation schemes whereby countries would distribute among themselves regional development projects? Could the countries of one region agree to share one large project, such as a power station, a steel factory or a textile plant, without each one wishing to have such industrial projects set up in their own countries? May I express my scepticism at this stage. It seems to me that French-speaking Africa constitutes an entity both in West Africa and in Equatorial Africa, and these entities can last if their governments wish it. English-speaking West Africa, even before the Nigerian chaos, has never had the same inducements to come together as French-speaking Africa. On the other hand, in East Africa there seems to be much greater scope for regionalisation and unity.

This book, therefore, raises several problems, but does not propose any solutions. The book's objective is to be, not controversial and passionate, but factual. It is an essay and an introduction to the history of Africa over the past ten years. It is written in full awareness of the limits of the sources and in particular of the lack of perspective which at this stage prevents an objective view being taken of the outstanding events in Africa since 1958. It would be impossible to try to give answers to the present problems and presumptuous to try to predict the future of Africa, which is first and foremost in the hands of the Africans themselves. But Africa's future is also in the hands of the developed countries and in their determination or reluctance to pursue their aid to Africa.

It is most likely that French-speaking Africa and Madagascar will continue to benefit from bilateral aid, as many donor countries (and primarily France) have vested political, cultural, commercial and economic interests. It is even more likely that multilateral aid will be expanded, particularly with the replenishment of the funds of the International Development Association, which should in principle be able to assist African countries more than hitherto.

There is inevitably a question mark over what will happen when 'the changing of the guard' (as it is called at the end of this book) takes place: the leaders of African politics will change, passing away like M'Ba of Gabon or dismissed like Yameogo of Upper Volta. In their hands power has shown signs of wear. Who will take over? The younger generation has heavy odds in its favour.

Indeed, Africa is definitively young, not only because independence came a brief ten years ago, but also because in most of the French-speaking African states 40 to 50 per cent of the population is under eighteen years of age. In twenty years' time this one phenomenon could upset all the basic facts of today's Africa. This is the major reason for trying to avoid any forecasts. Some slight warnings may, however, be given: Africa's future strength rests on its youth, but it must be trained and given jobs; it must become fully involved in the problems and realities of the respective countries, so that it acquires the sense of civic responsibility so badly needed in modern African societies.

G. L.

Part One

French-Speaking Africa becomes Independent, or de Gaulle's Africa

1. General de Gaulle and Africa

THIS BOOK could well have been called *De Gaulle's Africa*, since Charles de Gaulle has played a prominent part on the international stage for over a quarter of a century—indeed, even longer, for his military writings influenced a small circle of experts between the two world wars. Regardless of whether one likes or dislikes his political actions, it cannot be denied that he has left his mark on a whole generation of Frenchmen. More particularly during his two active periods—from 1940 to 1946, and since 1958—he has undoubtedly given a certain personal impetus to African affairs and African evolution.

Although as a young man he showed no particular interest in the colonies, Africa has played an important role in de Gaulle's destiny. On three occasions his fate was decided in Africa: in 1940 in Brazzaville, when French Equatorial Africa became the first important French territory to rally to the Free France Movement; in 1942 in Algiers, when the first Provisional government was formed; and again in Algiers, when the events of May 13, 1958, culminated in de Gaulle's return to power. Africa, in fact, provided his stepping stones to power. The evolution of Africa, in turn, depended for many years on de Gaulle's personality. His prestige, his unique stature and his grand manner greatly impressed the first generation of African leaders, while the masses were overawed by the outstanding role he was playing in French history.

Thus, in this analysis of French-speaking Africa since independence, the first task is to examine and assess the influence of Gaullism and de Gaulle's thought upon Africa. The first section of this chapter will show the Gaullist reaction to the colonial problem; the second section will analyse de Gaulle's attitude to decolonisation; and the concluding section will give a brief account of the short-lived 'Communauté'.

3

GAULLISM AND THE COLONIAL PROBLEM

De Gaulle belonged to that austere generation of Frenchmen who considered it their duty to redeem French honour, tarnished by the Sedan defeat in 1870. His upper middle-class family, from Lille in Northern France, was well-to-do (though not wealthy), hard working, honest and respectable, and held lofty views on morality, religion and duty to the country. Patriotism ran high, exacerbated, in those days, by the more and more overbearing demands of imperial Germany. Young Charles had strong reasons for joining the army and his uncompromising patriotism was reflected in his choice of regiment: instead of joining a fashionable cavalry regiment he chose the unglamorous, dangerous infantry.

De Gaulle never experienced—unlike some of his famous elders —a longing to explore overseas, to follow Faidherbe, Gallieni, Marchand and Lyautey. By the time he came of age, the period of conquest was over; Africa had been divided among the great powers at the Congress of Berlin in 1885 and an era of particularly bitter colonial competition was beginning. The colonial conflicts of the eighteenth century had been local and circumscribed; but by the late nineteenth century, so venomous were the clashes between the colonial powers that they were to prove, eventually, one of the causes of the First World War.

Undoubtedly, like most middle-class Frenchmen of his generation, Charles de Gaulle felt proud of the colonial conquests of France between 1875 and 1900.[1] Each newly-conquered territory meant enhanced prestige for France in the face of an overbearing German Empire. France threw itself enthusiastically into its overseas ventures and established a defensive network strong enough to make it respected among the world powers.

The end of the 1914–18 War brought victory for France, but only after appalling losses of French blood, so that between the two world wars the Empire with its hundred million inhabitants remained the only token of French world power. The French felt reassured in their jingoistic nationalism when they saw the French flag waving all over the world: in North Africa, in Black Africa with its still almost untapped resources, in the Far East and the Pacific Islands. So strong was France in its Empire that it could be really threatened by no one. In 1932 Colonel de Gaulle started publishing a series of books (*Le Fil de l'épée* in 1932, *Vers l'armée de métier* in 1934, *La France et son armée* in 1938), in which he gave a somewhat sombre assessment of French strength and military power, and criticised the obsolete means of defence; he commented favourably, however, on the importance of the great strategic roads throughout the Empire and on the enormous resources of manpower to be found in the North African and colonial regiments.

His realistic view brought him little gratification, other than the bitter satisfaction of seeing in 1940 how true his predictions had proved. By then General de Gaulle was Under-Secretary of State for War and a trusted friend of President Paul Reynaud. After the defeat of France, never wavering in his staunch decision to carry on the fight, he turned to Africa as the only possible refuge from which to continue. He lost no time in rejecting the new regime in France and the government's abdication in favour of Marshal Pétain, and on June 18, 1940, de Gaulle made his famous appeal not only to France but to the whole of the Empire: 'France is not alone. She has behind her a vast Empire. She can make common cause with the British Empire which still rules the seas and is still carrying on with the struggle. . . . This war is a world war. In spite of all the mistakes, all the delays, all the suffering, we have in this universe the means one day to crush our enemies. Nothing can be allowed to, and nothing shall, extinguish the flame of French resistance.'[2]

His position in London in June–July 1940 was extremely difficult. He stood almost isolated, with few followers and not a single front-ranking politician from the Third Republic to support him in his differences with Great Britain and clashes with the United States. He had only two assets at the time: the friendship of Winston Churchill, who stood by him throughout the war in spite of their well-known bickering, and the material resources of the African territories. These colonies, however, had not yet

5

rallied to him: he had to win them over and reconquer them physically and morally, a far from simple task. His success in doing so had tremendous consequences. With their assistance, he was able to continue the struggle which led ultimately to the liberation of the mother country. In the process he created in Africa the legend of de Gaulle. His prestige, and the aura surrounding his name, were to invest him with such authority that eventually he was able to carry Africa with him in his ideas for its decolonisation.

The defeat of 1940 had enormous repercussions overseas. It came as a great shock to the whole of French Africa. The young African intellectuals—such as Léopold Sédar Senghor, Félix Houphouet-Boigny, Barthélemy Boganda, Jacques Rabemananjara, Alioune Diop—were not the only ones affected. The ordinary African soldiers, the 'tirailleurs' from Upper Volta and Senegal, were also bewildered and sincerely sorrowful. They passed on the sad news to their friends who in turn relayed it to their relatives in the bush. Soon the whole of French Africa knew that the white man, the Frenchman, 'the boss', had been defeated in war, had failed. The African looked at the Frenchman with new eyes, eyes of doubt.

In 1940, the colonial administration, which had been liberalised between 1936 and 1939, returned to harsher ways. At the same time an unknown general was speaking from London, taking action, issuing orders, refusing to accept defeat, maintaining that France still lived in its Empire and that Africa could and must take part in a war that was far from finished. Admittedly, the feelings of the inhabitants of the French colonies seemed of little importance at the time, but the blunders of the Vichy administrators contrasted sharply with the forceful speeches from London. Gaullists arriving from London were able to find a few supporters among both the Africans and the French. These were particularly valuable, as the tragedy of Mers el Kebir (when the British fleet attacked the naval base of Oran in Algeria) had obviously alienated official and military circles. The Dakar expedition suggested by the British government to rally Senegal and French West Africa to the Free French had been another disastrous setback. It was little wonder that the Residents-General in North Africa and the Levant and the Governor-General of French West Africa adhered to the Pétain regime and refused to follow an unconstitutional leader, condemned as a traitor in France itself.

But on August 27, 1940, Captain de Hautecloque (who was to become General 'Leclerc') and Hétier de Boislambert crossed the border between Nigeria and Cameroun and in no time rallied the people of Cameroun to Free France. On August 28, Brazzaville, capital of French Equatorial Africa (AEF), went over to de Gaulle, following the action taken by Médecin-Général Sicé, head of the medical services of AEF, who put at the disposal of the Free French forces the important shortwave broadcasting station of Radio Brazzaville. Chad came under Gaullist administration when its Governor, Félix Eboué, born in the West Indies but an African at heart, placed himself at de Gaulle's orders; Governor Saint Marc of Oubangui-Chari soon followed Eboué's example. In Gabon there was some fighting between those for de Gaulle and those against him. It took several weeks for the capital of the territory, Libreville, to follow in the steps of the other capitals of Equatorial Africa.

Thus, in Africa, Free France had at last acquired a strong territorial base. French Equatorial Africa was to become a sort of springboard for de Gaulle. He felt he could speak more easily on behalf of France, and assert that his power was legitimate, in Brazzaville than in London. In Africa, he could indeed claim that he stood for the French state and eternal France,[3] for he was consolidating his position day by day. A council for the defence of the Empire was created and its first meeting was held in Brazzaville on October 27, 1940, in de Gaulle's presence. Throughout the war, both in this council and during his innumerable trips around Africa, de Gaulle exercised his authority 'on behalf of France, only to maintain its rights for the time being, and under the solemn promise to account for his actions to the representatives of the French nation, as soon as they [could] be freely elected'.[4] There existed no other legitimate French government: the Vichy regime was unconstitutional and under the invader's orders, and so he took upon himself the sacred duty of leading French efforts until the end of the war. The council had as its task 'to ensure unflagging loyalty to France, enforce interior security, promote economic activities and maintain the population in all the different territories of the Empire closely knit together'.[5]

At first, de Gaulle's sole purpose was to protect the existing ties between the Africans and the French so that both could be associated as closely as possible in the main task of *national* liberation; the French nation had, as it were, overflowed into Africa. This assimilation through common fighting was exemplified by African and French troops crossing the desert together in the Leclerc column to join the British Eighth Army, and later fighting in the battle of Bir Hakeim: France had become a combatant country again. Throughout the war, de Gaulle was to return again and again to the fundamental idea that the French and the Africans were completely assimilated. For the celebration of the Eleventh of November, 1942, he declared: 'We intend to gather together all our people and all our territories as we have already done with Chad and the Congo, Oubangui, Gabon, Cameroun, the New Hebrides, New Caledonia, Oceania, French India, Saint-Pierre and Miquelon. We have already liberated the Lebanon and Syria, who are now our close and true fighting companions, and we regard it our duty to do the same for that great French island of Madagascar, with the unflagging and selfless help of our great ally, England.'[6]

De Gaulle wanted to prove that there were no differences between the French from Marseilles, Lyon, Paris, Brazzaville, Beirut and London. 'The French nation at war is one.' He claimed the Gaullists had been able to win over the whole Empire and to obtain unwavering support everywhere. However, after the Allied landing in North Africa, he had a long and tedious struggle to supplant General Giraud[7] and win reluctant recognition from America; then alone could he stand as the one and only leader of Free France, the unquestioned head of the Committee of National

Liberation and later the first man in the Provisional government of the French Republic.

In this way the idea of the French Union, 'l'Union Française', grew among the little group of de Gaulle and his followers, during the hard years: a result of the part played during the war by Frenchmen 'white and black'. Vichy, and its colonial administration, had reactionary tendencies and kept to strict traditional ways. De Gaulle and the Committee of National Liberation broke away from the old methods and devised a more advanced colonial policy.

At the beginning of 1944, de Gaulle decided upon a great tour of Africa:[8] Rabat, Dakar (where he was received not with gunfire, as his troops had been two years before, but by cheering crowds), through Conakry, Abidjan, Lomé, Cotonou, Douala, Libreville and finally to Brazzaville, so dear to his heart. There the so-called 'de Gaulle's bungalow'* was put at his disposal when he arrived, on January 3, to open the Conference of the Governors-General and Governors of French Africa, which was attended by some members of the Provisional Consultative Assembly (Assemblée consultative provisoire), together with a few observers from Algeria, Morocco and Tunisia. The main leaders of the debate at the Conference, besides the General, were René Pleven, then Commissioner ('Commissaire') for the colonies, and Félix Eboué, who had recently become Governor-General of French Equatorial Africa.

De Gaulle's opening speech epitomised his ideas on the colonial problem at the time. He began by considering how fast the world was changing and how necessary it was to proceed to drastic revisions of established conceptions: 'Without wishing to exaggerate the reasons which urge us to tackle African problems in their entirety, we believe that the events at present shattering the world

* 'La case de Gaulle' still exists as the French Ambassador's private residence, somewhat renovated. Quite typically it stands apart from most European houses—on the banks of the Congo, far from the administrative, business and residential centre, and on the outskirts of one of the main African quarters.

9

are a warning not to delay.'[9] He then emphasised how the part played by Africa throughout the war should be acknowledged, and how it had earned the right to be respected; he hinted in a rather allusive way that changes were at hand: 'In this war, which has been to a large extent an African war, the issue has been the condition of man, and, under the impact of the psychological forces that have been released, the peoples are looking to the future and asking themselves what their destinies are to be. France has chosen to lead the sixty millions who are associated with her own forty million children into new ways, for the France of today is eagerly seeking rebirth.'[10]

Did de Gaulle mean that he would gradually give their freedom to the people hitherto administered, helped and educated by France? It is somewhat doubtful whether as early as 1944 he clearly realised the full impact of the renovating—even revolutionary— movement that was to sweep through all the colonies after the Second World War and to overthrow all the colonial structures. In a press conference on October 25, 1944, he merely expounded a French policy that would enable colonised people to develop faster, 'take administration into their own hands and—much later —govern themselves'. He could not have thought, in those days, that the African countries would sever all bonds with metropolitan France. He only foresaw the colonised peoples evolving towards new structures 'where each would play his own part within a French framework'. The Brazzaville spirit meant a slow integration of Africa into the French community in a process which would carry assimilation to its furthest conclusions. French civilisation, in de Gaulle's view, would prevail in Africa because it brought with it 'two precious boons: respect for the human personality and material welfare'.[11]

The Brazzaville Conference made some administrative, social and cultural changes. There were new rulings concerning African marriage, new labour laws (prohibiting enforced labour), and it was decided to terminate the native provident societies ('sociétés indigènes de prévoyance') and replace them with authentic production, credit and marketing co-operatives. It recommended a new emphasis on education and hygiene and it decided on the establishment of town councils ('municipalités'), the town councillors being chosen by the governors ('chefs de territoires') and in fact being notables: i.e., Africans of a certain income and education, whose task would be merely to advise on taxes, town-planning and various allowances. Yet no decisive political step was taken. No evolution was contemplated outside the French bloc nor beyond the strict framework of the Empire. No form of self-government was envisaged, even in the distant future.

The Brazzaville policy recognised that the African had a place in French civilisation and in the administration of metropolitan France—and, in consequence, African deputies and senators a place in the French Parliament. General Leclerc, one of de Gaulle's most trusted wartime colleagues, was sincere and honest when he wrote in a preface to E. Dehon's book: 'I dream of France radiating overseas, bringing civilisation and progress. Since 1940, the world has been surprised to watch our Empire fighting for the defence of the mother country. The first victories of our reborn forces were won in the Empire. . . . Their loyalty should now be duly rewarded. It is now our duty to show that the close union of all French territories is a fact, by the fusion of the Nation with the Empire which shared its woes so loyally.'[12]

General Leclerc, like so many well-meaning politicians and soldiers, failed to understand African aspirations. The Africans did not want to be treated simply as Frenchmen. They wanted to be recognised for what they were, and not to be patronised. They were prepared at most to accept a degree of supervision and control but it would have to be applied discreetly and tactfully. As time passed, however, the demands became increasingly pressing. We shall see in chapter 2 that the French were to concede more and more to no avail. Urged on by external events, outside influences and the normal development of ideas, the Africans had become insatiable.

As soon as the French Union, based on the Brazzaville policy, was officially proclaimed, events gave it the lie. On May 8, 1945, there were riots in Algeria, in the 'petite Kabylie', demanding better political conditions. In retaliation, Sétif was bombarded by the French navy. A terrible period of repression started, during which many thousands of people were brutally killed, and the very few Algerian political leaders were arrested and put in prison. In Madagascar, on March 29 and 30, 1947, Malagasy nationalists attacked a military camp and a rebellion flared up in several parts of the island: plantations were set on fire and the railway between Tananarive and Tamatave was sabotaged. The punishment meted out was swift and cruel: the army, the Senegalese troops and the police quelled the revolt. In all, 80,000 people were killed; the Mouvement Démocratique de Rénovation Malgache (MDRM), which had asked for more freedom within the French Union, was held responsible for the riots and outlawed and its leaders were put in jail.

Such ruthless repression was hardly in keeping with the French sense of duty to the colonies or with the spirit of Brazzaville. As early as 1944, French colonial policy became unimaginative, illogical and inconsistent. The Fourth Republic, on the whole, decolonised only under constraint. Only Pierre Mendès-France, when tackling the problems of Indochina and Tunisia, and Edgar Faure, when trying to solve the Moroccan affair, evinced some political flair and insight. Later it needed de Gaulle to solve the Algerian problem and he was able to do so only by resorting to irritating empirical methods, two steps forward, one step back. Moreover, in order to achieve his end, he was compelled to decolonise at full speed in Black Africa.

GAULLISM AND DECOLONISATION

By 1944 General de Gaulle had already predicted that the status of colonised countries would be greatly altered. He realised that a passionate desire to break all colonial fetters would sweep over the world, and that the first revolts in Asia would soon be followed by revolts elsewhere.[13] However, events moved faster than he had expected, and the sending of MPs and senators, black and North African, to the French Parliament proved to be no help.

Decolonisation was a process which could not be controlled, and the introduction of overseas politicians into the French Parliament, after Sétif and just before the quelling of the Malagasy rebellion and the war in Indochina, was ill-timed.

In 1944–46, General de Gaulle failed because he had no true control over the political parties—which he mistakenly imagined he could hold together in a Coalition government consisting of Christian Democrats, Socialists and Communists—because he was unable to cope with post-war economic and financial difficulties, and finally because many French political circles remained extremely reluctant to follow his liberal colonial policy. People approved of the United Nations Charter, which proclaimed the right of all peoples to self-determination, yet believed that what had been the 'French Empire' should still be held firmly under the new label of the French Union. There were violent reactions among the most colonialist groups and inside the ministries themselves against de Gaulle's mild reforms: for example, overseas, in the Ivory Coast, the European planters strongly opposed Governor Latrille and attacked him for his liberal tendencies and for having authorised the creation of a native trade union, led by a promising young doctor, Houphouet-Boigny.[14] In France, in July and August 1946, a meeting of 'Les Etats généraux de la Colonisation' was organised to muster all the conservative nationalistic forces, including numerous members of the Mouvement Républicain Populaire (MRP—Catholic Centre Party) and radical elements, against the Communist Party which was then giving its full support to the young African anti-colonialist movements. By October 1945, de Gaulle realised that the French political parties were not, as he put it to Léon Blum, 'in a suitable frame of mind' to support his reforms and he began to entertain grave doubts as to whether it would ever be possible to 'manage French affairs as they should be managed'.[15] On January 26 he tendered his resignation to the President of the National Constituent Assembly. So began his retreat into the wilderness which was to last twelve years.

It was also the beginning of a long period of political unrest and colonial crises. De Gaulle, though off the political stage, repeatedly expounded his ideas, especially in October 1952 at the national convention of the Rassemblement du Peuple Français (RPF), a political group which had been launched in 1946 under his patronage. There he declared that France should not merely await events, but should take the initiative and propose reforms in keeping with the new ideas, that it should lead colonial countries, particularly Morocco and Tunisia, towards some form of autonomy, that it should promote their economic and social development, while still containing them within a new loose framework in which, though freer, they would still feel closely knit to France. He endorsed Mendès-France's policy in Indochina, loudly disagreed with the devious procedure which led to the deposition of the Sultan of Morocco, and severely condemned the bombardment by the French air force of the small village of Sakiet Sidi Youssef, on the Tunisian–Algerian frontier. He also had a solemn farewell interview with the departing Tunisian Ambassador, Mohammed Masmoudi, when Tunisia broke off diplomatic relations with France. De Gaulle repeatedly explained to everyone who would listen how wrong it was to yield to the force of circumstances instead of paving the way to decolonisation in a calm, unhurried manner.

It was mainly because of his unrelenting criticism of the policies of the Fourth Republic that de Gaulle was recalled to power during the feverish days of May 1958 in Algiers. Such a crisis afforded the opportunity he was quietly awaiting, to step forward and save the nation once more. This time, though, he decided he would not, as in 1946, give up what he had undertaken without completing his task; and this time he would ensure that he was powerful enough to overcome petty party squabbles. His chief aim would be to give France its rightful place on the international stage.

Most Frenchmen—as it appeared from the results of the referendum of September 28, 1958—felt they could rest secure for they were at last putting the fate of the country in good hands: de Gaulle would untangle the Algerian knot and political stability would prevail at last. Nevertheless, there were still some who imagined that Algeria could remain French, or at least within the

French orbit, and had plotted for de Gaulle's return with this in mind. Others wanted to see an end to the war, but remained reluctant to face the prospect of an independent Algeria. A small minority considered it quite wrong for General de Gaulle to seize power in this unconstitutional way merely because the Algiers riots in May 1958 had forced the legal government away from true democratic procedure. According to their views, the only way of ending the Algerian war was to proclaim immediately the solemn right to independence of the Algerian people; the government team that had proved so weak and irresponsible on May 13 should be discarded, but no support whatsoever should be given to the Algiers plotters, Massu, Salan, Soustelle and others. However, from the moment that the crowds outside the Governor-General's office in Algiers shouted for de Gaulle, a strange succession of circumstances led inevitably to the agreement of the Section Française de l'Internationale Ouvrière (SFIO)—the French Socialist Party—and Guy Mollet to de Gaulle's return. The small fraction of the left which remained opposed found itself isolated and divided. It consisted of the Communist Party—many of whom voted for de Gaulle in the referendum—the purists such as Mendès-France and Daniel Mayer, the Parti Socialiste Unifié (PSU) of Edouard Depreux and the younger intellectuals. Yet de Gaulle, voted to power by a large majority, proceeded to follow a left-wing policy in foreign affairs, except in Europe.

The events of May 13 and their repercussions were watched in the French territories overseas with the closest attention, and their reactions were varied.[16] Business and military circles were greatly agitated: some felt it behoved them to defend the honour of Free France; others, wistfully looking to the past, would resort to some of the theories of the late Action Française or give vent to fiery nationalistic outbursts in the manner of Déroulède. Others, more bellicose, were quite ready to seize aeroplanes from the military airfields of Brazzaville or Fort Lamy, form them into fighting squadrons and sally forth to Algiera—and, who knows, to Paris—for an onslaught on the regime. But which regime was legal and should be acknowledged in Africa: Paris or Algiers? There was great irresolution; colonial leaders held meetings, uncertain of what they should do. Should they send the 'colonial troops'? Should events be left to follow their due course? At any rate connections were established between Algiers and the desert bases both in the Sahara departments and in the African countries bordering the Sahara on the south which were members of the Organisation Commune des Régions Sahariennes (OCRS).

French officers and NCOs of African regiments flared up, ready, if necessary, to support the 'pieds noirs' and the French army stationed in Algeria. The African population remained unconcerned, but the African MPs were worried, reacting, as usual, as if they were good French left-wing democrats. In a message to the President of the Republic, René Coty, they declared themselves deeply attached to the republican regime and to democratic liberties and eager to be members of a 'fraternal and egalitarian Franco-African Community'. The two French High Commissioners—Cusin in Dakar and Messmer in Brazzaville—remained on the side of the legal government although their sympathies were with de Gaulle. Their views reflected the Brazzaville spirit and the mystique of Free France. In spite of some cloak and dagger fever in Pointe Noire, the more sedate among the former Free French in Brazzaville advised their compatriots to remain prudent, watchful and unswervingly loyal to de Gaulle. The High Commissioner sent a telegram to President Coty, declaring his loyalty to the Republic but suggesting de Gaulle as the possible head of a government of National Union that would bring the Algerian tragedy to a fair conclusion. French Equatorial Africa placed implicit faith in 'l'homme de Brazzaville', and Jacques Opangault, the Vice-President of the government of the Middle Congo, was the first African to rally to the General 'in a secret message forwarded through the Ministry of Overseas France'.[17] A few months before these events, in February, Houphouet-Boigny, a minister in the cabinets of the Fourth Republic and a minister-to-be in the cabinets of the Fifth Republic, had begged, through his trusted friend Edmond Michelet, to be received by de Gaulle—a privilege he was granted.[18] On the whole, the African countries were in favour of de Gaulle's return: they were dissatisfied with the Loi Cadre of 1956 which, while giving semi-autonomous status to African territories, 'balkanised' and divided West and Equatorial Africa; they surmised that de Gaulle would prove more liberal and more amenable to their requests for self-government. However, they still wanted close bonds with France.

It became obvious that, once back in power, de Gaulle was quite willing to remain 'l'homme de Brazzaville'. On June 13, 1958, during his first broadcast speech, he announced that the structure of the French Union would soon be altered. On June 25 he agreed that in each African territory the vice-president of the executive council elected by the territorial assemblies should become president, whereas up to this time and under the 1956 Loi Cadre the president of this council had still been the 'chef de territoire', that is the French High Commissioner. A few days before the Fourteenth of July celebrations, two administrative decisions were taken modifying voting lists in the overseas territories and enabling local populations to participate in the referendum on the new constitution. During those celebrations, General de Gaulle sent a message of friendship to the populations overseas, 'for never [had] the men in those remote lands and those living in metropolitan France been closer'. The tone of the message was very hopeful: 'We have no doubt that bonds between our countries will be maintained in the future. We are going forward towards a new free Community. In 1958, we will establish new institutions.'[19]

In this hopeful atmosphere, General de Gaulle started his grand tour of Africa: between August 20 and 29, he visited Fort Lamy, Tananarive, Brazzaville, Abidjan, Conakry and Dakar. Everywhere, frenzied picturesque crowds gathered in their thousands to cheer and worship him. The only jarring notes occurred in Conakry, and in Dakar where some notices appeared demanding immediate independence. On the whole, the African crowds trusted de Gaulle and had faith in the changes he intended to bring about in Franco-African relations. After de Gaulle's tour,

17

Houphouet-Boigny went back to France with no further mis-givings about the deep feelings of the people of his country, who, he was certain, would vote 'Yes' at the referendum on September 28. Léopold Sédar Senghor's Parti de Rénovation Africaine (PRA) was not so wholeheartedly enthusiastic,* but in all those African countries with a local branch of Houphouet-Boigny's party, the Rassemblement Démocratique Africain (RDA), the majority would most probably vote 'Yes'.

In the General's view, those who voted 'Yes' agreed on the new-founded Communauté (Community) with the French Republic: that is to say, they spontaneously accepted the establishment of a union of France and the overseas territories, in which each territory would be completely free and responsible for its own government and administration, but would leave certain questions—foreign affairs, defence, economic affairs, commodities policy, finance and foreign exchange, justice, university education and transport—to be decided jointly with France.[20] It also meant that those African territories would acknowledge de Gaulle's two great principles: a prudent evolution towards self-government in internal matters and necessary alignment—due to prevailing circumstances—into large economic, political and cultural groupings.[21] On the other hand, voting 'No' would mean to him immediate secession; a brutal break with France; total isolation. He made it very clear, not without a touch of cynicism, that those who voted 'Yes' would be helped by France, whereas those who voted 'No' were 'forewarned that we shall not carry on helping them, but shall ignore them completely'.[22]

De Gaulle could not brook any refusal, could not believe that those youngsters waving notices saying 'Independence Now' were anything but hooligans. For the present, there was only one way:

* The PRA Congress held in Cotonou some time before the referendum had voted a resolution in favour of the 'No' vote at the referendum and, in addition, it is interesting to note that Senghor and Mamadou Dia, both major leaders of Senegalese politics, were absent from their country during de Gaulle's visit to Dakar.

the Franco-African Community. 'This is the era of efficiency, that is to say, of large well-organised units. This is not a time for demagogy; let the demagogues go, let them return to where they came from, where they are awaited. This is an era for those who can construct.'[23] In Tananarive, he said: 'Our Community is designed for the world in which we live, because this world, which has become so dangerous for us all, is troubled by currents which drag some from their homes to seek those of others. Every country lives under a terrible menace of upheaval and dreams of subversion. We can envisage events that would throw our world into a chaos more terrible than any which has gone before: all this our Community is designed to prevent.'[24]

In fact Chapter XII of the new constitution of the Fifth Republic, which established the Community, was the result of a compromise, suggested by the President of the Malagasy government, between the federalist proposals of Houphouet-Boigny and Senghor's concept of confederation. Those who drew up this Chapter had no doubt that it would be the starting point of a radical change.* The different paragraphs were flexible and non-committal enough to allow either for a real federation of equal states or for a vague form of confederacy. The right of states to some self-government was solemnly declared, but only in relation to internal matters such as administration and the management of the country. All matters of external policy, such as foreign affairs, defence, trade and finance, were to remain the responsibility of France. Therefore, although the states might be partly self-governing, they were not to be fully independent. The Community was to have an Executive Council presided over and represented by the President of the French Republic. The Council was to comprise the President and Prime Minister of the French Republic, the heads of government of each of the member states

* Among the members of the Constitutional Consultative Committee which had examined and canvassed the text of the constitution were prominent representatives of Black Africa, such as Senghor, Tsiranana, Lisette and Lamine Guèye.

and the ministers dealing with common matters. These arrangements considerably increased the importance of the French ministers, for they were in charge both of their metropolitan ministries and of the supervision of matters of common interest in the Franco-African Community. A Senate of the Community was established, invested with legislative power. There was also a Court of Arbitration (Cour arbitrale) set up to exercise judicial power and to settle any possible claims between the different members. It was undoubtedly a considerable step forward from the 1946 constitution and the Loi Cadre, all the more so since the new constitution made provision for the new countries to become completely independent if they so wished, but without letting them retain, in such a case, any bond at all with France. The Community was a half-way house between, on the one hand, a federation with one president, some common ministers and a senate, and, on the other, a confederation in which the prime ministers were loosely associated. It made some provision for common responsibilities.

African opinion, on the whole, was quite favourable to de Gaulle's new constitutional projects, as expounded by the Constitutional Consultative Committee, but French opinion remained totally indifferent. The French were preoccupied with their own politics and the Algerian war. Yet it was good news for them to hear how smoothly and peacefully overseas territories were evolving. However, people did not realise in the early months of 1959 what drastic changes were implied in the new laws, and that in fact the road towards independence was open to most of the former colonial countries, and not only those in Black Africa. Strange to say, de Gaulle's fiercest opponents at home on constitutional matters were those advocating the very same swift evolution overseas which de Gaulle was actually putting into practice. During de Gaulle's second term of power, only the left agreed with his overseas policy, although it consistently opposed his methods of government at home. The more conservative circles were alarmed; the weekly *Rivarol* published an indignant article pointing out how easy it would be for overseas territories within the new Community to obtain their independence. The Independents Party maintained that de Gaulle and his government were lightheartedly 'squandering the former French colonial Empire'.[25] Some feared that de Gaulle would walk out of Algeria as casually as he was walking out of Black Africa.

In spite of the gloomy forecasts of the world press, which was quite uncertain about the results of the referendum[26]—it was thought that the French had little enthusiasm for de Gaulle's moral dictatorship and arbitration—66·41 per cent of the voters in metropolitan France voted 'Yes'. Overseas, there was a landslide, with a 100 per cent 'Yes' vote in the Ivory Coast, Upper Volta, Middle Congo and Oubangui-Chari (today the Central African Republic); 98 per cent in Dahomey and Chad; 97 per cent in Senegal and Soudan; 92 per cent in Gabon; 78 per cent in Madagascar and Niger. Though in Africa votes might have been slightly 'swollen', yet the overall results reflect the complete faith and worship of the crowds for de Gaulle. There was only one unfortunate blot on this happy picture: the 95 per cent 'No' vote in Guinea. The reasons for the Guinean result demand investigation.

On August 25, 1958, General de Gaulle went to Conakry to meet President Sékou Touré: both delivered speeches that caused a great sensation at the time. It is still difficult to understand why de Gaulle's advisers were so badly informed and so unimaginative as to include Conakry in his African tour. It was a most unfortunate stop-over, for the Guinean leaders were so excited at the time that they were certain to take amiss anything he said. If Paris had been ready to meet Guinea on its own terms, to acknowledge its special position that stemmed from its outstanding economic potentialities and the fiery personality of its President, then de Gaulle should have been warned beforehand about the very different situation he was going to encounter. Had he been forewarned, he would either have avoided Conakry or have approached the situation with the utmost care, with greater understanding and political realism. Reading the declarations of the two leaders in their direct confrontation, one remains aghast: de Gaulle's speech emphasised that decolonisation should proceed by slow degrees and that a prudent co-operation with France should be firmly maintained, while Touré haughtily claimed independence at once.

If certain French circles in Conakry had ever entertained a malicious desire to sabotage de Gaulle's prestige in Guinea's capital, they could not have advised a more damaging course. Yet many French administrators, in Guinea or at the Ministry for Overseas Territories in the rue Oudinot, were aware of Touré's views: they knew that he held the country in his grip through the tight organisation of his Parti Démocratique de Guinée (PDG), the local branch of RDA, and that, whatever move he might make, Guinea would follow him to a man. The pyramidal structure of his party was flawless, with a political bureau at the top, village or district committees at the bottom, and efficient links between the two. Touré had much earlier revealed himself as a 'tough' trade union leader: first in Guinea, then over all Africa, when in 1956 he became president of the Confédération Générale des Travailleurs Africains (CGTA). These successes in the trade union movement had been a springboard for his more recent political career: he was elected mayor of Conakry in 1955, representative of Guinea in the French National Assembly in 1956, territorial councillor for Conakry in 1957, member of the Great Council for French West Africa in 1957 and finally vice-president of the Executive Council of Guinea.[27]

The flamboyant trade unionist and political leader was far from displeased to meet the General, but he thought he would leave to Conakry's joyful, rowdy, motley crowds the expression of Guinea's deep friendship for the great white chief; *he* was eager to come to the point: 'We want dignity more than anything else', he proclaimed. 'Where there is no liberty, there is no dignity. We would rather be poor and free than rich and enslaved. We cannot be persuaded to abandon our legitimate and natural right to independence.'[28] In this famous speech of welcome he also expressed somewhat more sedate feelings, which passed unnoticed in the

French press: he revealed tremendous admiration for the great soldier and wartime leader: 'For us, you embody the Resistance, but your presence here is also a token that a decisive period, a new stage of our evolution, is about to start.'[29] He felt deeply grateful for de Gaulle's effort to decolonise Africa once and for all. He was aware that Africa was one of de Gaulle's chief concerns, but the General must realise that Africa wanted immediate freedom. Touré believed that Africans, black or white, who had fallen or risked their lives on the battlefields of North Africa, Italy, France and Germany, had defended French liberty because it implied their own liberty. In countless speeches, he had harped on two themes: he felt deeply attached to France, but the time was now ripe and Africans should take their own revolution into their own hands; otherwise they would never be truly independent, they would never go forward. He did not beg for any help, though he probably needed it sorely; his foremost wish was to be understood. He believed that Africans could no longer be French citizens and that they should be allowed to develop along their own lines: he felt that, if France realised this before it was too late, it would not lose by granting Africa its independence.

General de Gaulle failed to see what Sékou Touré really meant. It was unprecedented that the petitioner should 'warn' the head of the French state and express such blunt demands; but Touré believed de Gaulle was wrong to try to shatter African unity, and to put in power, wherever he could, his own political creatures.

No head of state likes to be given a warning. Their viewpoints, though sincerely held by each, were too divergent—the clash was inevitable. De Gaulle had not expected such a reaction; he had no time to ponder and to prepare an answer. France, he said, well knew that Africa was a new continent. But, as the France of 1958 was a young country too, why could not the French and the Africans work side by side in one cultural, economic and social community? Nobody was required to join the Community, he went on. Let those who wanted independence by all means take it. But they must realise that if they voted for independence and against

23

the French constitutional project it would mean severing all relations with France. France would take a Guinean vote of 'No' at its face value. De Gaulle had been riled and hurt and he made it clear in his spiteful, piqued answer.

De Gaulle was never to forgive; he was to refuse any new contact with Touré at the level of head of state. On September 18, 1958, the chief of the French diplomatic mission in Conakry was instructed to pass on an official statement in which France took legal cognisance of the 'No' vote in Guinea (1,130,292 voted 'No', 56,959 'Yes') and recognised its de facto independence. The break with France was absolute; according to a hastily devised plan, French civil servants were to leave within two months. Guinea would receive no more help from the French administration, and no more equipment credits. Overnight Guinea found itself penniless.

At the time many political observers thought it was harsh treatment to mete out to a former colony. Even today it is hard to understand why it was so severely punished. From this time, France ignored Guinea, in spite of its economic potential, and in spite of French interests there. As a result Guinea had no alternative but to align itself with Nkrumah and join with him in a rabid anti-Community group; yet, only two years later, France was to let Mali become independent without such great ado. France, by breaking with Guinea, promoted Africa's balkanisation. In addition France's attitude unwittingly induced Touré to seek comfort and help where it would be readily given: from Soviet Russia and Communist China. Thus, for the next three years there was a general outcry throughout Africa against Touré, for turning Guinea into an African bridgehead for world Communism, though this was a somewhat inaccurate and exaggerated view. Moreover, Guinea's daring vote of 'No' became a burning pang of conscience for all French-speaking countries. Only in the future will historians be able to assess its decisive influence on African evolution. In 1957, the independence of Ghana—then the Gold Coast—had meant the demise of the Loi Cadre. In 1958, the independence of Guinea heralded the doom of the Community.

THE FRANCO-AFRICAN COMMUNITY

The Community was a short-lived venture that lasted only eighteen months. No sooner established than it needed 'renovating'; then it disappeared altogether, to be replaced by vaguer forms of Franco-African co-operation which lacked any precise legal basis. As early as December 10, 1959, at the sixth session of the Executive Council of the Community, de Gaulle agreed that international sovereignty should be granted to any state which requested it, and that new agreements on co-operation might be negotiated between African states and France. The race for independence had started. What were the major events of this very brief period, and why did de Gaulle's policy evolve so rapidly?

In the early months of 1959 the main legal institutions of the Community were established.[30] A Senate and an Executive Council of the Community were created, though in fact they were no great legal innovation but rather the logical outcome of the tendency towards assimilation traditional to French policy. Self-government at home was by this time becoming the rule rather than the exception, but African leaders and MPs were still 'taken in charge' by their French guardians. The President of the Republic, who was also the President of the Community, decreed that a general secretariat of the Community would be established, with its office in the Elysée, and Raymond Janot as general secretary. The secretariat of the Community provided the means by which co-operation between states could take practical form. It was responsible for arranging all councils and committee meetings, and for preparing the programmes of the Senate; it kept the President of the Community informed on developments in the political evolution of the new states and passed on the President's instructions and communications.

The head of the Executive Council was the President of the French Republic and its members were the thirteen heads of state, together with those ministers entrusted with matters of common interest.

The following members of the French government were entrusted with matters of common interest to the Community: foreign affairs, Couve de Murville; armed forces, Guillaumat; economic, finance and currency, Pinay; justice, Michelet; higher education, Boulloche; overseas and commercial transport and telecommunications, Cornut-Gentille. Relations between France and the African states and Madagascar were the responsibility of Lecourt, the Minister of State in charge of Inter-State Co-operation, and another minister of state, Jacquinot, was responsible for matters of trusteeship. Within the Executive Council, committees were established to cover each of these topics. They met not only when the Council itself met but also whenever a meeting seemed necessary. The result was a constant shuttling back and forth between Paris and the African capitals. French and African politicians and administrators, constantly meeting together and exchanging ideas, felt very close and friendly; but little time was left for the administrative machines in the new African countries to tackle their new responsibilities and get down to serious routine work.

It would be pointless to analyse here the work of each session, but it might be useful to quote some illustrations of the extent to which African states were bound to and dependent on France. It was de Gaulle's unswerving aim to rally the African states to his own international policy. As early as the second session held in Paris on March 2 and 3, 1959, the Council was given a detailed account of the international situation by the Minister of Foreign Affairs and was asked to declare the identity of its views with those of France, particularly regarding the Berlin crisis. During the third session on May 4 and 5, again in Paris, its members expressed the Community's 'complete agreement with France on the great international problems recently debated in Geneva'. Important decisions were taken on April 14, 1959, on military matters. The French army was required to organise the defence of the whole Community, under a unified high command. A defence committee was to be set up in each state, and strategic areas, often differing from the political territories of the states, were defined. The logistic and operational means were to be co-ordinated within each of them: the Central African area around the two military bases of Brazzaville and Fort Lamy, and the West African area around the bases of Dakar and Ouagadougou. Soon afterwards, at the fourth session in Tananarive, on July 7 and 8, an agreement was reached on the French atomic programme and the trial explosions in the Sahara. Many African politicians of the Community were invited to be present when the first bomb was exploded on February 13, 1960, at Reggane (in the depths of the Sahara); their presence was intended to demonstrate that they agreed with the French atomic programme, the keystone of their common defence policy. In many African states outside the Community, and among opposition elements within the Community states, this attendance, in fact only a formality, was condemned and reviled. Last but, considering the importance of its implications, by no means least, on May 14, 1959, an external security service of the Community was established, under the control of the French Prime Minister, to co-ordinate the political police in the several member states. It was a most potent weapon for eliminating troublesome elements in France and, above all, would provide protection for the established regimes throughout Africa against any opposition, especially from the political parties and from trade unions.

The Senate of the Community lacked any effective power: its function was merely deliberative and consultative. A bill was passed on February 9, 1959, which determined its composition: 284 members from the French Parliament and 98 from the Legislative Assemblies of the African member states, the number of senators from each state to be determined according to both its population and its importance within the Community. The Senate met only twice: between July 15 and 30, 1959, and between May 30 and June 3, 1960. France saw the Senate as a means of promoting friendship and co-operation between itself and the member states, but beyond this, as an instrument through which to influence and exert some pressure on its former colonies. In return for France's very substantial help in the economic, financial and cultural fields, it felt it was entitled to expect support for its international policy. Couve de Murville, speaking at a Senate meeting, expressed the wish that the African states should remain free, without committing themselves and becoming 'playthings or victims in a fight that was necessarily beyond them'. The young states must show that they were mature and sensible and not go to extremes; they must first learn the art of government.

The Fourteenth of July 1959 saw the apotheosis of the Community. Grandiose festivities were organised to celebrate the first year of power of this stronger and more stable regime which had earned the respect of the world beyond France. The celebrations centred on the President of the French Republic and the heads of state of the thirteen member states of the Community. André Malraux, who acted as master of ceremonies, had organised a torchlight procession from the Place de la République to the Champs Elysées, a solemn ceremony in which thirteen flags were presented to the thirteen states in the Place de la Concorde, a military parade and a vast reception. The national day of France now shone with a new lustre. However, on reading the contemporary newspaper accounts, one cannot help wondering whether in fact any really effective close contact had been established between the regime and the common man, or whether, in spite of all the glitter, the Algerian war did not cast a dark shadow over all the fine spectacles.

A year later the climate had changed. By the Fourteenth of July 1960, the Community had visibly evolved. The torchlight procession, the romantic excitement and the grand manner were gone. The tempo of decolonisation in Africa had been faster than anyone had imagined a year earlier. Thus, on July 11, the French Senate ratified the agreements reached with the Malagasy Republic and the Mali Federation transferring all powers which had hitherto been jointly exercised to the exclusive responsibility of these new states—thereby making them completely independent of metropolitan France. On July 12 similar agreements (accords de transfert) were signed with the four states of the Conseil de l'Entente: Ivory Coast, Niger, Dahomey and Upper Volta. The whole of French-speaking Africa was by now aspiring to and demanding independence, and it was being granted to them amicably. Self-government proved to be only a transitional phase of their evolution: independence was a right which they could now justly claim. It had, in fact, become a necessity, for without it they had no prestige on the international level. Independence meant a seat in the United Nations and the ability to sign bilateral treaties with countries other than France. Independence was also necessary to prevent African governments from being overtaken by the more progressive elements in their own countries, the opposition or the students. Finally, it was necessary in order to keep pace with other African states on the verge of independence, such as Cameroun (which achieved independence on January 1, 1960), Togo (April 1960), the Belgian Congo (June 30, 1960) and Nigeria (October 1960).

Senegal and Soudan began the move to independence, thus opening the second chapter in the short history of the Community. The Parti de la Fédération Africaine (PFA) was created on March 25, 1959, in order to establish a Federation of Mali, comprising Senegal and Soudan. On September 10 and 11, at the time the Executive Council of the Community was meeting for its fifth session, serious discussions took place about its possible future. Houphouet-Boigny again asserted that he was against any trans-formation of the Community into a confederation of independent states, but the leaders of the Soudan and Senegal maintained their positions and declared their intention of demanding independence under the terms of Article 86 of the French constitution, which granted to each member state of the Community the right to become independent. However, according to the terms of this article, any country becoming independent was automatically excluded from the Community, and both Mamadou Dia, Prime Minister of Senegal, and Modibo Keita, Premier of Soudan, wished to remain within it after independence. They both wanted independence, but they were determined that their independence should not lead to a complete severance of all the existing bonds with France, which would lead them to complete isolation—as had been the case with Guinea. The position adopted by Mali had profoundly important consequences—nothing less than an amendment to the constitution of France by modification of Article 86. It also meant a complete reorientation of de Gaulle's overseas policy. French law and French policy were altered to accommodate the wishes of the African leaders, as expressed first in Paris, and later at Dakar during the meeting of the PFA in September. In France the more liberal men of the left approved, for they realised that African aspirations could not be stifled; but the more conservative, many of de Gaulle's supporters from the centre, the Independents Party (which expressed the views of business circles), and, above all, the army, were afraid that independence for Black Africa would inevitably mean independence for Algeria. On December 10, 1959, General de Gaulle, opening the sixth session of the Community's Executive Council in St Louis, greeted the population of Mali and declared them to be entitled to independence within the Community. This speech marked the starting point of a succession of requests for independence during 1960, all of which were duly granted.

The first months of 1960 saw the gradual transformation of the legal institutions of the Community. A revision of the constitution passed by the French National Assembly after a debate on May 11 and 12, 1960, was subsequently submitted to the Senate of the Community at its second and final session, from May 30 to June 3.

Meanwhile the French government had been reshuffled. A State Secretariat for Relations with the Member States of the Community was established, with Jean Foyer as the first incumbent. He was to act as a link between the African states and the French ministries. A Committee for Relations with States of the Community was created, with the President of the Community as its head, and, as its members, the Prime Minister, the Secretary of State for Relations with the Member States of the Community, and the secretary-general of the Community, Jacques Foccart, who was to replace Janot. This committee was charged with the elaboration of French policy at the very highest level. At the eighth meeting of the Executive Council at the Elysée Palace in Paris on March 21, 1960, the main topic was the evolution of the

Community in the months to come. It proved to be the last meeting, as the Council was doomed to disappear as soon as the 'transfer agreements' were signed between France and Mali and France and Madagascar.

The constitution of the Franco-African Community was to be amended and a new name, the 'renewed Community' ('la Communauté rénovée') was adopted. For France, or rather General de Gaulle—as we shall see later—thought it wiser not to break with the countries who had requested independence. The constitutional bill proposed to add one paragraph to Article 85 of the French constitution. This paragraph would provide for the amendment of Chapter XII of the constitution through specific agreements between member states of the Community. It also proposed to add three new paragraphs to Article 86, which would make the following provisions. (i) A member state of the Community could become independent and yet still belong to it, something which previously, in the case of Guinea, had been considered impossible. (ii) Any independent state not a member of the Community (such as Cameroun and Togo) might still join it, without in any way impairing its independent status. This provision could equally have applied to Guinea, had it wished to come back and apply for it—and had de Gaulle relented. (iii) These provisions would be based on further agreements to be entered into with France. Further specific agreements were to define the relationship between France and the new independent states.

The bill which proposed these amendments became law in June 1960, when it was passed in the National Assembly by 288 votes to 174, and in the Senate by 144 to 127, in each case after a prolonged debate which clearly demonstrated where the different parties stood. The earlier stages of the debate were concerned with juridical issues, with the government being criticised for deviating from correct procedure. In fact, the government had resorted to the *original* text of Article 85 of the constitution which made provision for a revision of common institutions by simply passing bills in the Parliament of the Republic and the Senate of the Community, whereas the *established* text of Article 89 stated that any revision of the constitution should be canvassed and voted at a meeting of Congress (that is to say the National Assembly and the Senate sitting together as one body at Versailles), a three-fifths majority being necessary to pass a bill. To establish its point, the government had to overcome opposition from both the right and the left.

At the National Assembly, the spokesman of the Socialist Party expressed his alarm that the government should interpret the constitution so loosely rather than strictly follow its text; and the spokesman of the Communist Party believed this strange procedure to be an ingenious trick to salvage the last remnants of colonialism. An Independents MP expressed himself grieved 'to see French power in Africa crumbling'. Another MP made stinging attacks on the government for negotiating the transfer of responsibility to Madagascar and Mali *before* formally amending the constitution. According to yet another: 'All these agreements are likely to turn the Community into a kind of patchwork of different states with independence as the only common link.' In the Senate, the same arguments were used to oppose the reform—even more forcibly, for there the opposition was more active. The left stressed the government's totally anti-democratic procedure, whereas the right was greatly concerned with the consequences of the government's policy on Algeria, maintaining that the same policy would have to be applied there.

As spokesman for the government, Michel Debré emphasised the need to devise a new juridical framework for the renewed Community—a confederation of states which though independent would nevertheless maintain close affinities with each other. However, he also emphasised the political aspects of the proposed reforms: 'How idle it would be to equivocate over legal procedures when we are confronted with a major political problem: under the pressure of domestic forces as well as of ideological and strategic considerations, the former colonial empires are vanishing and the Black Continent fast changing.'

The two agreements between France and Mali and between France and Madagascar were ratified on June 9, 1960. The Socialist and Communist Parties, the Mouvement Républicain Populaire (MRP—Catholic Centre Party), and the Union pour la Nouvelle République (UNR—Gaullist) voted for it. Among those who voted against it were forty-six MPs from the Independents Party, some Radicals, and a few staunch opponents like Georges Bidault 'who will always refuse to share with the Government the responsibility for the destruction of the great work overseas which had been the pride of France during several Republics'. Earlier, on June 2, the Senate of the Community, then meeting for the last time, had praised General de Gaulle's far-sighted policy and expressed its gratification at seeing the Community evolving towards independence and enduring friendship with France, far from any bitterness and resentment.

The 'new' Franco-African Community was manifest in bilateral agreements with France, known as 'accords de coopération', on economic, financial, cultural and military matters. Once Franco-African co-operation was established, the Executive Council, the Senate and the ministers' committee ceased to exist; there were no longer any counsellors on African Affairs in the French government (posts given to Houphouet-Boigny and Senghor in 1958).

In fact, however, the Franco-African Community was not renovated; it was shattered. It had been an exciting idea, one which might have proved significant if it had been applied enthusiastically. But it remained no more than a half-hearted venture. The Ministry for the Colonies, first renamed the Ministry of Overseas France, then the Ministry of Co-operation, could not change its attitude so quickly; it needed a period of psychological preparation to overcome its ingrained reluctance to hand over authority. How can a centralising administration be asked, at the drop of a hat, to reorient itself to decentralisation? Besides, although the Community was based on egalitarian principles, the Senate of the Community had a French majority, which reflected the climate of the French Parliament. Had the Senate been given a more active role, not merely consultative, and had the African representatives been far more numerous, then the Community

33

might not have crumbled so quickly. However, no one could really imagine that the African countries would tolerate for long the shackles of the so-called 'common responsibilities'. The de-colonisation of Africa was a challenge to de Gaulle. Weighed down as he was by the burden of the Algerian war, with all its attendant external and internal problems, he was eager to demonstrate that, in spite of Algeria, France remained true to its century-old tradi-tion of assisting nations in obtaining their freedom. This is what he meant when he declared at his Press Conference of November 10, 1959, that French policy rested on two great principles 'as vast as the world': the right of the peoples associated with France to choose their own forms of government; and their just and growing desire for a higher standard of living in the face of the material progress and prosperity of the present day, which they were seeing for the first time.[31] In his broadcast speech of June 14, he harped on the theme of France's vocation. He said that one might be nostalgic and recall the colonial Empire of old, one might 'dream of the soft glow of oil lamps and of gallant sailing ships',[32] one might be apprehensive over the outcome of all the sterling efforts being undertaken in Africa for the benefit of black popula-tions. But dreaming and hard facts are two different things. The world has changed. It is France's duty to realise that it, too, must change. Some political circles and some businessmen, distorting Raymond Cartier's dramatic articles in *Paris Match*, wanted to abandon those territories formerly bound to France and let them fend for themselves. Far better, they said, to provide technical assistance to the underdeveloped parts of France itself and deploy its resources at home. But, for de Gaulle, this would be wrong: 'To my mind, these men's advice is not in keeping with the vision France has of herself nor with the vision the world has of France. We have always maintained a high sense of duty to humanity and we still hold it. Our political deeds must reflect the spirit of our country.'[33]

De Gaulle was true to his word. Decolonisation in Africa was to him a swift transition, a complete transformation achieved without bloodshed or violence: a direct contrast with Algeria. Because de

Gaulle knew that problems in Algeria and in Africa south of the Sahara could not be dissociated, he rightly felt that time was short, that he had to act quickly by granting independence to Black Africa and hence by creating a very important precedent for the future of Algeria.

His policy was to demonstrate to the Algerians and the Front de Libération National (FLN) that he was fully capable of understanding and accepting, even of promoting, the political development of the French territories overseas. The impasse in Algeria strengthened de Gaulle's hand in Black Africa and left him no option but to rush matters there. He needed an independent Black Africa to clear the name of France in the eyes of the Third World: 'The Community is both a model for and a consequence of the Algerian situation', as Alfred Grosser wrote.[34] De Gaulle repeatedly pointed out the analogy: the Algerians had resorted to violence as the only way of asserting their desire for liberty; down in the tropics violence was futile as independence had already been offered to the Africans. At the time, French public opinion was so preoccupied with North Africa that it hardly noticed the developments in Black Africa. Yet the changes gradually accustomed public opinion to the idea of decolonisation—which was exactly de Gaulle's purpose. A rapid process of decolonisation was the only way to ensure that France retained some significance overseas.

France was able to change its political, economic and military status in Black Africa, and yet retain the former colonies within its sphere of influence. 'The incorporation of the African countries into the ranks of sovereign states was welcomed by the technologists both in the nationalised and the private sectors of industry, who saw the new states as providing a stable basis for heavy capital investment, both public and private.'[35] If France played its cards well, Africa would still be a market in which it retained a highly privileged position—a ready market for French manufactured goods and itself exporting a wide range of raw materials (notably groundnuts, palm oil, tropical timber, iron, manganese bauxite, aluminium and uranium). Moreover, this new market would be within the French currency area and tariffs could discriminate in favour of France—even though many of the products would be heavily subsidised by France if they were to be competitive in the international market. Moreover, the exports of the African states would be paid for in francs, not in hard currency—a great advantage to the French balance of payments.

The great companies, most of which belonged to international groups, soon appreciated the new situation. The authorities encouraged them to deal with the former member states of the Community as customer-states—French-speaking Africa would remain French-buying Africa. Consequently these companies became strong supporters of rapid political change in Africa. They believed that friendly relations between France and Africa could be maintained if the new African states mastered the art of wise government and remained loyal to their former mother country. The companies were therefore ready to adapt their constitutions to accord with the emergence of the new states. They gradually adopted the status of locally-based companies and invited African politicians to join their boards. It is interesting to read the minutes of the general meetings and the board meetings of companies such as Société Commerciale pour l'Ouest Africain (SCOA), one of the leading trading companies in French-speaking Africa, which has steadily increased the volume of its business over the past ten years. Its report for 1960–61, for instance, reflected a completely new attitude among its managers and shareholders; similarly with other influential companies, such as Compagnie Française d'Afrique Occidentale (CFAO) and Charles Peyrissac and the Equatorial African agencies of these companies, and all the agents of important firms such as the United Africa Company (Unilever) and Pechiney. As soon as the African states had achieved their independent status without any major upheavals, a climate of optimism prevailed. It seemed that they were reaching political maturity by a process of steady and cautious development; the recently signed agreements for co-operation with France guaranteed the perpetuation of friendly relations, both economic and cultural. It is true that business interests were rather disturbed at the tendency of local politicians to direct and regulate private enterprise but the SCOA report was confident that the new states would not be so rash as to inhibit the essential flexibility and viability of industry and commerce. Some measure of Socialist-inspired intervention should not be misinterpreted; this Socialism, in economic matters at least, was no more than a manifestation of the strong community spirit prevailing in African society.

It is worth noting that the first to fall into line were the big international trusts and banks with branches in West and Equatorial Africa, rather than the strictly colonial establishments—the 'établissements de traite' (trading companies), public works enterprises, timber companies, transportation companies, factories of every kind, and chambers of commerce. The French business circles behind the colonial trade remained very reluctant to adapt themselves, believing that the decolonising policy was 'squandering' whatever was left of the former Empire, but they were eventually forced to accept independence, as there was no alternative. They were soon gratified to find Africa still remained quite dependent on the French monetary system, and were finally persuaded to stay when the African governments guaranteed their continued survival overseas.

By thus maintaining the closest possible relationship between French-speaking Africa and France, de Gaulle's policy arrived at another objective. The French colonial Empire of earlier days had survived by successively taking on different shapes: first, the Community; then the modified Community; then Franco-African co-operation. Now it envisaged a 'Eurafrica' with France as its leader. Later in this book the present situation will be analysed and the way in which the former French colonies are now subsidised, not only by French credit, but also by subsidies from the other five members of the EEC, will be demonstrated.

Such was the unfolding of events that led by degrees from the Community to Franco-African co-operation. An attempt has been made to explain those principles on which de Gaulle's policy rested; we must now try to change sides and see how Africans saw the great changes which carried them from colonialism to their present position, ten years after independence.

2. The Birth of the New African States

By 1958, French-speaking Africa had gradually become accustomed to the intricate machinery of the Loi Cadre. In the months following the September referendum, political developments rapidly gathered momentum and constitutional changes were rushed through. The old Ministry for Overseas France was required at short notice to change its former colours and to abandon the rusty machinery of colonial administration, with its set procedures so inappropriate to a policy of change and progress. Government officials were suddenly required to become the daring advocates of an entirely new colonial policy based on the sovereignty of the new-born African states, while all the time they remained convinced that the former colonial status of these countries was essential for the maintenance of French power overseas. Within Africa, too, the colonial administrators were quite unable to grasp the broad implications of the new concepts of decolonisation, international co-operation and the establishment of new inter-racial communities. The transformation was no less bewildering for the African politicians who were finding themselves transformed from advisory representatives into 'députés' (MPs), town councillors, ministers, heads of government, changes which brought new and heavy responsibilities.

A Frenchman visiting Africa in those early days of 1959 would find himself in a world that was in a complete state of flux—just as in his native France a new regime had recently been established. At first he might not realise the historical significance of the moment at which he had chosen to arrive. Many of the longer-established colonials were surprised to meet newcomers from France at a time when they themselves were undecided over whether they ought to leave. 'What on earth are you doing here?' they enquired. 'Do you mean to replace us and serve those who were formerly our servants? Spare us your criticisms, please; you don't know the first thing yet about Africa. You shouldn't expect much from *those* people. They want to be independent; good luck to them. They don't know what they're losing. . . .' Such were the bitter, spiteful comments of some of the old-fashioned businessmen and of the lower-middle-class European mechanics and petty tradesmen ('les petits blancs') who were afraid of losing their jobs and were sorry to see the end of the opportunity of adding to their nice little pile of savings (in valuable CFA francs). There were also disillusioned reactions from certain of the colonial administrators, who could not brook de Gaulle's new policy, who refused to trust the Africans, and who accused the mother country of irresponsibly squandering the national heritage.

Nevertheless, a newcomer to Brazzaville in April 1959 would find everything quiet and peaceful, in spite of the recent racial riots between two hostile tribal groups, the Balali and the M'Bochi. The government had not yet been completely transferred from Pointe Noire, which in the days of the Loi Cadre had been the capital of Moyen-Congo, where the territorial assembly met. Already, however, the former Vice-President of the government, Abbé Fulbert Youlou, now *primus inter pares*, and his ministers, were settling in Brazzaville. Yvon Bourges was still the High Commissioner General for French Equatorial Africa, bridging the gap between the end of the Federation and the new administrative machine of the Community. In the name of de Gaulle (whose minister he was later to become) he prepared to relinquish most of his powers with dignity and efficiency and without presumption. He saw it as his duty to do all he could to help the Congolese government towards self-determination as a model example of the spirit of the Community and of Gaullism—a manifestation of the spirit of Free France which still found effective expression in the daily broadcasts of Radio Brazzaville. In fact, the Federation of French Equatorial Africa (AEF) had had its day, but it did not completely vanish. There was no sudden break; on the contrary, the four states wanted to remain associated with each other in some way as yet undetermined. The shrewd, crafty, pleasure-loving Father Youlou soon saw what additional power and prestige he would gain from a continued association of the four constituent countries of the former AEF. His great rival, both in politics and in the Church, Barthélemy Boganda (the former leader of the Central African Republic), had just died in a strange accident, and Boganda's successor, the youthful David Dacko, was rather a lightweight.

In Dakar, at this time, the situation was more complicated. Of course, every Senegalese was looking forward to the end of colonisation, and independence to him meant more than to a Gabonese or to a Congolese from the great equatorial forest. But the end of the Federation of French West Africa (AOF) involved enormous political and economic upheavals in Dakar, the proud, glamorous capital. Senegal was seeking more from independence than it would obtain merely by voting 'Yes' at the referendum. It wished to be autonomous within the Community; but, beyond that, the leading Senegalese politicians envisaged the Community as the point of departure of a new kind of association between a federation of the newly-independent states and the former mother country, with Dakar the capital of the new federation. The new High Commissioner General, Pierre Messmer, was facing no easy task, for most African leaders were strongly opposed to Léopold Sédar Senghor's plan.

Tananarive was overjoyed with its status and sought nothing further. Madagascar was not losing—quite the contrary; it would be gaining national sovereignty; it would soon be independent with a seat at the United Nations. The President, Philibert Tsiranana, a wily peasant who does not himself belong to the aristocratic Hova tribe from the high plateaux of Tananarive, devoted himself to making the other independent African states aware of the Malagasy personality. He succeeded so well that everyone was forced to make frequent reference to the old Malagasy civilisation.

These three countries—Congo-Brazzaville, Senegal and Madagascar—were the kernel from which the Community developed. Its evolution accelerated in the years 1958–60—symbolically, precisely the period when jet aircraft were introduced on to the

African services. Henceforth Africa would play an extremely important role in world affairs. The birth of the African states may have been, in the end, a hurried and a precipitate process, but it cannot be understood without an appreciation of how the concepts of freedom and independence had gradually and imperceptibly become recognised by the African peoples, and of the events and the personalities involved in the slow evolution towards independence. To Paris, London or Brussels, these developments might well have seemed incomprehensible, but seen from the Gulf of Guinea, the wilds of the Sahel or the banks of the Congo river they were obvious and inevitable.

INDEPENDENCE, OR GOVERNMENT BY CONSENT

The transfer of power had been effected swiftly and smoothly, from the stage of the earliest negotiations through a succession of increasingly progressive agreements until the final stage was reached: a referendum organised by the colonial power. Those who voted 'Yes' would be granted national sovereignty in close association with France, within the framework of the Franco-African Community: those who voted 'No' could obtain independence but at the cost of cutting themselves off completely from France. No country was expected to take so rash a step. Did African peoples vote for this association with France with as little conviction as they had voted in the days of the French Union and the Loi Cadre? Perhaps, this time, they were inspired by the personality of de Gaulle, whom they trusted implicitly; certainly, this time, they voted fully realising what was at stake. But apart from the aura surrounding de Gaulle, what did independence mean for the ordinary man in Africa?

The sociologist, film-writer and director Jean Rouch is one of the white men who best know Africa. With great sensitivity and objectivity, he has tried to show how Africans were motivated, and to express, not through words but through pictures, the new motivations which colonialism had given them. In his first full-length film, *Moi, un Noir* (I, an African), a model of its kind, he examines the fundamental problems of underdeveloped peoples: their longing for freedom of expression and for unrestrained happiness; their daily struggle for the bare necessities of life; their frustrations and their resentment against the modern way of life, introduced into Africa by the white man for his own ends, with which the Africans must necessarily become involved and which they enjoy, particularly those happy few with a regular job and a monthly salary; the new black middle classes—the clerks, the civil servants, the messengers, the shop-assistants, etc. Rouch's poor Abidjan docker does not enjoy all those good things. He sweats and grumbles, he has a hard life and an empty stomach, like hundreds unemployed or under-employed in the new African towns. But he keeps smiling, he laughs, he jokes, he pretends; he pretends he is a great cinema actor like Edward G. Robinson, or a paratrooper fighting a war, expressing his pent-up resentment in dreams of violence. The poor docker sees himself as Edward G. Robinson just as the small clerk longs to become a fully-fledged Corsican customs officer, or as the new deputy adopts the clothes, bearing and smooth manners of a Radical Socialist or Christian Democrat deputy.

Apart from the flag, the new anthem, the new leader, the new feeling of prestige and satisfied vanity, what change has independence brought for our 'Edward G. Robinson'? Daily life is the same as ever: looking round for odd jobs, constant insecurity, bitter competition with all the other unemployed, low wages and, in the towns, a high cost of living and all the hardships and temptations of urban life. Certainly, there were a few who could aspire only to menial tasks under the colonial regime who were now becoming more important, getting a share of the newly-won power and considerably improving their lot; but many others did not agree to this independence by consent and reacted against it and they themselves were to pay a heavy price for refusing to adapt to the situation.

In fact, obtaining national sovereignty did not disrupt Africa as deeply as had, some fifty years before, the sudden forcible entry of the white man upon the African scene, especially in the heart of the forest, as in Congo, Gabon and Cameroun. At that time the Africans were panic-stricken, and displayed typical defence mechanisms, clinging desperately to their tribal groups, trying to merge into larger units. Once colonisation became established, with the imposition of a foreign way of life and the establishment of unfamiliar urban communities, the Africans felt a deep though suppressed resentment. They resorted to a kind of double life: on the one hand, they complied with the new order, with its unfamiliar way of life and its Christian ethics; on the other hand, they remained faithful to their traditional tribal groups, continuing to observe their long-standing practices either openly in cultural associations and fraternities or clandestinely within secret societies.[1] But once colonialism had become established—once it had created its large towns and sent out its administrators to run them, once harbours and airports had been built—then the new ways were adopted: first by a few, and then the infection spread like wildfire. Improved communications and the introduction of the radio led to an intimacy of contact between European colonialism and African tradition and, in spite of the survival of tradition in remote villages and even in some corners of the towns, the way of life and the long-standing beliefs of an entire continent were very largely swept aside.

I remember visiting a village in the region of Boko, in the Lower Congo, in 1959. It was the birthplace of a Congolese deputy, a member of the Union Démocratique de Défense des Intérêts Africains (UDDIA), Youlou's party which was then in power. In his village, the deputy was regarded as a local boy who had managed to rise to the status of the white man in earlier days. To the headman of the village, he represented a power parallel with the headman's own traditional authority. He was accepted provided he did not assert his authority beyond that of the earlier colonial administration. The situation was in any case beyond the grasp of the headman of the village, his wives or the other village elders. However, they all expected 'presents' and 'advantages' from their deputy. They saw him as a protector: not that they needed his support within the village, where the clan provided a protective framework, but they needed him at the 'sous-préfecture', the point at which they came into contact with the central authority. In that village, so remote from the capital, the deputy was a far more significant person than at the National Assembly. In carrying out his duties to his constituents, he was in direct contact with the realities of Africa.

African political life has evolved mainly in the towns. However, even today, 90 per cent of Africans live in rural areas and 80 per cent depend on agriculture and animal husbandry for a living. Political life first reached the villages in the guise of party workers, canvassers, territorial or municipal councillors and finally deputies, all promising roads, dispensaries, schools and wells. Inevitably, the contact was only superficial, because of the great size and sparse populations of the electoral districts, particularly in such countries as Chad, Niger, Mali and Mauritania. The base of the political pyramid was subject to the head; it was never able to express its views spontaneously, but was conditioned, even coerced, from the top. The modern political system was superimposed on the traditional system of discussion within the clans, tribes or ethnic groups. The two systems co-existed, just as the subsistence economy went on existing side by side with the monetary economy. Modern political institutions gained ground between 1946 and 1960, but the traditional structures did not crumble away. Customs and ancestral habits persist and act as a brake to progress, fortunately perhaps, in areas which are neglected and backward, lacking in technicians and administrators and poor in means of communication.

The monetary economy has made giant strides forward in the past fifteen years because of two essential factors: the outside demand for the basic commodities (cocoa, coffee, bananas, palm oil, groundnuts, wood, manganese, bauxite and iron ore); and the birth of an African middle class, small but increasingly powerful, holding salaried employment in the public and private sectors, which soon became eager to acquire the means of obtaining the material comforts of Western civilisation.[2] This middle class, concentrated in the urban and semi-urban areas, was the first

44

politically-conscious group to press for independence. It is not engaged in big business, being still at the stage of negotiating for immediate profits; it is not individualistic, however, for as political evolution favours its own development, it supports the state. Its existence has had important consequences: firstly, it has, quite involuntarily, attracted to the towns a young unskilled working population eager for the advantages of this same middle class; secondly, it has promoted an intensive educational programme. This, in its turn, has had two important results: the creation of a class of intellectuals, students educated for the most part in Europe with a view to obtaining key administrative posts, and who will come to clash with this same middle class that initiated the political development of their countries; and the creation of another class of local school-leavers, unemployed or under-employed, bitter and desperately jealous of the advantages of those who have come into power with independence. The situation briefly sketched here is by no means exceptional. It recalls certain stages of the political, economic and social development of the developed countries.

The legacy left by colonialism to the newly-independent countries has been heavy. Not only did the colonial powers destroy the structure of native African society but they imposed their own traditions, ideas and ways of thinking. These ways and traditions today fashion the African people.

Two phases of development can be recognised among the Africans—at least among those who succeeded in making their voices heard during their exchanges with the French colonial power. In the first stage, the Africans tried to carry the French principle of close association and assimilation to its furthermost limits. French policy had at first aimed at providing a logical legal basis for the colonial policy, and in the year II of the French Revolution a decree ordered that the same egalitarian principles should apply both in France and in the four 'communes' of Senegal: St Louis, Rufisque, Dakar and Gorée. According to this decree, any man living in one of the (then few) French colonies was considered to be a French citizen. During the nineteenth century, when France considerably expanded its colonial holdings and created the Second Empire, it reverted to traditional rather than statutory law in its colonies: authority was vested in the 'commandant de cercle' (district commissioner) whose power and effectiveness depended on close and friendly relations with the local tribes. In February 1944, the Brazzaville Conference established assimilation and association as the guiding principles of French colonial policy in the years to come. The Conference regarded such an evolution in the status of the colonies as a reward to those African territories which gave such decisive aid to de Gaulle during the war and never wavered in their loyalty (see chapter 1, pages 9–10).

In fact these reforms were overdue at the beginning of the war. The French principle of assimilation and association, formally reasserted at Brazzaville in 1944, had already inspired some earlier political decisions. As early as 1917 the first African deputy, Blaise Diagne, was sitting in the French Parliament; later, in 1931, he was to become Under-Secretary of State for the Colonies. The vogue in African art in the 'gay twenties' following the 1918 Armistice, the first Pan-African congress held in 1919, the colonial exhibition in 1936, Gide's books on travels through the Congo and Chad with their forceful criticisms of the colonial administrations, all made progressive Frenchmen aware of the people and the problems of French-speaking Africa. Yet, at the same time, France was implementing its colonial policy—in this respect so different from that of Great Britain—of introducing its own ways of living and its own mentality among its overseas peoples. The part played by French schools and French schoolteachers in shaping the leaders of French-speaking Africa cannot be overemphasised. The motivations that were, much later, to urge Africans to demand decolonisation and demand independence were largely acquired in French elementary schools from French teachers.

In *The New Societies of Tropical Africa*, Guy Hunter examines the consequences of the European penetration of Africa and the social problems which followed independence. He considers that the European mentality which pervaded Africa was typical of the

Protestant West and North—'self-assured, capitalist, industrial, scientific'—rather than the traditional Catholic outlook of Southern Europe. At first, the schools were the sole source of this European influence. Though originally aimed at training only clerks, instructors and foremen, nevertheless the young French schoolmaster, isolated in the heart of Africa, could not help but unconsciously impart his own dreams and ideals.

British policy had always been to maintain a sort of *Pax Britannica* in its colonial territories by relying upon some trusted native overlords, whose powers were usually very limited; their ultimate intention was always that one day—when, they themselves of course would choose—they would withdraw and leave an African society to African rule. The French, on the other hand, naively convinced that their own system was perfect, dreamed of reshaping Africa on the model of France; and just as any little boy from Toulouse, Brittany or Flanders learned to say 'Our forefathers, the Gauls . . .' so did the little African. France intended its African territories to change gradually into tropical versions of a French province. The French administrators saw this as a task for the schoolmaster; the French educational system, free, secular and republican, was to create black Frenchmen. The young African pupils learned of all the noble heritage of modern France: the 'immortal principles of 1789'; Rousseau's concepts of freedom and equality before the law; the Jacobinism of Robespierre and Saint-Just; finally Babeuf's utopian—and French—version of Communism or Proudhon's gentle, mild Socialism. Some of the schoolmasters may indeed have been members of the Communist Party, and therefore influenced by contemporary Marxism, but in fact they were much more nearly the embodiment of the ingenuous revolutionary tradition of the France of 1789, 1848 and the Commune of 1870, which still remained a living force among the classes from which they originated and which still pervaded the teachers' training colleges. Unconsciously, they passed on to their African pupils their radical principles—a profound distrust of the French upper classes, and the idea that, beyond the errant, unworthy France of the present time, there existed an eternal transcendant France ready and willing to share its lofty ideals with the outer world. It was from learning of ideas such as these that the African elite of today—the schoolmasters, higher civil servants, the trade unionists and, soon after, the politicians—absorbed an ingenuous sentimental admiration, in the best style of Rousseau or Proudhon, for the concepts of justice and democracy, at least until they found themselves saddled with power and with the need for keeping it.

Thus a strange marriage took place between the French left-wing anti-clerical schoolmaster, little subject to racial prejudice, and an African elite, longing to educate itself and to take over power, but also ingenuous, idealistic, eager to break free from the narrow, over-restrictive African tradition; incapable, at least for the time being, of adapting itself even to the first stage of assimilation into the European world. A first generation of African leaders (mostly from French West Africa) were trained in this tradition at the Ecole Normale Supérieure William Ponty (higher training college) in Gorée, the island off Dakar. The school had in the nineteenth century replaced the rather reactionary Ecole des Fils de Chefs (school for chiefs' sons), in St Louis.* This generation of William Ponty students included Ouezzin Coulibaly (who was to become Dean of Studies in the school, before the Second World War), Auguste Denise, Modibo Keita, Diallo Telli, Mamadou Konaté, Houphouet-Boigny, Diallo Safoulaye—the first prominent politicians of the French West African territories, the first generation of African members of the professions (schoolmasters, doctors, civil servants), the first to lay down the foundations of modern African society. The students and former pupils of William Ponty College published a magazine, *Genesis*; they organised discussion groups, such as 'La voix du Montagnard'; their former pupils' association provided a cover for the first union

---

* Such schools also existed in Bamako (Soudan), Bingerville (Ivory Coast), Conakry (Guinea) and Porto Novo (Dahomey). However from 1917 onwards, a centralised and more methodical system of education was organised at William Ponty to increase the number of African schoolmasters.

of African elementary schoolmasters. Others set up Marxist discussion groups in Dakar, Conakry, Abidjan, Bamako and Bobo-Dioulasso, where Africans could meet left-wing Frenchmen and argue interminably about decolonisation. This first generation of young independent Africans was influenced by both the Popular Front and the French Resistance—both of which seemed to represent perfectly natural reactions in defence of those noble principles they were proud to subscribe to and ardently wished to apply in their own countries. In spite of the defeat of 1940 and the humiliating presence of reactionary French representatives from the Vichy government, especially in West Africa, they had remained loyal to France in Dakar and Abidjan, because they believed that de Gaulle and the Free French were fighting for a better, nobler France, which, once the war was won, would grant Africa its freedom.

At the end of the war, in 1945–46, the leading African intellectuals gave at first their unquestioning support to de Gaulle's Coalition government, and, in spite of its innumerable anomalies, accepted the constitution of the Fourth Republic, which established the French Union. The constitution gave equality of voting rights to the Africans, it is true; but at the same time an electoral college was set up on a dual basis, by which the Africans, though they were indeed represented in Parliament, did not enjoy an electoral status equal to the French. Some authority was transferred to the Africans, but the colonial administration remained the supreme power. France agreed that the intellectuals of new Africa should be able to make their voices heard, and hoped that they would continue to play an increasingly important part; but in fact very little real responsibility was accorded to them (apart from a very few African members of the French Parliament), and many of the hopes of Africans were frustrated. It was clear that the French colonial administration was not prepared to recognise the post-war trend throughout the world towards national autonomy, except in the cases of the two former mandated territories, Cameroun and Togo, now transferred to the trusteeship of the United Nations (which had just solemnly proclaimed in its charter the right of nations to choose their own form of government). The Sétif massacres in Algeria and the savage repression of the Madagascar rebellion had gone unnoticed in France, except by a very few, but they did not escape the attention of the William Ponty men in Africa.

The movement towards independence was sweeping onward irresistibly in other parts of the world. It was nothing less than a logical step in the course of history, a sequel to the Second World War in which soldiers of all races and colours fought in the Allied armies against the Axis powers, and in which at one stage the Asian had proved victorious over the European. The proclamation of independence in India and in Indonesia, the Bandung declaration, the war in Indochina and later in Algeria, all had a profoundly traumatic effect on African thought. Despite the generosity of much of post-war European colonial policy, Africans nevertheless came increasingly to resent the affectations of superiority of so many Europeans, especially the 'lower whites' who were flocking in to take jobs in administration, in business and in the army. These repeated humiliations gravely offended the susceptibilities of the Africans, who came to be sorely disappointed in France.

The day-to-day practice of the colonial administration bore no resemblance to the lofty ideals that had been laid down for it, which the administrators themselves should have taken to heart far more than they did. The 'colonised' African had once been proud that assimilation was offered to him; now he found that, in practice, it was refused, and that his efforts to identify himself with the European were often greeted with derision. Finally he came to realise that he could never hope to be fully accepted as a metropolitan Frenchman.

He had hoped for complete assimilation but nearly always gave up, realising the exorbitant price that he would have to pay—a debt that he could never discharge. He was also horrified when he realised fully what it would mean. The dramatic moment would come when he would find himself looking at his own people with the eye of the colonial power, with all its prejudices and criticisms. Of course, his people were not perfect. They had their failings, and sometimes he would, reasonably enough, become irritated by their foibles. Much of what they valued he would come to regard as antiquated, inefficient, ludicrous. And yet! they were still his own people, he belonged to them and would always belong to them! The unvarying way of life established over the centuries, the food so good to his mouth and his stomach—they were part of his people, they were part of him. Was he throughout his life to be ashamed of all of him that was truly his own, of everything in him that had not been borrowed? Why should he be eager to disown his own blood? Was this perpetual frustration an essential part of his liberation?[3]

He may have been offered a new language and a new culture, but the barriers remained, the barriers of wealth, of the colour-bar, of social distinctions. He came to realise that he was still on his own and that he must find his way out of his dilemma.

If France had redoubled its efforts to establish an African elite to provide more widespread education and greater opportunity to become fully Europeanised, it is probable that the Africans would not have wanted to break away from what they would have come to consider their own world. It is even possible that, if the British colonies in Africa had not started breaking away into independent states in 1957, the French negro intellectuals would have been content to evolve some kind of Franco-African federation, rather than face the issue of an actual separation.[4]

This may sound plausible enough, but it is hard to believe that sooner or later, whatever kind of federal system were adopted, the African would not come to want unfettered independence and would not sever finally any kind of connection with France.

On the other hand, it is true that many African intellectuals felt fully at home in Paris and were tempted to turn their backs on the fundamental problems of Africa. Quite a few refused to return to their own countries, which were losing their individuality and their robustness in the enervating isolation of an over-centralised colonial administrative structure.[5] Many Africans, after spending a number of years in France, found themselves unhappy, at a loose end, out of their element, when they returned home to their fellow-countrymen. They were torn between the desire to keep to their 'European ways' and their duty to conform to their traditional customs. This is why French-speaking Africans, in spite of having become so much more intellectually integrated than their English-speaking brothers, nevertheless tried to rid themselves of the insidious all-pervading influence of French culture, by organising themselves first on a cultural rather than on a political basis.

They had been taught to admire the principles of liberty, equality, fraternity and justice; they had learnt the significance of formal procedure and the power of the spoken word. But to what purpose? Was it only to become 'white negroes', mere disciples of the white man? So it was that the African, although he had learned to become a part of, and to love, the French way of life that dominated his existence, turned back and reasserted his own African culture, hoping to provide a counterpoise, in his philosophy of 'negritude', to the spreading influence of the West. This enthusiasm for African ways soon became a cry of protest against colonialism. This spirit is well expressed in one of Aimé Césaire's poems, for, though a West Indian rather than an African, he accurately reproduces the feeling of jarring contradiction which, in spite of the French aim of complete assimilation, spurred on African intellectuals to recapture the true spirit of Africa:

> We are standing, my country and I, our hair streaming in the wind, my small hand in its huge fist; and our strength is not of us, but above us, speaking with a voice that resounds through the night. And the voice declares that for centuries Europe has fed us only lies and filled us with pestilence. . . .
>
> For it is untrue to say that man's task is now ended,
> That there remains nothing more to do in the world,
> That we should only drag along with the rest of the earth;
> Only now has man started his work,

And it remains for him to overcome all restrictions
Driven into the corners of his eagerness;
No people has a monopoly of beauty, wisdom or strength.[6]

At the end of the war, Alioune Diop, a Senegalese living in Paris, founded the Société Africaine de Culture, with its magazine *Présence Africaine*, and gathered around himself a number of African artists, poets, thinkers and politicians, the foremost among them being Léopold Sédar Senghor. Relentlessly and repeatedly, through meetings and rallies, they drove home to the intellectuals of Europe and the Third World their message that colonialism was undermining the African personality. At the time of the Paris Congress of Negro Writers and Artists, Alioune Diop wrote:

> Negritude was born of the resentment of black intellectuals at not being able to identify themselves fully with Western humanism. Confronted by European parties, by European churches, by classical works of art, even by the richness of the French and the English tongues (all of which set out, in all good faith, to be the heritage of men of every race), the black man could not help feeling frustrated. . . . No culture can thrive on colonialism: it will frustrate some, while others will feel condemned; and the black peoples feel they have suffered long enough the woes of racism, slavery and colonialism.[7]

Nevertheless, in spite of the repeated assertions of the spirit of Africa, in spite of the constant indictments of colonialism, Africa did not rise in a general revolt. North Africa arose, it is true, especially Algeria, which fought for its freedom through blood, violence, murder and war. Algeria found itself, and in the end threw off the yoke of colonialism. Whether its revolution ultimately failed to reach its aim is another matter.[8] From an ideological viewpoint, as the model of a nation awakening to rebel against its former colonial master, the Algerian War was a historical event as essential to Africa as was the American Revolution to the United States, or the French Revolutions of 1789 and 1848 to Europe. One can pursue the analogy and maintain that men like Ferhat

53

Abbas, Ait Ahmed, Boudiaf, Ben Bella, and those who were tortured to death (such as Ben Mehidi or Didouche Mourad), were pure nationalists and revolutionaries, following the tradition of those of the second half of the nineteenth century. Wartime Algeria was the scene of heroism and of great feats of arms; the Algerian revolt spelt total war, as it did with the Indonesians and the Vietnamese. The African, however, had neither the wish and aggressiveness nor the opportunity to throw himself into a similar all-out war.* A passionate spirit of nationalism sprang up in the Third World wherever communities had been disrupted by violent upheavals or had proved incapable of adapting themselves to sweeping social and technological change.[9] In Africa, on the other hand, dissatisfaction took the form of a growing impatience with the restrictions imposed by the white man, largely because of his patronising, smug superiority, and yet at the same time of a desire to share fully the material advantages enjoyed by the white colonists: social welfare; a salary for the African administrator equal to that of his French expatriate counterpart; motor-cycle police escorts ('les motards'), and a Mercedes for the President of the Republic just like any European head of state. Far from practising a violent and extreme form of nationalism, the African was ready, once he had been granted some degree of independence, to retain some Europeans in his government service and to have Europeans represent his country overseas—for instance, on the Council of the French Union.

In Africa south of the Sahara, there were no national revolutions, possibly because nationalism is essentially a European concept, involving long-established frontiers and national languages, cultures and philosophies, and the spirit of national loyalty. By contrast, the frontiers of the existing African states had been arbitrarily laid down by the colonial powers, long before anyone dreamed of independent African countries, and without any respect for ethnic divisions or for economic facts. In this way

* Except, of course, in four cases: the Malgache revolt; the Bamileke revolt in Cameroun, the Mau Mau revolt in Kenya; and the present fighting in the Portuguese African territories.

colonialism deprived Africa of the natural balance between its earlier frontiers. Consequently nationalism could express itself only in limited local tribal uprisings, as in the case of the Mau Mau or the Bamileke. Africa was to labour long under the handicap of its 'balkanisation', a point to be examined later in this chapter.

Yet it must be said that today the concepts of nationhood and of nationalism are becoming outmoded. From the struggles of the people of the colonies has been born a new principle of *collective nationalism* in which frontiers play no part.[10] The twentieth century has taught us that it is economic considerations that, above all, determine the fate of a country. No country can afford nowadays to live proudly isolated within its frontiers, its language, its customs, and remain self-sufficient. If a healthy national spirit is essential for survival, today economic and technological efficiency is even more important. The nationalism of former colonies will overflow their frontiers, as will be shown in Part Three.

The colonial powers were wise enough to arrive at a kind of unspoken 'non-aggression pact' with the African leaders, by which they would aim at a solution of the colonial problem which was to the best economic and political advantage of each side. Such a compromise would avoid sabotage, destruction, lawlessness and repression. The Africans soon came to realise that the major preoccupation of the colonial power was to retain its preferential economic position in these areas, and they realised that they would have to make concessions in that direction if they were themselves to enjoy the economic and social advantages that would result from such an arrangement. So, as Frantz Fanon has pointed out, the African leaders and political parties compounded with the French and thereby compromised themselves.[11] They conceded, in some measure, their national sovereignty. Later, after establishing themselves in power with the help of the 'neo-colonialists', they tried to rid themselves more completely of foreign control. This time, however, they were aiming not at political revolution but at equality of economic status. They maintained that if they were to be fully independent politically, it was essential that they should enjoy the economic privileges previously denied them.

55

POLITICAL STAGES OF INDEPENDENCE

We have examined the motivations which led to the birth of an independent modern Africa. We must now consider how Africa, in the event, put these ideals into practice.

In fifteen years Africa achieved a degree of political evolution which in France had taken over a century; the convulsions of 1946 to 1960 are quite without precedent in the entire history of nations. They were due primarily to the French anxiety to avoid a major disturbance at any cost, and yet at the same time to create a new Africa after France's own image. Naturally enough, the first concept to be introduced was of a parliamentary government, which became established in the towns, with the traditional African feudal system restricted to the depths of the bush.

The first stage came in 1946, with the establishment of the French Union. Its political structure was not dissimilar from that adopted at the Restoration in France: territorial councils elected under the 'double college' system, the two Grand Councils (in French West Africa and in French Equatorial Africa) and, right at the top, besides the French National Assembly, the Council of the French Union, the Holy of Holies. In 1952, the Africans, after considerable difficulty, gained the enactment of a 'Code du Travail' (Labour Code), granting them right of association and negotiation. Finally, in 1956, notwithstanding the continued supervision of the governors and of the elaborate superstructure of the French colonial administration and in spite of the continuing flow of instructions from Paris, Africans were 'allowed' to organise their own government councils and territorial assemblies. One might have thought that this stage of development would mark the end of African ambitions—a parliamentary system had been established and African politicians were learning all the niceties of party political life from their French counterparts.

In fact, however, the Loi Cadre was outdated the day it came into effect, since the French government, under pressure from the United Nations, had already gone so far as to concede full self-government in Togo and Cameroun. The events of 1958 in France saw a complete upheaval of policy: thereafter, greatly encouraged by pressures from political parties and trade unions, a sudden surge towards independence set in.

The Political Parties and the Trade Unions

Three works by Thomas Hodgkin—*Nationalism in Colonial Africa, African Political Parties*, and *French-Speaking West Africa in Transition*—provide an excellent guide to the intricate tangle of the African party political system.[12] We shall mention briefly the more important points.

First, it must be emphasised that the elaborate administrative mechanism set up by France (i.e., territorial councils and assemblies, the Grand Councils of the two French-African Federations, the Council of the French Union) provided an ideal training-ground for African intellectuals. Later, French-speaking African politicians at the United Nations and other international bodies made a deep impression with their familiarity with political procedure. These institutions had given the first generation of an African political and intellectual elite the chance to try out its talents. France had trained politicians rather than civil servants. Once a Negro could become a Member of Parliament or Senator of the French Republic, the prestige of the white man as a politician disappeared: now it was only his professional expertise—economic, administrative or technological—which earned the respect of the African. Under the Fourth Republic, 84 out of 620 Members of the National Assembly and 71 out of 320 Senators were representatives of African overseas territories. France might boast that it had spread its culture and civilisation through its primary schools, or might be proud of its great advances in secondary education after the Second World War, but the main outcome of its efforts was to produce a crop of young students following general legal studies with an eye on a career in politics rather than in one of the other professions. For politics, with its high-sounding speeches and endless cavilling, has much in common with the palavers of the everyday life of traditional Africa, is easier to learn and practise than the sciences or medicine, and not as mundane as administration or teaching. Power and prestige—a ministerial portfolio or an ambassadorship—are considered the due reward after a course at the Law Faculty or the Institut des Sciences Politiques, after a year or two at the former Ecole de la France d'Outre-Mer, or, for the exceptionally gifted, after a 'short course' at the Ecole Nationale d'Administration, in Paris. This was in marked contrast to the practice in English-speaking countries. There, as self-government was the rule and self-help the order of the day, the British, whose main interest was to maintain their control over national trade and commerce, had to rely on a strong and able administration, and at an early stage began to train civil servants and to establish local colleges and universities. Makerere College was opened in 1921 and given university status in 1949. Fourah Bay University College, at Freetown in Sierra Leone, the oldest teaching institution at university level in Africa, was established in 1827: later, in 1876, it was affiliated to Durham University in England. Achimota, and the more recent University of Legon, near Accra in Ghana, took students from all over West Africa. Nigerian students flocked there until the establishment in 1948 of the excellent University of Ibadan in Western Nigeria. Moreover, in English-speaking Africa, the chiefs, having retained some administrative authority under the British system of indirect rule, welcomed the creation of a nucleus of responsible civil servants. The Alake of Abeokuta in Western Nigeria, one of the most powerful Yoruba chiefs (who died in 1963), used to send, at his own expense, promising young Yoruba to complete their university studies in the United Kingdom. To young Ghanaians, Nigerians and other English-speaking Africans, the main concern was 'a degree', which would bring them 'a good job' either in the public or in the private sector. As a consequence of this aspect of British colonial policy, big firms like Shell or Unilever very soon were training and employing African junior personnel, who had the prospect of rising within the firm. The English-speaking elite learned more and thought less, so to speak, than their French-speaking counterparts and remained much less politically-minded.

In French-speaking Africa, the political parties and trade unions have provided the strongest motive forces behind African political life. In English-speaking Africa, by contrast, political parties often originated in a group of bright young disciples gathered round a prominent African leader: such was the case with the Nigerian National Democratic Party, founded in 1923 by the engineer Herbert Macaulay, and the National Congress of British West Africa, organised by the lawyer Caseley-Hayford. These groups were first a kind of club for members of the intellectual elite, well-to-do, holding moderate views and advocating comparatively mild reforms. Things began to change slightly around 1930 with the advent in Sierra Leone of Wallace Johnson, and in Nigeria of Azikiwe who soon became very popular in and even outside Nigeria. Their followers were younger, more numerous, more anxious to obtain a greater measure of self-rule—in fact, true self-government. Their ideas spread and germinated and led to the formation of a multitude of new parties, usually centring on the local chiefs or village elders, the traditional leaders of the African communities. In 1944 Azikiwe founded the National Council of Nigeria and the Cameroons (NCNC); the People's Party in Sierra Leone appeared at about the same time. These national or local organisations tried to gain influence at the lower end of the social scale, to get through to the villagers and make them more aware of their status as colonials, and more and more active in politics. Their tactics led to the emergence of comparatively well-organised political parties and had a profound influence on the development of the post-war generation. They came to realise, as did, for instance, Sékou Touré in Guinea, that only well-disciplined parties, with a large popular membership (especially from the bush villages) could apply real political pressure on the colonial powers. Such influence was beyond the tiny groups of urban intellectuals, who were closely connected with the leaders of traditional Africa. But English-speaking politicians had two great assets; their newly-founded parties were never closely associated with British political parties and they were backed by a strong, dynamic local political press. In 1950, twenty-three newspapers, with a total circulation of 185,000, were being published in Ghana; in Nigeria, thirty-five newspapers with a circulation of 471,000. The influence of the English-speaking press is a very important factor in the emergence of modern Africa, even if it cannot compare with the power of the press in highly-developed countries.

In French-speaking countries, a local press hardly existed. Such papers as existed were generally owned and written by Frenchmen, mainly for Frenchmen, like *Dakar Matin*, with a circulation of 15,000, and *Abidjan Matin*, with a circulation of 12,000. (Moreover, the paper from which these two evolved was originally called *Paris-Dakar*.) Their appeal was almost exclusively to urban readers. No journalistic tradition had been established in French Africa at the time of independence. A vast number of bulletins, with a very limited circulation, appeared erratically. On the other hand, the weeklies published by the Catholic missions were more successful, and their popularity continued even after independence: for instance, *Afrique Nouvelle* in Dakar (circulation 15,000) and *Semaine Africaine* in Brazzaville (circulation 12,000). The Malagasy press was the only exception, with two hundred papers in the Malagasy language with a circulation totalling 50,000 and fourteen French-language papers with a total circulation of 23,000.[13]

In spite of the absence of a true political press, active political life began in French-speaking Africa as early as in English-speaking Africa—perhaps even earlier. However, it must be stressed that, in contrast to their English counterparts, all the political parties and trade unions of French-speaking Africa maintained close affiliations to the corresponding organisations in metropolitan France.

In those days a rigid policy of assimilation was being applied, so much so that Edouard Herriot (the famous politician of the old Radical Socialist Party, mayor of Lyons and President of the National Assembly from 1947 to 1954) could open a debate on the French Union by jokingly saying that if the principle of assimilation were pushed to the point of absurdity, France would be in danger of becoming 'a colony of its colonies'. Senghor, at an inter-parliamentary Europe-Africa meeting in October 1959, made the very same point in a much more serious spirit when he said that in 'a true federation, half the members of the government and of Parliament should be Negroes or Arabo-Berbers. France is not racially-minded, but its reluctance to become a colony of its colonies, in order to meet their expenses, is quite understandable.' The policy of assimilation could not be taken that far, but it dominated Franco-African relations until 1958–59. Because African political parties were required to remain branches of their French counterparts, to boost their numbers within the French Parliament, they could not function as true representatives of the African people.* The people voted because they were given the right to vote and they were proud to do so, but the candidates for whom they voted were usually eminent men who had adopted French manners and the French way of life. Sometimes they were not even Africans but came from the French West Indies or even from France.

As early as 1930, the sfio had a section in Dakar, organised by the lawyer Lamine Guèye: it was the sfio also which stimulated the beginnings of political life in Senegal. In 1945, after four unpleasant years of the rigours of the Vichy regime, which deprived the Senegalese of their greatly-valued right of French citizenship, a discussion group (comité d'entente) was established at which the older Socialists, the followers of Lamine Guèye, could meet the younger representatives of a Marxist group, les Groupes d'études Communistes. Senghor was a member of this discussion group. A new political party, le Bloc Africain, was founded, which remained affiliated to the French sfio and sent Senghor and Lamine Guèye as representatives to the first and second Constituent Assemblies. At the same period, the African planters of the Ivory Coast became organised under the leadership

* This is perhaps an overstatement since the rda party launched by Houphouet-Boigny in 1946 (see pp. 63–4) could be called a 'mass' party. Initially, the main purpose of this party was to suppress forced labour effectively all over French-speaking Africa, an objective which appealed to the African peoples.

of a bright young African doctor, Houphouet-Boigny, who, at the end of 1945, founded the Parti Démocratique de Côte d'Ivoire. Like Senghor, he was elected to the two Constituent Assemblies as a member of the Union Républicaine et de la Résistance, a nebulous fellow-travelling organisation closely related to the Communist Party. In 1946 in Brazzaville, following the example of the Bloc Africain, Cazaban-Mazerolles, a Frenchman, founded a local section of the SFIO. In Oubangui-Chari a Mouvement de l'Evolution Sociale de l'Afrique Noire (MESAN) was organised, and in Dahomey a Parti Républicain Dahoméen: both voted with the MRP, the Christian Centre Party. De Gaulle's party, the Rassemblement du Peuple Français (RPF) also had affiliated local parties in some areas: for instance, the Union Démocratique Tchadienne. The Parti Social-Démocrate de Madagascar was yet another Socialist stronghold. Thus, immediately after the Second World War, all the major African political parties were connected with one of the three great French political parties, the Communist Party, the MRP and the SFIO, with the latter extending the closest welcome to the African parties. Later, some were also to join the Union Démocratique et Sociale de la Résistance (UDSR) and the RPF.

This close association with the political parties of France, though it seemed unavoidable, nevertheless proved to be a great disadvantage, for the African parties became involved in French political squabbles which deflected their attention from the problems of the African people. At the time, France was in a perpetual flurry of elections, with a new one virtually every eighteen months between 1946 and 1958. The SFIO was resisting the advance of the Communist Party, even aligning itself with the right in its attempts to stem Communist influence. At about this time, moderates and French business circles in Africa were becoming alarmed at the trend of events and mustered a right-wing body called les Etats Généraux de la Colonisation. To counteract them, Houphouet-Boigny made use of similar tactics and called for the establishment of a body to protect purely African interests. He won the support of five other African political leaders, all of whom had been disillusioned by the second constitutional project of 1946. Unfortunately, Houphouet-Boigny's idea was opposed by the SFIO, which suspected the influence of the Communist Party exercised —doubtless very discreetly—through Raymond Barbé, a counsellor of the French Union with special responsibility for overseas matters, who was urging Houphouet-Boigny to establish an alliance between the Communist Party and the new African body. When Houphouet-Boigny decided to convene a conference at Bamako in October 1946, the SFIO, and particularly the Socialist leader Marius Moutet (then Minister for Overseas France) discouraged its political allies in Africa from attending it. Houphouet-Boigny therefore founded the Rassemblement Démocratique Africain (RDA) without the support of his Socialist colleagues—the Senegalese, Senghor and Lamine Guèye—and even without Apithy from Dahomey and Fily Dabo Sissoko from Soudan. Thus began the intense rivalry between Houphouet-Boigny and Senghor that was to prove such a bane and was ultimately to defeat the hopes of a Franco-African confederation. The two great African leaders were never to join forces and each went his own way, even after Senghor parted with the SFIO in 1948 to found his own party, the Bloc Démocratique Sénégalais (BDS), which aligned itself with the Indépendants d'Outre-Mer in the French Parliament, and after 1950 when Houphouet-Boigny, anxious to follow his own path and not to rely on the possibility of a Communist victory in France, broke away from the French Communist Party. Houphouet-Boigny's party reached its apogee at its second congress at Bamako on September 25, 1957, which was attended by 800 delegates and observers, among them thirty-two African ministers, sixty-seven territorial councillors, and the French ministers Edgar Faure, Pierre Mendès-France and François Mitterand. Houphouet-Boigny's RDA very soon showed itself to be an impressive organisation, well managed, with a clear awareness of what Africa needed, and yet unanimous in its desire to maintain friendly relations with France. The RDA was hailed all over French-speaking Africa as the greatest of African political parties.

Things did not work out so smoothly for Senghor and his (then)

63

friend, Mamadou Dia. The first party which they set up, the Convention Africaine (1947), was reorganised a year later into the Parti de la Rénovation Africaine, which itself in 1959 became the Parti de la Fédération Africaine (PFA). All these political bodies lacked the efficient administrative structure of the RDA. They were more intellectual, and advocated a more extreme socialism than the RDA. Their influence was less widespread than that of the RDA, extending only to Senegal and Soudan, and to a lesser degree to Niger, the Upper Volta and Dahomey.

In the same way as the African political parties at first found it difficult to exist without leaning on the support of their French counterparts, the trade unions depended in their early days on the central unions of France. The right of association, first granted by the Front Populaire and then denied by the Vichy regime, was solemnly restated by the 1946 constitution, and the three major French unions—the Confédération Générale du Travail (CGT), the Socialist Confédération Générale du Travail-Force Ouvrière (CGT-FO) and the Christian Democrat Confédération Française des Travailleurs Chrétiens (CFTC)—felt it their duty to initiate, help, train and support the first African trade unions. As the French trade unions were, in their turn, members of the great international trade union confederations—the World Federation of Trade Unions (WFTU, Prague), the International Confederation of Free Trade Unions (ICFTU, Brussels) and the International Federation of Christian Trade Unions (IFCTU)—these affiliations were automatically extended to the newly-founded African unions. Here is another contrast with English-speaking Africa, whose trade unions never became affiliated to the United Kingdom Trades Union Congress (TUC). On the other hand, as trade unionism developed in English-Speaking Africa, the unions were more and more courted by the great international confederations, which coaxed them to join as soon as their countries became autonomous.

It became quite obvious, both in French-speaking and in English-speaking Africa, that even if their demands became more and more politically-minded between 1945 and 1956 the unions often held the clearest views on economic and social problems. Of course, this was no more than their duty, as the only representatives of the urban proletariat (for trade unionism was virtually unknown in rural areas), but they also played a fundamental part in the struggle against colonial rule, demanding, through innumerable strikes and mass meetings, that the rights of African workers should be respected and that strict legislation regarding labour should be introduced throughout Africa. One may cite the great strikes in 1945 in Nigeria; the first general strike in French West Africa, in 1946; the Bamako-Dakar railway strike; the 1950 strikes in the Gold Coast; the great trade union protest meetings in 1952 all over French West Africa, especially in Guinea and the Ivory Coast: all of these had a decisive political effect. The African unions also became involved in the bitter rivalries between the international confederations, especially between the WFTU and the ICFTU. Like the political parties, the French African trade unions wasted their energy on remote ideological conflicts of little concern to them and were continuously exposed to the political instability that prevailed in those years both in France and all over the world.

As soon as the African countries became independent, one of their first moves was to disaffiliate their trade unions from the international confederations, but it was too late—the African unions remained suspicious of one another. In Guinea, the Union Générale des Travailleurs d'Afrique Noire (UGTAN) maintained orthodox Marxist views, though independent branches of UGTAN in other countries were less radical; the Confédération Générale des Travailleurs Africains (CGTA) had lost most of its power; the Force Ouvrière was not very active and preoccupied chiefly with political issues; probably the Confédération Africaine des Travailleurs Croyants (CATC) alone was sincerely trying to do what it could for the African worker.

For all their failings, however, the African trade unions served a very important purpose: they translated the traditional tribal spirit of Africa into modern language. They counterbalanced the trend towards a narrow nationalism by refusing to view independence

65

as an ultimate end, but focused public opinion upon more fundamental issues such as underdevelopment and the economic consequences of colonialism. Their attitude was authentically revolutionary, as they spoke for the proletariat of the colonial world. Their weakness lay in the fact that they represented so few people.

In fact, the day-to-day life of both political parties and trade unions was concerned primarily with political matters and industrial questions always took second place. It would be dangerous to over-simplify the very complex political history of Africa between 1946 and 1958, but the history of French West and Equatorial Africa of those years was dominated by the struggle between two opposing concepts: confederation versus federation. The leading proponents of these conflicting concepts were Houphouet-Boigny and Senghor. Houphouet-Boigny maintained that the African countries should preserve their own direct links with France and retain their own national sovereignty, whereas for Senghor, the two great primary federations of West Africa and Equatorial Africa should be no more than associates of France within a large Franco-African group. From an economic viewpoint, the one theory would still balkanise Africa, as it was after the Loi Cadre, into a number of weak economic units, whereas according to the other, the international sovereignty of African states would be to some extent limited, but a certain degree of economic unity and a common market would be established. As we have already seen in the first chapter of this book, confederation or federation or indeed any other type of association was in the event abandoned in favour of the Community, a more matter-of-fact, pragmatic body. Yet even the Community did not survive. Both the crisis in Mali and the policy of Houphouet-Boigny launched an irresistible movement towards independence among the African states: each of them, one after the other, refused to concede any part of its autonomy to the communal body and demanded comprehensive diplomatic power, including independent representation at the United Nations and other international bodies. The only thing that remained unchanged with independence in all the new states was currency; the only thing to be managed on a communal basis was transport and communications.

Houphouet-Boigny, disillusioned by the turn events had taken and bitterly disappointed by de Gaulle's readiness to concede the demands of Soudan and Senegal, decided to demand independence for the Ivory Coast while not committing himself to any agreement as to future co-operation with France. Having taken up a position 'completely outside the framework of the Community', he started negotiations, which continued for nine months before an agreement was finally signed on April 24, 1961. He carried the other states of the Conseil de l'Entente with him: Dahomey, Niger, and Upper Volta.

It is interesting to note how two men, both of them brought up under the same educational system, came to adopt diametrically opposing views on the development of French-speaking Africa. Senghor would fervently extol the lofty ideals of 'negritude', so remote from the mundane everyday problems of the new states; he saw a great and noble Africa marching forward to play its part among the nations of the world, assuming its role face to face with other civilisations: an Africa that the whole universe would have to reckon with. Nothing could be more remote from Houphouet-Boigny's dry, dispassionate appreciations of the grave economic problems confronting Africa.

The first concern of Senghor and his friends in the Parti de la Fédération Africaine was to define accurately the relation between France and Africa. In an address to the Dakar Congress in March 1959, Doudou Guèye said:

> The Community must come to help the African nation, not to disrupt it. If it is to do that, we must first set up a well balanced Franco-African Community. No such balance will be possible if France finds itself facing a number of tiny, struggling states; we intend that France should take as partners, not a dozen weak states, but powerful combinations of states. If this is to be our objective, then the political parties of yesterday, like the PRA and the RDA, are not adequate for our purpose, for they all

disintegrated in one way or another when confronted by the unexpected test of the referendum.

The second concern was to obtain independence that was truly effective, as Senghor declared when he received de Gaulle on December 13, 1959, at the Mali Assembly: 'Beyond constitutional independence, we want to reach actual independence. We intend to leave legal considerations behind and to establish with you, the people of France and the other nations of the Community, new active relations of friendship and co-operation that will guarantee true independence.' Professor M. Hamon in *Les partis politiques africains* points out how Senghor's lofty vision of independence was akin to de Gaulle's. Did not de Gaulle tell his host during a visit to Dakar in December 1959: 'Independence is a yearning, a frame of mind, an intention. I would rather call it international sovereignty. For the main thing is to exist on one's own, as one's own country and in one's own country; there can be no international existence without a national existence first. There will never be a country that matters, there *is* no country that matters, that does not contribute something to the technical progress of this world.' And Senghor replied: 'You are a true twentieth century revolutionary. You have realised that to free peoples is the great design of our century, just as to free individuals was the design of the French Revolution; and when speaking of the Algerians you have declared that self-determination was a fundamental concept of our times. And you have declared that the universal wish to raise the standard of living is another characteristic of our times. For our part, we have never maintained anything else.' At the end of the meeting of the Executive Council at St Louis in December 1959, de Gaulle granted the Federation of Mali (Soudan and Senegal) full independence; thereafter Mali became fully responsible for matters previously administered jointly. The decision was to have enormous consequences, for no self-governing French-speaking African country now felt that it could ask for less for itself. Six months after the meeting of the Executive Council and the Dakar Congress (to be exact, on the night of

August 19, 1960), Mali became independent, but the Senegalese and Soudanese were never able to agree on the election of a President of their Mali Federation. The great vision of Senghor faded away, and Senegal once again was, though independent, no more than one of many small members of the renewed Community, which was doomed shortly to crumble away. But Senghor did not abandon his abstract principles, and he and his Prime Minister, Mamadou Dia, tried to defend their attitude, first in their native part of Africa and later to the Brazzaville bloc which was set up in December 1960. 'What matters most', Mamadou Dia wrote in *Nations Africaines et solidarité mondiale*, 'is not to give a people words and slogans, but the "know-how" and technical knowledge. To harp on the theme of liberty is useless; they know that tune well enough. In short, it is useless to try to tell Africans something that they know already and not to instil in them the efficiency essential to give practical effect to their knowledge and their attainments.'[14]

On economic matters Dia was not so far from Houphouet-Boigny, who had declared at the Abidjan Congress in 1959: 'I stay apart from the battle of slogans; Africa is surfeited with slogans; it wants more solid nourishment.' Nevertheless Houphouet-Boigny's party, the RDA, was far less theoretically-minded and doctrinaire than Senghor's Parti de la Fédération Africaine. The RDA was concerned, first and foremost, with practical matters—getting on with the job of running Africa.[15] It put tangible achievement before fine theories, such as 'negritude'. Houphouet-Boigny was going to make a modern state of his country. He wanted to lead the way along a new path of international and inter-racial co-operation, within a new political framework, freed from any taint of colonialism, and to establish firm economic and cultural links with the former colonial power —first between the French and the Ivory Coast, then between the French and all Africans (at any rate, those Africans who were prepared to follow him and not to be enticed by the blandishments of Senghor's exquisite poetic fancies). In January 1960, Houphouet-Boigny declared: 'We must bring together the White and the Black, all the different tribes, the young and the old, we must bring everyone together—old and young, let us join hands.' In this characteristic speech, one can detect Houphouet-Boigny's particular brand of idealism and sentimentality. From a political viewpoint, he has nothing against traditional tribalism; provided the tribal chiefs acknowledge him as the supreme head of state, sympathise with his ideals and do not stand in his way, he will not try to destroy their power as did Sékou Touré in Guinea. On the other hand, Houphouet-Boigny has no faith in the unity of Africa and Pan-Africanism; he cannot conceive any close federation of African states. The alternative to Pan-African liberty that he has to offer is economic liberty: 'They want Pan-African liberty, but Pan-Africanism they will never get; instead they will get isolation and poverty; poverty will breed political insecurity; and with political insecurity there will be no more liberty.'[16] Houphouet-Boigny had joined the French Communist Party, not so much because the doctrines appealed to him, coming as he did from the African upper-class elite, but as a matter of tactics. Later, his stately progress took him to the French centre (though he did not align himself with the Radicals on his way), and in 1956 he became a minister in Guy Mollet's Républicain government. Later he became one of de Gaulle's ministers of state. Throughout his life in French politics he vacillated between left and right (although, of course, this classical antithesis of ideologies means little to Africa). In the end, the former fellow-traveller of French Communism came to be almost *persona grata* among French business-men in the Ivory Coast.

The political struggles between the great African parties, parti-cularly the RDA and the PFA, can be understood only in the context of Africa's economic position. Sékou Touré displayed remarkable courage when he refused to associate himself with France, preferring to stay independent and poor. By contrast, many African states shrank back from the complete independence within their grasp, for fear of losing the important economic and technical advantages of retaining some kind of association with France.

A few figures will serve to demonstrate the extent of this

economic dependence. An investment fund for the economic and social development of the overseas territories, Fonds d'investissement pour le développement économique et social des territoires d'outre-mer (FIDES), was set up in 1949. From 1949 to 1955, France contributed 1,340,000 million francs ($3,800 million) to its overseas territories; in the same period the World Bank disbursed no more than 700,000 million francs ($2,000 million) to developing countries. In 1954, 68,700 million francs ($196 million) and in 1955, 72,200 million ($206 million) of public money was invested in overseas France (excluding North Africa and overseas departments). In addition, very substantial loans were made by French finance houses, including the Caisse Centrale de la France d'Outre-mer (now renamed Caisse Centrale de la Co-opération Economique). It was estimated that more than 8 per cent of the total annual investment of French capital was disbursed overseas. There were also substantial local investments which in all overseas territories amounted in 1955 to 32,000 million francs ($91 million). Metropolitan France, as well as bearing the cost of overseas capital investment, also bore expenses incurred overseas, such as administrators' salaries, transport and communications, and the maintenance of the armed forces. Pierre Moussa points out that 9 per cent of the French metropolitan public revenues and 8 per cent of its capital investments were granted overseas but that the share taken by overseas territories of the Gross National Product was no more than 1 to 1·3 per cent.[17] To counterbalance this, however, large transfers of funds took place from overseas territories to metropolitan France.

Thus French investments had become *a habit* with African countries. They were used to having France stop the gaps in their budgets, embark on prestige building projects, and grant heavy subsidies to certain basic commodities such as cocoa, coffee and groundnuts. They were used to being in a privileged position compared with other tropical countries. The existence of a 'franc area' meant that both African exports and French imports were protected. The French policy of protection led to much higher prices than in the English-speaking African countries; while the

Ghanaian or Nigerian pound was at parity with sterling, the CFA franc was worth no more than two old French francs.

Moreover a far higher proportion of French held executive positions in government or private business, or worked in supervisory grades or as skilled labour in industry than was the case in English-speaking Africa. During the period from 1946 to 1956, the number of Europeans (mostly Frenchmen) in French West Africa increased from 32,000 to 90,000. In 1951, there were 42,500 civil servants, of whom 5,300 were Europeans (and only 2,000 of them in administrative posts). In 1956, there were 56,000 civil servants, of whom 5,500 were Europeans. Another feature of French Africa, which was to have grave repercussions and lead to deep resentment, was the large number of 'petits blancs' who, attracted by the 'expatriate bonus' and the better promotion prospects, had left low-paid jobs in France for comparable but better-paid jobs in Africa. French non-commissioned officers' wives were eager to take any job suited to women, thereby barring the way to employment for the few educated African women. These 'petits blancs' proved a real obstacle to the development of the new Africa. On the other hand, the presence of senior administrators and experts never caused any criticism; even after independence they were accepted and sometimes welcomed, as long as they had changed their label and were seen to be working not for the 'colonial' but for the new co-operative administration.

In 1958 African leaders were influenced by their wish to hold on to all the economic and financial advantages which the French colonial system had brought. The political and economic affairs of all the territories had been centralised and co-ordinated by the French ministry in the rue Oudinot and the poorer territories were supported by their richer neighbours. Prior to their reaching self-government under the Community, and their independence, the Ivory Coast and Senegal provided classic examples: with its large exports of a very wide range of basic raw products, the rich Ivory Coast made an important contribution to the overall economy of French West Africa, whereas Senegal (whose capital, Dakar, was the seat of the federal government) contributed little, but received 30 per cent of all the revenues of French West Africa. In 1956 Senegal and the Ivory Coast, whose combined population totalled one quarter of that of all French West Africa, were responsible between them for more than half of the trade output of the entire region; but Soudan, Niger, Mauritania and Upper Volta, with 60 per cent of the total population of the federation, accounted for only a quarter of the total trade output. The wealth of the region was so unequally distributed that national interests were bound to clash. In fact there had been very little inter-African trade prior to independence: exports between the countries of former French West Africa amounted to only 10 per cent of their total exports. On the other hand, movements of labour between the different countries were very heavy: at the time of the groundnut harvest, Guinean labourers would flock into Senegal; 200,000 migrant workers would work for a few months in the Ivory Coast, having travelled down from the neighbouring and relatively poor country of Upper Volta. Dahomey, Senegal and Togo provided large numbers of junior administrators for the whole of what was formerly French Africa.

There had been no economic unity, no real attempt at building strong economic blocs. The erratic partition of Africa was the iron rule and the arbitrary division into AOF and AEF had reinforced this trend. Why, for instance, should Chad be a part of AEF, when in ecological terms it belonged with Niger and the rest of AOF? It was obvious that all countries in the Sahelian and pre-Sahelian belt, stretching from Mauritania to Chad, had common economic problems. All these countries were hot and dry and contained large tracts of desert land. They had few natural resources to provide the basis of economic wealth; their only asset was cattle breeding. By contrast, the countries bordering the Gulf of Guinea were richer. They were smaller and rather more densely populated; their climate was tropical and wet, and they all possessed natural resources capable of future development. However, communications between east and west were never properly organised; the road and rail system had a pronounced north-south orientation. A well-organised air traffic network would have improved matters, but at this time it was not very effective, with very few flights scheduled between West and Equatorial Africa.

Confronted with the prospects of autonomy and independence, the African leaders did not hesitate for long. However well-justified in theory the alteration of the existing frontiers might have been, in practice it was too large a pill for them to swallow. To them, immediate independence meant that they gained control at once of the government, economy and finances of their countries. But what did this really add up to in practice? As a result of the break-up of the West African Federation, the poorer countries could no longer depend on the support of their richer neighbours. Few at the time were prepared to face up to the major economic issues. The order of the day was simply liberty, and that meant a new flag, a new national anthem, and, somehow, all the advantages the Europeans in Africa had previously enjoyed. In such a heady climate, who was going to tackle economic problems, to exercise foresight and plan for the future, to organise agriculture, communications and industry, and to decide where among all these developments the priorities should be focused? Apart from a very few African economists in Senegal and the Ivory Coast, who cared about such things? France had always been a plentiful source of capital: why should it stop now? 'When we joined the Community', said Tsiranana, the head of the Malagasy government, 'we were promised help and support, and we hope that the help that we get in the future will be even more important than we got before.' Internal price levels were fixed by France: the currency was supported by the French franc, which, after many years of crisis, was becoming increasingly strong; the Common Market, at that time being set up in Europe, was to establish an important fund for the development of overseas countries; all salary scales, social security regulations and family allowances were modelled on those of France: it was all so simple and easy. Why make independence so drastic a matter, as Guinea did; why interfere with the existing economic system?

At the time the Community came into being, most African leaders thought that their countries were too young and inexperienced to become completely independent states, interconnected only by a very loose kind of federation. Moreover, the African leadership was not yet ready to control its own economic destiny: M'Ba, the Gabonese President, succinctly summed up his colleagues' point of view: 'As we have not enough African administrators and technicians, I prefer the present form of internal sovereignty, which will enable Gabon to prepare itself efficiently to meet its international responsibilities, to a complete theoretical independence, which would undoubtedly plunge Gabon straight back into neo-colonialism.'

This was the climate in which the new African states were preparing for independence. As a result, even when the African states had severed their political bonds with France, they found themselves still closely tied to its economic system from sheer necessity.

The Political Regimes

There were two stages in the setting up of the new regimes. First, shortly after the referendum, between January and April 1959, a series of constitutional formulae were defined; and then, at the end of 1960, after the clash between Senegal and Mali, formal constitutions were drawn up and enacted by the constituent assemblies of the various countries, establishing the national and international sovereignty of the new states. With the exception of the Guinean constitution, which was influenced by the constitution of the United States, they were all very obviously modelled on the new French constitution of 1958. All referred to those basic principles which the French and the Africans alike, through the influence of their French educational background, had been taught to respect.[18]

(i) *The will of the people should be respected.* 'National sovereignty belongs to the people of Cameroun': article 2 of the Cameroun constitution of September 1, 1961. 'Sovereignty belongs to the people': article 2 of the constitution of the Central African Republic. 'National sovereignty stems from the people': article 3 of the Gabonese constitution. 'National sovereignty belongs to the people': article 3 of the Malagasy constitution. Every constitution embodies the principle of 'government for the people and by the people' and contemplates the use of the referendum as the means of directly gauging the measure of public support.

(ii) *The rights of man and of the citizen* are solemnly restated in the preambles to most constitutions. Often the declaration of the Revolution of 1789 is quoted, and also occasionally (as in the Malagasy constitution) the Universal Declaration of Human Rights of the United Nations. Similarly, the constitutions of both Guinea and Cameroun refer specifically to the United Nations charter. The freedom of the individual is recognised and the right of free association is granted; most of them prohibit racialist propaganda.

(iii) Most regimes proclaim themselves to be *republican, democratic, social and 'laïc'* (secular, not subject to any religious influence). Only the constitutions of Gabon, of Madagascar and of Mauritania refer explicitly to religious beliefs. Article 8 of the Gabon constitution reads: 'the right to establish associations and societies, institutions of social interest or communities is recognised for everyone, within the conditions prescribed by law. Religious communities are to manage and administer their own affairs without interference, provided they respect national sovereignty and public order.' The opening of the Malagasy constitution proclaims its 'belief in God and in the dignity of Man', and the Mauritanian constitution proclaims its affinity with both the Muslim faith and the principles of democracy.

(iv) The 'liberté, égalité, fraternité' of the French Revolution has its counterparts: 'Peace, work, country' in Cameroun; 'Unity, dignity, work' in the Central African Republic; 'Unity, work, progress' in Congo-Brazzaville; 'Union, discipline, work' in the Ivory Coast; 'Liberty, country, progress' in Madagascar; 'Brotherhood, work, progress' in Niger; and 'One people, one goal, one faith' in Mali.

(v) In order to protect 'liberty and individual rights' in the tradition of the judicial system of the West, a system of 'cours d'Etat', supreme courts, and, in the case of Cameroun, federal courts, is provided for in each country.

(vi) Finally, one feature is common to all the constitutions except those of Cameroun and Madagascar: they all emphasise the need for African states to become closely associated with each other, and proclaim African unity as the ultimate goal.

It is understandable that the new African constitutions should borrow widely from the French constitution of 1958, for the politicians who drew them up had often had experience of the working of the Fourth Republic. Some, indeed, had known the Third Republic, so that they had had ample time to observe and to come to appreciate the advantages of the bicameral parliamentary system, but also to deplore the instability of the Third and Fourth Republics. Some maintain that this instability was caused primarily by the existence of a large number of small political parties, rather than of two major parties, one in power and one in opposition, representing each of the main trends of public opinion, and also by the absence of a strong executive power invested with the authority to dissolve Parliament.

Many Africans approved of the much stronger executive powers which characterised the French constitution of 1958 and concluded that a similar system would be appropriate to their own countries. As a result, it was only in exceptional cases that African governments could be called to account in Parliament. For instance, in the constitutions of the Ivory Coast and of Gabon, a second reading of a bill could be compelled only by a majority of two-thirds (article 12). In the constitution of Chad of 1962 (article 43) a motion of censure against the government could be carried only if it was signed by one-third of the members of the Assembly and passed by a two-thirds majority. Other constitutions expressly stipulated that the head of government could commit the entire cabinet to a matter of policy once it had been debated by the council of ministers. In these cases a motion of censure needed to set out a complete new political programme and cite the name of the new leader for whom the support of Parliament was sought: article 34 of the constitution of Mali; similar provisions appear in the constitutions of Upper Volta and the Central African Republic.

Most African constitutions laid great stress on the right of dissolution of Parliament, which in some cases was automatic, and in others was in the hands of the government. Article 38 of the French constitution of 1958, which augmented the powers of the executive by authorising the issuing of regulations (though for a limited period only) on 'matters normally falling within the field of law-making', directly inspired similar provisions in each of the new African constitutions, as did article 47, dealing with money bills: 'If Parliament has reached no decision within seventy days, the provisions of the Bill may be put into force by ordinance.'

The essential ingredient common to all the early African constitutions was recognition of the need to establish 'a rationalised parliamentary system, with extensive power vested in the executive'.[19] The framers of the African constitutions had followed the French example of a close affinity between the executive and the legislature, but as a result the classic concept of parliamentary government with the separation of the three powers could not be fully adopted. The legislature was subjected to restrictions in order to stabilise and strengthen the executive.

This led to some criticism of the 1958 French constitution, and of the African constitutions modelled on it, which were considered to embody the anomalies of the dualist 'Orléanist' regime established in France by the July monarchy of 1830 in that they conferred powers of a dual character on the executive while leaving little authority in the hands of Parliament, and at the same time granted wide emergency powers to the executive (the famous article 16 of the 1958 French constitution).[20] The wish of the African states to maintain a powerful executive, and so to achieve stability in government, was evinced even more strongly in the second spate of new constitutions, which were drawn up after the countries had arrived at full national and international sovereignty. The links between the governments and the national assemblies became still more tenuous, and there were no longer any provisions for a mechanism by which the governments' policies could be challenged. Motions of censure were ruled out. Above all, the executive power was fully vested in the President of the Republic, since he was also the head of the government. Like the President of the French Republic, he was elected by a system of universal suffrage, either directly or indirectly. Together with the deputies in Parliament, he had the power of initiating legislation. In fact the President had become the keystone of the new regimes. Such a presidential regime seemed a necessity to most African leaders, not only because it satisfied their craving for power, but also because it seemed the best means of ensuring the well-being of their countries, whose limitations they knew so well. Moreover, the concentration of all governmental responsibility in the hands of one man was in the spirit of the African tribal tradition: to have a supreme head of the executive seemed quite natural both to the people themselves and to their representatives in the assembly.

In fact, this crop of strong regimes was no more than yet another instance of taking imitation of France to its extreme. The 'myth of de Gaulle' was undoubtedly the inspiration of the African leaders. They well remembered that French Equatorial Africa had been the starting point for his liberal policies for overseas France. Their belief in a strong executive was as strong as de Gaulle's, so explicitly described in his war memoirs:

In my opinion, there must be a head of state, that is to say a leader whom the nation can look up to, above fluctuations, a man entrusted with the fundamental decisions, responsible for the national destiny. For the executive, whose only purpose is to serve the community as a whole, cannot proceed from Parliament, where the representatives of diverging private interests are gathered. Such requirements imply that the head of state should never come from one party, should be designated by the people, be endowed with the right to refer to the nation and should choose the ministers, either in a referendum, or in the election of the Assemblies, and finally should have the right— in case of danger—to preserve the integrity and independence of France. Apart from those circumstances that might compel the President to step forth and take decisions, the cabinet and the Parliament should work together, the latter controlling the former and being entitled to overthrow it; but the supreme magistrate should act as umpire and have the right to turn to the nation as the ultimate judge.[21]

We can divide African constitutions into three main classes.[22] First, there are those which establish '*a controlled and nationalised parliamentary regime*', such as the 1960 Mali constitution. Executive power is in the hands of the government, a unified body responsible to the National Assembly. The leader of the government is at the same time the head of state (article 9). He is chosen by the President of the National Assembly at the beginning of each session, but this choice must be approved by the Assembly. In the case of a divergence of opinion between the government and the Assembly, a vote of confidence may be put (article 34), and, should two ministerial crises take place, the Assembly is automatically dissolved (article 37). (Incidentally, since 1967 this procedure is completely changed, due to the political evolution of Mali—see chapter 11.)

Secondly, there are those which establish '*strengthened presidential regimes*'. This is the case nowadays in most French-speaking African countries: the four countries of the Conseil de l'Entente, the former territories of French Equatorial Africa, and Mauritania. Even Senegal, which until 1960 inclined strongly to Radical Socialism, has adopted a presidential regime since the referendum of March 1963: 'the President of the Republic, the guardian of the constitution, alone exerts executive power. He determines and administers the overall policy of the Nation': article 3 of the Senegalese constitution. 'The President of the Republic is the head of the State': article 10 of the Mauritanian constitution; 'and exerts the executive power': article 12. 'The President of the Republic is the head of the state and of the government. He determines and carries out the policy of the nation. Executive power is vested in him alone. He sees to it that the constitution is respected': article 5 of the constitution of Chad. 'The President of the Republic assumes the entire executive power': article 12 of the constitution of the Central African Republic. The head of state also has a share of legislative power. He can gainsay the decisions of the Assembly, and either appeal directly to the nation through a referendum, or quite simply dissolve the Assembly. If he disagrees with the tenor of any bill before the Assembly, the head of state may demand a second reading, and the bill would then be passed only if it gained a majority of two-thirds, or, in some cases, three-fifths. Such provisions are particularly notable in articles 12 and 13 of the Congolese constitution (second reading, vote with a two-thirds majority, referendum); in articles 13 and 14 of the Ivory Coast constitution (second reading, vote with a two-thirds majority, referendum); in articles 12 and 16 of the Gabonese constitution (second reading, two-thirds majority and referendum). Finally, all these constitutions provide for emergency powers 'whenever circumstances warrant it': article 17 of the Gabonese constitution; article 14 of the constitution of Chad; article 47 of the Senegalese constitution; article 19 of the Upper Volta constitution, etc.

Regimes of the third category follow a middle course between a strengthened presidential regime and a controlled and rationalised parliamentarian regime. The constitutions of Madagascar and Cameroun fall within this category. Madagascar had to maintain the precarious balance established among its ten provinces, each with its own Assembly, by the constitution of 1946 and ratified under the Loi Cadre. The political set-up in Madagascar, therefore, was similar to a federation; as well as the government and the National Assembly, the organs of centralised power, there existed the Senate which was actually a council of communities. Two-thirds of its members were elected, the same number from each province, by the representatives of the provincial, urban and rural communities; the remaining one-third of its members, representing economic, social and cultural interests, were nominated by the government (articles 27 and 28). Madagascar had adopted a bi-cameral system, but nevertheless the executive power rested in the hands of the President. He could resort to 'special powers' in time of emergency, just as his African colleagues could:

81

article 12. He could dissolve the Assembly, but not before seeking the Senate's advice: article 15. The President of the Republic could commit the government to any policy: article 43. On the other hand the National Assembly could over-ride the government by a vote of censure, provided it was signed by one-fifth of the members and ratified by an absolute majority: article 44. The other example of a 'mixed' constitution is that of Cameroun. It is interesting to note how, in spite of their different political philosophies and forms of government, their language barrier and the wide diversity of their economic and social circumstances, East and West Cameroun could unite within a federation. One can easily imagine the problems confronting the attempt to integrate the two systems. Clearly the only solution was a federal type of regime functioning at two levels. The higher level dealt with many matters, such as nationality, the status of foreigners, national defence, foreign affairs, internal and external security, plans for national development, the overall organisation of the economy, finance, currency, the federal budget and taxation policy, university education, scientific research, radio and other mass media, postal services, and civil and criminal law. It is a long list which shows how far the leaders of the two former parts of Cameroun, Ahidjo and Foncha, were able to go towards agreement. The ruling power of the regime was vested in one chamber only, the National Federal Assembly, whose members were representatives of the federated states, elected by direct universal suffrage: article 16. Cameroun is, however, another example of a 'strengthened' presidential regime, for the President—always from East Cameroun—wields the executive power: he must ensure that the federal constitution is duly respected, ensure that the Federation remains closely united and, with the help of his vice-president (always elected by West Cameroun), manage public affairs: article 8. As has been seen to be the case elsewhere, the President enjoys special powers. He acts as head of state for both parts of Cameroun and nominates the prime minister of each part, who must be approved by his respective assembly. Each of the federated states is free to set up what instruments of government it chooses: for instance, the former British part has retained an assembly of traditional chiefs. As a result there was no abrupt discontinuity in the government of the two federated states.

To sum up: all the new African constitutions had one thing in common—they all led to the establishment of strongly authoritarian regimes. In the second part of this book, the history of these countries in the first decade of independence will be discussed, and we shall see that this latent authoritarianism has become increasingly pronounced, with power more and more concentrated in the hands of one man and his followers.

Part Two

Evolution since Independence

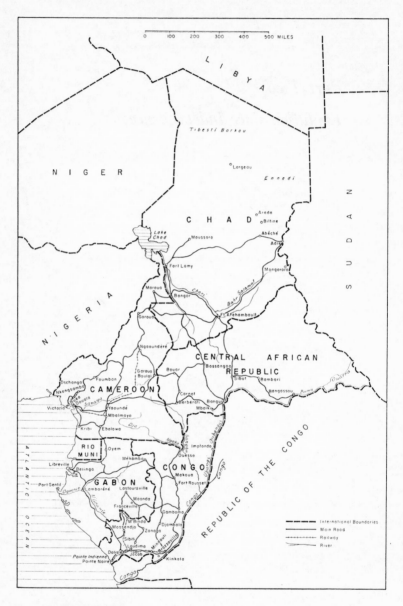

2. Equatorial Africa

Introduction

THE FIRST and the last parts of this book deal with French-speaking Africa as an entity; in this part, the main developments in each of the states of French-speaking Africa are discussed. Similar factors led to the process of decolonisation in different parts of Africa, and the reactions to decolonisation also had much in common: moreover, the problems left in its wake are broadly similar. Even so, each of the fifteen French-speaking African countries has evolved in its own particular way, and each must be discussed separately. Some rough idea of their recent political and economic evolution can be gleaned from the major events of their history in the past decade: but this is no more than a cursory glance at each country. There are certain basic questions which must be given some answer, however brief, in the study of each of the fifteen countries. Firstly, what are the fundamental factors determining the condition of each country? In some, geographic, demographic or economic considerations predominate: in others, wider political considerations may over-ride all other factors. Secondly, what regime is in power? Who are the personalities dominating it? Is there a political opposition? If so, has it any real significance and what measures are taken to recognise or, perhaps, suppress it? Is the country showing signs of fusion into a true nation or are there strong tendencies towards political disintegration? What are the major national events of the past decade? Thirdly, has the country become richer since independence? What is the nature of its economic development, if any?

In the case of countries whose recent development has been sudden and dramatic, with events culminating in a sudden 'coup', the account will cease with that moment; but where evolution has been steady and the political scene stable, the account will, correspondingly, extend over the period since independence. In the third part of the book, there is a discussion of the recent

development of the new African states, and some provisional conclusions. The most significant forces influencing recent developments in the history both of each individual country and of Africa
generally are emphasised and highlighted.

The primary concern in Part Two is not with chronology or
statistics, but to give a terse, clear account of recent developments.
The next few years will see more and more documents becoming
available to the historian, both inside and outside Africa, and, as
the archives become accessible, current developments will be seen
in clearer perspective. I shall try not to pass judgment, as the
time is not yet ripe, but since I was involved in African developments some years ago, it will not be easy to suppress my hopes
and sympathies.

Specific sources relating to the detail of each chapter will be
given in the Notes and References section at the back of the book.
The more general sources which have been drawn on—other than
personal recollections and records—will not all be listed. Among
the more important are: *Chronologie Africaine* (1961–66) from
the Centre d'étude des relations internationales in the Fondation
nationale des Sciences Politiques, Paris; *Année Africaine* (1963,
1964 and 1965), a team survey prepared by the Centre d'étude
des relations internationales, the Centre des Hautes Etudes
Administratives sur l'Afrique et l'Asie Moderne (CHEAM), also
located in Paris, and the Centre d'Etude de l'Afrique Noire of
the University of Bordeaux (CEAN); *Année politique africaine*
edited by Pierre Biarnès, Philippe Decraene and Roland Itey;
the Economist Intelligence Unit issues on former French overseas territories from 1963 to 1967; and the monograph on
thirty-one African countries edited in 1962–64 under the sponsor-
ship of the Compagnie générale d'études et de recherches pour
l'Afrique (COGERAF), Paris, for the Union Africaine et Malgache de
Coopération Economique (UAMCE).

3. Equatorial Africa

As soon as the member countries achieved independence, the former Federation of West Africa (AOF) disintegrated. By contrast, the former members of the Federation of Equatorial Africa (AEF) —Gabon, Congo-Brazzaville, Chad and the Central African Republic—strove to maintain their association with each other, despite the strong forces towards separation which were then prevalent. Although they achieved independent status individually, and not as a federation, they wished to avoid the complete balkanisation of Africa. Twice they embarked on bold projects aiming at unification: the first of these failed, the second met with some degree of success.

A natural consequence of the formation of the new institutions that the African countries agreed upon in 1958 was the dissolution of the Grand Council of the AEF. Shortly afterwards the prime ministers of the four countries that had formed the Federation agreed that they should meet at regular intervals, should set up a permanent secretariat, should maintain in being the several administrative bodies common to the four countries which already existed (for instance, the Agence Transatlantique des Communications and the Institut Equatorial des Postes et Télécommunications) and establish a customs union (Union Douanière Equatoriale) as the first stage of the gradual establishment of an Equatorial Common Market. Later, the so-called 'Conference of Prime Ministers of the States of Equatorial Africa' was established; in 1961 it was redesignated the 'Conference of Heads of State'.

Such a planned and integrated economic development of the four countries had two aims: first, to ensure that the economic interests of any one country would not be adversely affected by the activities of its neighbours, and second, to establish a single body which could negotiate with international economic institutions such as EEC and GATT.

In June 1961, one year after the customs union was established, the four Equatorial heads of state agreed to include Cameroun in their deliberations as an observer and decided on the following actions: (i) to establish a common external tariff which would be presented by the countries as a single bloc to GATT; (ii) to unify the regulations relating to financial investment throughout the four countries; and (iii) to confer frequently with a view to making consistent the tax structures of the four countries.

These schemes proved successful. As will be seen later in this chapter, Congo–Brazzaville, Gabon, Chad and the Central African Republic have maintained in being their customs union of Equatorial states and have built it into one of the strongest international organisations of French-speaking Africa, in spite of minor differences and of individual developments potentially fraught with difficulty. At a later stage the very wealthy neighbouring state of Cameroun was admitted to full partnership, and the new union was named the Union Douanière et Economique d'Afrique Centrale (UDEAC).

The second plan to achieve a degree of unification was, by contrast, almost stillborn. In 1960 the Premier of the Congo, Abbé Fulbert Youlou, had tried to coax his neighbours into a political coalition whose final goal was to be the formation of a Union des Républiques d'Afrique Centrale (URAC). In such a union, each of the partners was to concede part of its autonomy in international affairs, with the URAC to be responsible for the foreign policy and the defence of each of the four member states. This was a considerable step beyond the idea of a customs union. The scheme was originated by Congo–Brazzaville and for a time the Central African Republic and Chad were attracted by the prospect of a political union; indeed, the National Assemblies of all three countries ratified it. However, it was never acceptable to Gabon. If it had been put into effect, it would have meant Youlou's playing a leading role in its policies: as promoter of the scheme, he expected to be its natural leader. Fears that it could undermine the customs union, together with the firm decision of Gabon not to participate, led to second thoughts; in the end, the four countries of Equatorial Africa pursued their separate paths towards complete independence.

CONGO–BRAZZAVILLE

Congo–Brazzaville lies in the thick forest areas of Equatorial Africa, straddling the equator. Its population of about 900,000 is spread over 135,000 square miles but is concentrated mainly in Brazzaville, the capital (where more than 130,000 people live), in Pointe Noire, the harbour on the Atlantic (about 80,000 inhabitants), and along the 320 miles of railroad between Pointe Noire and Brazzaville, especially in the fairly rich Niari Valley, an important livestock and sugar-producing area. Other important centres are the Sangha Valley around Ouesso, in the north, where palm oil is the major cash crop, and the region of Makoua-Fort Rousset, the main area of the so-called 'cuvette congolaise', which might in the future be an interesting area to develop in spite of its swamps.

When it became self-governing in 1958, Congo (formerly known as the Middle Congo and part of the AEF) was confronted with two problems. The lesser one was that Brazzaville, on the Stanley Pool, had to relinquish its status of federal capital. In fact, this was not really a serious matter; Brazzaville had never rivalled Dakar, had never been rebuilt as a modern city, but had always retained the quaint simple houses and the tranquil life of a colonial outpost.

A much greater problem was to find a government appropriate to this country. The Middle Congo had never proved a political problem to its French administrators (who rarely showed much enthusiasm for their posting there, considering it very much second best to West Africa); the local politicians meekly followed the line laid down by their counterparts in Dakar or by their French overseers. But neither had much account been taken of the strong tribal rivalries between the two major ethnic groups, the M'Bochi and the Balali.

The M'Bochi, from the areas near the frontier with Cameroun

and the Central African Republic in the north, had founded a political party, the Mouvement Socialiste Africain (MSA). Their leader, Jacques Opangault (himself a Northerner, of course) held views corresponding to the Socialists of metropolitan French politics, which meant that the MSA had a tendency towards Socialism, anti-clericalism and republicanism. The Balali (or Lari) in the Congo river-Stanley Pool area of the south, together with kindred tribes on the coast, had gathered round Abbé Fulbert Youlou, an ambitious young priest who, with the support of the Catholic missions and of the RDA, had founded the Union Démocratique de Défense des Intérêts Africains (UDDIA), a party in the Christian Democrat tradition, as a counterbalance to Opangault and his party in the North.

In the absence of a strong central administration, the Congo was faced with the problem of maintaining a balance between these two groups which divided the country politically as well as ethnically. At the time of the Loi Cadre, the MSA of the north, the older of the two parties, was in power with a very tenuous majority. The MSA held 23 seats, and the UDDIA held 22 seats, in the 45-seat National Assembly (which sat in the local capital of Pointe Noire). Then, after the referendum in 1958, during a very memorable stormy session at the Territorial Assembly, one representative from a minor tribe (who had formerly supported the MSA) was persuaded to change sides, and M. Youlou (as *Le Monde* styled him)* gained a majority in the Assembly and became head of the government.

The Northern reaction was utterly unexpected. Three days of chaos broke out in Pointe Noire and Brazzaville in January 1959, during which the two tribes set out to massacre each other, casually dumping the corpses into the Congo river. A few months later, equally unexpectedly, the mild, composed, diffident Lari, known as good traders and diligent peasants, suddenly appeared as an

---

* *Le Monde's* editor is a Catholic, and the paper refused to refer to Youlou as 'Father' after he had been suspended by the Catholic hierarchy for refusing to obey his (French) bishop's order to discontinue his political career.

irresponsible blood-thirsty tribe and once more indulged in butchery: this time of some of their own fellows, the Matsouanists,* an obscure sect which had refused to comply with the fiscal and administrative regulations of the government. From the start, Youlou's regime, based as it was on parliamentary rule of law, was compelled to take very strict and somewhat dictatorial measures against these tribal outbursts; for instance, Opangault was arrested. Gradually, the diminutive, megalomanic, champagne-loving Abbé—who, at official receptions, would affect Dior cassocks of white† piqué—became the unquestioned ruler of the country.

Power soon became concentrated in his hands and in the hands of a few trusty henchmen from his Lari tribe. With the replacement in March 1961 of the constitution established by the laws of 1958 and 1959, Youlou's administration took a form in which extensive powers were vested in the executive; the President was elected by the whole country on a basis of universal suffrage; special emergency powers were reserved to him; and ministers were made responsible, not to the National Assembly, but to the head of state who had appointed them. In March 1961, Youlou was re-elected, receiving 97·56 per cent of the total votes cast. He ruled the country with such a firm hand that tribal rivalry lost some of its venom; during the peaceful, happy years of his reign the two tribal groups learned how to live side by side and forget their fears of each other. In 1960, Youlou thought that it would be a subtle move to include a few 'wild' Northerners in his government, including Jacques Opangault (who had been Vice-President of the Executive Council in 1958, before Youlou came to power) who was by this time no longer a serious political danger.

But it was all too easy for Youlou. Everything went along

* A syncretist sect, half animist, half bizarrely Christian, founded by a Congolese usher of the Ministère des Colonies, Simon Grenard-Matswa. He was later imprisoned by the French administration, and he died in prison.

† He even wore a pale blue one on the first anniversary of independence in 1961, on August 15—the Feast of the Assumption.

smoothly; economic problems would be dealt with . . . tomorrow; the Congolese were happy to live under the trees of the forests as they had always done, and de Gaulle's France was ready to meet the annual deficits of the budget. Youlou, who had much less to worry about than his neighbours, considered that the time was ripe for him to take a hand in their affairs and to play a leading role on the international stage. He could not disguise the fact that he wanted to replace as leading statesman of the area the extremely astute Central African statesman, Barthélemy Boganda (also a former priest). Youlou wanted to reconstitute the colonial Federation into a confederated union, the Union des Républiques d'Afrique Centrale (URAC), and he would be its unchallenged leader. Looking to the south, he had tried to extend his gracious advice to Kasavubu (who, apart from a Chinese grandfather, belonged to the same tribe as himself) with the remote hope of gathering together the Balali on both banks of the Stanley Pool, from the former Belgian Congo and the former French Congo, into a State or Confederation of Balali. This dream was rudely shattered when, soon after independence, chaos overwhelmed the Belgian Congo and Lumumba, a dangerous man to Youlou's way of thinking, emerged as Prime Minister and a 'Communist envoy'. At that time Katanga was politically isolated, for the countries of Africa had turned a cold shoulder on the sly Moïse Tshombe, with his blatantly neo-colonialist policies. Consequently Tshombe and Youlou had only each other to turn to and frequently visited one another. Youlou gained some personal profit from his association with such a rich man, but at the cost of a very evil reputation among other African leaders, especially after Lumumba's murder. He had turned against Kasavubu, his blood brother, and, in the teeth of African public opinion, was backing Kasavubu's arch-enemy.

However, Youlou was so carried away by his anti-Lumumba frenzy that he was easily persuaded to make his country the focal point of African anti-Communist feeling. Of course, those were the days when Sékou Touré had incurred the General's wrath, and Youlou—than whom there was no more faithful supporter of de Gaulle—thought it was wise to continue to sound the chord of anti-communism to placate the kind former masters who were so generously relieving him of much of his financial worries. Strange characters, men who had been French police inspectors under the German occupation, were to be found settling in Brazzaville to keep an eye on Congolese political and student leaders, to screen Youlou from many of his friends and to organise anti-Communist propaganda. Under these conditions it was inevitable that a Communist plot should be uncovered—in Brazzaville in May 1960. It was alleged that contacts had been established between the very few left-wingers in the Congo and the French Communist Party, with the intention of forming a Communist Party in the Congo. Matsika, the secretary-general of the African Communist trade union, the Confédération Générale des Travailleurs Africains (CGTA), was arrested, with a former president of the World Congress for Peace, Simon-Pierre Kikounga N'Got.

Meanwhile, throughout 1959 and 1960, a series of repressive laws had been enacted. They were aimed against the opposition to Youlou, which was growing daily: the poorly-paid clerks and shop assistants in the towns, the urban unemployed, and all those with mild tendencies to Socialism who had criticised the Abbé's policy —for instance Gilbert Pongault, the leader of the Union Panafricaine et Malgache des Travailleurs Croyants (UPMTC), a Congolese M'Bochi who had been responsible for setting up the headquarters of the union in Brazzaville.

Students returning from France or from countries within the Eastern bloc were quite rightly considered a threat to the regime, for they were better qualified than Youlou's trusted followers and had every intention of superseding them. They were young and impetuous, and ready to voice their contempt for what they thought was their slumbering backward country and its irresponsible leader. They despised the widespread system of patronage by which any post, obscure or important, was given to tribal friends or to party colleagues; they criticised the absence of any economic and social planning, for, unlike some other African countries, Congolese administration had remained unaltered since

95

independence; they indicted the regime for its lack of financial responsibility, for its squandering of money on Mercedes cars and modern Swedish furniture. The national budget increased from 4,500 million CFA francs in 1959 to 7,200 million CFA francs in 1962. In 1963 the National Assembly voted an annual expenditure of 8,188 million CFA francs: 45 per cent of this went on administrative expenditure, while capital expenditure amounted to only 386 million, 211 million of it for new housing. True enough, France had agreed, once and for all, to meet any deficit; however, the young radical newcomers argued that, although the Congo might be poor, it was in a much better position than any other equatorial country except Gabon. In 1960, timber accounted for 60 per cent of the total value of its exports; in 1961–62, there was a dramatic increase in the value of exports, attributable to the export of diamonds—both produced at home and smuggled from Congo–Léopoldville—which reduced the proportion of all exports attributable to timber to only 36 per cent of the total. Together, these represent the major exports of the Congo; in addition there is some palm oil and mineral oil. The main causes of the overall trade deficit are the heavy imports of foodstuffs (19 per cent) and the still heavier imports of capital and manufactured goods (42 per cent). In 1963 the Gross National Product was 34,000 million CFA francs, representing 40,000 CFA francs, or $140, per head of population. Agriculture's contribution to this figure, less than one-half, was low in view of the fact that 85 per cent of the 'active' population was engaged in agriculture; while the revenues from public and private administrative services were comparatively high at 40 per cent. It is extremely difficult to estimate the global balance of payments of each individual former AEF country. It is, however, much easier to assess the balance of payments in relation to countries outside the franc currency area. Strangely enough, in view of an adverse balance of trade and a budget underwritten by France, this part of the balance of payments of the Congo has been favourable since 1960, mainly because of loans from the United States Steel Company to the Compagnie minière de l'Ogooué (COMILOG) for the transport of manganese from Gabon.

Youlou's pet project, the basic—and, indeed, the only—economic concept of his regime, was the Kouilou scheme for building a hydro-electric barrage on the coast, to harness a small river and thereby to produce 7,000 million KW a year for the processing of alumina—imported from Guinea within the framework of an industrial complex to be established at the harbour of Pointe Noire. This project, which had been studied before independence, was to make the Congo the producer of one-tenth of the world's aluminium—twice the output of France. Such a project would cost $40 million (200 million French francs); Congo is still looking for foreign capital to finance it. The trump card of Youlou's economic policy was no more than a pipe dream. The only economic consolation for Youlou before his fall was the establishment thirty miles from Pointe Noire of the Congolese potash company of Holle, following the discovery of important deposits in 1960. (The exploitation of these deposits began at the end of 1967 and they are expected to produce 500,000 tons a year.)

In spite of his last-ditch efforts to maintain his position, Youlou's final fall was dramatic enough. First, he tried to veer towards the left and to align himself with one of the Congo's former arch-enemies, Sékou Touré, the spirit of revolution incarnate. In August 1962 an envoy from Sékou Touré, Diallo Telli, visited the Congo, and in October 1962 Youlou paid a state visit to Conakry. Second, Youlou, admittedly under pressure from some of his fellow heads of state, abandoned his support of Tshombe. Third, he tried, belatedly, to overhaul the financial situation of the Congo by making drastic cuts of 10 to 50 per cent in the salaries and allowances of ministers, MPs and 'chefs de cabinet'. At the same time he ordered the dissolution of all associations of an ethnic or regional character and declared them to be illegal. Only the two government parties, and a minor pro-government party in the Pointe Noire area, the Parti Progressiste Congolais (PPC), were allowed to continue. Finally, in July 1963, Youlou made two announcements: that on August 15 all political parties would be merged into a single government party; and that

97

he was negotiating with President Salazar of Portugal over elections that were to take place in Angola in September (this incredible news revealed the alarming turn Youlou's megalomania was now taking).

Revolution broke out in the Congo in August 1963—August 13, 14 and 15 were to go down in the history of the Congo as its 'trois glorieuses'. The trade unions took the initiative. They had never forgiven Youlou for arresting their captivating Pan-Africanist leader, Gilbert Pongault, and they could not tolerate the increasing restrictions on their freedom of action. They roused all the discontented elements in Brazzaville, Pointe Noire and Dolisie, the three main towns—the shop assistants and clerks, embittered by their low salaries and the rising cost of living in the towns, the unemployed, all those who had slowly come to realise over five years that independence had done no more than to transfer wealth and power from the whites to a very restricted circle of sycophantic followers of the party in power. Before long the few Youlou loyalists had fled and there was nothing to check the widespread street rioting. The small Congolese army stood by unperturbed. France did nothing—Youlou's regime had long since become both a bad joke and a heavy economic liability. Youlou disappeared, arrested with several of his ministers by the new President of the Republic, Alphonse Massemba-Debat, who had been President of the National Assembly in 1959–61, and later Minister of State until his dismissal a few months before the revolution. Youlou's successor was acutely aware of, on the one hand, the demands and aspirations of the extreme Marxist left-wing of Congolese politics and, on the other, of the ideas and intentions of the young and enterprising Christian Democrats; there was to come a time when he was forced to choose between them.

Under President Massemba-Debat, an efficient team of young technicians began to take an active part in government (Pascal Lissouba, Director of Agriculture, and Paul Kaya, an economist and planner) together with trade unionists from both the Christian trade union, like Okiemba, or the Marxist union, like Matsika, and Bikouma, an old friend of the new President. Rather unexpectedly the country shifted its sympathies from the African 'moderates' to the so-called 'revolutionary' side. Institutions conforming to strict Socialist principles were set up, and many a Congolese found himself sorry for the change. They soon came to forget the irresponsibility of the Youlou regime ,with its squandering of public funds and its autocratic measures against the trade unions. The streets—day and night—were in the hands of the unemployed school-leavers who had become members of youth movements ready to take any action on behalf of 'Socialism' and of the 'national revolution'. The moderate elements like Kaya and Okiemba were soon compelled to resign, being superseded by a radical element led by Pascal Lissouba, the Prime Minister, and by Matsika, Minister of Public Works. Whereas the Congolese had risen against Youlou for trying to establish a one-party system, they now had to accept *one* political party, the Mouvement National de la Révolution, led by André Hombessa, and several other new 'leftist' organisations such as the Jeunesses Ouvrières, a sort of civilian militia, which was under the direct control of the party's political bureau. The new President of the Republic, Massemba-Debat, stood on the sidelines during the formative years of the new regime (1963–65), but soon found himself compelled to abandon any idea of compromise and to follow the stringent measures proposed by his severest followers to punish those responsible for the dissipation of the wealth and resources of the previous regime. A large part of the Congolese population was soon alienated and conceived a nostalgia for the 'good old days of Fulbert Youlou';* the numerous Catholics in the Congo were uneasy and disillusioned; pamphlets were circulated in 1963–64 signed by a Comité antifasciste de défense des libertés congolaises; members from the Lari ethnic group rioted against the government in February 1964; it was rumoured that commandos trained on the other bank of the Stanley Pool were preparing for a crossing of the river at a moment's notice. The government,

* With the help of former followers, Youlou escaped to Léopoldville, which he later left for Rome and Spain.

meanwhile, was tightening its grip on the country; youths just out of school and the urban unemployed were rounded up and despatched to quasi-military organisations. The nationalisation of the means of production was planned, to take place at some unspecified time in the future; the countries of the Eastern bloc were now numbered among the Congo's closest friends. But though it was leaning towards the revolutionary group, the Brazzaville government nevertheless avoided breaking with either OCAM or France. The Brazzaville government did not demur at an apparent contradiction between the radical measures applied at home and a far more tolerant foreign policy;[1] Congo was not the only country vacillating between the two orientations. (For details of the late 1968 coup, see chapter 11, page 372).

GABON

The political evolution of Gabon in recent years must be examined within its proper geographical and economic context. First it must be emphasised that Gabon was the wealthiest colony of the former French Equatorial Africa. Its trade provided the main source of revenue for the AEF Federation. Gabon was in the same position within the Federation as was the Ivory Coast in the Federation of French West Africa. Gabon's privileged position was a result of its natural resources, the part played by Europeans and its geographical situation. It is not isolated from the outer world; through the basin of the River Ogooué, it has access to the Atlantic Ocean and therefore an easy channel of communication for both imports and exports.

Europeans were first attracted to this readily-accessible country at the turn of the century—not only colonial administrators, but also representatives of trade and industry. There was no trouble with the 'native population' in Gabon, for the good reason that the country was underpopulated. It is still underpopulated today: an area of 102,317 square miles supports a population of only 463,000, most of them in the coastal areas: the central parts of the country are almost uninhabited. Moreover, the population growth rate is only one per cent. It is a strange experience to fly over the Gabonese forest and not see a clearing—that is, a village—for miles. The country includes many tribes, but most of them belong to the same large ethnic group, the Fang. The country is essentially rural: Libreville, the capital, has only 30,000 inhabitants compared with Brazzaville's 135,000. Thanks to the remarkable developments of recent years, 80 per cent—a large proportion—of the population receives some education, although few continue to the secondary and post-secondary level, and for a long time the teachers could not reach the agricultural population widely scattered in the vast primeval forest. Hence Gabon, with more material than human resources, and with a very small fully-educated and trained elite, relied for its development in the past, and still relies, on Europeans—engineers, administrators and managers.

Gabon produces no agricultural crops of any economic importance.* The country is a forest and its main source of profit by far is from timber. Nine-tenths of the country is covered with forests, and okoumé—from which the best plywood is made—is the country's main resource. In 1965 its timber exports reached 6,445 million CFA francs, constituting 29 per cent of all revenue from external trade. A thriving wood industry was bound to develop rapidly: sawmills, plywood, sliced and peeled veneers. One of the largest plywood factories in the world has been built in Port Gentil, the second largest town in Gabon, by the Société de Gestion de la Compagnie Française du Gabon.

Gabon also promises to be a source of minerals and oil. An important manganese deposit, near Moanda in South Gabon, has been actively exploited by the Compagnie minière de l'Ogooué

---

* The country is trying to develop its cocoa output, which totalled 4,300 tons in 1965–66. However, the fluctuations in the world prices of cocoa do not give much incentive to Gabonese farmers: the purchase price to the producer was only 48 CFA francs per kilo in 1965–66, whereas it had been 80 CFA francs per kilo the previous year (see Banque Centrale des Etats d'Afrique Equatoriale et du Cameroun, *Rapport d'activités, 1965–1966*).

(COMILOG) and exported via the Congo. A 48-mile long ropeway transport system crossing the Gabon-Congo frontier carries the manganese ore to the Congolese railway between M'Binda, Dolisie and Pointe Noire. The production of manganese has increased so steadily—from 200,000 tons in 1962, the first year of exploitation, to 1,150,000 tons in 1965—that its export value (approaching 6,400 million CFA francs) rivals that of timber. Very near the manganese deposit, and at roughly the same time, work started on an important uranium ore deposit, the output of which is also removed through the COMILOG ropeway. By 1965, the annual value of sales reached 2,145 million CFA francs, but both the output and the commercial prospects have since been limited by a glut on the world market and by an agreement between the development company, the Compagnie des Mines d'Uranium de Franceville (CMUF) and the French Commission for Atomic Energy.

As a mining country, Gabon is full of promise. In Mekambo, in the north-east of the country, two deposits of very high-grade iron-ore have been discovered and are proving of great interest to the European steel industry. Reserves are estimated at 1,000 million tons. However, the development and transport problems associated with a deposit of this size are severe, and studies are now being carried out under the supervision of the World Bank to assess the technical and economic prospects of the construction of a railway from Belinga, close to the mine, to Owendo, on the coast south of Libreville. It seems that the building of the Owendo-Belinga railway could be justified on economic grounds if it also transported timber and thereby encouraged the exploitation of the forest reserves of Central and Eastern Gabon.

A few years before independence, the Société des Pétroles d'AEF (SPAEF)—now the Société des Pétroles d'Afrique Equatoriale (SPAFE)—struck oil during explorations along the coastal strip of Gabon and the Congo. Between 1959 and 1961, the output of oil in Gabon was about 70,000 tons per year, and is now well over a million tons annually: overseas sales in 1965 amounted to 1,281,000 tons.

In spite of the heavy imports of foodstuffs and of capital goods required for the development of its forestry, minerals and oil, Gabon is now among the very few French-speaking African countries with a favourable trade balance—9,000 million CFA francs in 1964, 10,000 million in 1965, 9,300 million in 1966 and 13,870 million in 1967. At $250 per head of population, its GNP is the highest in Africa (excepting South Africa and Libya). However, the Gabonese economy is precariously balanced. Overproduction or excessive stockpiling of okoumé timber or of manganese ore in the world would upset it: there is insufficient diversification and Gabon has no alternatives to turn to. It relies on the outside world to feed its population; here again it could be hit hard by fluctuations in world markets. To develop its latent riches, Gabon must depend on the good offices of European industry, which, in turn, 'expects to find' a favourable attitude among the local people and a reliable and stable government. European industry is not committed to Gabon, as most of the industries are conducted by Gabonese subsidiaries of international firms. If anything happened to displease or to alarm the head organisations, they could quite easily close down the Gabonese branches. Should Gabonese okoumé timber cease to be competitive on world markets, or should political unrest complicate the exploitation of the forests, the healthy state of Gabon's economy would very quickly disappear. For it is neither the only country producing okoumé—Asia is a large producer, particularly Malaysia—nor is it the only country with manganese—Gabon is in fact the world's third largest producer after South Africa and India.

These over-riding economic considerations force the country to be docile and submissive, and leave little scope for freedom in Gabonese politics. That is the reason why French troops acted with such brutality in Gabon in February 1964, as they did nowhere else, to stabilise the existing regime, which had been established in 1958 and had survived six apparently uneventful years.

Léon M'Ba, who was appointed head of state when Gabon became independent, acted like so many other African leaders in steering his country to a 'strong regime' with a constitution very similar to that of the France of 1958. M'Ba came from the predominant ethnic group, the Fang; he was the loyal supporter of Houphouet-Boigny's great party, the RDA, and had called his Gabonese section the Bloc Démocratique Gabonais (BDG). His fellow tribesman and only rival, Jean-Hilaire Aubame, had from 1946 to 1958 become so involved in colonial politics in the French Parliament that he spent most of his time away from Gabon and was easily overcome in domestic politics. His party, the Union Démocratique et Sociale Gabonaise (UDSG), tended to follow Senghor's policies. The elderly M'Ba—he was born in 1902 and thus was much older than Dacko, Tombalbaye, Ahidjo, etc.—was elected mayor of Libreville in 1957, Vice-President of the Government Council in 1957, Prime Minister in 1958, and finally, after independence day, on August 17, 1960, President of the Republic.

Although he had clashed in his earlier days with the French colonial police, he had never been a rabid radical and he realised that Gabon could achieve nothing, for a time, without European help. European capital was essential if the ambitious industrial developments contemplated by Gabon were to be implemented. He therefore sought a process of quiet evolution: the well-being of the country would be ensured only by a policy of conservatism. Free enterprise was the order of the day. Investment was to be encouraged by all possible means: on November 3, 1961, an investment code law was passed to promote the entry and transfer of foreign capital. However, he saw it as his duty as the head of state of Gabon to ensure that his country participated in this investment on a basis equal with that of international business and finance.*

* (*a*) Creation in June 1962 of the Union Gabonaise de Banque (Banque Gabonaise de Développement; Crédit Lyonnais; Morgan Guaranty International Corporation; Deutsche Bank; Banca Commerciale Italiana). (*b*) Creation in November 1962 of GABECO-Société Commerciale Gabonaise, in which the government and the main trading firms in Gabon have an interest. Its purpose is to import and sell foodstuffs at reasonable prices to the population, to improve the marketing system, and to facilitate the collection of customs duties on imported goods in transit from neighbouring countries.

The Gabonese opposition, also, had an obvious line of policy—
to oppose M'Ba's abrogation of his country's interests to those of
world finance, his so-called 'neo-colonialism', his tyrannical concentration of power in his own hands and among a few trusted
party followers. But who exactly was the opposition? Certainly
none of M'Ba's party. There had, it is true, once been an internal
party quarrel with one of his colleagues, Paul Goudjout, President
of the National Assembly and secretary of the government party,
which had ended with Goudjout's arrest. However, even Aubame,
M'Ba's major political rival, was following the party line; he had
accepted the portfolio of Foreign Affairs in M'Ba's cabinet, and
had obtained ministerial posts for some of his own followers. But,
even though their leader appeared to have given up the struggle,
Aubame's party had not given up. The most severe critics of the
M'Ba regime were the trade unionists, especially those affiliated
to Gilbert Pongault's Union Panafricaine et Malgache des
Travailleurs Croyants, and students back from the 'red' Latin
Quarter or from African universities such as that of Brazzaville.
The strong, well-organised, Marxist-tinged students' associations
had, in the past years, been the bane of more than one African
leader.

In many ways, having members of the thoroughly-cowed
official opposition inside his government proved to be a hindrance.
As M'Ba could not organise the campaign in favour of the one-
party system as he would have liked, in February 1963 he persuaded a member of the 'other' party, François Meye, the Minister
of Labour, to initiate it. This move proved to be a grave political
error; on February 19 the two parties fell apart and the opposition
was wiped out—except for the over-complaisant Meye. Aubame
became a liability; appointed President of the Supreme Court—
'kicked upstairs'—he refused to resign his seat in Parliament as
M'Ba wished him to, and in January 1964 the National Assembly
refused to enact a law forbidding a member to hold other offices.
M'Ba felt that the National Assembly was becoming altogether
too unruly, for it had also refused, in December 1963, to vote the
1964 budget, which made provision for cuts in the salaries and

allowances of MPs and of the President of the National Assembly. M'Ba could not brook such near-rebellion; he decided to dissolve the Assembly and to proceed forthwith to a new election on February 25, without any electoral campaign.

On February 18, 1964, there was a general uprising. The Gabonese army seized power; a revolutionary committee was created and a temporary government hastily formed under the leadership of Aubame. M'Ba was placed under arrest. The Vice-President of the government, Yembit, asked French paratroopers to intervene. By February 21, M'Ba had the situation once again under control. The 'revolutionaries' were arrested, and were put on trial in Lambaréné later that year, on September 10. Aubame was condemned to ten years of hard labour and ten years' banishment.

The French government justified its action on the basis of the agreements on co-operation and defence between the two countries. It emphasised that M'Ba's was the *legal* government and the uprising had not been a mass movement (that is to say, not as had been the case in Congo–Brazzaville). Indeed, the plot had been engineered by the elite and watched with indifference by the people, who took sides neither with the revolutionaries nor with M'Ba. A few soldiers and trade unionists had taken to arms, and some were killed, but they signified little. What mattered in Gabon was not the regime itself, but the large economic interests, which were convinced that if M'Ba were kept in power the economic climate would remain favourable to them; and that remains the case today. Yet political dissatisfaction still remains, as is shown by the strikes of March to May 1964 and street demonstrations against both the government and the French; by the creation, under Germain M'Ba,* of a Mouvement National de la Révolution Gabonaise; by the expulsion or removal of several Gabonese and French Catholic missionaries, since the clergy was charged—not

---

* Germain M'Ba, who has no direct family tie with the President, was the secretary-general of the UAM till his resignation following the French intervention in his country. He fled and sought refuge in various parts of Africa.

unjustly—of siding with Aubame and with the 'syndicats croyants' (believers' trade unions);* and finally by the unexpected success in April 1964 of the opposition, which won sixteen seats to the BDG's thirty-one and polled 44·75 per cent of the total votes cast. The opposition was not formally suppressed in 1964; but in March 1967 the opposition was forbidden to participate in the election—the government party, the BDG, drew up a single list of candidates.

Léon M'Ba died on November 28, 1967. He had been wise enough to prepare his succession: in 1966 he had created a Vice-Presidency, choosing for this office one of his most unswervingly loyal supporters, Albert Bongo, a very capable young man of thirty-two. Bongo had been, prior to M'Ba's illness, his 'directeur de cabinet' and later a member of his government, and on his death Bongo became President of the Republic of Gabon. On taking office, Albert Bongo had two assets: first, his youth, which may make him more aware of the position of those elements, less conservative than the late President, which have been thwarted in the past and which might view Germain M'Ba as their possible leader; secondly, the economy of Gabon, which is still developing in the way described earlier and which is likely to continue its progress. However, if his government is to survive and to remain

* The 'syndicats croyants' were initially called Christian trade unions since they were affiliated to the French Confederation of Christian Trade Unions. But these unions realised progressively that they had to gather together not only all Christian workers, but also those who belonged to and *believed* in other religions, particularly the Muslims. For this reason they became known as 'syndicats croyants', 'believers' trade unions'. Just before the Loi Cadre these trade unions decided to form independent confederations directly affiliated to the International Confederation of Christian Trade Unions. Hence the creation of the African Confederation of 'Travailleurs Croyants' of West Africa in July 1956, of Cameroun in December 1955, of Equatorial Africa in January 1957. A link was however maintained with the French Confederation, which has since provided advice, technical assistance and training, particularly when this type of trade unionism became Pan-African with the establishment in January 1959 of the 'Union Panafricaine des Travailleurs Croyants' under the chairmanship of Gilbert Pongault.

a stable unit, he will have to deal with a major problem: Gabon's take-off benefits only the elite and the middle-class in the towns; the rural masses of Gabon remain isolated, slow-moving and completely cut off from the economic development of the country, which is still controlled by European business and industrial interests.

CENTRAL AFRICAN REPUBLIC

In Oubangui-Chari, the country known as the Central African Republic after it became independent in 1958, geographical considerations dominate the country's economic prospects. The Central African Republic (CAR) is land-locked and cut off from sea trade: a riverway, 800 miles long, stretches between Bangui, its capital, and Brazzaville, the nearest large city,* and from Brazzaville men and materials must travel a further 320 miles by rail to reach Pointe Noire on the coast. Thus the price of cement, to take one example, rises steadily along this lengthy route until it is tripled by the time it reaches Bangui. The CAR is now trying to establish better communications by cutting through Cameroun: both countries have agreed to embark on a joint study of the prospects for a Douala–Bangui railway, under the auspices of the World Bank and the United Nations Development Programme.

The CAR is poor and underpopulated—1,301,000 inhabitants eke out a poor living, most of them in rural areas, in an area of 234,000 square miles (a little over five inhabitants per square mile). The rate of increase of the population is slow and the future seems to hold little economic promise, as no crops of substantial commercial value are grown and there are no large mineral deposits. Its main export is diamonds. Thanks to a dramatic increase in the output of diamonds, the economy has slightly improved and the Gross National Product has risen slowly, from 31,000 million

* A boat company, the Compagnie Générale des Transports Africains (CGTA), a branch of the Banque d'Indochine, reigns supreme over this waterway.

CFA francs in 1961 to 35,300 million in 1964. But diamonds cannot provide the basis of a stable economy, since the diamond reserves, experts have announced, will soon be exhausted and no alternative source of income is likely to arise in the near future. The CAR grows hardly enough foodstuffs to support its population, which still exists, for the large part, at no more than a subsistence level. The only possible commercial crops would be cotton, coffee, palm oil and groundnuts, but the prospects for the development of these are very limited. Cotton exports have steadily decreased in the past ten years; the value of the coffee crop in 1965 was only half that of 1964. There is a small project for palm oil tree development, that would enable the CAR only to cut its present necessary imports in this field, and a small cocoa project, both of which are under study. Only cattle breeding, fishing (for local purposes) and forestry could—over a period—be intensified on a profitable scale: the forests in south-eastern CAR have interesting species such as limba and safelli that could find substantial markets provided adequate means of transport existed.

The CAR imports more than it exports and its trade balance has steadily deteriorated since 1960, apart from temporary improvements:

millions CFA francs

1960	*1961*	*1962*	*1963*	*1964*	*1965*	*1966*	*1967*
—1,532	—2,109	—3,699	—1,085	—229	—289	—1,032	—3,740

As in many other African states, the cost of administration and government is shockingly high (80 per cent of current expenditure, out of which as much as 11 per cent is for national defence): every year the country must contend with a budgetary deficit, which was, however, reduced from 1,000 million CFA francs in 1960 to 500 million in 1962.

Hence the political life of the CAR is overshadowed by the country's depressing economic condition. Nevertheless, for several years it remained comparatively stable—from March 1959, when the great CAR leader Barthélemy Boganda was killed in a mysterious plane accident, to December 1965, when Boganda's young cousin and successor, David Dacko, resigned in favour of another cousin, Colonel Bokassa. During these quiet years nothing striking happened to influence the life of the country.

Two political rivals contended for Boganda's position at his death: Dacko, comparatively young and little known and Abel Goumba, Boganda's former Minister of Finance, who provisionally took over after his death. But Boganda's party, the Mouvement de l'Evolution Sociale de l'Afrique Noire (MESAN) decided to push Goumba to one side and to recognise Boganda's cousin as a more suitable spiritual heir. It was, thus, a fateful coincidence (Boganda's death and the fact that Dacko was related to the 'father of independence of the Central African Republic') that brought Dacko to power. He started life as an earnest school teacher and an active trade unionist; later he was elected to Parliament and was appointed Minister of Agriculture by Boganda. He was not ambitious or particularly well prepared for the subtleties of political life: his staunch supporters had to intrigue on his behalf. However, he was a worthy man, a fine character and a pleasant personality full of buoyancy and commonsense. He stayed in power for six years without any elections, as he knew only too well the limitations of his country, and took action against 'nefarious elements' only when absolutely necessary.

His main concern, similar to that of Boganda, was to build up a nation, to establish a common sense of purpose among people who had been arbitrarily drawn together within the frontiers established by the colonial powers, and to make his countrymen conscious of their responsibilities. He had little difficulty in dealing with the opposition. The frustrated Abel Goumba formed a new party but could not enlist any popular support, and his followers constituted no more than a fraction of the elite; he soon found himself isolated and his party banned; an order for his arrest followed, but he escaped to France with the aim of completing his medical studies. Once the opposition had been eliminated, Dacko gradually transformed his strong parliamentary majority into a single-party system—a move endorsed in the constitution of November 26,

1964, which was based upon the highly original notion of the party as the fountain of the life of the nation.

Dacko's concept of the new independent regime demanded active participation from every level of the 'social pyramid'. At the top, the head of state was to live for his country; below him, a national elite, the equivalent of the 'upper middle classes' of foreign countries, was to become aware of its responsibilities; and, at the lowest level, the hard core of the working class, who did no more than survive, were to be helped to improve their living conditions. It was the party's duty, as the country's fundamental institution, to establish harmony between all three social levels. So, for instance, the President nominated ministers only after having sought advice from the party's governing committee; similarly, the constitution could not be amended without the agreement of the governing committee. Furthermore, MESAN's budget was included in the national budget. It was intended that MESAN should be a mass movement; all local organisations, village communities, youth clubs, trade unions, tribal associations, were to be gathered together within it in a nation-wide union. Most of the active population were expected to become members of MESAN. Membership fees were established for all levels: 10 CFA francs a month for a child, 20 for a woman, 50 for a man; honorary members and active party members were required to pay 100 CFA francs a month; and MPs, ministers, directors and senior administrators were to give the party 10 per cent of their total income. Dacko tried to use MESAN as a means of checking tribalism. He also set out to curb the trade unions, and advised them to break away from the international trade union confederations. He wanted them to stop their futile social agitation, since their small numbers and their concentration within the towns greatly restricted their effectiveness; they were expected to become loyal supporters of the party and the nation. The trade unionists, however, were uncoöperative, and in April 1964 the Congress of MESAN had to force them to unite into one centralised union, the Union Générale des Travailleurs Centrafricains, a federation which included all the unions based both on the public service and private business.

Dacko's hopes for this union remained a pipe dream, and the atmosphere around him became less friendly. There had been no rapid economic improvements, in spite of a two-year plan launched in 1964, which made provision for investments of 28,000 million CFA francs and for an increase in agricultural production of between 5 and 20 per cent, and in spite of extensive technical assistance from abroad. The so-called elite was never won over. For many administrators, technicians and managers, independence meant soft jobs, big profits, and those enviable situations which the French had previously enjoyed. For most, President Dacko's 'national ideal' remained a remote concept. Thus, when Dacko levelled his sights against African neo-colonialism, showing how exploitation of the masses had been re-established, not by the whites, but by the Africans themselves, and when he thundered against those trouble-makers who used rumours and slanders to rouse the people, he was doomed to failure. He entreated MPs to set an example for the nation—no whisky and champagne, no European meals or luxury cars—but they turned a deaf ear. He had no real control over his administration and his lack of authority was obvious at every level. Dacko was only too conscious of the injustices rampant throughout Africa in those post-independence years: why should an African peasant toil for fifty-five weary years to save what a casual civil servant, in a cool office, earned in a year? Why did 4,000 civil servants pocket 300 million CFA francs in the form of social security benefits, while 51,000 wage-earners in the private sector received no more than 150 million CFA francs, and one million peasants nothing at all for their children? When Dacko refused his civil servants state-provided housing, cut their salaries, reduced administrative expenses and in 1964 waived France's standing undertaking to meet the budgetary deficit, all was of very little avail: in fact, this proved to be a very dangerous move. His path was not made any smoother when he tried to move his policies to the left, deeming MESAN to be a Socialist movement. The ambassador from Nationalist China was asked to leave and was at once replaced by an ambassador from Communist China; as a 'reward' Communist China granted the CAR a subsidy of 1,000 million CFA francs—no small boon. However, Dacko soon realised that the Communist Chinese, though they might be generous, could prove difficult customers to handle. To add to Dacko's worries, all his neighbours were showing signs of restlessness: a state of anarchy in Congo-Léopoldville, just over the river; the constant threat of a coup in Chad; and open rebellion in Sudan, with thousands of refugees from Southern Sudan being forced across the frontier of the CAR by the Sudanese government.

Probably Dacko meant well, but he lacked the means and the energy to enforce his policies and to hit hard enough at the country's major evil—corruption in the civil service. He dismissed a few administrators, but was powerless against inefficient, dishonest provincial administrators, when at least twenty of them should have been jailed for embezzling state funds.*

Dacko's last battle ended when, to raise a compulsory government loan, he compelled all civil servants to refund 10 per cent of their salaries to the state. This raised such a wide outcry in Bangui that the head of the police forces, Commandant Izamo, thought fit to engineer a coup. He invited Colonel Jean-Bedel Bokassa, Chief of the General Staff, and all the senior army officers to a big New Year's Eve party. But Bokassa, Dacko's cousin, decided to foil Izamo's 'revolutionary schemes' and, since the President had by this time lost control of the situation, to seize power himself on New Year's Eve. Dacko, under house arrest, was easily persuaded to resign in favour of Bokassa—whereupon Bokassa publicly extolled Dacko's great honesty! Bokassa dissolved the National Assembly on January 1, 1966, and abrogated the constitution; on January 6 he broke off diplomatic relations with Communist China, ordered all Chinese citizens to leave at once and seized large stocks of arms, and also documents, which, he said, provided

* In an article in *Le Monde*, January 4 and 5, 1966, entitled "Esquisses centrafricaines", Michel Legris pictures some CAR 'mandarins', the secluded civil service caste, living riotously, exploiting the masses, engaging in diamond-smuggling on a large scale.

113

ample evidence that the Chinese were preparing to set up a popular army and to murder Dacko. (The so-called 'Chinese plot' was put forward later by well-informed observers as the true motive for Bokassa's coup.) The country desperately needed administrative reform; law and order were no longer enforced, and Dacko's authority had been frittered away. The army—the only authority left—stepped in. The situation in the CAR contained all the classical conditions for a military coup, a recurrent feature in the development of the young independent Africa.

CHAD

François Tombalbaye has been head of state of Chad since independence. As Chad is one of the most unstable countries of Africa and one of the most difficult to govern, so long a spell in power is a most creditable achievement. Few African countries, when they first raised the flag of independence, found themselves confronted by so many handicaps. The soil is poor or even non-existent. In the south, Chad comprises a not very fertile part of the Sudanese savannah belt; the country then stretches for a thousand miles to the north into the Sahel and desert. Chad has the rather doubtful privilege of having within its borders the extraordinary desert mountain sites of Tibesti, rising to over 10,000 feet, where no human being can normally live. Few African countries are more distant from the sea—the nearest possible harbour would be Port Harcourt, in Eastern Nigeria, over a thousand miles away, or perhaps Lagos (via Kano), 1,250 miles away, or Douala, in Cameroun, at about the same distance. The disposition of frontiers under colonial rule made Chad an equatorial region, and forced it into the colonial Federation of Equatorial Africa; its normal trade route is still via Bangui and Brazzaville, over 1,800 miles of road, waterway and railway. As a result, petrol is eight times as costly in Fort Lamy as on the Gulf of Guinea, and cement costs four times as much. Imported goods are more expensive at Fort Lamy than anywhere else in French-speaking Africa; conversely, exported local goods (mainly meat and cotton) are subject to heavy transport costs. Even if local products were plentiful—and they are not—marketing them under such conditions would undermine their competitiveness.

Chad is fairly thinly populated, with a population of about 3,300,000 in an area of 487,920 square miles, an average density of just under seven inhabitants per square mile. The density is slightly higher in the huge Lake Chad basin area where two great African rivers, the Logone and the Chari, meet, but it falls sharply as one goes north. Moreover, this sparse population, which is growing only very slowly, is not homogeneous. There is a very marked division between North and South, which over the years has been the source of acute problems and constant political tension. Most Northerners are fairly light-skinned with some Arab blood in their ancestry, devout Muslims, living and dressing in the traditional Muslim manner; in the South, the largest ethnic group, the very dark-skinned Sara, either animists or, nowadays, quite often Christian, were for centuries harassed by invasions and slave-raids from the North.

Therefore, in facing up to the difficulties of economic development, Chad cannot even rely on national unity. Its resources are scanty: no exploitable minerals and meagre food-crops, all consumed locally. Fishing, and more particularly cattle-breeding, could be developed, but at present they are undertaken inefficiently, trained and reliable personnel are sadly lacking, and marketing has not yet been organised effectively. The French colonial economic service had set very great hopes on cotton. From 1928 onwards its cultivation was developed by the Cotonfran Company until, by 1965–66, yearly production had reached 87,000 tons.[2] Cotton became, and remains, the only commercial crop, accounting for 80 per cent of the total value of exports. Somehow, however, the peasants of Chad showed little enthusiasm for the cultivation of cotton, and a great deal of encouragement and forceful persuasion was required, first from the French and then from the government of Chad, to make them till their plots.

It is no wonder that under such adverse circumstances—the

heavy cost of transporting imported foodstuffs, such as sugar and rice, and the comparatively low level of productivity in agriculture and cattle breeding—the trade balance of Chad should show a cruelly large deficit varying between 2,000 million CFA francs in 1959 and 3,300 million in 1962; only after very stringent budgetary measures were taken did it fall to 2,000 million CFA francs in 1964 and 982 million in 1965, but it rose again to 2,114 million in 1966 and to 3,566 million in 1967. As the country is huge and heterogeneous, it must support an extensive administration and a comparatively large army, and the expenditure for their upkeep is such a burden that the annual budget shows a debit balance, compensated, as usual, by a general subsidy from France —the so-called 'subvention d'équilibre'. Chad is now trying hard to improve its fiscal policy and increase its revenue from taxation.

Under these circumstances, even more than elsewhere in Africa, it seemed essential to avoid dissipating energy on party politics and to have a strong central executive if the so-called 'benefits of French colonialism and civilisation' were not to evaporate within a few years and the country return to its previous history of misery and murder. A very serious young leader suddenly emerged in 1959, earnest and austere behind the striking Sara tribal gashes across his cheeks. That François Tombalbaye has managed to maintain himself in power so long is a feat in itself. He is quiet, apparently humourless, and a fighter. He has struggled hard, first to assert himself over possible competitors, then again and again to avoid tribal friction and secession. He is still fighting armed rebellion on the north-east desert borders— local uprisings, no doubt supported and encouraged by neighbours. For to his long list of discomforts must be added the problem of border troubles: anarchy and chaos among his western neighbours in Nigeria, and armed rebellion and dissension to the east in Southern Sudan.

The great political figure of the early days of Chad's independence was Gabriel Lisette, a brilliant half-caste from Guadeloupe in the French West Indies, who, after serving as a French colonial civil servant, represented Chad as an RDA member at the French National Assembly. In 1957 he was elected mayor of Fort Lamy, and later that year was appointed vice-president of the government council. After the September 1958 referendum he became Prime Minister. However, he made several false political moves, siding too obviously with the Northern politicians, and on March 24, 1959, Tombalbaye assumed power, having managed to oust his rival. It was unthinkable that Tombalbaye should rule with so senior a figure at his elbow as Lisette, who became his second-in-command of both the party and the government. In August 1959, while Lisette was out of the country, Tombalbaye dismissed him from office and forbade his return. Next, Tombalbaye moved against a clever Chadian half-caste, Jean Baptiste, who was also looking for support from the North and unabashedly exploiting North-South rivalry. When it came to dealing with the elected representatives of the North, Djebrine Kerallah and Ahmed Koulamallah—men of fine intelligence and integrity—Tombalbaye had to watch his step and wait his time before acting. First he joined with them in forming a new coalition party, thereby forestalling any opposition that might have arisen within his own majority party. Then, as the Northerners could not tolerate the prospect of playing second fiddle to the young Sara upstart and were continually involved in plotting and scheming for a Northern leadership, they were, first one, then the other, detected in a 'plot', arrested, and, notwithstanding their high calibre, excluded from active politics or any form of public life. It was the country which was thereby the loser, but regionalism and petty tribalism had to be eradicated at all costs. Even so, Tombalbaye was a more honest man than some among his political rivals. He never lost faith in the idea of national unity, and incorporated Northerners in his frequently reorganised cabinets. (At present—late 1968—the cabinet has a fair distribution of ministers from both communities —seven Christians and eight Muslims.) Moreover, when necessary, he could be just as severe with members of his own ethnic group, as, for instance, when he dismissed Silas Selingar, accused of dishonesty, and when he exiled the army's strong man, Lieutenant-

Colonel Djogo, from Fort Lamy by appointing him 'préfet' of a Northern desert province.

Since he considered that any election campaign of an opposition party would provide a pretext for the cunning Northerner to exploit the rivalry between North and South, on January 18, 1962, Tombalbaye banned all parties and held new elections on a one-list system. The new Assembly, elected in this way, agreed to enact a new constitution of the presidential type and to reinforce President Tombalbaye's powers. Only the one large national party, the Parti Progressiste Tchadien (PPT), was capable of combining the separate aims of the North and the South. In January 1963, at the congress of the PPT, it was decided to insist on a compulsory merger of all unions into a government-sponsored confederation of trade unions—another instance of the strengthening of the government's control of all aspects of the life of the nation.

Repeatedly, in recent years, Tombalbaye has been confronted with even more distasteful tasks, which have involved not merely ousting a small number of potential political rivals such as Mahamat Abdelkrim, the President of the National Assembly, and Outel Bono, a leader of the opposition intelligentsia, but also the suppression of widespread upheavals among the masses. The economic situation had caused great discontent; the measures taken by the government to suppress corruption among the slightly better-educated lower middle classes had proved highly unpopular. Following the arrest of Kerallah, Koulamallah and Baptiste, leaders of the Muslim Parti National Africain (PNA), riots broke out in Fort Lamy in September 1963 and stern measures were needed to suppress them. After an interval of peace, relations between the North and the South again became strained; street-brawls broke out between Southerners and Northerners in Fort Lamy and in different parts of the country. Armed bands crossed the north-eastern frontiers of Chad from parts of Sudan, intending to provide support for the Northern opposition muzzled in Fort Lamy, and fleeing back into the Sudan whenever pursued by the Chad army. The nomads in the Northern desert province of Ouadaï, refusing to obey government orders, attacked the frontier post of Adré in December 1965; this disturbance led to more than a hundred casualties, according to official estimates. Sporadic fights along the frontier occur even to the present day, and Radio Cairo in its daily broadcasts still tries to rouse the Muslim inhabitants of Northern Chad; there have been unconfirmed rumours of a 'Muslim government of Chad in exile'. The friction and countless incidents between Chad and the Sudan have led them to close their mutual frontier, though lately both countries have tried to establish better relations. More recently, too, Northern provinces, particularly the desert area beyond Largeau, have grown quieter, held in the firm grip of their new 'préfet', Lieutenant-Colonel Djogo.[3]

Tombalbaye has been ruthless, but he also knows the value of compromise and can forgive his opponents, as in 1965 when he incorporated some of them into his administration. Perhaps he realises that there are subtle influences at work behind the antipathies between Muslims on the one hand and animists and Christians on the other.* But he is very isolated. He is feared,

---

* At this point one should note an interesting letter by Mme. V. Pâques (in *Le Monde*, April 12, 1967), which considers the evolution of Chad. First Mme. Pâques emphasises that disturbances did not come to an end with the one-party system. Universal violent dissensions have led to widespread discontent and unrest, not only in town circles but also in the remotest bush villages. As politicians and administrators are constantly replaced, the traditional authority of the old chiefs has remained unimpaired. She points out how unconcerned the government has shown itself with the traditions and the needs of its Northern citizens. Prior to independence the major activity of the province of Ouadaï—and its main source of food—was big game hunting, which is now forbidden. The brave hunters of old are left with no occupation but fishing—and they are even taxed on part of their catch! The result is a scarcity of meat among the villagers. On the other hand, the growing of cotton is compulsory and those who refuse to comply are heavily fined. It is not surprising that they wonder what good independence is to them. It was hailed as a panacea for all the social ills stemming from colonialism; it would permit them to follow the two most noble occupations of man— hunting and fighting; once more their traditional rulers and their Muslim customs would be respected; compulsory labour would be abolished.

and he is supported because he is feared—and also because he is backed by France. In April 1964 France had been requested to withdraw all its troops after certain French officials had been accused of interference in the domestic politics of Chad, favouring the North, with whose proud nomadic desert tribes they felt a strong traditional affinity. Even after independence, the French had maintained strong administrative and military responsibilities in the Northern regions of Chad. The officers of the French army were in fact 'running' the North as they had done during the colonial period. Hence some French circles—military as well as civilian or even religious—were not at all in agreement with Tombalbaye's policy vis-à-vis the Muslim minority groups. A letter from the Northern Chad Committee was addressed to General de Gaulle criticising this policy. On April 19, Tombalbaye declared that this letter had been written by 'evil Frenchmen who are trying to divide Chadians'. He condemned on the same occasion the activities of the believers' trade unions, who were backed by the Catholic Church although defending the ideals not only of the Christians but of all who belonged to a religion and more especially the Muslims, and who objected to joining a single pro-government trade union. On April 28 a resolution was approved by the National Assembly asking for the withdrawal of French military bases. Tombalbaye did not follow up this resolution as he was not keen to provoke a diplomatic crisis with France. However, according to the overall French policy on military bases in Africa, the French troops were withdrawn, but not entirely: a military base is still maintained in Fort Lamy, discreetly designated the 'stop-over for French flights in Central Africa'.

Many fine speeches are made about liberty of religion and the development of the nation. Children are sent to French-speaking schools, where for a few hours they hear and speak French; when they come home, they return to a completely different world and have no chance of using their French. Children are brought up at school in a strange milieu, which they must accept if they want to obtain the primary school certificate and enter the modern world—a world so alien to their family ways and traditions.

Even though François Tombalbaye may have repeatedly disregarded all the conventions of democracy, he is probably the best type of leader for the Chad of today. It is true that the peoples of the North could be treated better; their fundamental rights should certainly be recognised by the central government. But if the Muslims of the North were not curbed and muzzled at the present time, chaos, anarchy and guerilla warfare would probably prevail over yet another area of Central Africa.

However, a Front de Libération du Tchad was constituted, which led to the incidents of Am Timan—375 miles east of Fort Lamy—on February 22, 1967, of Salamat near the Sudanese border in April, and in the Batha district on July 27. Worse than these incidents was the plot discovered by Tombalbaye in December. Its leader was Silas Selingar, the former Minister of the Interior and the most important member of the government after the President, a Sara and hence not a Muslim. Although imprisoned for embezzlement he seems to have succeeded in organising this plot, according to sixty-six letters addressed by him to friends. How then would François Tombalbaye cope with opposition both within his own party and from the Muslim front?

A final and quite striking fact: French troops were called in during August–September 1968 under the defence agreement between France and Chad to help the government crush a 'rebellion' among nomadic guards and regular soldiers in the Tibesti. In an interview given to *Jeune Afrique* (number 308, August 1968), Tombalbaye explained the situation by saying: 'I do not agree that this should be called a rebellion. . . . We are faced, not by rebels, but by highway robbers. This is a coalition of feudal elements who have been disappointed in their political ambitions and have deliberately placed themselves at the service of foreigners.'

CAMEROUN

Cameroun covers an area of 183,381 square miles. From its 125-mile coastline on the Gulf of Guinea in the south, it stretches 800 miles northwards to Lake Chad. This explains the diversity of its climate and ecology: from the hot, wet, equatorial climate and thick forests of the south, to the hot, dry savannah belt in the north. The population today is estimated at about 5,300,000, belonging to some eighty different ethnic groups. The largest of these are the Fang or Pahouin in the southern region bordering Gabon; the Bamileke on the south-west coast (Douala-Nkong-samba) and in the west on the former border of British Cameroons; the Bamoun, also in the western region; and the Fulani and the Kirdi in the northern regions. About half the population is animist; the rest of the population is divided roughly equally among the Catholics, the Muslims and the Protestants.

Cameroun, with a colonial history different from that of its French-speaking neighbours, has evolved in a different way. Furthermore, its development in recent years has been hampered by subversion. Until 1918 it was a German colony; after the defeat of Germany it was divided into two territories, which were administered first under a mandate of the League of Nations, and since 1945 under the trusteeship of the United Nations. The larger and more densely populated of these territories was administered by France; the other, which was divided into two parts which had common frontiers with Eastern and Northern Nigeria, was administered by Britain. Therefore, the major problem in the way of establishing an independent country was the reunification of the French-speaking and the English-speaking parts. Against this, however, there was a body of opinion in 'British' Cameroons which was in favour of a merger with Nigeria. The colonial administrations of both France and Great Britain were far too cautious to intervene.

The larger French-speaking Eastern part of the country had since 1955 been rent by internal rebellion, ruthlessly conducted and never fully overcome. The Cameroun section of the RDA, the Union des Populations Camerounaises (UPC), had developed under fiery leaders—Dr Roland Félix Moumié, its president, and Rueben Um Nyobe, its secretary-general—into a revolutionary body, chafing under the restraints of compromise and caution and

demanding immediate independence and reunification of Camer-
oun. They were constantly organising meetings and street demon-
strations and making repeated representations to the Trusteeship
Council until they were outlawed by the colonial administration in
July 1955. The banned leaders were at once actively supported by
Nasser in Cairo, and later by Nkrumah in Ghana and by Sékou
Touré after Guinea had pronounced the fateful 'No' in 1958.
Operating from headquarters outside the country, the UPC's
leaders stirred to guerilla warfare some of their most fiery, bellicose
and determined countrymen, in the Bamileke region and in
the Sanaga maritime province, east of Douala along the Douala-
Yaoundé railway line. The Bamileke became the most aggressive
since they were suffering so much from the chiefdoms and more
especially from the chiefs (called 'fons') who, with the consent of
the French administration, acted as sheer autocrats. Their tax
practices and their abuses in distributing the land created widespread dissatisfaction. This discontent amongst the Bamileke was
cleverly used by Moumié, who had only to stir up hatred against
the French and the fons to create a state of guerilla warfare. For
the Third World, the warriors of the UPC in Bamileke became a
symbol; they were extolled and encouraged at the United Nations
in melodramatic motions from the Afro-Asian bloc.[4] However, no
nation-wide insurrection with massive popular support took place,
as in Indochina or Algeria. Cameroun counted for little on the
international scene because it was too remote and too poor; it
never became the basis of an international political issue. The
fighting remained sporadic, unplanned and irregular, but it was a
great burden on Cameroun, where it occupied several thousand
French and Camerounese soldiers till 1962–63.

When autonomy came in 1958, Cameroun was governed by a
wise man. Ahmadou Ahidjo is a Northerner and a Muslim who
had founded his own party, Union Camerounaise, to counteract
the UPC, but was anxious to avoid all tribal cavilling. While the
aim of his policy was closely similar to the UPC's—independence
and unification at once—his attitude and the means he intended to
adopt were different. He had already ousted a more moderate

politician, André-Marie M'Bida, the Prime Minister in 1957 during the period of the Loi Cadre. M'Bida was well versed in the ways of French parliamentary life, but had vacillated in the face of the spreading Bamileke rebellion instead of striking hard at it. Once in power, Ahidjo demanded immediate independence, something M'Bida, dominated by his French senior colleagues, would never have dared to do. Ahidjo's move was well-timed: de Gaulle, recently returned to power, realised that France must grant Black Africa its independence. Consequently, at the thirteenth session of the General Assembly of the United Nations, the French delegation asked for the Cameroun trusteeship mandate to be terminated. On January 1, 1959, Cameroun became self-governing, with France remaining responsible for matters of defence, finance and foreign affairs.

Independence, unhappily, did not end the Bamileke rebellion, which remained as active and insidious as ever, after its leader Um Nyobe was killed in an ambush; nor did it end dissension in and around Douala, or even in the Sanaga maritime province. However, one of the Bamileke chiefs, Mayi Matip, began to establish a 'legal', 'reconciled' UPC. Félix Moumié, the leader of the UPC, requested from Conakry that general elections should be held under the control of the United Nations; M'Bida, President Ahidjo's former rival, decided to align himself with the UPC and sought a self-imposed exile in Conakry beside Moumié.

On January 1, 1960, before the Secretary-General of the United Nations, Dag Hammarskjöld, and the personal representative of General de Gaulle, L. Jacquinot, Cameroun celebrated its independence. On the same day, a UPC commando unit attacked Douala airport. There can be no doubt that the granting of independence gravely disturbed Moumié, as Ahidjo had now procured what the UPC had been steadily demanding for the last five years. The uprising of the Bamileke could now have little purpose. Ahidjo believed that there was no point in antagonising the Western world: he saw that it was far better to maintain friendly relations and still get what you want in the end. The general elections held on April 10, 1960, showed that Ahidjo had chosen the right course and that the whole country approved of it: his party won 59 seats, the 'legal' UPC only 18, and M'Bida's Parti Démocratique Camerounais (PDC) 11.*

Unification became Ahidjo's next target. It would add to his own and his country's prestige and would leave the rebellious elements completely circumscribed. Unification depended on the result of a referendum, to be held on February 11 and 12, 1961, which had been proposed by the United Nations for the Northern and Southern sections of the British Cameroons. The more populous Southern section voted in favour of becoming a part of Ahidjo's Cameroun—a triumph for John Ngu Foncha's Kameroun National Democratic Party (KNDP), which supported Ahidjo, over its rival, the Kameroun National Congress (KNC) of Dr Emmanuel Endeley, which campaigned for incorporation as a separate state of the Federation of Nigeria. The Northern section, by a landslide vote of 140,000 to 18,000, elected to become part of Nigeria. There was, at first, some bitterness in Douala and Yaoundé at this result and there were suggestions of irregularities in the ballot. However, the division was made and the frontiers of Cameroun were settled. As with British Somaliland and Somalia, two African territories, arbitrarily partitioned by the colonial powers, had decided to join forces; now for the first time, English-speaking and French-speaking Africa, in seeking unity, had disregarded the differences of language, legal systems and living habits. Unification has proved a success—and perhaps an example for the future. The country has accepted bilingualism. The metric system, the CFA franc and the right-hand traffic rule have been adopted without any great difficulty. The excise and taxation systems are being brought into line with each other. It will, however, be some considerable time before the administrative structures of the two countries are fully harmonised.

On October 20, 1961, Ahidjo was elected President of the Federal Republic of Cameroun and Foncha, the former leader of British Cameroons, Vice-President. A federal National Assembly

* M'Bida had come home from Conakry: he seemed sufficiently apologetic to be forgiven by the magnanimous Ahidjo.

was formed on April 3, 1962, consisting of 40 MPs belonging to the Union Camerounaise, Ahidjo's party, and 10 belonging to the Kameroun National Democratic Party of Foncha. The minority parties were not represented in it. The days of inter-tribal strife were over; Ahidjo had been proved right. A man of dignified and gracious appearance, the President of Cameroun had demonstrated his unswerving determination and unflagging authority. It still remained for him to assert his position as the sole leader of his country, and to overcome any possible obstacle in his path.

He turned first to the trade unions, which were then divided into rival factions, telling them to unite into one body and to stop troubling the government with trivia. He told them that they must collaborate with management and with foreign business interests in a joint effort to reach the economic targets specified in the government's development plan. As a result, in January 1963 a federation of Cameroun trade unions was established. Fortunately, the senior trade union leader in Cameroun, Jacques N'Gom, had been persuaded to co-operate. He was the former secretary of the Union Générale des Travailleurs Camerounais, the largest trade union, which at one time was affiliated to the CGT in France. The trade union affiliated to the so-called free trade union (of the CGT-Force Ouvrière brand in France) soon followed. Only the trade union belonging to the Union des Syndicats Croyants wavered and kept out for three years, till a new secretary-general, Michel Tina, decided it was time to join the government sponsored union.

Next it was the turn of the opposition political parties: the 'legal' UPC of Mayi Matip, the PDC of M'Bida, a new party launched by Bebey Eyidi, a well-known doctor from Douala, and a small party led by the former Foreign Minister, Charles Okala. Already, in November 1961, during a press conference, Ahidjo had expressed the wish for a joint programme of all the existing parties so that a single unified national party might be established for the benefit of the nation. The 'legal' UPC, at its congress in January 1962, rejected this proposition and stated that it was the only party to have really fought for independence and should therefore share power with the Union Camerounaise. The congress was thereupon dissolved by a decision of the President of the Republic, particularly for having paid one minute of homage to Moumié, who had been mysteriously poisoned in Switzerland. Charles Okala was against the idea of a unified party, favouring the formation of a 'unified front' which would be a coalition of parties in which each group would retain its individual personality.

On April 20, 1962, Ahidjo addressed the nation over the radio to explain his position:

> We should understand that the era of micro-parties and ideological quarrels based on slogans void of content is over. Ideologies certainly respectable in themselves are apt to end by missing the national ideal. It is therefore of urgent necessity that we should rally round one ideal, rally round one programme. . . . I am firmly convinced that the Cameroun masses ardently desire this union which is indispensable for national reconstruction. To mar it, for reasons of self-interest and personal ambition, would be to undermine the building of our state.

On May 15 the opposition answered this appeal with an open letter to Ahidjo, signed by M'Bida, Eyidi, Okala and Mayi Matip, rejecting the one-party system as leading to dictatorship and fascism. Ahidjo was of a different mind, and battle was joined. Ahidjo did not beat about the bush. On June 19 he denounced the 'ambitious and outmoded petty politicians who have been spoiled by the Fourth French Republic'. On June 29, 1962, all those who had expressed such loud dissent from his policy—Mayi Matip, Bebey Eyidi, Okala and M'Bida—were arrested and sentenced to thirty months' imprisonment. To eliminate the opposition seemed easy enough. Ahidjo waited, however, four years before carrying out his ultimate purpose. In June 1966 a unified party, the Union Nationale Camerounaise, was formed from a combination of his own party, the Union Camerounaise, with the political parties of Western Cameroun. The English-speaking Vice-President played an important part in this development by persuading both his own party and the opposition parties of Western Cameroun, especially Endeley's KNC, that it was the only sensible course to follow.

Ahidjo proved to be a great unifier. For instance, in April 1963 he went to the Bassa country, where the UPC had some very solid strongholds, and invited the population to join him in his political efforts to unify Cameroun; he asked them to forget the divisions and squabbles of the past, paying homage to the late patriot Um Nyobe. But he wanted also to be a moderniser; he rejected the example of some of his colleagues in neighbouring countries, who relied on one single party over which their own ethnic group had a firm grip. When he said he favoured a unified party, he meant a party where there would be no differences of opinion based on religion or race. As a Northerner, he did not want his Union Nationale Camerounaise to be the stronghold of the Northern tribes; he knew quite well that he had to be able to count on the Southern groups and above all on the Bamileke.

The spirit of rebellion has gradually faded away, receiving less and less support from abroad, apart from some encouragement from Red China. Ghana and Guinea had enough domestic problems on their hands, and patched up their feud with Cameroun. Cameroun established good relations with the countries of the Eastern bloc, exchanging missions for trade and information. This was stimulated in March 1965 by the appointment of Etoungou, Ambassador in Moscow, as Minister of Foreign Affairs. In September 1965, Peking sent a mission and Ahidjo intimated that he was ready to establish normal diplomatic relations between the two countries, provided that China did not try to interfere in Cameroun's internal politics. With the murder of Félix Moumié in Switzerland in September 1960, the UPC had lost all its great former leaders, and the outlawed party divided into pro-Russian and pro-Chinese factions. In Douala, the rebellion was crushed and the local commander caught and shot. Yet the fire has not been completely put out; here and there, in the Bamileke and Mungo departments, it still smoulders.[5] Government forces are still at the ready, prepared to go into action to maintain peace at home. The government has even been criticised for offering too many blandishments to the Bamileke peoples—who represent one-quarter of the entire population of the country—to the prejudice of other, more amenable, peoples. The ambitious and sturdy Bamileke are given the best appointments: the administration is staffed largely by them and other tribes retire resentfully to the background. The country has not yet overcome all its ethnic problems, but Ahidjo's outstanding political success is largely attributable to his complete lack of ethnic favouritism.

It is also attributable to his determination to run the country on the basis of very strict financial rules. He could never (as he had already stated in a general note sent to the administration in early 1962) accept the lack of responsibility of civil servants. He could not allow his country to fall into anarchy; neither could he accept undue criticism from certain officials. They had to choose between staying and serving the government and the country or resigning.

Ahidjo also sternly denounced corruption and embezzlement. In November 1966 he asked for the resignation of Victor Kanga, the Minister of Information, who had previously been Minister of Finance. In December Kanga was condemned to four years imprisonment, together with two of his assistants: the former permanent secretary of the Ministry of Finance and the assistant director of the Camerounian Broadcasting Corporation. Following this delicate case, President Ahidjo recommended a policy of rigorous financial measures, reforming the whole system of public accounts in July 1967 and in particular establishing a better control of public expenditure and an improved fiscal system. A 'technical committee for the distribution of imported goods' was created to enable the government to eliminate those import firms which were notoriously cheating the state.

Another reason for the success of Ahidjo's presidency is to be found in the striking economic progress of his country during his six years in office. Paradoxical though it may seem, the rebellion did not hinder the economic development of Eastern Cameroun, but rather stimulated it. From 1958 to 1964, the trade balance showed a strong credit balance.* This thriving financial situation was the result of several favourable factors. Firstly, Cameroun is a producer of aluminium. The output and export of aluminium ingots increased so rapidly that by 1964, with a production of 51,500 tons, Cameroun was the fifth largest producer in the world. The output for 1966 was estimated at 50,000 tons. This aluminium is smelted from the alumina imported from Guinea (FRIA plant) at the ALUCAM works, established by the Pechiney company in 1957-58, using the electricity produced by the dam of Edea. Secondly, the production of cocoa has been improved and increased with such effectiveness that, here again, Cameroun ranks as the fifth largest producer in the world, with 80,000 tons in 1965–66. Moreover, agriculture is much more diversified than in most African countries, incomparably more so than in any other country of Equatorial Africa. Cameroun is Africa's fourth largest producer of coffee, after Ivory Coast, Angola and Ethiopia, and on a par with Congo-Kinshasa. It is the third largest banana exporter in the 'franc area', after Martinique and Ivory Coast; as the West is the main source, this economic trend appeared only after reunification in 1962. It also produces tobacco, some tea (especially in the West) and limba timber. Finally, Cameroun is one of the few African countries which seem to have 'taken off' industrially. Quite apart from the aluminium production of ALUCAM, thirty-two industrial firms were established in varied sectors between 1960 and 1964: a chocolate factory, noodles, soaps, beer, bicycles, radio sets and transistors, textiles, paints and varnish, and small agricultural machines. Secondary industries accounted for 31 per cent of the national income in 1964, compared with 20 per cent in 1960.

Only 1965 was a difficult year, with a trade deficit of 3,700

* In 1958, 839 million CFA francs surplus; in 1959, 6,613 million; in 1960, 3,511 million; in 1961, 486 million; in 1962, 375 million; in 1963, 2,391 million; in 1964, 1,444 million (from the Report for 1965–1966 of the Banque Centrale des Etats de l'Afrique Equatoriale et du Cameroun). IMF statistics indicate a 3,700 million CFA francs deficit in 1965 and an 11 million surplus in 1966.

million CFA francs, because cocoa prices dropped unexpectedly and imports of capital equipment increased sharply. For instance, Cameroun started work on the projected Trans-Cameroun railway, which will establish a trade link from northern Chad to Douala, the important Cameroun port. Cameroun's economic expansion should continue; in 1966, a five-year plan was launched which made provision for investments totalling 165,000 million CFA francs and aiming at a yearly increase of 5·75 per cent in the Gross National Product. The country has a number of untapped resources, such as a bauxite deposit in Northern Cameroun and probably some oil.[6] The present plan will emphasise the development of fisheries and cattle-breeding, increase palm oil production and launch a project for the production of rice. The country still relies heavily for its future development on French technicians, of whom there are now 12,000, but the young intellectuals of Cameroun have been very successful in French universities and technical colleges. It is hard to believe that such a protracted and steady increase in economic efforts could survive if President Ahidjo's strictly authoritarian rule were to be challenged, no longer by terrorists, but by the intellectuals who are growing impatient of the dominance of foreign business interests, usually labelled 'neo-colonialist'.

When the opportunity arose, Cameroun readily entered into association with its four equatorial neighbours, which provided a large and readily accessible outlet for its increasing production. Since January 1, 1966, Cameroun has been a member of the Union Douanière et Economique de l'Afrique Centrale (UDEAC). The treaty, which was signed two years earlier, makes provision for co-ordinated development in each of the five member states with the establishment of eleven industrial projects, giving due consideration to the needs and present production of each country; for common customs and tax tariffs; and for harmonised fiscal systems and investment regulations. Because of its existing assets, and because of the wide diversity of its future industrial and agricultural prospects, Cameroun should benefit more than any other member from the formation of the UDEAC. With Gabon, to which similar considerations apply though to a lesser extent, it should both derive immediate benefits from the existing stage of development and also provide an incentive for the other three countries. The UDEAC has made provision for a 'solidarity fund' based on the following levies from each of the member governments: Congo–Brazzaville and Gabon, 500 million CFA francs each; Chad, CAR and Cameroun, 300 million each. This aims at an equitable reallocation of all revenues levied on imported goods and is to act as a kind of clearing house for all goods transported through the coastal countries inland, since the former are profiting from the latters' import trade. In 1966, it was agreed that from this source Chad would receive 1,175 million CFA francs, CAR 665 million, Congo 57 million, Gabon 2,850,000, and Cameroun would receive nothing.

UDEAC should be hailed as the first serious, down-to-earth reorganisation of African countries. However, the wide differences between the five members—one of them wealthy, one fairly wealthy, and three much poorer—represent a considerable practical difficulty. For instance, what policy should be adopted for the establishment of new industries? To implant textile mills in all five countries would be absurd, yet who will agree to go without? The less well-favoured countries will inevitably feel resentful and reluctant to co-operate; for instance, soon after the treaty was signed, Chad considered that it was the loser in the taxation arrangements established with Cameroun. So stimulating an economic undertaking for all its members can survive only if each member maintains political stability and retains its confidence in its fellow-members.

4. The Entente States

THE LONG-STANDING RIVALRY between Houphouet-Boigny and Senghor may well have been one of the main reasons which led Houphouet-Boigny to persuade Upper Volta and Dahomey to abandon their idea of an association with Senegal and Soudan in a 'Federation' of Mali, and instead gradually to establish a political bloc consisting of Ivory Coast, Dahomey, Niger and Upper Volta, a group later to be known as the Entente states. The heads of state of Upper Volta and Dahomey maintained that the short-lived Mali Federation could have been to their countries' benefit. The National Assembly of Upper Volta went as far as to ratify the federal constitution, but the country was so closely associated economically with the Ivory Coast that the head of state, Maurice Yameogo, finally abandoned the project. Dahomey wavered for quite a while but finally refused to join in view of Upper Volta's defection. Niger, because of its particular differences with Bamako, never agreed to join.

At this psychological moment, Houphouet-Boigny intervened with proposals of new alliances that from geographical considerations seemed more realistic. Negotiations were slow and at first resulted only in bilateral agreements in April 1959 between the Ivory Coast and Upper Volta, and between the Ivory Coast and Niger. A conference of three heads of state then followed, and Dahomey was persuaded to join. The association soon abandoned its first title, Union Sahel-Bénin, which could have been ambiguous, and opted for the vaguer 'Conseil de l'Entente'. As a French jurist analysed it: 'It was never intended to be a federated state, but merely a co-operative association intending to give a practical form to economic solidarity and to establish the common utilisation of certain public services.'[1] It has no reality as a concrete institution and involves no division of responsibilities. Only certain services are jointly managed: the Cotonou and Abidjan

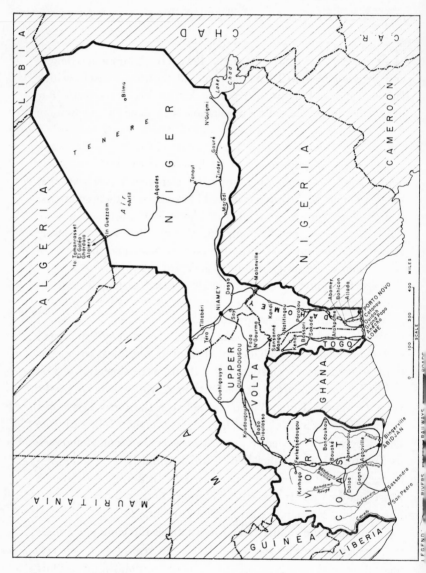

3. The Entente States

harbours, and the Niger-Bénin and Abidjan-Niger railway lines. Yet the striking economic discrepancies among the four states has made it necessary to establish a solidarity fund: each state will pay one-tenth of its yearly budgetary receipts into this fund which is to be divided among the four member-states in inverse ratio to the amount of receipts: one-sixteenth to the rich Ivory Coast against five-sixteenths to each of the other three less affluent states.[2] The Council meets twice a year in each capital in turn. Decisions are taken 'in common': that is, only if the four Presidents unanimously agree. Such a loose association was consistent with Houphouet-Boigny's often expressed theories: African states should not for the moment relinquish any degree of sovereignty nor join any federation (as had been Senghor's fervent wish), but should restrict themselves to friendly economic relationships.

The Entente has survived, in spite of some moments of conflict. Its success and its very realistic basis attracted a fifth African state, Togo, which had hitherto remained aloof: hence it will also be considered in this chapter. Togo joined formally on June 9, 1966. During the same session which welcomed Togo as a new member, the Conseil de l'Entente decided to change the solidarity fund into 'fonds d'entr'aide et de garantie des emprunts' (a fund to assist member countries and guarantee their loans), which was to receive 650 million CFA francs yearly: 500 million from the Ivory Coast, 42 million from Niger, Upper Volta and Dahomey, 24 million from Togo. The Ivory Coast was not to draw on the fund during its first five years of operation, in order to allow the maximum assistance to be given to the investment programmes of the other members. The novel feature of this fund is that it may be used to warrant or to guarantee loans contracted or issued both by public or semi-public organisations in the member-countries and by private firms whose headquarters and main field of activities fall within them.

IVORY COAST

The Ivory Coast was the richest of the French colonies in Africa south of the Sahara, and this relative affluence has dominated the history of its ten years of independence. Another feature unique to the Ivory Coast was the unquestionable aura of prestige surrounding its great political leader, Dr Félix Houphouet-Boigny.

A few statistics will show more clearly than any discussion the importance of this wealth to the Ivory Coast's recent history. In 1953–55, when the value per capita of exports from French West Africa as a whole was $18, the corresponding figure for the Ivory Coast was $47. The corresponding figures for imports were $20 and $33 respectively. While only 1·4 per cent of wage earners in French West Africa (AOF) were concerned with activities other than agricultural, the figure for the Ivory Coast was 2·8 per cent. In the year 1955 the total of taxes and other levies in the Ivory Coast amounted to 10,972 million CFA francs. This was, of course, for the benefit of the whole Federation and, under the federal arrangements for the division of income, only 2,729 million CFA was fed back to the Ivory Coast.[3]

The Ivory Coast's great wealth, that in part went to support its colonial associates, was equalled by its leader's tremendous prestige. An intelligent, shrewd, well-read man, fully aware of African realities because of his early experience as a planter and a doctor, Houphouet-Boigny soon became a leading figure of French political life, an experienced MP and a minister in several French cabinets, without ever losing contact with Africa. With its great economic potential, the Ivory Coast might well have proved one of the most difficult French-speaking African countries to govern, due to what may be termed 'antagonismes permanents' (permanent difficulties) such as tribalism, a widely diverse population and a strong student force, and probably only so exceptional a character as Houphouet-Boigny could have controlled the country with a strong hand. About sixty different ethnic groups are scattered over its territory. Two of the most numerous, the Agni and the Baoule, find it difficult to live side by side. For example, in 1959, the Agni group decided to secede and create an independent state, Sanwi; a delegation went to negotiate with the French government, was arrested, to comply with a request from the Abidjan government, and shipped back home.

The economic growth of the Ivory Coast has attracted labour from its poorer neighbours. Mossi from the Upper Volta have come to work in agriculture, and Senegalese and Dahomeans in office jobs. As a result, small cliques of foreigners have proliferated in the towns of the Ivory Coast—youth clubs, sports clubs and the like. The idea spread to the people of the Ivory Coast who, perhaps in self-defence against the foreigners' institutions, themselves formed large numbers of clubs and associations; for instance, in Abidjan, the Association des Originaires de Daloa, the Association des Originaires de Bouaké,* the Union des Originaires des Six Cercles de l'Ouest, etc. These clubs and associations provided forums where they could debate, criticise and scheme together. The people of the Ivory Coast came to realise that so many minority groups of foreigners were a danger to them and, as soon as their country became self-governing, most of the foreigners were told to leave. These were mainly the Senegalese and the Dahomeans, not the Mossi who were needed for agricultural work.

The large number of young men who were sent to study abroad were determined to play their own part in the political life of the country. The younger generation provided an opposition to the government in the Ivory Coast much earlier than in any other African country—and a very unruly opposition it was, for the students tried to agitate within their own tribal groups, supported radical motions within the country and generally disagreed with their famous leader, who to them was an elderly conservative. Houphouet-Boigny, who was, of course, the leader of the RDA all over French-speaking Africa as well as of the local branch, the Parti Démocratique de la Côte d'Ivoire (PDCI), did not want the country to be disrupted in any way when it became self-governing: he believed that the administrative framework and economy should be left alone to function as before. He felt there was no

* Daloa and Bouaké are two inland towns.

137

point in prematurely sending away useful French technicians or administrators and speeding up Africanisation, and no point in picking fights with traditional chiefdoms when they could so easily support the party platform in bush villages. The student opposition felt otherwise. With the support of the strong Fédération des Etudiants d'Afrique Noire en France (FEANF), the students of the Ivory Coast campaigned during the referendum for a vote of 'No', as did the leading trade union of the Ivory Coast, the Union Générale des Travailleurs de l'Afrique Noire (UGTAN). The students and the unions did not represent a large part of the total population of the Ivory Coast, but, since there was only one organised party at the National Assembly, Houphouet-Boigny's PDCI, the students and the trade unions came to be the major active and intelligent opposition to 'the black bourgeoisie which had established itself in power'.[4]

Opposition of this kind necessarily led to some constraint on the government. However, Houphouet-Boigny's prestige stood so high—particularly in the bush where his party was very well-entrenched—and the economic record of the country had been so impressive, that Houphouet-Boigny was in the end able to overcome it. But the struggle proved to be tedious and long-drawn-out, against hidden opponents and against his earlier supporters who would waver and then furtively abandon him, denigrating his authoritarian, pro-European attitude and his neo-colonial undemocratic party. Some merely disagreed with him; some envied him and dreamed of ousting him; yet others actively plotted his downfall. His former supporters abandoned him, until finally he was left with only two of the 'old-timers'—the unflinchingly loyal Auguste Denise, and the 'Number Two Strong Man' of the country, Philippe Yace, the President of the National Assembly and secretary-general of the PDCI. Houphouet-Boigny's ministerial team of loyalists was now composed of much younger, brilliant men: Diomande (Minister of the Civil Service), Usher (Minister of Foreign Affairs), Tanoh Lambert (Minister of National Education), Diawara (Minister of Planning) and Raphael Saller, the founder of the modern Ivory Coast, a former 'Governor' in the French colonial civil service, who was disliked for the very 'colonialist' measures that he advocated but was accepted for his remarkable achievements. Born in the French West Indies, he was the only coloured non-Ivorian in power. He remained a kind of 'Lord Treasurer' of the country for eight years, until he was persuaded to resign in 1966.

First there were minor skirmishes with students and trade unionists, especially with members of the believers' union. Several students were arrested in 1961 and released six months later only after they had given certain undertakings, including acknowledging one students' union, the government-patronised Union Nationale des Etudiants de Côte d'Ivoire en France—the Fédération des Etudiants d'Afrique Noire was held too leftish. All the Ivory Coast trade unions were 'required' to hold their meetings jointly. The believers' union refused to comply for they considered this would lend support to the government's policy of supporting free enterprise, leaving private business unchecked and observing without demur the flood of foreign capital into the economy of the young Ivory Coast. Before long, strikes were decreed to be illegal and all the demands of the unions were rejected. The unions threw in their hand* for the sake of the public interest, combining in 1962 into one governmental trade union federation (which did not include the believers' union). In fact economic considerations were predominant in the first two years after independence and the potential opponents of the government were reluctant to do anything that might hinder its extraordinary expansion. During this period, Houphouet-Boigny showed his lack of concern for all the discussions and conferences about African unity. Sometimes he attended and paid lip-service to the cause, thus reinforcing it, for such was his prestige. However, he

---

* They had been divided since the 1958 split of UGTAN into two tendencies: one a unitary front following Sékou Touré and hence outlawed in the Ivory Coast, the second an autonomous body with very limited means of action and influence.

would not commit himself and was much less active on the international stage than several of his colleagues. He seemed interested only in strengthening the ties with his neighbour-partners of the Conseil de l'Entente.

In the following years (1963–64) Houphouet-Boigny was confronted with more serious difficulties, for the opposition that then reared its head came from within his own party, from his closer associates. Was it prompted merely by human weakness—vanity, pride, thwarted ambition, suppressed envy for the glory and success of their President? Or were his opponents, stirred by idealist motives, meaning to rid the country of an increasingly autocratic regime? Or was it simply tribal rivalry that underlay such attempts at subversion? The plots of January and September 1963 did not rouse the masses, and both were foiled in good time by the very efficient police service of the presidency. The plotters were arrested and tried in April 1963 and December 1964, in each case in Houphouet-Boigny's native village, Yamoussoukro, and condemned for subversion, attempted murder and attempting to overthrow the regime.

The first plot, of January 1963, was engineered by a variety of people, including several important public figures; those attending secret meetings used to wear penitents' hoods so that they could not be identified. In January 1963, a captain in the customs administration, Anaki, was the first to be arrested. He was supposed to be the 'brain', together with several police officers, some with well-known Communist leanings. Soon afterwards the 'leaders' were found out: Joachim Bony, Minister of Education; Amadou Kone, Minister of Health; and Charles Donwali, Minister of Agriculture. A variety of innocuous-looking organisations made the preparations for revolt: for instance, the 'Association du RDA du Nord', and 'Les Amis de la Culture', which had the active support of a number of students back from France and even some of the technicians sent by France to assist development. The plot was a perfect cross-section of every possible type of opponent to Houphouet-Boigny's regime. Students and members of the younger generation were attacking (and even despising)

Houphouet-Boigny for ideological reasons; Northern Ivorians were resenting the influence exerted by the Southern tribal groups and particularly by the Baoule, the President's tribe. The plot had two consequences for the activities of the party. A drastic purge expelled many of its members, and ethnic and advisory committees were set up within each ministry. Since the army had proved unreliable, it was also dramatically reduced in size—from 5,500 to 3,500 men—and the soldiers were posted to stations at the frontiers and partly replaced in 1964 in the interior by a special militia of 6,000 men.

The announcement of the second plot, of September 1963, was followed by arrests and by a further 'purge' of the party. Still, it was doubtful whether there really had been a second plot or whether the police had uncovered a sequel to the earlier plot and come upon hitherto undiscovered accomplices and supporters, some of them prominent in the government's hierarchy. Ironically, J. B. Mockey, Chief Justice at the first political trial in Yamoussoukro, was one of those implicated in the second plot, along with five other ministers: Jean Banny, Minister of Defence; Camille Gris, Minister of Labour; Alaou Kacou, Minister of Housing; A. Thiam, Minister of Information; and Tidiane Dem, Minister of Production. They were all arrested and, in December 1964, were sentenced to death; these sentences were later commuted to life imprisonment.

After so many leading supporters of Houphouet-Boigny had proved unfaithful, suspicion was widespread and the tension was in no way relieved by a huge 'spontaneous' demonstration of loyalty set up by the party in September 1963, when 200,000 party members were brought into the capital from all over the country.

A more tragic event was the suicide of the President of the Supreme Court, Ernest Boka, on April 7, 1964, following his arrest for yet another attempt to overthrow the President. The government announced he had left a political testament which showed him to be ambitious, dishonest and repeatedly plotting to overthrow Houphouet-Boigny's authority, ever since a Muslim marabout had foretold that 'he was destined to reach a very exalted station'. The President, officially commenting upon this latest defection, remarked sadly that what seemed to a European mere rigmarole still carried great weight in Africa and was the source of daily tensions and drama. He said that fetishism was still the core of the problem, together with the fear of being poisoned.

By the end of 1964, the opposition had been thoroughly suppressed. The government was then free to embark unopposed on modern reforms: the outlawing of polygamy, of the so-called 'dowry' or bride-price, and of inheritance in the female line. (According to the old customs, prevailing chiefly in the south, the deceased's inheritance went not to his children but to his sister's children.) The government was shrewd enough to arrange to have all anti-tribal measures introduced and supported by traditional chiefs and leaders. The government team and the party could now at last devote their time and energy to their main concern: developing the Ivory Coast into a modern state and the richest country of French-speaking Africa.

In the Ivory Coast, sudden economic expansion is neither a dream nor a fiction. However, the economy is still fragile, for it still needs many more reliable, well-trained, efficient, honest managers and technicians capable of replacing Europeans. The Ivory Coast could not be what it is today without the presence of a large body of Frenchmen, both in administration and in private business. Houphouet-Boigny and his team have been policy-makers of undeniable worth. They staked their all on big business and foreign capital. The brilliant potentialities of the country are a challenge and their answer to that challenge is undoubtedly 'neo-colonialist' in spirit. In economic terms, it is a tremendous success: in 1964, the Ivory Coast was the largest African producer of bananas (114,000 tons), of raw timber (1,450,000 tons), and of coffee (261,000 tons), making it the third largest producer of coffee in the world; in that year its output of cocoa reached 98,000 tons, making it the fourth largest cocoa producer in the world. Between 1960 and 1964, the credit margin of its trade balance doubled.[5]

millions CFA francs

	1960	*1961*	*1962*	*1963*	*1964*
Exports	37,300	47,100	47,700	56,800	73,200
Imports	29,600	41,800	38,500	41,900	58,100
Yearly surplus	7,700	5,300	9,200	14,900	15,100

The per capita Gross National Product increased from $100 in 1960 to $210 in 1966. The balance of payments showed a profit of over 800 million CFA francs on total transactions of 112 billion.[6]

millions CFA francs

	Debit	Credit
Goods and services	95,395	100,379
Transfers	9,712	4,813
External accounts	6,965	—
External liabilities	—	7,752
	112,072	112,944

Of course, this incredible boom was dependent, as is the case with most African economies, on the fluctuations in the world prices of exported foodstuffs, which until 1965 were very favourable. In that year the rate of expansion fell sharply. The annual rate of increase of the GNP, which between 1960 and 1964 had been as high as about 10 per cent, fell to 5 per cent. Exports shrank somewhat to a figure of about 68,400 million CFA francs and profits totalled only 10,100 million. The government immediately reoriented its economic policies to meet these rather less optimistic economic prospects. It recognised that the Ivory Coast was already producing too much coffee; in order to protect the country from price fluctuations, it has lately considered a decrease in production, for fear that world stocks should become alarmingly high and world markets reluctant to accept coffee from the Ivory Coast. For several years it was able to circumvent the restrictions of its coffee export quota set by the International Coffee Organisation by quietly disposing of its excess production through Liberia, especially in 1964 when the coffee crop increased dramatically.

Several serious endeavours have been made to diversify agriculture: by developing palm oil, rubber, cotton, tropical timber (that could be trans-shipped in much larger quantities through the new harbour of San Pedro in the west of the country), tropical fruit and fisheries. Although not as favoured as other African countries in its mineral resources, the Ivory Coast has an excellent manganese deposit that has recently been developed. Production increased from 105,000 tons in 1964 to 171,000 tons in 1965.

The Ivory Coast recently started on a new four-year development plan (1967–1970) in which public investment in agriculture is given top priority and will be quadrupled. One of the plan's targets is to give each region within the Ivory Coast a more balanced agricultural output. Pro-foreign economic liberalism is still the order of the day; however, the intention is, whenever possible, to replace foreigners by well-trained Ivorians in the industrial sector.

After the pause of 1965, the economic situation is once again flourishing. In 1965–66, the Gross Domestic Product increased from 223,000 million CFA francs to 242,000 million, the strikingly good figure of a 9 per cent increase.[7] Exports in 1966 totalled 76,610 million against 63,610 million for imports. In the past four years the Ivory Coast has greatly enlarged its industrial production and new factories have been set up to produce light electrical goods, chemicals and oils, timber, textiles, building materials, shoes and noodles. The overall industrial turnover has quadrupled: 12,700 million CFA francs in 1960 and 51,400 million CFA francs in 1966 (excluding building and public works).[8] Prospects for the 1967–68 harvest seem favourable. It is estimated that 240,000 tons of coffee will be marketed compared with 130,000 in 1966–67, and 40,000 tons of cotton compared with 22,000 tons; 250,000 tons of paddy are likely to be produced, which will apparently cover local consumption.

When Raphael Saller, the brain behind the boom, was asked to leave in 1965, European businessmen were somewhat annoyed: their concern has proved groundless. The expansion continues. To dispell any fears among the French and to demonstrate where his fundamental concern lies, the President has recently assumed, together with the portfolio of Defence, full responsibility for the two main ministries concerned with the economy: Agriculture, and Economy and Finance. One of his most trusted associates, Konan Bedié, is Minister of Economic Affairs and one of Saller's assistants, Diawara, is in charge of the four-year plan.

Formally, at least, all political dangers are a thing of the past. The former leading conspirators, J. B. Mockey, Amadou Kone, Alaou Kacou, Camille Gris and Jean Banny, who were sentenced at first to death, then in 1965 to life or to shorter terms, were released in May 1967.[9] For the fortunate Ivory Coast, future prospects seem rosy.

UPPER VOLTA

Upper Volta is a comparatively small country, with a total area half that of France. It is an enclave surrounded by the Ivory Coast, Ghana and Togo to the south, Mali to the west and to the north, Niger to the east, and Dahomey to the south-east. Consequently Upper Volta is not land-locked and isolated, but is rather a cross-roads or a trade route for the whole of West Africa. It has a much more important network of roads than most African countries (which carries with it the financial burden of keeping it in good repair), and the important Abidjan-Ouagadougou railway line carrying goods to or from the Gulf of Guinea. Being a trade route for Ivory Coast, Dahomey, Niger and Togo, Upper Volta readily entered into a treaty—the Conseil de l'Entente—which aimed at regulating and integrating trade between them. The country cannot afford to quarrel with any of its neighbours. At the beginning of 1961 there was a slight tension when—according to Upper Volta—the Ivory Coast refused to repay part of the taxes levied at Abidjan harbour. There was also a period, before the Conseil de l'Entente was properly organised, of political flirtation with Nkrumah during which the removal of all customs barriers between Ghana and Upper Volta was contemplated.

Upper Volta is poor and over-populated, with a population of

145

4·7 million, an average density of population of about 47 per square mile (reaching 180 in some richer parts). There is one main ethnic group, the Mossi. Some 450,000 work in neighbouring countries, remitting money back to Upper Volta. Of these, some 100,000 work only as seasonal migrant labour, returning to Upper Volta for a part of every year. Supplies of food and outlets for labour have always been inadequate, and foodstuffs imported from the coast, such as sugar and cola nut, have always commanded very high prices. As a result, it has been a long-standing custom among the Mossi to leave their country temporarily to seek money for food in the richer coastal countries. These migrations, which may well date back to pre-colonial days, were encouraged by the French and English colonial administrations. For so many years have the Mossi migrated to Ghana that they have an old proverb which says: 'Si tu n'as pas été à Kumasi, tu n'as pas vu le paradis' ('If you have never been to Kumasi [in Ghana] you've never seen Paradise'). Half of the migrant labour in Ghana is French-speaking, most of them Mossi from Upper Volta. Many other Mossi go to the Ivory Coast; private organisations recruit migrant labourers in Upper Volta and convey them to Abidjan.[10] Another outlet for migrants in colonial times was the French colonial regiments, wrongly known as the 'tirailleurs sénégalais', who were mostly Mossi from Upper Volta. In fact, the deficit in the balance of payments of Upper Volta was not (and is not) as great as might be expected of so poor a country, because of the existence of the large so-called 'invisible revenues': the pensions of former French soldiers (still a charge on the French budget) and money remitted from abroad by migrant labourers. In a study of economic accounts published in 1962, the Société d'Etudes pour le Développement Economique et Sociale (SEDES) estimated that these revenues totalled 4,700 million CFA francs for the period 1954–59.

However, apart from this peculiar economic factor, there is little that is encouraging about Upper Volta's economy. It produces no crops of economic significance, and traditional agriculture is hardly sufficient to feed the country (as has been noted already, the most costly foodstuffs—sugar and cola—are not produced locally). In addition, the former soldiers and migrant labourers have returned with meagre savings and many expensive acquired tastes, such as alcoholic drinks, tobacco and wheaten bread. Some 2·5 million acres of good agricultural land could be reclaimed if they were not in a particularly unwholesome area, where malaria and bilharziasis are rampant, along Upper Volta's border with Ghana and the Ivory Coast. In the middle of the country, over-cultivation is slowly destroying the soil. Mineral deposits are meagre, with only one significant deposit, manganese at Tambao, 220 miles from Ouagadougou, in the extreme north-east of the country. An estimated 2,200 million CFA francs would be needed to develop these deposits, without taking into account the transport and evacuation problems.*

As a result there is a deficit all along the line, both in the national budget and the trade balance, and France is obliged to fill the gap by providing a balancing subsidy that amounted to 900 million CFA francs in 1962, 1,000 million in 1963, 573 million in 1964, and 500 million in 1965. The cost of administration constitutes a very high proportion of the budget: 72 per cent of the total budget in 1962 and 65 per cent in 1963. In 1962, the deficit of the trade balance was 6,900 million CFA francs, rising to 7,400 million the following year. In 1964, it was 6,800 million, 5,500 million in 1965, 5,300 million in 1966 and 4,500 million in 1967.

Economic prospects are thus somewhat depressing. Cattle breeding, the only substantial potential export, cannot at present be developed for want of water and because of endemic tripanoso-miasis. The first obvious target is to reduce recurrent expenses,

* According to the Economist Intelligence Unit's *Economic Review for former French Tropical Africa*, October 7, 1965, the Ministry of Economic Affairs was expecting financial assistance from Japan to build a railway line 225 miles long that would evacuate the manganese ore (reserves 15 million tons, a 50/54 per cent grade; an initial yearly rate of production of 150,000 tons). But according to the 1965 report of the Banque Centrale des Etats de l'Afrique de l'Ouest, these projects were not going to be realised in the near future. The UNDP is at present studying this project.

particularly those incurred for maintaining an over-large administration; the second, to increase the production of foodstuffs.

Independent Upper Volta has evolved for ten years against this depressing economic background. Political life has not been very active, with few major events, except the somewhat unexpected overthrow of the regime initially established by Ouezzin Coulibaly, who, together with Houphouet-Boigny, was one of the top RDA politicians. When Coulibaly died in 1958, he was succeeded by Maurice Yameogo, who was later elected President of the Republic in December 1959. His party, the local branch of the RDA (at first called the Parti Démocratique Unifié, and later the Union Démocratique Voltaïque), reigned supreme, winning 64 seats out of 75 at the April 1959 Legislative Assembly elections. There was very little actual opposition. It centred on one brilliant leader, Nazi Boni, head of the Parti National Voltaïque (PNV), who advocated association with Mali at the time of the vote on independence. His party won only 11 seats at the April 1959 elections, yet the government thought it prudent to outlaw it. Boni sought refuge first in Bamako and then in Dakar. The PNV was more or less replaced by the Parti Républicain de la Liberté, which in turn was banned in January 1960 and thereafter compelled to resort to clandestine activities.

Maurice Yameogo was quite popular. He was famous for his trenchant outspoken speeches and his courage when confronting his opponents, whether 'on the left'—the trade unionists and students—or 'on the right'—the tribal and religious chiefs. The following quotations illustrate this: 'Government is not a gang of old pals having it good on nice fat jobs at the expense of the people.' 'No one here will hold his job for life, not even the head of state.' 'A marabout is a stupid lazy swindler who has a dangerous hold on benighted minds. That should not be confused with the good influence of Muslim priests.' He forbade all the external signs of the traditional hierarchy, such as the wearing of special caps or pagnes, thus showing how he disparaged tribalism and regionalism. But his MPs, 'préfets' and senior administrators, who were supported by the tribes and regions, showed less concern for the loftier interests of the nation. President Yameogo might have been somewhat dictatorial, but he meant well; he tried hard to rid his country of its traditional tribal system, although this proved impossible. When in power he had an eye to his own interests, but at the same time he had the welfare of his country at heart. He fought hard to assert his authority, to outwit his enemies, or perhaps only to push to one side rival families who showed too much enterprise. There had been an age-old feud between his own family—a prominent one in Ouagadougou—and the Ouedraogo family from Bobo-Dioulasso. On June 18, 1963, Maxime Ouedraogo, the Minister of Labour, was arrested for maintaining, out of public funds, a private armed guard as well as his own personal choir of marabouts. One of Ouedraogo's cousins, Ouedraogo Bougouraoua, the Minister of Public Works, was obliged to resign when he was confronted with the charge of embezzling funds from the national consumers' co-operative.

Yameogo tried to undermine those who wielded any rival influence on the grounds that they were subversive. First, the Church: in April 1964 he decreed that the powers of Church and state should be separate. Shortly afterwards, he attacked the trade unions, especially the Christian trade unions, despite the fact that he had started his political career as a leader of those very unions.

The people approved and cheered when he travelled through the bush, stopping in tiny villages to deliver fierce speeches on the necessity of being austere and self-sufficient, levelling his shafts against corrupt civil servants who were careless of their duties to the nation, repeating again and again his dictum that the head of state should stand alone and unchallenged. In October 1965, after he had revealed a plot organised by a 'movement of national liberation', he was re-elected with 99·7 per cent of the votes; in the following November, his one list received 99·97 per cent of the votes—a landslide victory.

Only a few days later, on January 3, 1966, he was overthrown and the army had to step in. The forces which ejected him were few: discontented civil servants and trade unionists, whose resentment had developed rapidly, even if their motives were not of the loftiest; radical students and teachers like the historian Joseph Ki-Zerbo; and the minority tribes of the west. Yameogo had tried, on December 30, 1965, to carry an austerity budget that might have done away with the need for a French subsidy. All civil servants' salaries were to be cut by between 10 and 20 per cent. The rates at which family allowances were paid were to be the same for both public and private sectors. All promotion in the civil service was to be frozen for a year. It was the unionists who first reacted, speaking for the others; they proclaimed a general strike on December 31, 1965. Yameogo was preparing to fight back to counteract the strike, by proclaiming a state of emergency, on the grounds that there was a 'Communist plot' afoot. But the real leader of Yameogo's wrathful enemies was in fact a former President of the National Assembly, yet another member of the rival clan, Joseph Ouedraogo. Students from the Union Générale des Etudiants Voltaïques marched through the streets demonstrating against Yameogo, the arch-foe of the nation; on January 2, the situation was getting worse, with everyone in the capital on strike, refusing to obey orders and to end the chaos. On January 3, the commander-in-chief of the Upper Volta armed forces, Lieutenant-Colonel Sangoulé Lamizana, seized power.

At first, Yameogo congratulated the army for intervening as umpire to maintain order. However, Lamizana dissolved the Assembly, suspended the constitution, and on January 8 formed a cabinet in which he kept most ministerial portfolios for himself (National Defence, Foreign Affairs, Interior, Youth, Veterans), entrusting only a few others to certain technicians and soldiers. He created an Advisory Committee of forty-one members which included ten officers and five trade unionists. Joseph Ouedraogo was also on this committee, but was not given a portfolio. The coup d'état led to no change whatever in government policy. It was ironic that, although Lamizana pushed Yameogo aside, he implemented exactly the same financial measures. On February 17, 1966, one month after the coup, an austerity budget, closely similar to Yameogo's, was passed, making drastic cuts in civil servants' salaries in order to reduce administrative costs that Upper Volta could not afford.

NIGER

Niger shares with Chad the doubtful privilege of being the most continental of French-speaking African countries, but it has one great advantage over its neighbour: its lines of communications to the Gulf of Guinea are shorter and easier. Like Chad, Niger extends over a wide area, two and a half times that of France. Its climate is Sudanese-Sahelian—first a strip of savannah, then large expanses of desert extending northward towards the more mountainous part of the Sahara which lies within Algeria. It is almost as sparsely populated as Chad, with only 4,034,000 inhabitants or 8·3 per square mile. Muslims constitute 85 per cent of the population, about 14 per cent are animist (small tribes in the south-western region) and one to two per cent belong to other religious groups (Catholics and Protestants). The ethnic groups are broadly separated by the river Niger. The comparatively rich district of the Djerma in the south-west contains about 20 per cent of the total population. The most numerous of the peoples of the savannah and the desert are the Hausa, constituting half the people of Niger; there are also the nomadic pastoral Fulani and, in the north, the picturesque 'blue men', the Tuaregs of the Sahara.

On the whole, Niger is a poor country. Drought is a fundamental problem; lack of water means that only 2 per cent of the soil is cultivated. Groundnuts are the crop with the greatest economic importance, representing half the total exports, and the people eke out a bare existence by growing their own food. In spite of this, Niger has to import a large part of its food, especially cola, sugar and rice, with the usual adverse effect on the trade balance. As was the case in Chad, cattle breeding, the second most important export industry of Niger, might well become a more important source of wealth if competent experts could be found to advise on all aspects of animal husbandry. This particular area of development certainly holds out great prospects; it is, moreover, the only one where reasonably bright hopes can be entertained for the future.

The prospects for the exploitation of mineral resources were, until recently, discouraging. President Hamani Diori has entertained an ambitious scheme for establishing an iron industry in the country, using the iron ore found at Say (near Niamey), but his ideas cannot be taken very seriously for expert opinion holds that it could not possibly be justified economically. Recently, however, a deposit of uranium of exceptionally high quality has been found in the desert in the region of Arlit, which is dominated by the mountain range of Air. The governments of France and Niger have entered into an agreement for the development of this deposit, under which the French atomic energy authority will be responsible for its exploitation. The Arlit deposit has reserves of 20,000 tons and will be able to produce uranium at a price of less than $8 per pound of oxide delivered in France. Because of the difficulty of access to the deposit, its exploitation and transportation will involve major communications developments. Production will start in 1973 with an annual output of 1,000 tons, but will require the shipment of 30,000 tons of equipment per year and very deep drilling for water.

Apart from his rather wild hopes for an iron industry, President Diori has seldom made a mistake. Since gaining independence in 1958, Niger has avoided serious crises; it has kept the same President; the same head of the party, Boubou Hama, who is also President of the National Assembly; and the same Minister of the Interior, Diamballa Maiga. Hamani Diori ranks among the wise men of French-speaking Africa, for from the start he has enforced a rigid economic policy, whatever the short-term cost. Public expenditure has been rigidly controlled and taxation has been kept as high as the country could sustain. The result of this austerity has been a rise in the national income from 2,300 million CFA francs in 1958 to 6,300 million in 1963, and, although a 'balancing subsidy' had been necessary and had been granted by

France in 1962 and 1963, when the gap was over 800 million CFA francs, the domestic budget was met in 1964–65 and in 1965–66 without the need for any subsidy—a shining example for the rest of the African states. France has continued to meet the budget for capital expenditure, either in part or in whole: 416 million CFA francs in 1964, the whole of that years' budget; but only 250 million in 1966, out of a total of 800 million.

However, the balance of trade is still an acute problem, as is seen from the following table:

thousand million CFA francs

	1962	1963	1964	1965	1966	1967
Exports	4·8	5·3	5·3	6·3	8·6	6·3
Imports	6·8	6·0	8·1	9·3	11·1	11·3
	− 2·0	− 0·7	− 2·8	− 3·0	− 2·5	− 5·0

Consequently, the primary concern of the four-year plan over the period 1965–68 is to develop production capacity. The investment of 43,000 million CFA francs—a considerable sum for a relatively poor country—is contemplated. Of this, 43 per cent is to be devoted to improving the infrastructure, principally the road system, and 42 per cent to increasing production capacity. Niger is still desperately searching for external sources of finance, both public and private, but who is anxious to invest where the returns are so uncertain?

Meanwhile Hamani Diori has unswervingly stuck to his declared economic policies. He has tried to keep down public expenditures and to maintain imports at a low level, cutting them further where-ever possible. He has sought to develop the country by increasing the credit available for agricultural purposes and by giving strong encouragement to cattle-breeding and to the cultivation of cotton and exportable foodstuffs such as tomatoes and onions, all of which would find export markets in neighbouring countries. Cotton could be exported from Niger to Bouaké in the Ivory

Coast to be processed there. The intensive cultivation of millet and of groundnuts, also potential export commodities, has been encouraged in what few fertile areas there are in Niger, near the river.

Niger now enjoys stable political life that may well enable such courageous, far-reaching, economic measures to be carried out, but almost continuously from when he first took office President Diori had to contend with subversive activities organised by his great rival, Djibo Bakary, and the Sawaba 'freedom party'. This movement had been organised several years before independence, in 1945, as a local section of the RDA, which at that time was affiliated to the French Communist Party and included Hamani Diori among its members. In 1951, when the RDA broke with the French Communists, the Niger RDA split: one part became the Parti Progressiste Nigérien (PPN) and remained under the control of Diori and Boubou Hama, while the other, under Bakary's leadership, assumed the name Union Démocratique Nigérienne (UDN).

When the poll on the Loi Cadre took place, Bakary campaigned in its support and, with the help of another small party, the Mouvement Socialiste Nigérien, won the elections of May 1957 and became Vice-President of the Executive Council. Diori, though the favoured candidate of the traditional chiefs, had lost the elections. He then changed the label of his party to the Union pour la Communauté Franco-Africaine (UCFA) and began campaigning vigorously for a pro-Gaullist policy and a vote of 'Yes' at the referendum, thus differing from Bakary who called on the electorate to vote 'No'.

The poll resulted in an overwhelming 'Yes' majority (358,000 votes to 98,000) and overnight Diori found himself on the winning side. At the legislative elections following the referendum on December 14, 1958, his own UCFA, with its 'new look', now affiliated to the RDA, won 49 seats out of 60, as opposed to the mere 18 it had taken at the earlier poll. Bakary's party, which had by this time changed its name to Sawaba, lost the election. Diori, who had become the country's leader, refused to let his country become a member of the Mali Federation. He had won his campaign as the most strongly pro-French candidate and the French troops stationed in Niger appeared, for the time being, to be affording him necessary protection.

Once in power, Diori was harried for many years by the major rival whom he had defeated and expelled from the country. The fact that Bakary had sought refuge in 1959, when his party was outlawed, in Mali, the very country that Diori refused to join in a federation, did not help matters. However, Bakary's Sawaba party never gained the support of the masses. (Indeed, neither Bakary nor Diori was able to win real support from the most influential ethnic group, the Hausa.) All Bakary could do was to foment temporary unrest, but always with the ultimate purpose of overthrowing the government. His activities had their effect, and Diori's political line was always in part dictated by the need to foil his brilliant rival in exile, who had the ardent support of the Arab and Socialist countries of Africa.

The Saharan desert extends to Niger, and Algeria and Mali, also desert countries, had spoken to Bakary in friendly terms. Diori was astute enough quickly to invoke the 'fraternity of the Sahara' for his own ends. He maintained that the independent countries which bordered the great desert should co-operate: the former Organisation Commune des Régions Sahariennes (OCRS), which after the Algerian War had been reorganised by France and Algeria as the Organisme Saharien, to develop the mineral resources of the Sahara, should also concern itself with the non-Algerian parts of the desert. The Sahara—or, more precisely, the collaborative development of desert lands and the welfare of the nomadic peoples—provided an excellent meeting point for the Black Africans and the North African Arabs who had so seldom previously found common ground for sincere and whole-hearted collaboration. In such terms Diori made overtures of friendship to his Saharan neighbours. In March 1963 he invited Mauritania and other countries bordering the desert to a meeting at which they grappled with problems concerning the Sahara common to them all, in an effort 'to avoid a balkanisation of the Sahara'.

Unfortunately, he was inclined to indulge in pipe-dreams. He suggested that a pipe-line be built across the desert to bring the oil of the Sahara to the southern parts of Africa—a project that would have proved astronomically expensive. He felt that an inter-governmental organisation should be established to deal with Saharan problems, but when he and Ben Bella met in June 1965 in Tamanrasset, mid-way between their respective countries, he proved very suspicious of the friendly advances of the Algerian leader, because Ben Bella was giving protection to Bakary's expatriate party headquarters in Algiers.[11]

At the same time Diori was not prepared to appear as a tame satellite of the Western camp. He made deliberate overtures to the Eastern bloc, despatching and receiving information missions and entering into cultural or commercial agreements with Poland, Czechoslovakia and, most significantly, the USSR, with whom he signed a trade agreement in April 1962 and a cultural agreement in September of the same year. Boubou Hama, Diori's second-in-command, paid a visit to Communist China in 1962. It was necessary—partly to counteract the influence of Sawaba—to patch up the old feud with Mali, where the outlawed party had at first been welcomed. In the early months of 1963, diplomatic relations were resumed between the two countries. The two presidents first exchanged kind greetings; then, in March 1964, Modibo Keita visited Diori and assured him that Mali would no longer support or harbour the Sawaba party. It seemed that each of Diori's political moves was another sly blow dealt to his arch-foe, Bakary, who retaliated by fomenting unrest inside the country from which he had been exiled.

Diori had been careful to extend the range of his support. His first supporters had been the traditional chiefs, but he later increased his popularity and introduced his party throughout the country, except among the nomads of the north. New cells of his party were founded at every level of urban society to control the masses living in the towns. The party and the administration were closely interconnected and operated together. Consequently, Bakary's relentless attempts to overcome the ruling regime never succeeded. First, in December 1963, a plot was engineered, within a regiment of the army commanded by Captain Diallo. It seems that the Minister of African Affairs, Zodi Ikhia, was implicated in it. It was exposed as a plot against public security; as a result, eighty people were arrested and the opposition for the time being was inactive. Within a year, however, further attempts at revolutionary action again flared up in several parts of the country.

There was considerable terrorist activity, such as the attack against the outpost of Maradoufa on October 4, 1964, and against the outpost of Bosso on October 8, both of them close to the frontier with Northern Nigeria. The terrorist organisation was cleverly built up from small secret training camps just across the frontiers; small military detachments infiltrated into the country to make daring sorties, which had a profound effect on public opinion. In its issue of April 24, 1965, *Marchés Tropicaux*, a French economic weekly specialising in African affairs, drew a telling parallel between the methods of Sawaba—its techniques of training in psychological warfare, and its oath of unquestioning loyalty—and those of the Mau Mau. A large consignment of arms was discovered in the southern town of Zinder on September 15, 1964; and on October 27 several skirmishes broke out on the frontier near Téra between the rebels and the national army and police forces. The government forces remained completely loyal, but Diori thought it prudent to create a special militia ready to crush any uprising that might occur. The repressive measures taken after these organised outbursts of violence were very harsh. They were explained as an example necessary 'pour encourager les autres', to make 'excited minds' think twice next time before they took up arms against their government. On October 13, 1964, seven 'terrorists' were court-martialled and shot in public in Niamey. In all, twenty-three others were sentenced to death and executed as a consequence of the 1964 demonstrations.

On the whole, 1964 was a very difficult year for the government. Tribal unrest was causing new worries, and the government was reshuffled to give an equal number of portfolios to the Djerma and the Hausa. The Hausa came from those areas of Zinder and Maradi where Sawaba propaganda was active and where demonstrations had taken place. By altering the construction of his government, Diori had deprived Sawaba of one of its main propaganda points among the Hausa: the party had alleged that the distribution of ministries and honours was quite inequitable in view of the Hausa's numerical importance, and had called on the Hausa to overthrow their Djerma 'oppressors'. Moreover, the new ministers were much younger than their predecessors and perhaps less conservative in outlook.

Yet Sawaba refused to give up. The party's only hope was to get rid of its redoubtable opponent at the head of the country. An attempt on his life was made with a grenade at the Tabasqui mosque in Niamey on April 13, 1965. By sheer good luck, Diori came out unscathed. A terrorist, Amadou Diop, was arrested, and the government maintained it could prove that the murderer had first crossed the Ghana-Togo frontier, then the Togo-Dahomey frontier, then into Nigeria and, finally, into Niger, with the active help of the Ghanaian police. Diori made the most of this information and hinted that Ghana, with the help of Communist China, was giving shelter to all rebels and outlawed political movements. Most of the French-speaking African leaders expressed their sympathy, especially those of the Ivory Coast and Upper Volta, and it was decided that the heads of all the governments should join in a united effort against similar attempts at subversion from outside.

Dahomey did not join in this unified plan, for at the time it was engaged in a rather pointless dispute with Niger over the ownership of the tiny Lété island in the river Niger. In reply, Niger felt compelled to expel, in December 1963, 769 excellent Dahomean civil servants, the backbone of the Niger administration. Their departure led to great disruption of public services in Niamey. This unfortunate dispute also had the effect of bringing to a premature halt the activities of the Organisation Commune Dahomey–Niger (ocdm), set up for the administration of jointly-used railways and harbours. The customs arrangements between the two countries were interrupted and communications between them came to a standstill, with the result that Niger's groundnuts could no longer be transported to the coast. After a lull in the early months of 1964, when it seemed to the deeply-concerned neighbouring countries that Niger and Dahomey were going to patch up their differences, there was a relapse: a second crisis arose when Niger accused Dahomey of giving shelter to terrorists of the Sawaba. The Ivory Coast President felt obliged to intervene and, in January 1965, he invited the two presidents of the disputing countries to his native village, Yamoussoukro, to bring the feud to an end and to persuade the Dahomeans to rejoin the Conseil de l'Entente.

In September 1966, Diori was re-elected President for a further five years: ample proof of his great popularity and his very successful political manoeuvring. For this reason, like his colleague and friend Houphouet-Boigny, Diori was merciful and decided in August 1967 to commute to life imprisonment the death sentences passed on Captain Diallo and the former minister Zodi Ikhia.

Travellers in Niger in recent years are often struck by its atmosphere of earnest endeavour, and it is often cited as an example in view of its ability to meet ordinary budget expenditure from national revenues alone and for its efforts to cut down the deficit in the balance of trade. In spite of the heavy economic and social handicaps under which it labours, Niger stands a good chance of reaching the point of balancing its budget.

DAHOMEY

Dahomey is a small country. Its strange shape has been compared to a giraffe's head, or to an arrow darting from a narrow coastal strip up into the heart of Africa. Over its 47,000 square miles all the ecological areas of Africa are to be found, from the palm groves along the sand beaches of the Gulf of Guinea to the pre-Sahelian savannah on the border with Northern Nigeria, where the country is over 150 miles wider than on the narrow coastal strip. Dahomey's population is estimated at 2,365,000 inhabitants (about 45 per cent under 15 years of age), divided into several ethnic groups: in the south, the Fon form the largest group, followed by the Adjon, with the Yoruba a minority concentrated along the Nigerian border; in the north there are the Somba around Natitingou, the Bariba in the central north, and the Fulani up towards Niger.

The Dahomeans were well-known throughout colonial French Africa, either as clerks in the administration in Brazzaville or Dakar, or as small tradesmen. With their quick minds and smiling manners, they already had established a long tradition of adaptability to European ways of life, and it seemed an excellent idea to the French to encourage the spread of education in the well-populated parts of Dahomey, making it the 'Latin Quarter of Africa'. However, this also proved to be a serious handicap. Was it all worthwhile? Did this essentially agricultural country, with 90 per cent of its population living in rural areas, need so very many educated men: doctors, male nurses, judges and clerks? For over twenty years before independence it had been difficult to find well-paid employment in the towns, where competition to enter the privileged administrative class was ruthless. While many of its intellectuals were going abroad, things were not too difficult for Dahomey. But, with the spread of independence in Africa, many Dahomeans were thrown out of the former colonial administrations, especially from Senegal and the Ivory Coast, to be replaced by indigenous inhabitants. The Dahomeans had assimilated only too well the colonialist principles of their former masters. When they returned home, they found it difficult to get suitable employment, for their education had made them unfit for the life led by their forbears. They have been a heavy burden to their country ever since. Nevertheless they constitute a political and administrative elite capable of action. The uncomfortable fact is that Dahomey has far too many civil servants employed in its administration (including three to four thousand supernumeraries), and consequently the administrative expenses of the country are incredibly high.

Moreover, there seems little prospect of improvement, for the educational system still turns out thousands of potential unemployed every year. It has never been adequately adjusted to meet the real agricultural needs of the country. A large proportion of Dahomeans have read Molière and Corneille but few are prepared to become agricultural engineers, supervisers, extension workers or village headmen. More and more young men are reluctant to leave the town where they have studied: they linger, full of bitterness and frustration, in Cotonou or Porto Novo, job-hunting, living—or rather starving—by their wits, relying for their daily bread on some luckier cousin who has found himself a soft job in the administration. The problem does not end there. This so-called 'lucky' cousin with the theoretically well-paid job must keep ten, or even twenty, poorer relatives. He has no incentive to improve his condition: if he did so, the hangers-on would only increase. He dreams of running away from tribal ties, of going to France and finding a job, any small job on which he could easily keep his wife and children. The phenomenon prevails all over French-speaking Africa, but is particularly striking in Dahomey because of the exceptional unemployment. In 1964, 1,500 were registered unemployed in Cotonou alone, despite the big public works for the construction of the harbour.

Dahomey is overcrowded, particularly in its narrow coastal strip: the towns—Porto Novo, Cotonou, Abomey, Bohicon and Ouidah—are bulging with inhabitants, and the rural areas around them, which can contain as many as 250 inhabitants per square mile (as, for instance, around Porto Novo), are so thickly populated that they are nearing saturation. Individual holdings have been divided into lots too small for efficient agricultural methods to be applied. The soil is overworked by the traditional methods of husbandry and is rapidly becoming exhausted, making impossible any organised planning of crops for home consumption or for export. This agricultural problem is, or ought to be, the primary preoccupation of any Dahomean leader.

The smart pleasant Dahomean one used to meet in the towns is now likely to be an embittered pessimist ready to explain why his country is doomed, why it cannot improve in spite of its high intellectual level, why the economic and financial situation is so tragic and political life so unstable, although he himself will be doing little or nothing to try to effect a change.

It must be said that, even on a continent where deficits in the budget are as common as malaria, Dahomey's financial plight is appalling. Although revenue from taxation has increased very sharply during the period under consideration, the cost of the rapidly-expanding administration has also risen steadily. The ordinary budget rose from 3,220 million CFA francs in 1958 to 6,688 million in 1963, the year President Maga fell. These figures reveal a yearly increase of 20 per cent between 1958 and 1963. There was a slight reduction in the rate of increase, to 10–15 per cent, between 1963 and 1965. Despite drastic cuts in 1965 and 1966, the ordinary budget totalled 8,183 million CFA francs in the latter year. These deficits have been met by the usual panacea: a subsidy from France. In 1962, this subsidy came to 1,000 million CFA francs, dropping slightly to 950 million in 1963, dropping again to 750 million in both 1964 and 1965, and falling sharply to 50 million in 1966. The subsidy is only one aspect of French help and takes no account of any credit granted for the development budget of Dahomey or of the technical assistance of French personnel paid by France.

Why does Dahomey spend so much? Partly for the reasons given above—because the administration is very extensive and elaborate, the social services (hospitals, schools) are excellent, the army and diplomacy can vie with those of any of its richer neighbours, and the upkeep of an over-developed infrastructure of roads, bridges, etc.—a heritage of colonial times—is a heavy burden on the economy. The ruling caste in Dahomey are lavish spenders, who do not allow lack of finance to deter them. What matters to them is national prestige. They consider it a duty to their country to erect lofty, impressive buildings, and regard preferential treatment of their loyal supporters as quite natural.

In 1950 the trade balance was very slightly on the credit side, but since then it has invariably shown a deficit. Before the war Dahomey used to export maize and millet, but now it ekes out a bare existence and has to import a large proportion of its food. The main exports, palm-kernels and palm-oil (which together amounted to 60 per cent of the exports in 1961–62, and 70 per cent in 1964), used to vary both in quantity and in value. Since 1963 they have remained steady: after reaching a value of 4,513 million CFA francs in 1960, they have levelled out at around 3,500 million, showing that agricultural production has stagnated in recent years. By contrast, imports have steadily and markedly increased: from only 4,329 million CFA francs in 1958, they reached 6,600 million in 1962 (with an exceptional peak of 7,600 million in 1960, because of the Cotonou harbour public works) and 8,500 million in 1965. As has been pointed out already, the towns were expanding rapidly and the educated unemployed were acquiring expensive tastes such as wheaten bread, tinned sardines and fancy soft drinks. But, in addition, the agricultural north has experienced difficult years of drought and has also been forced to depend on imports of food, especially maize and rice. There is also an increasing demand from the growing wage-earning population for consumer goods that the simple rural communities of former days did not want: fabrics, shoes, tobacco, bicycles and transistors.

Hence an enormous deficit in the trade balance looms as a threatening cloud over Dahomean life: 3,000 million CFA francs in 1960, 5,000 million in 1963, 4,500 million in 1964 and 5,000 million in 1965. As the Minister of Finance, Bertin Borna, has said (rather understating the case), the problem of Dahomey's external debts is alarming: it incurred a total of 575 million CFA francs between 1958 and 1963; the debt rose by 360 million in 1964 and rose again by 657 million in 1965.[12] The recession in the economy has been accompanied by a slowing-down in commercial activity, particularly since the French withdrew their military bases. (Wherever French military bases were maintained in Africa after independence, their final withdrawal always proved a blow to the local economy.) There are very few commercially sound industrial projects in the offing and, as a result, Dahomey has for years hovered on the brink of bankruptcy, always being rescued at the last minute by the helping hand of France. No doubt this unfortunate situation is in part a result of economic and financial factors, but it also (and perhaps principally) stems from the political situation.

When, in Abidjan, Houphouet-Boigny decided on a stately palace, with opulent offices, huge air-conditioned reception rooms, marble steps and statues, though a luxurious residence had already been built for him in the fashionable district of Abidjan, many in Africa and in Europe derided this diminutive 'African Versailles'. But who could object? The standard of living has improved for many in the Ivory Coast and the country could afford this luxury, and more. However, when President Maga, intending to keep up with his famous—and incomparably richer—colleague, spent 1,000 million CFA francs on his own palace, it became for any observant critic of the new independent Africa the perfect symbol of African improvidence, casual unconcern for financial matters, complete lack of political responsibility, and complacent readiness to be 'kept' by the former colonial master for ever after.

The political life of Dahomey is greatly complicated by its elongated geographical shape, and a policy of constant compromise with the innumerable ethnic and social groups was the only way in which any leader of Dahomey might hope to remain in power. Hubert Maga, President at the time of independence, came from Parakou, and his party, the Rassemblement Démocratique Dahoméen (RDD), founded in 1957 as a result of a sequence of political mergers and integrations, represented the entire northern area. In the more densely populated south-west, political life centred on the Union Démocratique Dahoméenne (UDD), a local section of the RDA, headed by Justin Ahomadegbé. Its head-quarters were in Abomey, formerly a royal seat but now only a village. A third party, Sourou Apithy's Parti Républicain du Dahomey (PRD), represented the south-east and the town of Porto Novo.

Furtive disputes and struggles could well have gone on for a long time, for none of the three parties had an influence spreading over all the country. At the April 1959 elections Apithy's PRD won 37 seats, Maga's RDD 22, and Ahomadegbé's UDD 11. However, many of the results were challenged. New elections were held, with Maga and Ahomadegbé temporarily joining forces against the winner; the new results were: PRD 28, RDD 22 and UDD 20. Houphouet-Boigny, in the role of the African sage adjudicating between the contenders, encouraged Apithy to give way and to let his rival Maga lead the government. However, the opposition groups were aggrieved and resentful, and did their utmost to stir up their followers and the two trade unions (the 'believers' and the pro-Guinean). Apithy never forgave Ahomadegbé for having taken sides against him. Ahomadegbé at that time was adopting a more forward-looking Socialist policy than the government, and found an eager response among the unemployed urban intellectuals. As a counter-move, President Maga formed a new alliance with Apithy, and together they founded the Parti Dahoméen de l'Unité (PDU) that won 468,000 votes at the 1960 elections as compared with 213,000 for Ahomadegbé's UDD. To add insult to injury the UDD was dissolved by a presidential decree in April 1961 and Ahomadegbé's arrest was ordered in the following May, under the time-honoured pretext of a plot against the government. (He was released in November 1962.) This arrest did nothing to solve the problem of the three-cornered political struggle, with each of the three antagonists resorting to any means to get the better of his rivals. The temporary alliance between Maga and Apithy proved to be no peaceful marriage. Apithy, who had become Vice-President of the Republic, would give vent to his ill-temper in bombastic declarations to the press, especially in February and March 1962: 'I am the leader, mark you, of a radical wing in Dahomey.' Though he still privately regarded France as a privileged ally, he would declare in public that non-alignment was his principle, that he would seek new associations with the Eastern bloc and would send goodwill missions to the USSR, Czechoslovakia and Poland. Maga felt obliged to respond to this left-wing challenge and to prove himself yet more radical than his fiery Vice-President. He announced that the main target for his four-year plan was land reform, but in fact he had no truly progressive policy: collectively

owned land was still to remain the property of the village communities and would not be transferred to state ownership. The
believers' trade union, the Confédération Générale des
Travailleurs Croyants (CGTC), was banned: an application of the
official state doctrine of anti-clerical Socialism. In Dahomey, as
elsewhere in Africa, there was a great temptation at a certain stage
of political evolution to adopt a one-party system. On August 29,
1963, Apithy appeared to give his agreement to a merger between
his and Maga's parties, for the first and only congress of the new
Parti Dahoméen de l'Unité, but he refused to let his presidential partner become the predominant party leader and rule the
new party. Theirs was contractual association, he said.

Meanwhile, the financial and economic situation was deteriorating and social unrest was growing in the towns. There was even,
after a severe drought, a peasant uprising in Nikki, a village to the
north-east of Parakou, and its MP was wounded. But the trade
unions were to become the more aggressive group, though they
had little public support since only 3 per cent of the adult population were wage-earners. However, trade unions have always played
a big role in Dahomean politics, for they belonged to the elite,
concentrated as they were in urban and suburban districts. They
became involved in the struggles between the UDD, PDU and RDD,
particularly when, after the creation of the UGTAN in 1957, the
CGTC–Dahomey joined the new federation of the Union Nationale
des Syndicats des Travailleurs du Dahomey (UNSTD). This
federation supported Ahomadegbé's UDD and consequently formed
part of the opposition to Maga and also to Apithy, who was not
particularly sensitive to trade union problems and activities. In
October 1960 UNSTD called a general strike which was broken by
the troops and armed police. Both UNSTD and Ahomadegbé's UDD
were dissolved. A new trade union, the Union Générale des
Travailleurs Dahoméens, was established under PDU's firm
control. However, affiliates of UNSTD started holding secret meetings and even the tame government-sponsored union became
concerned at the rising cost of living and reduced salaries. Consequently, there was a conjunction of labour forces belonging to both

tendencies. Strikes broke out in October 1963, with trade unionists and students frantically marching and shrieking in many of the towns.

Following what was by this time almost a standard pattern in Africa, the army felt the time had come to curb the excess of popular feeling. On October 27, 1963, Colonel Soglo, the head of the Dahomean army, took things into his own hands and ordered the arrest of all the members of the government, including Maga and Apithy, and also Ahomadegbé. But Soglo's power was not entirely unchallenged. The trade unions were holding the towns, and they compelled him to accept the creation of a revolutionary committee. On October 28, Soglo suspended the constitution and dissolved the National Assembly; on October 29, he constituted a new government in which the three leading politicians— Maga, Apithy and Ahomadegbé—shared among them the different ministerial portfolios. At this stage complete chaos reigned. No one knew why such a coalition should be established. Was it the result of an obscure and dishonest political game? Was it due to the ambiguity of Soglo's actions? The coalition was short-lived and did nothing to curb the prevailing resentment against President Maga. The intellectuals of the towns denounced his luxurious way of living, his lavish spending of public money, the appointment of his unknown supporters to ministerial posts, the growing external debt totalling 20,000 million CFA francs, the complete disregard of social questions and of the fundamental problems of the country. No one would tolerate Maga in power much longer, even under military supervision—his arch-rival Ahomadegbé least of all. Two months later, in December, Maga was compelled to resign and was put under house arrest, under the now standard pretext of a plot to assassinate Colonel Soglo.

It proved clear that the Dahomean army leader did not lust for power. Once more the army had intervened with a show of power, to initiate the new change, only to withdraw on January 5, 1964, in favour of a new civilian government of a presidential type—not unlike Maga's, though more democratically inclined. The trade unions played a part in the transitional stage, participating in the constitutional conference side by side with the army officers. It seemed that the trade unions chose Ahomadegbé as leader, though the concept of personal power did not appeal to them. He became both head of the government and Vice-President, with Apithy as President of the Republic. A new constitution was adopted. Stimulated by Ahomadegbé, a new national party was founded: the Parti Démocratique Dahoméen (PDD).

This second attempt at presidential government proved as unworkable as the first, and unrest continued. The two leaders, having ousted the third competitor, now found themselves face to face and frequently clashed. Apithy wanted his country to extend its relationship with the Eastern bloc and to recognise Communist China; Ahomadegbé, on the other hand, leaned towards the Conseil de l'Entente and Houphouet-Boigny.[13] Ahomadegbé made some attempt to overcome the fearsome financial situation, to cut down expenses and to stop the recession. All civil servants' salaries were reduced by 20 per cent, but this measure proved highly unpopular and the trade unions embarked once again on their round of strikes and street demonstrations. Who was going to maintain order in this bizarre two-headed government? According to the new constitution, the Vice-President, the head of the government, was responsible for public order and security, whereas only the President could take special measures in an emergency. The party, under Ahomadegbé's grip, had passed a vote of censure on the President of the Republic and expelled him. No rapport was possible between the two partners in power. One of them had to go, and neither had the slightest wish to do so.

Once again, the army had to act as referee to stop a fight. In November 1965, for the second time, the army dissolved the government and compelled both Apithy and Ahomadegbé to resign. Once more it refused to meddle with political affairs and tried to find a suitable politician to leave in charge. This time they chose Tahiron Congacon, the former President of the National Assembly. Once again the urban intellectuals dissented; they shouted their disapproval in unruly street demonstrations. What could the man in charge do, restricted as he was and rendered powerless by local intrigues? For the third time in Dahomey's short history the army stepped in. This time Colonel (now General) Soglo thought it his duty to stay, 'considering the endless strife between those responsible for the political life of the country'. On December 23, 1965, he formed a government composed only of soldiers and technicians. (A few months later, in Paris, journalists were called to witness a touching scene: Maga, Apithy and Ahomadegbé meeting for a solemn reconciliation, with smiles and hearty hand-shakes, now that the worries of governing Dahomey had been left behind!)

The most recent economic information is still depressing and seems to show that there is as yet little change in Dahomey, even though political rivalry has come to an end and the army maintains discipline. Why should Dahomey be still a 'doomed' country as most of its intellectuals consider it to be? There is considerable scope for agricultural development in the different climatic belts stretching between the coast and the northern border. Agriculture could be, and could remain, the corner-stone of a policy of intensive development. First, at the village level, intelligently organised small-scale efforts could improve the food crops and make the country virtually self-sufficient. At a second stage—and this target appears as top priority in the 1966–70 four-year development plan—cash crops could be encouraged: first palm-oil, then groundnuts and cotton. The development plan's main target is a 12 per cent increase in the output of food over the four years contemplated, with the result that the import bill for food should be lower and less of a burden to the country.

To sum up, there are certain prerequisites for the future of Dahomey. Firstly, the budgetary deficit must be cut by reducing administrative expenditure. Secondly, the trade deficit must be reduced by increasing agricultural exports and, particularly, by restricting imports of food. But to implement this will be a burdensome task, as the deficit has increased over recent years. The most important requirement, however, is to re-establish and maintain a more stable political climate (see chapter 11, pp. 365-71).

TOGO

The two dominant factors in any consideration of Togo are its geographical peculiarities and its political status in the days before independence. It is a long narrow corridor squeezed in between Ghana and Dahomey, 375 miles in length, at its widest 90 miles across, but with a coastline of only 35 miles. Though small (21,000 square miles) it has no one climate, but rather seems to be a complete cross-section of every possible climatic and economic condition to be found in West Africa from the Gulf of Guinea to the savannah belt. In the centre, a series of plateaux, the highest of them reaching to almost 4,000 feet, divides the country approximately into two, the North and the South, each with its own ethnic groups: the Ewe and Paragourma in the South; the Kabre, Adele and Akpossa in the North.

The population of Togo is 1·7 million, producing the very high density by West African standards of over 80 inhabitants per square mile. In the South, Togo is even more over-populated than Southern Dahomey, especially in the towns and villages, chiefly because of traditional migration from North to South. The people of Togo also migrate to Ghana: an average of 100,000 per year between 1956 and 1963. Unemployment is rife: in December 1961, 170,000 were unemployed in rural areas and 300,000 in urban areas.

The fact that Togo, like Cameroun, was a German colony before the First World War, and that it was a neighbour of the former Gold Coast, made the political situation of Togo difficult and complex, especially since—by a resolution of the League of Nations and an agreement between France and the United Kingdom—the former German Togo was divided into two mandates. The larger area was put under French mandate; the rest, the most westerly part of the country bordering the Gold Coast, was made the responsibility of the United Kingdom. This division of Togo into two parts split the most important, turbulent and industrious ethnic group of Togo, the Ewe, and even before the Second World War it led to contention and strain between the French and British administrations. As a result, after the Second World War, the United Kingdom supported the nationalists of the Gold Coast in their desire to annex Eastern Togo, mainly the Ewe areas. The French, of course, objected strongly to any merger of their part of Togo with the Gold Coast.[14] The question of Togo's relationship with the Gold Coast was one of the major topics of discussion of the United Nations Trusteeship Council when in 1945 Togo and Cameroun came under the United Nations, with France and the United Kingdom remaining the administrating powers. The Togo problem was on the agenda of the UN General Assembly and the Trusteeship Council for many years, with the delegations hearing representations from both Togos, and debating on them. Finally, in 1956, a referendum reaffirmed the rights of the French-speaking Togolese in their part of Togo and ratified the absorption of the British part of Togo into the Gold Coast. The status quo thus remained unaltered. The Ewe stayed separated from each other, living in two different countries.

France proved quite a liberal trustee in its administration of the 1946 constitution which associated France with Togo, but took no notice of those Togo politicians who wanted to reunite the two Togos and to end the trusteeship arrangements. During the final years of the trusteeship, from 1950 to 1958, France resisted any attempt at a premature termination of its administration. The movement which favoured a reunification was supported at that time by the Comité de l'Unité Togolaise (CUT) of Sylvanus Olympio. In 1941, France had approved the creation of the Comité as a discussion group. It was not until 1946 that it emerged as a political party. Olympio was an Ewe, and his newly-formed party had been associated with the All-Ewe Conference set up in the Gold Coast by Daniel Chapman with the intention of reunifying the two separated parts of Togo. Within the CUT, a radical wing, the Mouvement de la Jeunesse Togolaise (Juvento), led by Arani Santos and Abalo Firmin, demonstrated actively for reunification. France was at the time lending discreet support to a more conservative party, the Parti Togolais du Progrés (PTP), which had won the majority of seats at the Assembly from 1952 to 1958. Its leader, Nicolas Grunitzky, was Premier. It was supported largely by the conservatives of the North, whereas the CUT, the opposition, was more dependent on the South and the Ewe.

These various strains and stresses played an important part in the unique, and rather erratic, political evolution of Togo. At first, it was dominated by Olympio; then came an interregnum during which power was in the hands of the army; this was followed by a second stage, with Grunitzky's regime supported by the army; finally the army, disillusioned in its protégé, took over control of the country.

Under constant pressure from the United Nations, France took the opportunity afforded by the 1956 Loi Cadre to grant self-government to Togo. A Togolese republic, associated with the French republic, was established. It seemed that CUT, the dynamic opposition party, had finally achieved what it had long been pressing France for, and it easily won the April 1958 elections, with 33 seats out of 43. Sylvanus Olympio took over from Grunitzky as leader of the country. In many ways he was a good choice. He was an experienced politician, having been President of the Territorial Assembly from 1946 to 1952; he had had a Franco-English education, a sound business training and experience inside the Unilever Company (manager in Lomé) and close contacts with Gold Coast leaders. The new government was constituted on May 6, 1958, with two simple political principles: independence, and then co-operation with France. Togo became 'de jure' self-governing on January 1, 1959, as a result of the new French constitution. France officially notified the United Nations that it was ready to terminate the trusteeship in 1960. The Trusteeship Council approved the French proposal on July 14, 1959, and decided that Togo would become independent on April 27, 1960.

At first all went well for Sylvanus Olympio. A bilateral agreement was signed with France in June 1960; Togo was to remain within the franc currency area, and France would help Togo build up its armed forces. The CUT won every seat at the next elections in April 1961 and the opposition no longer had any means by which it could make its views known. Olympio was elected President of the Republic with an overwhelming majority. Then, two years later, on January 13, 1963, Olympio was murdered. The army had meant to seize power in a midnight coup and an NCO had shot him 'by mistake', according to the official version, as he was escaping into the United States embassy. Public opinion, both in Africa (particularly in Guinea) and in the whole world, was outraged. But inside Togo there was no mass reaction to this absurd murder, either on behalf of the late President—hardly anyone mourned him—or against his murderers. There was only embarrassment on the part of the elite of Lomé at such an unexpected outburst of violence.

What had been Olympio's real influence on the country? He was a relatively old man to lead a young country; he lived a quiet unassuming life, diffident and reluctant to pass judgements on his fellow African heads of state, being unwilling, it seemed, to appear as an elderly schoolmaster. To his credit, he favoured and implemented a very austere policy. He refused to have many embassies and representatives throughout the world, to travel on state visits, to attend any of the great inter-African conferences—in part because, basically, he was following a policy of isolation. He strongly favoured drastic restriction of expenditure and in the year of his death the national budget was almost balanced. Thanks to the 'open door' policy practised by Togo, trade developed rapidly: Togo was the only French-speaking country with the privilege of free trade with any country outside the franc area. Exports had increased by 35 per cent in volume over five years. Economic development was slow but promising. It relied mainly on the phosphates recently discovered and exploited; as they were situated on the coast, they were easily and cheaply transported abroad. By 1962, 185,000 tons were being exported and the estimate for 1963 was half a million tons. Germany had shortly before this agreed to build a modern harbour in Lomé— only 45 miles from Cotonou in Dahomey, where a harbour was being built by France.

However, in spite of these achievements, most people stood in awe of the stern, reticent, elderly politician. President Olympio gave the impression of being without human feeling and his obstinate realism was considered inappropriate and met with little general approval. Other countries could not understand his utter lack of interest in inter-African affairs, in spite of the fact that Togo was confronted with severe domestic difficulties that might have been solved by a more co-operative attitude towards its neighbours.

As soon as Togo became independent, Ghana seemed to forget the good relations it had entertained with Sylvanus Olympio, and the bonds between the CUT and the All-Ewe Conference. When Togo 'expressed the wish' to receive back the slice of the original Togo which now formed part of Ghana, Nkrumah replied by declaring that he would seize part of Western Togo. There were several skirmishes on the frontier between 1960 and 1963. According to Lomé, Ghana took repressive measures against the Ewe from the annexed part of Togo, and, in 1960–61, over 6,000 refugees flocked into Togo. In spite of the friendly intervention of President Maga of Dahomey, it was never possible to bring together Olympio and Nkrumah. In 1962 Ghana was openly giving shelter to elements of the Togolese opposition, who could mount raids into their former country from secret bases.

At home Olympio was losing popularity. He refused to appease the North by appointing Northern ministers to his cabinet. A new opposition party, the Union Démocratique des Populations Togolaises (UDPT), began to grow up. It had been created in October 1959 after a merger of Grunitzky's PTP and the Union des Chefs et des Populations du Nord. Grunitzky had gone to live in Dahomey, apparently indifferent to what was going on in Togo. However, in May 1961, the UDPT leader, Antoine Meatchi—a protégé of Nkrumah—was arrested for conspiring against the safety of the state. The radical wing of Olympio's own CUT, the Juvento movement, broke away in July 1959, soon after independence; it disagreed with the President's foreign policy, maintaining that Togo had an international role to play and that a federation of Ghana and Togo might solve many problems. In 1961 Juvento allied itself with the young UDPT to form the Mouvement Nationalist

Togolais. Since the new opposition was becoming increasingly active, Olympio brought it to a halt. A 'plot' was exposed in December 1961, and Juvento was dissolved in January 1962. Olympio's harsh treatment of his former followers no doubt added to the popular resentment. Santos, the leader of Juvento and a minister of Olympio's government between 1958 and 1960, was arrested, imprisoned in a cell and regularly beaten.

Olympio's achievements on the domestic front were being severely criticised, as were his economic policies which bore down heavily on everyday life. But, try as he might, Olympio could never turn Togo into a rich country. Its poor soil produced hardly enough food to meet local consumption. As throughout Africa, agricultural development had occurred against the background of mere subsistence. A few plantations of coffee and cocoa provided some return to the economy, and the exploitation of phosphates had, fortunately, proved a successful venture, but nevertheless the trade deficit was fairly high: 2,900 million CFA francs in 1960, 1,900 million in 1961, and 2,500 million in 1962. The reasons for such poor performances were the same as in every other small poor African country with an unbalanced economy: the fluctuations of commodity prices, particularly the downward trends of coffee and cocoa; the need to import foodstuffs; the eagerness to obtain the amenities of modern life, which increased the demand for consumer goods such as cotton fabrics and beverages. It must be said, however, that a large part of the trade deficit was due to the importation of equipment required to exploit the phosphate deposits.

Olympio could well have stayed in power had it not been for the collaboration of two small groups of dissatisfied Togolese: the still dynamic Juvento opposition, and a few soldiers, former NCOs in the French army, who had travelled and thought a little and were becoming ashamed of the small part played by their country on the international stage, of its isolation and poverty, and were furious that Olympio had refused to join the Union Africaine et Malgache. The two central figures, Sergeant Etienne Eyadema and 'Adjudant-Chef' E. Bodjollé, were completely unknown and not ambitious, merely angry and humiliated. They were utterly dissatisfied at Olympio's unwillingness (for budgetary reasons) to build up a large army. They intended to do no more than depose Olympio and act as caretakers until a satisfactory successor could be found. A minor incident roused many of their friends against the President. They felt that they would be supported, not only by all present and past Togolese soldiers of the French army* and by a few active Juvento members, but also by all the Northerners, and particularly by the Northern chiefs, all of whom had been deprived of power. Olympio, a Southerner himself, had appointed mostly Southern ministers and encouraged economic development in the South alone.

The revolutionary committee established in January 1963 never looked for new men as possible successors. They timidly turned again to the best-known former politicians—Grunitzky, the one-time Premier, in exile in Dahomey, and Meatchi, in exile in Ghana—and for three years supported a new governmental team which certainly did little better than Olympio. The French government seemed satisfied, and asked for no more. For three years Grunitzky vacillated and compromised over the successive economic and political difficulties as they cropped up.

Ghana had first to be placated: the earlier inter-Ewe relationships across the border, which had been forbidden for several years, were resumed. One result of this was an improvement in Togo's trade: cheaper imports were made available from Ghana, and profit was also derived from the transport of goods across Togo. However, the idea of a reunification of Togo and Ghana, which at one time had been nurtured by Juvento, was left in abeyance as being rather too daring. Since Olympio's death, Nkrumah seemed to have given up gloating over Togo. On January 20, 1963, Ghana recognised the Grunitzky government, and six months later, on July 15, the new President of Togo paid

* Three days before the coup, Olympio had again warned that the country could not afford to take all former soldiers of the French army into the new Togo army. Seven hundred of them would not be retained; they would have to live on their small French 'pension'.

a state visit to Ghana. On the other hand, all was not peaceful between the two neighbours from 1963 to Nkrumah's fall in 1966. There were ups and downs in Ghanaian-Togolese relations: frontier skirmishes and then attempts at a reconciliation. The frontier was repeatedly opened and closed according to the whim of the Ghanaians.

Under Olympio, Togo had ostentatiously ignored all inter-African relationships and turned down all invitations to attend inter-African conferences. The new regime, by contrast, tried to end this policy of isolation. Togo joined the so-called Brazzaville group (UAM). More and more Togolese observers attended sessions of the Conseil de l'Entente, though they remained reluctant to commit their country any further. Grunitzky, who had blamed his predecessor for this isolation, would have joined readily, but some members of his government remained suspicious of this and all international groupings.

On the other hand the economic situation improved scarcely at all. The value of exports rose for two years, from 4,500 million CFA francs in 1963 to 7,400 million in 1964, because of the appearance on the world market of Togolese phosphates: 440,000 tons in 1963 and 801,000 tons in 1964. Coffee exports rose slightly in volume but, as world prices slumped, receipts from this crop fell in 1963. Togolese exports were left dependent predominantly on phosphates; cocoa and coffee became of only secondary importance, because of the fluctuations in the world markets. If the value of Togolese phosphates slumped, economic collapse would follow immediately, for, while exports remained roughly at the same level, imports rose in frightening proportions. The demand for supplementary foodstuffs, capital goods, and light luxury goods such as soft drinks, wine and spirits, and tobacco increased alarmingly, from 7,200 million CFA francs in 1963 to 11,100 million in 1965. As a result, in 1965 there was a deficit in the trade balance of 4,400 million. The government certainly tackled the situation with great vigour. It cut down on unnecessary imports, and stepped up the export of phosphates even further so that they came to represent 40 per cent of the total value of Togolese exports. The deficit was reduced to 2,800 million in 1966 and to 3,200 million in 1967.

The Olympio regime had grown unpopular for having in a few instances exerted a brutal show of authority and for having ignored all the conventional external procedures of democracy. Grunitzky was careful to do the opposite. Harsh police action was forbidden, political parties were allowed freedom of expression, and the new President proceeded to set up a national government, generously inviting members of Olympio's former party (the CUT, hastily renamed the Parti de l'Unité Togolaise) to join. Northerners were no longer the poor relations and, when Grunitzky went the rounds of Northern villages, he was welcomed and cheered. Even the Ewe chieftains in the South were reconciled to Grunitzky's political line.

However, the Grunitzky golden age was not destined to last long. At first he was protected and cherished by the French administration, which had found that Olympio, a true nationalist, was not easy to manipulate, but political dissension soon re-emerged. Several of Olympio's supporters, notably his former minister Theodore Mally and the lawyer Noe Kutuklui, had refused to change their allegiance and to accept ministerial portfolios. The murdered Olympio was regaining some of the popularity he had lost in life. Whispered criticism was again to be heard in the Lomé cafés, and Ghana, so close at hand, provided once again a convenient hiding place for conspirators. The Juvento intellectuals, who had played so large a part in Olympio's fall, found the new government's policy somewhat too conservative for their taste and became resentful, but they carried little political weight. Discontent arose in the trade unions, for the standard of living in Togo had not greatly improved since independence. In 1964 the army took alarm and forbade the May Day parade as a dangerously Marxist movement, though the tame Union des Travailleurs Togolais, the principal trade union, was an active supporter of the government. Unrest continued, however; there were too many unemployed in the towns and too much unease among the peasants.

Finally a new crisis broke out on December 20 and 21, 1966.

The army once more intervened and dictated orders to the government. The army that was supposed to shield Grunitzky, as its own chosen candidate, had not had a very clear position in recent years. 'Adjudant-Chef' Bodjollé (promoted to Commander after the coup) had been dismissed in 1965 as Chief of Staff. Former Sergeant Eyadema (now Lieutenant-Colonel) remained in sole charge; consequently, he was the strong man of the country. The conspiracy, engineered by the young dynamic lawyer Kutuklui, tried at first to confuse public opinion by spreading, on the Togolese radio, the false rumour that the army was turning against the government. Thousands of rowdy demonstrators surrounded Grunitzky's house, shrieking for his resignation. At that time, however, it had not been the army's intention to intervene. On the first day of the rising, Lieutenant-Colonel Eyadema protested that the army would support only the government. But Nicolas Grunitzky was frightened; he dissolved the government and shared all the ministerial portfolios with his colleague Meatchi, the Vice-President of the Republic.[15] Such an arrangement could be no more than makeshift. On January 13, 1967, Eyadema stepped in, pushed Grunitzky aside and took over control himself.

Grunitzky had tried his best to govern the country with the help of the growing power of the army, and his policy had been merely to avoid Olympio's mistakes. Olympio's followers were furious after the failure of their coup. They claimed that Olympio's murderers should be put on trial, and by now the masses were growing nostalgic for their 'good old President'. Finally Grunitzky, who came to be accused of neglecting the North (and most soldiers were poor Northerners), made one final blunder when he recommended that the army budget should be cut down as a national economy. The army is the only power left in Togo. Lieutenant-Colonel Eyadema has enough allies, both among the army and among his Northern countrymen, to support him—at any rate for the time being—in whatever he chooses to do. In fact, some of those who were formerly loyal followers of Olympio have agreed to accept portfolios in Eyadema's cabinet.

5. Guinea

For saying 'No' to General de Gaulle at the 1958 referendum, Guinea was immediately severed from France and from the rest of French-speaking Africa. This dramatic first gesture of Guinea's modern political history at once became symbolic. Guinea stood for the principle of uncompromising, unrestrained independence and had only contempt for economic compromise. Sékou Touré, the handsome, daring, passionate, enthusiastic, straightforward leader of Guinea, known long before independence as a great coiner of fiery slogans, was looked upon as a harbinger of the free Africa in the making, a defender of the colonially oppressed, a pillar of anti-colonial strength, and a great African hero. The Guinean venture was seen as a challenge to the rest of Africa and to the Third World: a country starting without help, beginning everything from scratch, gathering together all the national effort within one strong nation-wide party that would reach out to and rouse everyone, even in the remotest bush village. Guinea was dizzy with wild hope. Many Africans outside Guinea watched enviously, almost shamefacedly, and economists, whether African or non-African, followed events with sympathy. The Guineans were tough—Guinea might make it. The country possessed a much stronger base than most of its neighbours from which to launch so dauntless a course.

Around President Touré there was an integrated team, intelligent and selfless; responsible party members were few but earnest and hard-working. In the towns, in the bush, people were busy organising party cells, passing on slogans. Youth brigades built bridges, village women brought their crops, everyone toiled, with or without recompense, for the country's sake. As early as 1956, before independence, Sékou Touré, then a young trade-union leader and party dialectician, had argued that human investment, so easy to come by in Africa, could replace or at least supplement the financial investments from overseas. An underdeveloped country could 'take off', even if the population had to work with their bare hands, provided that no energy was wasted in futile disputes and everyone was ready to co-operate and to toil hard. Fortunately, Guinea could count on a population of over 3 million inhabitants that was youthful (40 per cent under fifteen years of age) and strong, specially the Fulani of Fouta-Djallon and the Soussou of Lower Guinea. So what did it matter if the French

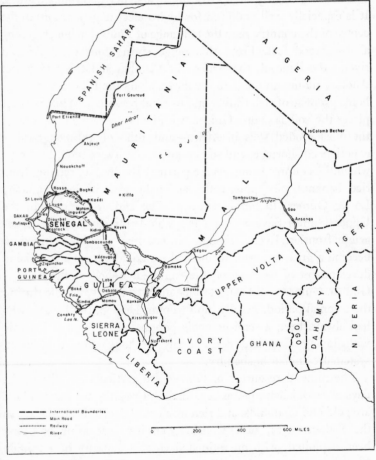

4. Senegal River Basin

administrators and technicians had walked out, leaving Guineans to their own devices? The task was gigantic. Everything had to be devised afresh: a new administration, new laws, a new diplomacy, a new army. Nothing frightened the Guineans. They recognised that they lacked the experience, and that mistakes were unavoidable; but they were tough, they would manage.

Guinea, luckily, was not poor. Its economic potentialities were reasonably good, for it has a varied soil, vegetation and climate. The country is fairly large, covering an area of 95,000 square miles. It is especially well endowed for hydro-electric generation: in the centre of the country rises the tall range of Fouta-Djallon, reaching almost 5,000 feet. From this range spring four great African rivers: the Senegal, the Niger, the Gambia and the Konkoure. Another mountain range to the north, along the Liberian frontier, holds promise of rich timber and mineral resources. While in most places the soil is poor—Guinea, with its heavy rainfall, has one of the most eroded soils in Africa—and although the country has experienced shortage, and sometimes a scarcity, of food, the crops which the country produces are particularly diverse, ranging from rice, bananas, pineapple, coffee and palm-trees in damp, marshy Lower Guinea, to fonio (cereal), millet and groundnuts in the Upper Guinea Savannah, on the table-lands close to the Senegalese frontier. Even although Guinea may not be destined to become a great exporter of food, there could yet be a surprising development of fisheries on the continental shelf of the Gulf of Guinea. Guinea could export much more timber than it did during the colonial period. Finally, up in Fouta-Djallon, the Fulani, who had always been a semi-nomadic population, tended their cattle with loving care and could easily be taught more efficient, systematic animal husbandry.

The mineral resources of Guinea are particularly rich; in the days of colonialism, it was regarded as a wealthy territory. There are gold and diamonds, and rich iron ore and bauxite deposits. In the Kaloum area, near Conakry, an iron ore mine has long been exploited, with an estimated current capacity of 1 million tons a year, and a potential output of 3 million tons a year. A second as yet unexploited deposit has been discovered in Mount Nimba, the same ore field as has been developed in Liberia. One of the richest bauxite deposits in the world is to be found on the tiny island of Loos, opposite Conakry, on a hill which is easily worked. Other rich bauxite deposits are to be found at the Fria mines in the western part of Guinea, and in the reserves of Boké. Thus Guinea possesses the two necessary ingredients—bauxite and water (for hydro-electric power generation)—for a very important aluminium industry.

Guinea started immediately on the road to economic independence of the colonial power. Successive economic difficulties arose and were dealt with in an ad hoc manner, and Guinea often found itself with its back to the wall. However, the most startling developments and the most severe struggle for Sékou Touré were in the arena of domestic politics. The three aspects of Guinea's evolution—economic, international relations and internal opposition—must now be discussed and their mutual influence on each other demonstrated.

Economic Decolonisation

In the economic field, Guinea had to reorganise in haste. The French, offended by Guinea's rejection of de Gaulle's proposals, withdrew rapidly, and their sudden departure shattered all the institutions of the country. In one sense, France's sudden departure made things easier for Guinea, for if the colonial power had pulled out gradually and diplomatically, it might have been harder to shake off all the legacies of colonialism. Starting with a blank sheet, Guinea could begin everything afresh on new Socialist lines. The broad programme was outlined by the political leaders, and then elaborated by a team of Guinean and foreign economists, under the guidance of the French economist, Charles Bettelheim. As a beginning, a three-year plan was launched (1960-63).

As Guinea had broken its ties with its customers of colonial days, new buyers and new outlets had to be found very quickly, as well as new sources of the imported foodstuffs, materials and manufactured goods Guinea needed. This extremely delicate task was entrusted in January 1959 to a newly created department, the Comptoir Guinéen du Commerce Extérieur. Later, in April 1960, a second department, the Comptoir Guinéen du Commerce Intérieur, was established to control commerce at home. The creation of two such bodies was intended, on the one hand, to provide a bulwark against domination by foreign commercial interests—particularly in the marketing of crops for export—and, on the other, to eradicate the chaos of local trading conditions and eliminate the petty middlemen who took their cut to the detriment of the producers. This action was exactly analogous to the government's struggle against the pointless power of the traditional chieftains. It was all a manifestation of the policy of the revolution: one party, undivided power, one leader.

As a next stage, the government took the necessary measure of by-passing and making powerless the foreign trading interests, before evicting them from the country, as it was able to do now that their protectors had withdrawn. Furthermore, state control of trade made it easier to negotiate with the Socialist countries of the Eastern bloc, the only trading partners Guinea had been able to find in these difficult days.

There was of course a great temptation for offended national pride to sever Guinea's financial connections with the country which had so humiliated it and to withdraw with inconvenient alacrity from the franc area. Economists could also argue that no stringent economic measures could be enforced without a national currency that would frustrate attempts at currency smuggling and fraud. However, a small group within the government team diffidently pointed out, in January 1959, that it might be advisable to define the new currency in relation to the franc and that it might even prove less costly to remain within a strong currency area. These objections were taken seriously: France and Guinea held discreet discussions in January 1959, but it proved impossible to re-establish any formal relation. Both countries were angry. Guinea blamed France for disrupting all its trade: the French banks had temporarily suspended their short-term loans and the effect of this was aggravated when the first crops after independence proved to be very poor indeed. The peasants and the leaders were equally resentful. General de Gaulle, who had assumed personal responsibility for all decisions concerning Guinea ('that Communist country'), refused to withdraw from his position. Matters were exacerbated when Guinea violated the French exchange regulations by obtaining from Ghana an urgently-needed loan of 10 million pounds. Then France devalued its currency and created the new franc, without giving any warning to Conakry—another blow to the economy of Guinea.

As a consequence, on March 1, 1960, Guinea haughtily withdrew from the French franc area, and decided to establish a State Bank and create its own Guinean franc, the equivalent of one CFA franc. The new currency was to be the corner-stone of the new Socialist economy and a status symbol that would put to shame all Guinea's pusillanimous neo-colonialist African neighbours. It was the fine gesture, no doubt, of a man whose pride had been scorned, but it is questionable whether Sékou Touré appreciated and had considered all its day-to-day implications and consequences.

Guinean wealth depended on its mineral potential. In this Guinea was unique among African countries, in that it had first to develop industry to provide the wealth necessary for agricultural development. The mines were being exploited by three important French firms: the iron ore by the Compagnie Minière de Conakry, the bauxite deposits of Loos island by the Société des Bauxites du Midi, and the Fria bauxite by the Société FRIA. All three firms could well cease their activities if the country in which they were operating were to exclude itself from the franc area. Moreover, Sékou Touré was heavily dependent on a big dam to be built on the Konkoure river to provide the electricity necessary for the further development of the extracting industries. The dam project was a realistic concept. It had been studied before independence, and could prove highly profitable in view of its closeness to the very rich Boké bauxite deposit (estimated to contain 15,000 million tons of ore) which had been made the responsibility of the

Société des Bauxites du Midi. The Conakry government came to an agreement with the two international firms (both associated with the French Pechiney group) over the exploitation of the Guinean bauxite. FRIA would not be touched by the Guinean trade measures and would continue selling to Europe and supplying alumina to the aluminium factory of Edea in Cameroun, also a part of the Pechiney group. Once again the cloud on the horizon was the scheme's dependence on the goodwill of French capitalist firms, who might well reconsider their decision if the economic conditions in the country in which they were operating did not suit them.

The creation of an independent Guinean currency caused some concern but it seemed that, as FRIA had its headquarters outside Guinea, it would not be inconvenienced by the new Guinean exchange regulations. On the other hand, relations between the government and the Société des Bauxites du Midi underwent some strain. Guineans became suspicious of this French capitalist company which was over-riding the principles of their Socialist economic revolution. They were concerned that the development of the mine and the erection of the extraction plant might not begin in sufficient time to meet the official deadline for completion, July 1964. On November 23, 1961, the government ordered the Société des Bauxites du Midi to cease all its activities, a decision that placed all the plans for the industrialisation of Guinea in the melting pot once more.

Guinea has never been so near to total collapse as it was in 1961. It is to the credit of the country's leaders that they did not give up, that they had the courage to fight on. Economic difficulties were mounting. The agricultural output was lower than in colonial days, and remained so. The external trade system was unsatisfactory as it rigidly excluded any business with countries outside the Eastern bloc; even with them, trade agreements were usually on a basis of barter, so they did not help Guinea's foreign exchange position. Aid agreements with Eastern countries enabled Guinea to start on its industrial programme—brick and cement factories, a light hydro-electric plant, printing works—but they worked, at the beginning especially, at a low capacity. The peasants were apprehensive and refused to co-operate; though they had been severely warned against it, they preferred to sell their crops to middlemen, who sold them at black market prices or smuggled them over the frontiers in order to be paid in more desirable currencies. Consequently, there was a great scarcity of goods in the towns, where the almost empty shops sold only second-rate merchandise from Hungary or Eastern Germany. The peasants and the townsfolk were equally dissatisfied.

Food had to be imported but how was it to be paid for? Guinea had so little to sell and needed so much capital equipment for industrial development. Even though exports of iron, bauxite and alumina had shown a promising rise, they still could not overcome the heavy deficit in the trade figures.

The government fought hard in this trying year. It tried to thwart smugglers and black-marketeers by repressive measures and to increase the degree of state control. Later, in 1963, the government finally closed all the frontiers. But it was too late and these efforts were all in vain. Unrelated as it was to any firmer currency, the Guinean franc soon came to have little meaning as a medium of exchange. It lost any pretence of real parity with the CFA franc. The result was a spate of illegal transactions, with the black market rate of the Guinean franc running at between 1950 and 1200 to the dollar as compared with the official rate of 250. In an attempt to overcome its currency problems, the government decided to print new notes and compulsorily call in the old currency. The reserves from abroad of 7 billion Guinean francs lost their value overnight—another bitter blow to the economy.

This desperate situation and disillusionment with and perhaps even suspicion of his allies led Sékou Touré to seek help from new sources. He made overtures to the United States, which responded at once by shipping large quantities of rice and flour from food surplus stocks, thus saving the urban population of Guinea from starvation. In 1962 alone, American aid totalled $16 million, half of it in the form of food imports. Encouraged by its new-found friends of the Western world, the government of

Guinea thought it prudent to put its Marxist principles to one side, for the time being at least, and a new policy was devised that would encourage the investment of foreign capital in Socialist Guinea.

The quest for foreign capital at last bore fruit. On October 2, 1962, an agreement related to the Boké scheme was signed with Harvey Aluminium for the building of three factories—one for bauxite, one for alumina, one for aluminium—a harbour and a railway line. The firm was also granted exploitation rights for the bauxite deposit of Kassa on Loos island. Of course, the agreement with this company, jointly owned by American and Canadian interests, was for no more than an option. It will be a long time before all these schemes come to fruition. In 1965, Alcan Aluminium, a Canadian firm, joined Harvey Aluminium in the proposed exploitation of Guinea's bauxite. The only condition required of Guinea was that it should build at its own expense the means of transporting the bauxite over the hundred miles to the sea. These arrangements remained intact throughout the strain in relations between the United States and Guinea in 1965–66.

In late 1967–early 1968, an international consortium known as the Compagnie Bauxite de Guinée was established, in which the government will have 49 per cent of the shares and receive 65 per cent of the profits. The other shareholders are: Harvey (26·01 per cent), Alcan (8·925 per cent), Alcoa (8·925 per cent), Pechiney-Ugine (3·06 per cent), Vereinigte Aluminium Werke AG (2·55 per cent) and Montecatini Edison (1·55 per cent). The private firms are to spend between 60 and 70 million US dollars on the opening of the mine. It is expected that 5–7 million tons of bauxite will be exported per year.[1] In September 1968 the World Bank approved a loan of $64·5 million to the government to finance the foreign exchange costs of the construction of the railway, the port and the township required to develop the Boké project. The Compagnie Bauxite de Guinée, which will construct and work the mine, will invest about $100 million.

On the domestic scale, in everyday life, Guinea has done little more than survive, and then only with the help of foreign aid. It is believed that only the big aluminium developments will bring in the currency needed to develop Guinean agriculture. Meanwhile, the output of food, both for domestic consumption and for export, has shown little improvement: it has not reached even the levels at which it stood in colonial times. However, it is very difficult to know exactly how much Guinea is producing, firstly because few economic statistics are available abroad, and secondly because part of the Guinean production is smuggled over the frontier. The Economist Intelligence Unit, in its 1966 *Annual Supplement*, estimates that in 1962, the last year for which figures are available, there was an imbalance of 5,100 million Guinean francs. Consequently, even the increase in the production of alumina (484,000 tons in 1964 against 400,000 in 1960) and of iron ore (701,000 tons in 1964 against 342,000 in 1959) has been insufficient to achieve a favourable trade balance. Even when these new economic projects are realised, however, the weak, unsupported, unconvertible currency of Guinea will always be a serious handicap to its development.

Political Developments and Foreign Policy

The leaders of Guinea, above all the fervent Sékou Touré, would dearly have liked to prosecute a diplomatic policy which did not tie them to any particular group and which would not be hindered by day-to-day considerations. They could not. In 1958, Guinea was compelled to seek new allies. The first African friend to appear was Kwame Nkrumah's Ghana, which expressed its sympathy with a very substantial loan at a time when the Guinean treasury was empty. Then, in 1959, Ghana suggested that revolutionary Africa should combine in a Ghana-Guinea-Mali Union; this proved a purely symbolic gesture which had no material repercussions. At an early stage Nasser also sent friendly messages to Guinea and there soon became established a group of radical countries including Ghana, Guinea, Mali, Morocco and the United Arab Republic.

France had turned its back on Guinea, and the West generally was suspicious of Sékou Touré's quasi-Marxist slogans, but the countries of the Eastern bloc and China made approaches. There were exchanges of good wishes, goodwill missions and a small trickle of Eastern technicians arrived in Guinea: engineers who would help to build small factories, and a group which was to build a stadium and a university in Conakry. Some material aid came from the Eastern bloc—food and manufactured goods—but many things, especially the trucks, were of a very poor quality. The Russians sent such huge quantities of capital goods—tractors and lorries—that the Guineans did not know what to do with them. For a time, Conakry harbour was packed tight with rusting spare parts from Russia. The Russian specialists who came did not appear to relish their appointment to Guinea: the language barrier proved a severe problem and they hated the climate.

As early as 1959 Guinea made it clear that it did not want to become rigidly associated with the East to the exclusion of the West, but, with the aid from Russia in the early years of revolution, it was in fact deeply committed to the Soviet bloc. Guinea's political evolution soon reached a second stage in which it tried to shake off any permanent commitments: indeed, in December 1961, because of a misunderstanding, the Russian ambassador, Daniel Solod, was expelled from Conakry. As has been noted already, the extreme economic difficulties of 1961 compelled Guinea to approach the USA. This was during the Kennedy era and Guinea felt innately en rapport with the young President who had indicted colonialism with such vigour; moreover, the American ambassador in Conakry at that time was William Attwood, an energetic liberal. American aid was sent almost immediately, most of it in the form of food, which was particularly welcome. We have already seen how Guinea's friendship with the United States induced Guinea to modify its investment policies and how American and Canadian capital was greatly interested in the abundant reserves of bauxite in Guinea. This friendship has had its ups and downs, but, in spite of temporary strains, it has endured over the years. Although Guinea may not relish the fact, the United States has provided almost as much support to Guinea

—Socialist though it may be—in its early years of independence as France has provided. The void left by the French on their departure has been filled by American capital.

During this second stage of its political evolution, Guinea abandoned its hostility towards France. For one thing, fighting had ceased in Algeria, providing the opportunity for polite messages of congratulation to General de Gaulle. Sékou Touré's lieutenant, Diallo Safoulaye, was sent to Paris to settle disputed claims between France and Guinea, in discussions with the French minister, L. Joxe. Two agreements were signed on May 22, 1963. The first granted what Guinea had repeatedly claimed from France—the payment of 3,000 million old francs to Guinea, as retired soldiers' pensions—and Guinea agreed to pay some of its debts to the French treasury and to expelled French firms. The second agreement dealt with technical co-operation, arranging for the training in France of some Guinean administrators and technicians, and missions of specialised experts.

In contrast to the time when it had been isolated among African countries (apart from its role in the Ghana-Guinea-Mali Union), Guinea began to play a leading part in encouraging the concept of African unity, which became an established principle of its diplomacy. Overtures were made to the Brazzaville group in the hope of merging the Brazzaville and Casablanca groups, the two major alignments among African nations. Among other things, Sékou Touré expected the dissolution of the specialised organisations created by the Brazzaville group. Later, when the Organisation of African Unity (OAU) was created, Guinea succeeded in having one of its brilliant young diplomats, Diallo Telli, adopted as secretary-general. In 1963, just before the establishment of the OAU, Guinea pronounced officially that it considered there was a contradiction in belonging to both the OAU and Brazzaville group, for the latter had been founded with the purpose of dividing up Africa.

The new conciliatory climate led to rapprochements with several African states. Guinea readily agreed to participate with Senegal in a joint committee for the development of the Senegal river. Strange as it may seem, Sékou Touré paid a state visit to Brazzaville in mid-1963, to reciprocate Youlou's visit to Conakry in October 1962. Houphouet-Boigny visited Touré in Conakry, thus putting an end to the six years' tension between Guinea and the Ivory Coast, and Houphouet-Boigny invited all the founder members of the RDA—Sékou Touré, Modibo Keita, Maurice Yameogo, Hamani Diori—for a sentimental get-together at Bouaké in the Ivory Coast in April 1964.

This idyllic period soon came to an end. After 1965, Guinea once again changed its political line and kept the friends of yesterday at a distance. Perhaps Touré had been disappointed in his attempts at friendship with the West, or perhaps he was harried by uncompromising Marxists at home who could not tolerate such indiscriminate flirtations. Aid from the United States continued, but US-Guinea relations became lukewarm, probably as a result of President Johnson's policy in Vietnam.

The French-speaking moderates in Africa had stubbornly maintained their UAM association, separate from the OAU, though Touré had made it quite plain in 1962 that he considered it an instrument of pro-French neo-colonialism. They failed to heed his warning and he reacted violently: hence his renewed attempts to gather the truly revolutionary Africans around himself; hence his frequent visits to Nasser and to Modibo Keita and his long official trip to Moscow, at the end of July 1965. The Russians proved more understanding and co-operative than ever before, for they promised to build a £70 million barrage on the Konkoure river with an electricity output estimated at 3 to 6 million KW per year (as compared with the Aswan dam's 10 million KW) and an aluminium factory with an output of 50,000 tons a year.[2] The Moscow trip was followed by a series of trips, exchanges, missions, visits to and from China and Eastern Europe.

Was it Touré's aim to maintain a delicate balance between East and West? Was it a very shrewd and realistic foreign policy? Or did he and his followers act on impulse? One cannot avoid drawing the latter conclusion from Touré's break with France and with the Ivory Coast in 1965, affected in the most undiplomatic manner possible. At the end of that year, the French diplomatic mission in Conakry was asked to leave, and the Guinean mission in Paris recalled, even though right up to that time the government of Guinea had appeared very eager to overcome any difficulties which arose between Paris and Conakry, and had shown no reluctance in accepting aid from the French Fonds d'Aide et de Coopération. The official reason was that the French had participated in a plot designed to overthrow the Guinean government. Houphouet-Boigny and other leaders of the Entente were held responsible too. Had not Houphouet-Boigny encouraged other African moderates to join OCAM, thereby once more introducing rivalry and division in Africa?

The next move was a reaction to events outside Guinea rather than on the initiative of Touré. In February 1966 Nkrumah was overthrown by a military coup and a few days afterwards sought refuge in Conakry, where he was welcomed by his old friend and offered a share in the highest offices of the Guinean state and party. Guinea was now to be a country headed by twin leaders: Sékou Touré and Nkrumah. All this was a symbol, yet another fine dramatic gesture. It sheds a new light on Touré, who remembered his debt to his sympathetic friend and showed himself a true African nationalist who respected deeply all that Nkrumah had stood for, especially his views on Pan-Africanism.

To Sékou Touré, the United States appeared over-eager to recognise the new regime in Ghana: an unforgivable sin. A new crisis broke out between Guinea and the United States, which was charged with being no more than an accomplice of the new Ghanaian government. The Guineans were infuriated when one of their missions (including Beavogui, Minister of Foreign Affairs) was arrested in Accra, and they held the United States responsible. Anti-American demonstrations were organised in Conakry, sixty-four Peace Corps volunteers were expelled, and a substantial part of the American aid was rejected, though it had amounted to $70 million over the previous four years, half of it in the form of food surpluses. It was replaced by increased aid from Eastern Europe and China. However, up to the time of writing, the aluminium

193

agreements with American capital seem to be still valid. At the beginning of 1967, the differences between the United States and Guinea were patched up, an American ambassador returned to Conakry and American aid was resumed, though on a less important scale. It amounted to $6·8 million in 1966–67 ($4·4 in actual aid and $2·4 in food surplus) as against $24·6 million in 1965–66.

At first sight Guinean foreign policy appears vacillating and inconsistent, determined by the mood of the moment. No doubt the Guinean leader is a most mercurial man, but his political policy throughout has been a difficult, ad hoc compromise between the logical course demanded by the concepts of a Socialist revolution and the need to solve the economic problems of the moment. It reflects a desire to be unfettered and free of permanent association with any particular bloc, and, at the same time, a desperate quest for active supporters who would promote the well-being of Guinea and make possible rapid industrial expansion.

Opposition

Meanwhile, with the passing of time, Guinea's leaders had to face growing difficulties at home. Virtually nothing would have been beyond them and the country could have embarked on quite novel adventures, if only the great expectations of 1958 had not turned into bitter disillusionment, if the earlier enthusiasm had not faded away. The opposition at first came from traders, tradesmen, middlemen, lorry-drivers and the like. Guinea is a country of traders: the Diallo, from time immemorial, have traded throughout Africa. Yet the very first measures taken by the government interfered with all their habits; theoretically, all private trading was to disappear within a short time. No account was taken of the astuteness of the small traders of Guinea, many of whom became smugglers and black-marketeers. Everyone concerned with trade, great or small, appreciated much more quickly than did his leaders that the introduction of a national currency was a catastrophe and that it would soon be worthless. Consequently, many traders did all they could to accumulate and hoard CFA francs and other foreign currencies—anything but the Guinean franc. Naturally, this did little to help the economy, and the inexperienced administrators and those in power wasted much time and energy in vain efforts to prevent smuggling, dishonesty and fraud, which dissipated what little credit the party enjoyed.

In 1961 new measures were taken to encourage more active participation by the private sector in the government's policies: they proved useless. Clandestine businesses were flourishing widely and all the restrictive measures had proved to be of no avail. They merely provoked widespread resentment and encouraged all the traders and primary producers, who had long since decided to turn a deaf ear to the government's efforts at reorganising the country, to embellish their cunning schemes. In November and December 1961, discontent and anger led to the first incidents in Labé, which were incorrectly described as a 'plot' by official propaganda. The army was called in to stop street demonstrations and there were three deaths and many other casualties.

Then a second form of opposition arose, much more dangerous than the first. It was a matter of much graver concern for Touré, for he was being criticised on ideological grounds: not for the party doctrine itself, which was generally approved, but because he was considered too timid in putting it into practice. He was blamed for failing to follow slavishly the pattern of the Russian or the Chinese revolutionaries.

As a consequence of all this unrest, certain social groups were denied full freedom of expression. This meant that the party had failed in one of its major aims, for the idea of its founders was that the fundamental purpose of the Parti Démocratique de Guinée (PDG) was the expression of every possible viewpoint. Something was wrong with the party. It was no longer the monument of fiery determination of 1958; instead, it was becoming the stronghold of a privileged faction. Was there not—critics would cruelly ask—a kind of selective mechanism in Guinea, as everywhere else in Africa, rejecting the 'unworthy' from the party ranks? The opposition could not help but notice that it was the party members who found their way into all the easy, relatively well-paid, administrative jobs in the vast number of state organisations, or that the perquisites that were relics of 'nationalisation'—houses, cars and furniture—invariably found their way to trusted party members.[3]

The unexpected swing to the left in 1965 may have been occasioned in part by a desperate attempt to conciliate the critics on the left, the uncompromising Marxists.[4] Had not Touré been incensed by those who accused him of betraying the revolution and, in order to deny the charge, had he not dramatically (and rather pointlessly) broken with France and the Ivory Coast? Touré thought he had reasserted himself as the enemy of moderate 'neo-colonialist' Africa and that he still appeared in the vanguard of revolution on the African continent. However, Guinea did not, and could not, renounce its important undertakings with foreign capitalists, and, however indispensable for Guinea, these prospective heavy capital investments were a contradiction of the principles of Socialism. Because Touré met each difficulty as it arose, his political policy was bound to appear hesitant and contradictory.

In fact, none of the party leadership's efforts could arrest the growing resentment. The regime was beginning to totter; the party had lost its grip on the nation and could not spur it on any longer. The country had lost its hope and its determination. The administration, and even the police themselves, were not as reliable as before. After Fodeba Keita was moved from the Ministry of Defence and Security to the Ministry of Rural Economy, as a result of a partial reshuffle of the governmental team, half the officers of the police force, who were suspected of remaining loyal to Fodeba, had to be dismissed and replaced by younger party members. Many Guineans could not tolerate Nkrumah's welcome in their country as a leader *of Guinea*. There were rumours of frantic demonstrations by women in front of the presidential palace, demanding that Nkrumah be sent away.

Whatever may have been their motives, an alarming number of Guineans have escaped abroad. Many of them belonged to the elite and had shared the wild hopes of 1959, but they had watched the deterioration of the economic, financial and political situation since that time with growing dismay. There are now about half a million Guinean expatriates, 200,000 of them in the Ivory Coast and 300,000 in Senegal and in France.[5] Recently a Front de Libération Nationale de la Guinée has been founded abroad. One of the most active members of its provisional committee is David Soumah, the well-known trade union leader, a sound and clever man.*

Some had great hopes for and expectations of Guinea when it became independent, but it might have been foolish to expect too much, considering the gigantic task which faced the country. What other former French colony could have remained on its feet if it had been obliged to start with no help whatsoever—no administration, no experience, no money, no markets—if it had had to fight against such formidable odds? It could be said that it has taken ten years for Guinea to recover from the hasty departure of the colonial power. It is easy enough to be ironic and point out that the most Socialist country in Africa, though indeed greatly helped by the East, owes its survival and its prospects of future growth to help from the United States. One must bear in mind the poor soils, the meagre agricultural prospects and the strange paradox of the fact that the economy of Guinea—in this respect unique among African countries—can thrive only if the country first develops its industrial potential.

One of the few clear facts arising from this survey of Guinea's first decade of independence is that the economic policy was singularly unsuccessful. The most tragic aspect of the failure of

* President of the Confédération des Travailleurs Croyants de l'Afrique Occidentale, secretary since 1962 of the Confédération Syndicale Africaine, Soumah lives in Senegal, though he is of Guinean origin and a blood relation of Touré. The present author, who knew him quite well, had frequent discussions with him about the Guinean regime. In those days, he was far from sharing the author's enthusiastic sympathy for the Guinean experiment. Soumah would point out—and time has proved him right—that behind the gloss of Touré's great verbal felicity and facility, behind his brilliant expatiations on Guinea's bright future, there was an alarming disregard of everyday realities.

Guinea is the contrast between, on the one hand, the courage of its leaders, the coherency of the governmental team over a long period, and the determination of the trade unionists and the active party members, and, on the other, the ease with which the masses became disillusioned and discouraged. The fervour and the aspirations of 1958 were pitched in too high a key. The man in the street never appreciated what toil, hardships and difficulties lay ahead. The happy-go-lucky, cheerful people of Guinea soon tired of making personal sacrifices and all looked to their own selfish ends, leaving the revolution and the revolutionary leaders to follow their own burdensome way. The failure of the economic and commercial revolution of Guinea must in part be laid at the door of the people.

What is in store for Guinea? Once it has found the necessary capital, once its vast mineral wealth is exploited, once it becomes a major aluminium producer, rapid expansion will be possible. What will happen to Sékou Touré and to his friends? For the moment, they are quite isolated in Africa and are surrounded by suspicion and hostility which is partly their own fault and partly that of their neighbours. The army is not as reliable as it once was. Touré is no longer the unquestioned leader of his team. Minor disagreements have arisen and other names have been suggested as possible leaders: Fodeba Keita or Ismaël Touré.* However, it is still possible to say that in recent years Africa has seen few statesmen of the stamp of Sékou Touré.

* For later developments, see pages 373–5.

6. Senegal

SENEGAL is the most westerly part of French-speaking Africa, bordered to the north by the river Senegal, a natural frontier with Mauritania, to the south by Guinea and to the east by Mali. It is a flat country (nowhere more than 300 feet above sea level), with an area of over 76,000 square miles, of which half is semi-arid: in the Ferlo region and the eastern province. Most of the other parts of the country are devoted to groundnuts: the Diourbel, Thiès and Siné-Saloum regions as well as part of the river basin area. Most of the north-east is given over to livestock, and the Casamance, the region south of the Gambia enclave, is covered by forest and paddy fields. The economic and urban centre of the country is the Cape Verde region, with Dakar, the capital, and several industrialised satellite towns. The population of Senegal is nearly 3,500,000, half under 20 years of age. The Cape Verde region has over 2,000 inhabitants per square mile against 150 in the Thiès region and only 6 in eastern Senegal. The major ethnic group is the Wolof, concentrated around St Louis, north of Thiès-Diourbel, and in the Dakar region, followed by the Serer in the Siné-Saloum area, the Toucouleur in the south, the Fulani, found wherever there is some livestock development, the Diola in Casamance, and finally the Mandingo, also in Casamance, and the Sarakole, near the Guinean border. Initially an animist country, Senegal has been stamped since the thirteenth century by Islam and about three-quarters of the population is Muslim. Although the Catholics are very much a minority, totalling only 160,000 (according to the 1961 census), a high proportion of the elite are members of that church.

Senegal has always enjoyed a privileged position within French-speaking Africa, chiefly for historical reasons. The bonds between Senegal and the Mediterranean world are long-standing: the good Senegalese harbours, particularly St Louis, and the tiny rocky island of Gorée opposite Dakar, were among the first parts of the African Atlantic coastline to be reached by European vessels. Moreover, Senegal had seen Arab caravans from across the desert and veiled Almoravid warriors from Mauritania, farther north. Slave traders would set sail from the French village established on Gorée and carry their shameful cargo to Brazil and the Caribbean. Later, French explorers and soldiers would stop awhile in Dakar on their sea journey farther south to seize great tracts for an 'Empire'. Today, Dakar is trying hard to remain an important port of call for round-Africa trips and for South American sailings.

It is small wonder that the people of Senegal became accustomed at an early stage to the white intruders and their ways—not only the Senegalese who lived on the coast, but also those from inland who, from time immemorial, had travelled to and from the coast as migrant labour.* The Senegalese are intelligent, eager, alert, adaptable, volatile, argumentative, quarrelsome, ever ready to embark on endless political discussions, and their long association with the French has accentuated these characteristics.

As was mentioned earlier in chapter 2, four Senegalese communes were given certain rights at the time of the 1789 Revolution; as early as 1870, Senegal sent a French MP to the French Parliament, though only after 1917 was this representative elected by those few Senegalese who were French citizens, as well as the French who lived there. In this way, Blaise Diagne became the first African to represent a number of his fellow citizens and to be confronted with the difficult problem of which French party he should be associated with. Political life in Senegal itself started as timidly as elsewhere in French Africa under the all-powerful French administration, but it would seem that the Senegalese caught the infection more rapidly than others in Africa and developed a real enthusiasm for political debate. Indeed, after 1945, political life in Senegal was a long series of political quarrels. Everything was viewed from a political angle; parties were numerous, and the country was divided by hot party struggles that

* For instance, the Navetanie from Casamance leave home every year to go and pick the groundnut crop.

amounted to little else than personal rivalry. It was a perfect caricature of contemporary French political activity.

This political awareness was also a by-product of the French educational system, introduced to the Senegalese earlier than elsewhere. The Senegalese were the first Africans considered worthy by their French overlords to become schoolmasters or local doctors. On the island of Gorée, in the nineteenth-century scene of the small one-time slave-trading harbour, the French established the first African school for higher studies (Ecole normale), the Ecole William Ponty, where many of the African leaders of the first generation were educated. Some of the first African clerks and administrators in offices all over the two colonial federations came from Senegal. For a long time it was Senegal's claim to fame that it had given birth to the first African 'intellectuals', and today it is certainly Senegal's pride to have chosen an outstanding poet and inspired writer as its President.

Léopold Sédar Senghor is more the archetypal French-educated African than are any of his present African colleagues in other French-speaking countries. He went to school in Paris, at the Lycée Louis le Grand, where he studied with the former French Premier, Georges Pompidou; subsequently, Senghor had a brilliant university career, culminating in success in the stiff French competitive examination, the agrégation de grammaire. He was later appointed a teacher of French and Latin in a French lycée. A somewhat facile parallel is usually drawn between Senghor and Houphouet-Boigny, both of them fascinating and forceful personalities, both belonging to the same 'older' generation, both having had outstanding intellectual achievements and exceptionally successful careers as African statesmen and yet with sharply contrasted characters and divergent opinions on fundamental African issues. This is often explained simply by saying that Senghor's past history was predominantly French while Houphouet-Boigny grew up and developed within his native Africa and encountered its everyday problems at a very early stage of his career. But this is far too superficial. The poet of *Chants d'Ombre*, the extoller of 'negritude' as a significant factor in world civilisation, Senghor well understood the Africa whose spirit he expressed with such mastery; abandoning the prospect of a brilliant career in the French or the African academic world, he succeeded in becoming, within the confines of a smaller and a poorer country, in the teeth of grave political and economic handicaps, every whit as much an energetic and efficient head of state as Houphouet-Boigny.

It is true that Senghor spent the greater part of his life in France, that he learned there the rudiments of politics, that he fought in the war as a French officer and was a prisoner in a German prison camp, that he is a Catholic and married to a Frenchwoman. Only in 1945 did he return to Dakar, and even then, for the next thirteen years, he divided his time between Paris and Dakar, since he sat in the French Parliament as the representative of Senegal. His 'French past' had been one of the constant criticisms levelled at him by political enemies, especially by young students. He was too close, they would argue, to the former colonial power to resist the blandishments of French neo-colonialism. His highly poetic genius has sometimes been taken amiss and he has been accused of being a dreamer.

His concept, however visionary, does have a tangible impact and can reach and rouse the African masses.[1] He regards the virtues of the 'Negro' as a positive and important contribution to mankind. He considers that Africa had an important destiny, and feels that the countries of French-speaking Africa should have united in a federation. This idea, so dear to President Senghor's heart, has been abandoned, for a variety of reasons, and replaced by the new concept of a world French-speaking community. Senghor considers that the African way to progress is through Socialism, or more accurately, through an African version of Socialism, a version which his detractors feel is too lukewarm and half-hearted to be effective.

Léopold Sédar Senghor's gradual ascent to power has shown that the poet and humanist could become an efficient political leader, a head of state, a leader of men who could readily effect the transition from poetic vision to economic reality and still impress and convince his followers. At first he steered a very astute course among a vast number of tiny political groups and succeeded in attracting many to his growing band of supporters. For instance, although opponents contended that his being a Catholic was a grave disadvantage in a country with a substantial Muslim majority, he kept on good terms with the Senegalese Muslim leaders and became a friend of one of the highest, the general calif of the Mourids. He was thus able to introduce the nationalisation of land, or put an end to long-established practices of feudalism, after first persuading his very conservative Muslim friends that such measures were unavoidable and necessary. He devised and implemented a 'Code de la famille' (Family Code) that succeeded in having close similarities to both the French Civil Code and the Koran. Among Senghor's friends was a brilliant economist, Mamadou Dia, whom Senghor thought an ideal collaborator and colleague. Before long they were sharing the highest powers, the poet as President and the economist as Premier. This exceptional team should have been a great asset to Senegal, but in fact it proved a failure. The reasons for this deserve close examination.

The Senghor–Dia Team

Although, when a young man studying in Paris, Mamadou Dia tended more to the left than Senghor, they joined in 1948 to found the Bloc Démocratique Sénégalais, when Senghor grew impatient with the French Socialist Party which was giving its support rather too obviously to the old Bloc Africain created earlier by Lamine Guèye. After Senghor and Dia had succeeded in absorbing a number of smaller parties, they renamed it first, in 1956, the Bloc Populaire Sénégalais (BPS), and then, in 1958, the Union Progressiste Sénégalaise (UPS). This was the time of the great referendum held throughout French-speaking Africa and the two Senegalese leaders decided to campaign for a massive vote of 'Yes', though one of their followers, Abdoulaye Ly, disagreed and called on the people to reject de Gaulle's offer. Ly seceded and founded the Parti du Regroupement Africain (PRA-Sénégal), which was to remain the official legal opposition in Senegal for several years. At the legislative elections after the referendum, UPS won such an overwhelming majority that it gained all eighty seats in Parliament.

Soon afterwards came the Mali crisis (see pages 235–6) and Senghor's somewhat premature vision of a federated Africa collapsed. Senghor, who had been President of the Federal Assembly of Mali, remained President of the Senegalese Republic, and Mamadou Dia, formerly Vice-President of Mali (under Modibo Keita, as President of Mali) became the Senegalese Premier. We shall not here consider the reasons why this federation failed,[2] but we must try to explain why Senghor and Dia, an outstanding team endowed with contrasting qualities and talents, who had chosen to work together, came to disagree so bitterly.

They had carefully chosen a rationalised parliamentarian regime, in order to share governmental responsibilities between the two of them.[3] The President of the Republic was to be elected for seven years by an electoral body similar to that defined in the French constitution of 1958 and, as in the French constitution, he would assume responsibilities somewhat wider than those generally allocated to the head of state in a parliamentary regime. The Premier, on the other hand, had his powers voted by the National Assembly, once he had been chosen and designated by the President of the Republic. He determined and implemented the national policy and had sole responsibility for national defence, the administration and the armed forces. The Premier and his ministers—and this was to prove the decisive issue—were collectively responsible to the National Assembly, which could bring about their fall by a vote of censure.

The views of the two on the so-called 'African Socialism' were not so divergent as to lead to a clash over ideological principles. Both believed that an unadorned Marxist form of Socialism could never be applied as such in Africa, but would need to be drastically altered to fit the African picture.[4] The special circumstances of the new Africa must be taken into account—and here it was mainly

Senghor, the theoretician of the two, who was speaking—notably, that the Negro much more than his white fellow man was a deeply emotional being. He could accept and incorporate himself into a political group, provided his leaders never forgot that for him the first and most important group was his own family.[5] He was deeply mystic and had to feel that he played an integral part in the development of the universe as a whole. (Senghor had probably been influenced in this by the French philosopher, Teilhard de Chardin.) The Negro was quick to feel impatient of any restraint or restriction; he longed for the fullest freedom and yearned for spiritual inspiration. He was supported in his beliefs by the moral tradition of French Socialism, as he had assimilated it in French schools—in sharp distinction to the very alien materialist doctrines of Marxism.

It is difficult to divorce from Senghor's philosophical principles the economic concepts of Mamadou Dia: his ideal of African unity manifested in an African nation (see chapter 2, pp. 55 and 69), and his belief that planning was an essential ingredient of economic development. A modern independent Senegal could not be created without planning according to the ideas of Socialism; at the same time, planning, to be effective, should concentrate on putting right the existing status quo, in both the domestic and the foreign relations fields, rather than base itself on abstract principles.[6] Mamadou Dia's team of economic advisers or counsellors, such as François Perroux and the research workers from the Paris Institut des Sciences Economiques Appliquées, and Father Lebret, a French Jesuit, were responsible for the first detailed plan.

On a purely intellectual level the political vision of the two Senegalese leaders seemed to blend most happily, but on certain matters they found themselves in slight disagreement. The party meant different things to each of them. Senghor was loath to adopt the one-party system, for a party dictatorship was alien to his concept of a free Africa. His ultimate aim in the years 1960–62 was rather to encourage the stray lambs back into the fold of the UPS, the government party, making it the only strong party. Senghor, secretary-general of UPS, repeatedly made overtures to a new party founded after the split with Mali, the Bloc des Masses Sénégalaises (BMS), whose secretary-general was the Senegalese historian, Cheik Anta Diop. On the other hand, he entertained little hope of any reconciliation with Ly's PRA-Sénégal, although he considered it to be the only serious legally-authorised opposition to him. Infuriated by the aggressive Marxism of Mahjmout Diop's small Parti Africain de l'Indépendance (PAI), he declared it illegal, compelling Diop to seek refuge in Bamako. However disappointed Senghor had been with the leaders of Mali for what he considered the unnecessary balkanisation of Africa, he wanted to bury the hatchet and to re-establish the essential good economic relationship with Mali.

On the other hand, Mamadou Dia, assistant secretary-general of the UPS, could not countenance any agreement with the official opposition and was, indeed, in favour of treating harshly any kind of opposition whatever. It seemed to Dia that a one-party system was essential if a complex economic plan were to be successfully implemented. Only a single, pre-eminent national party could rally all classes and elements of the nation, and orient all its diffuse social ingredients towards one ultimate goal. (His ideas here were not very different from Sékou Touré's.)

During 1961 and 1962 the two men quickly came to realise how much they were in disagreement. Quite apart from the progressive concepts of Dia, his obvious interest in the East appealed to the younger generation, the trade unionists and students. The USSR, he would declare, is an invaluable example of Socialist develop-ment, even if it could not be imitated slavishly. He favoured such contacts, and in June 1962 he visited the Soviet Union where he signed several agreements on the diplomatic, cultural and economic levels. In March 1961 Senegal recognised Communist China, earlier than France. Senghor accepted contacts with Communist states as necessary ingredients of his policy of non-alignment, but he felt a careful balance should be maintained between East and West—always excepting the special privileged position to be accorded to France. Both among their political supporters and among the people of Senegal, open conflict was rife between the factions of the two leaders. The Muslim friends of Mamadou Dia—himself a Muslim—expressed their distrust of a Catholic President, a viewpoint difficult to maintain considering that Senghor was on friendlier terms with the general calif of the Mourids and the marabouts than was his more radical, though Muslim, Premier.

Ultimately, Dia forgot that within the Senegalese Parliament he had fewer reliable friends than his rival, and made the fatal mistake of haughtily disregarding a motion of censure supported by more than half the MPs to the effect that 'the free exercise of parliamentary duties was being impeded'. This motion was the sequel to a reorganisation of the cabinet, initiated by Mamadou Dia, which followed the resignation of two ministers, one a supporter of Senghor and the other of Dia. One of Dia's closest friends, Valdiodio N'Diaye, was transferred from the important Ministry of the Interior to the less important Ministry of Finance: the official line was that Senghor and Dia were both anxious to avoid any real clash. The same impression was given soon after, in December 1962, at the Colloque sur les Voies Africaines vers le Socialisme in Dakar, where the contributions of the two indicated closely similar viewpoints. The impression of the author, who at the time was on a short visit to Dakar, and of most political observers was that, at any rate officially, the crisis and Mamadou Dia's arrest came as a bolt out of the blue. The whole nation was aghast; nobody could believe that there was such deep dissension between the two, that Dia could dare to defy the President, or could violate the constitution with such brutal indifference. Dia was so shrewd and so honest, so punctilious over points of procedure and so deeply convinced of his responsibility to the people. His extraordinary behaviour was never satisfactorily explained. A formal official explanation included in Dia's indictment at his trial in May 1963* maintained that he had a sectarian outlook within the party. 'Arbitrary measures were replacing the law, and regulations, money and constraint were getting the better of free discussion.' The second charge was more subtle, being directed by

* Several members of Dia's cabinet were also in the dock: Valdiodio N'Diaye, Ibrahim Sar, Joseph M'Baye, Alioune Tall.

Senghor the theoretician against Dia the man of action. Socialism, it said, cannot be regarded as an all-embracing panacea. It was necessary to get down to routine practical matters such as countering the excessive expenditure and embezzlement of public funds. It seemed that the administrators were left very much to their own devices on financial matters in Dia's day, that they were inadequately supervised, and that dishonesty was as widespread as in many other African states. The third accusation against the former Premier was even more serious. The economic plan was already six months behind schedule. No mechanism existed for the supervision of the various ministries, which had shown no sense of urgency in implementing it.

Mamadou Dia's own defence at his trial threw a very different light on the feud and was conceived on a much higher plane. He believed in a strong party and maintained that party decisions carried more weight even than the constitution, since the approval of the party had to be gained before anyone could be appointed to a public office, and since the country's development depended on targets defined by the party itself. Therefore, he said, on December 17, 1962, he (Dia) had followed strict party doctrine; the MPs who voted against him without first seeking advice from the highest authorities of the party were mistaken, even dishonest, and he was entirely justified in correcting the error of their ways for the sake of the party. Dia staunchly asserted that he had never tried to engineer a 'coup', but had rather fallen a victim to a very devious plot to get rid of him and replace the system by a plain presidential regime. (The same reasoning was used by Gabriel d'Arboussier, Minister of Justice, in an interview to *Paris Presse* on December 27, 1962. Though officially denied, it was exactly the line taken by Dia when speaking in his own defence.)

Though the Attorney-General pleaded most earnestly for extenuating circumstances,* a severe sentence was passed on Dia, with no prospect of an appeal: Dia was condemned to detention

* 'I am persuaded that his intentions were blameless. At this one point, he believed he was doing right though there was a vast gulf between what he meant to do and the law.'

for life in a fortress. Valdiodio N'Diaye, Ibrahim Sar and Joseph M'Baye received sentences of twenty years' detention, and Alioune Tall a term of five years.

After the 1962 Crisis

The harsh treatment meted out to Dia and his followers staggered the people of Senegal. Even so, the effect of the crisis was to clear the political air: the subsequent strengthening of the powers of the President increased the stability of the regime. Yet President Senghor, now solely responsible for the fate of his country, did not always find life easy. The economy, for one thing, caused him great concern.

The 1962 crisis had not only emphasised the frailty of man, but had also underlined the fragility of the constitutional framework of Senegal in time of crisis.* A reframed constitution was the subject of a national referendum held on March 3, 1963. An overwhelming majority, 1,155,077 out of a total vote of 1,162,062, was in favour of it; only 6,340, mostly in Dakar and in the heavily urbanised area of the Cape Verde peninsula, voted against it. Senghor may well have had his reservations, but personal power seemed unavoidable in Africa, the only possible method of controlling a young developing country. He soon found himself treading the same path as most of his fellow-presidents. The new constitution involved a more logical separation of powers than had previously been the case. Legislative power was still vested in the Legislative Assembly, but it could no longer pass motions of censure. The President had almost unlimited authority in defining national policy and could assume special powers in times of emergency.

However, Senghor stubbornly resisted the temptation to adopt a one-party system. He still maintained that the government party should be no more than the 'dominant' party, and he clung to his favourite tenet that the constitution should be above political

---

* It also appeared, when time had elapsed and brought things into due perspective, that the Mali Federation had crumbled for exactly the same reasons: the executive power could not be shared between two men.

parties. The constitution, which had been conceived and drafted by the most eminent members of the government party, the UPS, ascribed a vital role to the party, but only within the framework of the constitution, which gave the party pre-eminence over the government, the Assembly and even the party leaders. Thus it was the constitution itself that strengthened Senghor's supreme power over the Assembly, the government, the party and the nation. A constitutional opposition was still tolerated, provided it deferred to the constitution. Any subversion would be promptly and ruthlessly repressed.

For some time after Mamadou Dia's trial, the government was very sensitive and vigilant. Later, it relaxed, and in September 1963 several political prisoners were amnestied, including those implicated at the time of the break with Mali. After three years of complete estrangement, there had been an historic meeting between Senghor and Modibo Keita on June 22, 1963. It appeared that Mamadou Dia had stood in the way of friendly relations between the countries, and once he had gone they could again be on good terms. The only sensible course for both of them was to establish a close economic relationship. It was a matter of regret for Senegal that Mali could not be persuaded to join the Union Douanière des Pays de l'Afrique de l'Ouest and to re-enter the franc area.

One of the immediate results of this rapprochement was that the PAI of Mahjmout Diop, the violent illegal opposition to Senghor, was expelled from Mali, where it had been operating, and compelled to transfer its headquarters from Bamako to Algiers (Algeria has proved a ready supporter of political parties in exile). There was some unrest in eastern Senegal, and in 1965–66 on the frontier with Portuguese Guinea, probably provoked by the widely-scattered independent bodies of armed partisans. Luckily for Senghor, the PAI was divided sharply between a pro-Russian and a pro-Chinese faction, and therefore did not become a real problem to him.

The government tolerated an opposition, but still tried to coax the dissidents into the ranks of the government party. The BMS and the PRA-Sénégal, the two small official opposition parties that were allowed to campaign for a vote of 'No' at the March 1963 constitutional referendum, were repeatedly told that they were dissipating their energies, and that only if they threw in their lot with the government party would they be able to exert any real influence. In October 1963, before the election, the BMS finally agreed, and a few small concessions were made to them as a reward: they were given two ministerial portfolios and their name was annexed to that of the government party, which now became known as the UPS-BMS.

The legislative and presidential elections in December 1963 were a success for the government, with 85 per cent of the votes for Senghor and for the new UPS, in spite of demonstrations and clashes in Dakar which degenerated into street fighting and led to several deaths. Among the street demonstrators were members of the PRA-Sénégal and certain elements from the clandestine PAI. One of the few political leaders who had stubbornly refused to join the government ranks, Abdoulaye Ly, secretary-general of PRA-Sénégal, had been arrested and condemned to two years' imprisonment on the day before the elections, on the charge that he had slandered the Minister of the Interior during the campaign. His opposition party was outlawed in October 1964.

The political fight had for two years been harsh and unrelenting, but it appeared that the President's prestige was constantly increasing among the Senegalese masses and that the army and police had always been loyal to a man.

President Senghor's major concern today is not empty political disputation with the few intellectuals who have stayed outside his party, with little between them in common, nor is it the frequent disputes with the ill-organised trade unions* or the rowdy students

---

* Senegalese trade unions had taken a long time to unite for cohesive action. They are still divided into the Travailleurs Croyants, affiliated to the Union Panafricaine, and the Union Générale des Travailleurs du Sénégal, affiliated to the ICFTU.

of Dakar University.* He had to take positive action to deal with them. He established a Youth Civil Service, which enlists young men between sixteen and twenty for two years' training in youth camps, where they are trained to become extension workers, village headmen, 'animateurs ruraux' (community development workers) in charge of agricultural development, in top priority areas. He banned strikes among the students, arguing that such strikes would merely impair the reputation of Dakar University without in any way advancing the students' interests. Even Senghor, despite his unquestioned prestige as a thinker and the extent of popular support that he enjoys as a politician, found it essential to take careful account of the political activities of the students, and occasionally to act to resist them; the views, the preferences and the possible actions of the younger generation have been a constant preoccupation. Throughout Africa, the opinions of the very young are much more important and exercise a greater influence on future developments than in any European country.

The major preoccupation of the Senegal of today is the social and economic situation. At the time of Dia's trial, the principal official charge against him concerned the chaotic condition of the civil service, its general dishonesty and lack of responsibility. A new regime and a new administration have, however, done little to improve matters. It is true that occasionally, when scandal became too blatant, the government has taken drastic measures against dishonest officials, and it has reorganised the state-controlled organisation for exports, the Organisation de Com-

---

* Dakar University has such an excellent academic level that it attracts students from all over French-speaking Africa. Over 1,000 read law, 600 arts, 550 sciences. Of course, they are easily excited over political problems, but such an attitude is viewed rather favourably by the President, except when they oppose the government with too much animosity. Senghor has been obliged at times to expel a few of them, especially foreigners from the Ivory Coast, Dahomey and Guinea, and to outlaw the much too political—to his mind—Union des Etudiants de l'Afrique de l'Ouest, which could not conceal its sympathy for the illegal PAI party. Probably, most members of the clandestine PAI are students.

mercialisation de l'Agriculture (OCA), which failed for want of competent management and due to a general lack of experience. The organisation has been renamed the Office de Commercialisation des Arachides du Sénégal (OCAS) and is now responsible only for the production and marketing of groundnuts. A new body is centralising the whole agricultural production: the Office National de Coopération et d'Assistance au Développement (ONCAD).* Another new body has also been created, the Société Nouvelle d'Approvisionnement et de Distribution (SONADIS), which is less ambitious in scope and less doctrinaire in outlook. Its activity is at present limited to relations with the Société Commerciale pour l'Ouest Africain (SCOA) and the Compagnie Française d'Afrique Occidentale (CFAO), but it may in the future expand to be responsible for most of Senegal's imports.

Senegal has been, and still is, burdened by a heavy budgetary deficit, as a result of the very large number of administrators which it maintains. The generally high intellectual level, the great number of school graduates, the cumbersome machine inherited from the days of colonial administration, are the reasons for the vast number of civil servants: 35,000 in a country of 3,500,000 inhabitants. (The Ivory Coast, with 3,800,000 inhabitants, has only 28,000 civil servants.)† Senghor's government has tackled the problem of cutting down this very high current expenditure, which amounted to an annual 34,000 million CFA francs from 1961 to 1964: the higher salaries have been cut and the other salaries frozen, and taxation has been increased as much as practicable. However, excessive prosecution of this policy runs the danger of leading to social unrest.

There is also a heavy deficit in the trade balance: 7,500 million CFA francs in 1961 and 1962; 14,100 million in 1963; 12,200 million in 1964; 8,900 million in 1965; 3,000 million in 1966; 6,000 million in 1967. The imbalance is mainly due to the economic recession and to fluctuations in price levels. The value

* ONCAD is in fact the merger of the several Centres Régionaux d'Assistance au Développement (CRAD).

† 1966 figures for both countries.

of exports has shown no real increase since 1962. Moreover, Senegal's export trade is insufficiently varied: 80 per cent is accounted for by groundnuts, groundnut oil and oil cake. Only the exploitation of the phosphate deposits of Taïba has prevented an even higher deficit: the value of phosphate exports rose from 1,300 million CFA francs in 1962 to 2,700 million in 1965.

Until the 1964–65 harvest, groundnuts from Senegal enjoyed the advantages of a protected French market and a 'supported' price. In 1964, France paid 52·50 CFA francs per kilo for Senegalese groundnuts, as against a price of 42·50 per kilo which Senegal received on the world market. For the five year period 1964–69, as a condition of its status as an associate of the Common Market, Senegal is required to produce more groundnuts, sufficient at least to equal the 1 million tons produced in the record year of 1964–65, and to sell them at the world market price, not under the favourable conditions of protected trade with France. Annual receipts have dropped as a result by 7,000 to 8,000 million CFA francs, a loss counterbalanced by EEC aid of 11,500 million over the next five years. Thus, it is essential that Senegal diversifies its food and cash crops, making use of the massive aid it receives from several foreign sources (the five years' EEC assistance, grants from France, and loans from the World Bank and from the USA).

The shortage of home-produced food is at present a great financial burden. Imports of rice alone accounted for 3,000 million CFA francs of the trading deficit. A large agricultural development campaign has been launched, primarily to induce the peasants not to abandon the land and add to the underemployed urban population, and also to persuade them to abandon their traditional inefficient methods in favour of modern techniques and to cultivate larger areas. Under the guidance of young village workers, headmen just out of Youth Camps, the country people are taught how to diversify their crops. Some parts of Senegal are quite fertile and could grow cotton, sugar cane and far more rice, as well as early green vegetables for the winter market in Europe. The agricultural services also try to improve pastures and to develop animal production and fisheries.

For Senegal, 1965 was a difficult year. The departure of the French troops meant a loss of 6,000 million CFA francs. The groundnut harvest was mediocre and no longer did the crop receive preferential treatment on the French market. Thereafter, matters could only improve after the initiation of the four year plan in July 1965. Over the period 1959–65 the GNP actually increased slightly, which is a good performance for a country which has sacrificed the economic advantages of participation within a colonial structure to become no more than a small, not especially prosperous, independent country. Senegal can probably do much better. The industrial output has steadily risen, which is unusual for post-independence Africa; from 1963 to 1966 the index of production (1959 = 100) increased from 131 to 160, a growth of 21·7 per cent in three years. The privileged position of Senegal as head of the West African Federation gave it the one asset of a good industrial implantation before independence, especially in the heavily urbanised Cape Verde peninsula area around Dakar: a cement plant, textile and shoe factories, preserves, brick factories. Since 1963, seventy-nine new industrial firms have settled in Senegal: tuna canneries; sugar plants; paint, phosphates, and match factories; new textile factories; off-shore oil research; fertilisers.[7]

The targets of the 1964–68 economic plan are to cut down or even eliminate food imports, to reduce industrial imports and to improve the currency reserves of the country. In the speech he delivered on the seventh anniversary of independence, President Senghor sounded most optimistic. Industrial output has shown a 12·9 per cent rise over the first two years of the plan (1964–65) and was reaching 150,000 million CFA francs by the end of 1966. In spite of all the difficulties faced by Senegal and its lack of economic resources, the yearly national income per capita is about $190, one of the highest in Africa. The latest figures from Senegal are encouraging: the plan is making headway and the country's economy is progressing.

The President's unremitting efforts over the years to convert rather than suppress his opponents continue to meet with success.

One of his last major political foes, Abdoulaye Ly, as soon as he had served his sentence of two years' imprisonment, agreed to forget the old quarrels and to incorporate the PRA-Sénégal within the national party. He has been rewarded with the post of Minister of Health and two of his followers received the portfolios of National Education and Cultural Affairs. This was a shrewd move in the President's strivings for national unity, for the small party, though dwindling, still retained a large measure of local influence in Casamance. It also seems that the President's few remaining opponents—Dia loyalists, such as the historian Cheik Anta Diop and his friends—might relent and abandon their position of isolation to play a more positive role within Senghor's party.

Nothing demonstrated more clearly President Senghor's prestige than the reactions to the attempt on his life in 1967. Apparently without any plot and because of personal grievances,* a lone adventurer, Mustapha Lo, First Secretary in Cairo, tried to kill the President with a dagger. There was a nationwide outcry against the would-be murderer's mad gesture and a wave of sympathy for the unscathed victim from all over the country. The strange incident enabled the UPS leaders to regain a firm hold on their followers and to call a temporary halt to the domestic squabbles—of the traditional Franco-Senegalese pattern in politics—and to redouble their efforts in preparation for the legislative elections of February 1968.

The President is most reluctant to become involved in the petty bickerings of party politics; he never dissipates his energy over nagging minor problems, but seeks to concentrate his attention on the grand issues of political life. It was the political life, with all its hardship and worries, that he deliberately chose rather than

* It has been rumoured that he was persuaded to make this attempt by Mamadou Dramé, former 'chef de cabinet' of Valdiodio N'Diaye, Minister of the Interior. But the generally accepted version is that it was in fact a solitary gesture from an embittered Dia follower. It was all the more stupid as Senghor was considering amnestying Dia. This was, at least, the view of a Radio-Senegal editorial, commenting on official news released by the Ministry of the Interior. (AFP cable and *Le Monde*, March 28, 1967.)

the academic career he could have had either in Africa or in Europe, and he declared in a recent interview[8] that he had never regretted the choice he had made. The champion of negritude and the great African humanist grasped the opportunity of himself putting into practice the principle he had enunciated: that of an African integrated into a modern world. When circumstances dictated, he did not hesitate to soil his hands with the dirt of practical politics. When he could he adhered to his lofty political ideals and his exalted concept of Man.

7. Mauritania

THE ISLAMIC Republic of Mauritania has affinities both with Arab North Africa and with Black Africa, and its recent history reveals the problems raised by this dual allegiance to the people of 'Sudan'—the land of the black man—and to those of 'Beidan'—the land of the white man. The country has attempted to be a bridge between them rather than a disputed frontier, but, ultimately, it resolved the problem by aligning itself with the Arab world while continuing, at the same time, to co-operate with Black Africa on a basis of friendship. This situation, yet another of the ambiguities of modern Africa, can be explained in terms of Mauritania's geographical and economic characteristics and its ethnic and historical background.

Like all other countries of the Sahel (Mali, Niger, Chad), Mauritania is huge and empty (just over one million people in an area of 418,810 square miles) and, apart from the Adrar plateau which rises to over 1,500 feet, mostly flat. Water presents a problem: there is water underground and a very few small oueds (water courses), but hydrological research and the building and maintenance of wells is a costly business. It is both difficult and expensive to provide water for the small but growing cities and to develop the country's agriculture, which up to the present has been virtually non-existent. Parts of Mauritania lie within the Sahara and exhibit the typical characteristics of a desert region.

The only region that can be cultivated is the southern strip, on the banks of the river Senegal which constitutes the 400-mile frontier between Mauritania and Senegal. There life is easier, water is plentiful, and the population is sedentary. The regular floods of the river are most welcome—although they should be controlled—for they fertilise the long narrow plain. But only one per cent of the total area of Mauritania can be cultivated and even this cultivation depends on large-scale and costly capital expenditure with low returns. Fortunately for Mauritania, its mineral resources are very rich and its entire economy is dependent on two important mines: the iron ore reserves of Fort Gouraud in Northern Mauritania (certainly 145 million tons if not 200 million—with a high grade, 52 to 65 per cent) which are under exploitation, and the as yet unexploited open copper ore deposits of Akjoujt, over 150 miles to the north-west of Nouakchott, the capital (7·4 million tons of oxide ore and nearly 20 million tons of sulphide ore, a total of 27 million tons of estimated reserves).[1] Prospecting for oil is currently in progress, though by 1968 none had been discovered; there is also ilmenite (estimated as of 3 per cent quality) in the coastal sands. Beyond these mineral resources, Mauritania may also develop its livestock-breeding* and fisheries so that they become economically viable.

However, problems of population are a serious limitation on the future development of the country. The population of 1·1 million is small and its density of less than three per square mile is the lowest of all French-speaking Africa. As a result there is a serious lack of trained personnel at every level, and the situation is aggravated by the fact that 75 per cent of Mauritanians are nomads. Since independence, with the creation of a capital and of the harbour of Port Etienne for the Fort Gouraud iron, movement to the towns has increased and the urban population is now 10 per cent of the total. However, this influx into the towns has led in turn to problems of unemployment.

The population of Mauritania includes two markedly different peoples. The present Moors are descendants of the Maqil Arabs who interbred with the native Berber population during the fourteenth century. According to official estimates, about 54 per cent of all Mauritanians are white Moors, 27 per cent black or mestizo Moors and the rest are black men from the areas near the river banks: 4·5 per cent Fulani, 14 per cent Toucouleur and

---

* Estimated livestock, 1963—11 million: 10 per cent oxen, 30 per cent sheep. At present, animal husbandry is inadequate. Mauritanians are great meat eaters: 46 lb. a year per capita, as against 18 lb. in Senegal.

Sarakole. Whereas in Chad the black element is dominant and recollections of Arab slave-raids are already distant, in Mauritania the Moors are more numerous and people can vividly recall the immemorial antagonism between the white-skinned nomads and the quiet Negro villages along the river, which they would attack and plunder.

From the very outset, the existence of an independent Mauritania was denied by its northern neighbour, Morocco, which appealed to history to support its claims over both Mauritania and the Spanish Sahara, Rio de Oro. The representatives of Morocco would declare at the United Nations that Mauritania was a part of Morocco and maintained its policy of 'SHIMQUIT' (the merger of Mauritania and the Spanish Sahara with Morocco). The king of Morocco was vigorously supported by the Muslim-Socialist group of countries, which accepted Nasser as their spokesman if not their leader. The African revolutionaries, Guinea and Mali, aligned themselves with the Muslim countries, maintaining with Morocco that Mauritania had no right to be independent and should not be accepted as a member of the United Nations. For a country to be admitted to the United Nations it must have the support of two-thirds of the member-countries. The so-called Casablanca group opposed Mauritania's application for membership, and they were supported (for rather different reasons) by the Eastern bloc. Several other countries hesitated, with the result that Mauritania had to wait some time before its admission, already recommended by the Security Council, was finally approved on October 27, 1961. On that occasion, Russia abstained and Morocco, Libya, the UAR, Guinea and Mali voted against admission.*

As soon as its independent existence began, Mauritania found itself isolated from the other countries of North Africa, but strongly supported by the countries of Black Africa. This was a difficult start for a country whose people were predominantly white. The head of the government was a fair-skinned Moor, Mokhtar Ould Daddah, a lawyer and a strict Muslim (though

* The Eastern bloc finally had not voted against it, having obtained, in its turn, the admission of Outer Mongolia.

married to a Frenchwoman). He was a founder of the Parti du Regroupement Mauritanien (PRM), the party representing the Moorish tribes, which had won the 1959 elections with an overwhelming majority and had gained all forty seats in Parliament. The internal antagonisms within Mauritania, together with the external political situation, made government a difficult task. Ould Daddah has remained in power because he has the national interest at heart and is careful to remain aloof from tribal strife.

Internal Policy

The internal political situation was not made any easier by the existence of two active pro-Moroccan political groups: the Nahda Party, founded in 1958 by Bouyagui Ould Abidine, which was closely linked to Istiqlal, the ruling party in Morocco, and which campaigned for a Morocco-Mauritania association; and an older pro-Moroccan group, loyal to Ahmedou Ould Horma, the former secretary-general of the Entente Mauritanienne who had voluntarily exiled himself in Morocco. The other leaders of the Entente Mauritanienne had in 1958 temporarily supported the PRM. The black sedentary peasants of the river banks did not really represent an opposition to the government. For a time, in 1959, they tried to launch a political movement supporting the inclusion of Mauritania in a large Mali Federation (Senegal plus the former French Soudan). Then, after Mali split up, this movement, called the Union Nationale Mauritanienne (UNM), allied itself, sensibly enough, with the government party, PRM, though it still aimed at a federated state in which the interests of the two populations would be represented on a proportional basis. For a time Mokhtar Ould Daddah and his colleagues were interested in this proposal, but the project was finally dropped. When the new 1959 constitution was introduced, with its provisions for stronger executive powers, the leaders of the black Southerners considered that parliamentary representation was inadequate and the interests of the black South were insufficiently safeguarded. One of the leading black personalities, Sidi el Mokhtar N'Diaye (for several years an African deputy in the French Parliament), resigned in March 1961 as President of the National Assembly because he considered that the executive power had full control of the state and that the Assembly was there only to register the decisions of the government. In addition to the pro-Moroccan parties and the black Mauritanians, the government party was also encumbered with a conservative wing that included all the Moorish traditional chiefs and the marabouts.

The only possible course for the head of state was to steer clear of party quarrels and to enlarge and reinforce the government party, so that all the other parties would be encouraged to align themselves with it. 'National Union' was a convincing motto, when the country stood isolated and persecuted by the rest of the Arab world and when it was all too obvious that the internal affairs of the country were being interfered with from outside—as witness some isolated attempts at subversion in Atar and Nouakchott, and foreign efforts to rouse nomadic tribes in the area nearest Morocco. In the hour of danger, it was essential that one party should embrace the black villagers of the river banks, the various political leaders, the traditional Moorish rulers and even some well-meaning elements of the Nahda party. Even the Southern leader, Sidi el Mokhtar N'Diaye, rallied round. On December 25, 1961, a single all-embracing nationalist party was constituted: the Parti du Peuple Mauritanien (PPM). It was a fine achievement, due no doubt to external circumstances, but nevertheless one that strengthened Ould Daddah's prestige. He had won over everyone to his side by careful, calm persuasion. Morocco, on the other hand, with a series of fiery, exaggerated pronouncements, had deeply wounded the Mauritanian national pride and thus unwittingly contributed to the advancement of Ould Daddah's cause. Throughout, France had given support and help to Mauritania by maintaining its troops in the desert of North Mauritania and by undertaking to provide essential technical aid.

Ould Daddah had always included two Black Africans in his cabinet, but, with the exceptions of Ba Bocar Alpha and Sy Seck, they had never been truly representative of the black movement in

Mauritania, which in fact had not evolved a strong political party to stand up for its rights. However, it is fair to say that, up to the time of Mauritania's admission to the United Nations, all colours of political opinion in Mauritania were truly united. It was later, when the threat of danger from outside had evaporated, that opposition to the government and political strife began to arise.

At first, Ould Daddah was criticised for his strict authoritarianism and the austere financial policy which he pursued, which had taken the form of reducing the size of the cabinet, and cutting down salaries (ministers and ambassadors had their salaries reduced by 20 per cent; the President of the Republic and the members of the Assembly had theirs cut by 25 per cent). The main spokesman of this opposition was Souleymane Ould Cheik Sidya, the former representative of Mauritania at the United Nations. The alliance between the government and the Nahda Party, previously in opposition, proved not to last and Nahda's leader, Bouyagui Ould Abidine, resigned in October 1962; he was also expelled at that time from the political bureau of the PPM. Ould Daddah, a fighter by nature, reacted by further strengthening the central authority. He maintained that the party should become even more important and that this importance should stem from the provisions of the constitution itself. As in the Central African Republic, the party should be officially recognised as the backbone and the focus of national life. Almost immediately there was a general outcry from his opponents, led by Sidi el Mokhtar N'Diaye, Souleymane Ould Cheik Sidya and Bouyagui Ould Abidine. All of them, whatever their differences, decided to unite into one opposition political party of a 'revolutionary' character named the Front National Démocratique. Ould Daddah responded by dissolving and outlawing the new party. This did not daunt his opponents, who sought to establish an opposition party under a different name. The government outlawed this party no less firmly, and, since the three opposition leaders temporarily disappeared from political life, Ould Daddah may be said to have won this round of the struggle.

But compared with the nation-wide outbursts which then

confronted Ould Daddah, these political struggles were no more than preliminary skirmishes. Hitherto there had been only minor incidents between the two major divisions of the people, but the situation was becoming increasingly difficult as the younger Moorish elements, inflamed by Pan-Arab propaganda, grew more arrogant, more intolerant and self-satisfied, and more confident of their own Arab superiority. Thus, in 1964, when the Association de la Jeunesse Mauritanienne held its congress, there was not one representative of the black population present and a motion was passed that Arabic should become the sole national language. In 1966 Arabic became a compulsory subject in all secondary schools. As a result the black pupils in the Nouakchott secondary school, already exasperated by the bullying of their Moorish fellow-students, staged a strike. A manifesto, signed by prominent black personalities and senior civil servants, pointed out that the peoples from the river areas were being gradually ejected from all key posts; that in 1965 a black minister, Ba Bocar Alpha, had been compelled to resign; that whereas the black population of the Senegal banks represented 20 per cent of the total population the proportion in the administration and army was much lower because of subtle discrimination against them.[2] If French were not maintained as the official language and Arabic insinuated into its place, the black Southerners would be severely handicapped, as Arabic was a language they did not hear or use.

The exasperation of the black peoples could not be canalised into the actions of an established political movement. It could manifest itself only in the actions of individuals, unsupported by any party machine. Such an individual was Mamadou Samba, the President of the National Assembly, who supported the black schoolboys in their struggle and who was compelled to resign after the events of February.

The young Moors of Nouakchott considered themselves to be offended by these events and in turn organised their own strikes which were supported by strikes among the Moorish civil servants. Demonstrations took place and, on February 9, 1967, the blacks and the Moors clashed in the streets. The schools were closed and the President was compelled to take very severe repressive measures. Discussion of racial problems was forbidden, and he decided, without committing his party, to change his government. He wisely refrained from introducing pro-Arabic elements or representatives from the South, but resolved his differences with his two important opponents, Sidi el Mokhtar N'Diaye and Souleymane Ould Cheik Sidya, and welcomed them into the fold of his own party, the PPM.

External Policy

At the same time, the black tribal groups from the South were alarmed by the increasingly pro-Arab foreign policy, which was entirely Ould Daddah's personal responsibility. His political line was a direct consequence of Morocco's blunt refusal to recognise his own country, which made it necessary to establish friendly relations with all who might rally to the support of an independent united Mauritania and to 'by-pass' Morocco in foreign diplomacy.

At first, the warmest support came from the heads of state of French-speaking Africa, but at a later stage Ould Daddah very gradually withdrew from so close a relationship in order to avoid identifying himself with any particular African group of countries. Meanwhile, for obvious economic reasons, Mauritania had to keep on the best of terms with the capitalist Western world. Between 1958 and 1960, the 'blue period', the only unfriendly Black African countries were the 'revolutionaries', Guinea and Mali, but the whole Arab League boycotted Mauritanian goods. Consequently, Mauritania was eager to attend any African interstate conference of countries more or less aligned with the West, whether of the Monrovia or the Brazzaville group.

However, it was impossible for a white man and a Muslim like Mokhtar Ould Daddah not to look forward to the day when Mauritania would once more be accepted among its Muslim North African neighbours—including Morocco. A significant resolution was passed in January 1962 at the Congress of Ould Daddah's newly unified party, recommending a policy of non-alignment

225

for Mauritania and recognition of the Gouvernement Provisoire de la République Algérienne (GPRA), which at that time was still fighting against France. Another friendly gesture about this time towards revolutionary Algeria was the refusal to attend any meeting of OCRS,* thus ensuring that Mauritania would not be associated with any decision to deny Algeria its rights over the Sahara.

Thus opened a second period—'pink' this time—in which President Ould Daddah, having arrived at a rapprochement with his former opponents on the home front and having increased the centralised power of the government, began making overtures to the allies of Morocco. The first countries to prove receptive were Guinea and Mali. In February 1963, in the town of Kayes in Mali, Modibo Keita and Ould Daddah met to debate difficulties which concerned the frontier between their countries. A few months later Mauritania and Guinea exchanged diplomatic missions. As we have already seen, Mauritania was a consistent supporter of revolutionary Algeria at the United Nations and on the international level. Soon after Algeria became independent, it quarrelled with Morocco, which laid claim to the barren area of the Western Algerian Sahara that contained the very important Gara-Djebilet iron ore deposit in the Tindouf district.† There was a great diplomatic flurry and even some physical clashes between Algerians and Moroccans. For the first time in some years, the North African Arab world was disunited. Nasser, who often acted as the senior member of the group, gave his support to Algeria. For Mauritania this was a real diplomatic 'break' as, by siding with Algeria, it could gain the friendship of the Arab countries and become the ally of Nasser. The usual round of visits, exchanges, missions and studies followed soon after, and on

* OCRS—Organisation Commune des Régions Sahariennes—which was to be replaced in September 1962, after Algeria became independent, by a Franco-Algerian organisation, the Organisme Franco-Algérien de Mise en Valeur des Richesses du Sous-sol Saharien.

† Very low-grade deposit (45 per cent) difficult to transport via Algeria, the only reasonable way being either through Rio de Oro, the Spanish part of the Sahara, or through a small port, Tan-Tan, in the southern part of Morocco.

October 21, 1964, the United Arab Republic officially recognised Mauritania as a sovereign state. As a result, Ould Daddah could appeal to Morocco as one sovereign state to another, in an attempt to resolve their differences and to prepare for future co-operation, though his overtures did not succeed initially.

There was no reason now why Mauritania should not look to the Eastern bloc. In 1965, Russian and Yugoslavian embassies were established in Nouakchott. Mauritania broke off diplomatic relations with South Korea and Nationalist China and in July 1965 recognised the People's Republic of China.

But Mauritania's new political orientation led it gradually to become estranged from its former supporters in Black Africa. First Ould Daddah refused to allow the UAM to become involved in political matters and, in the spring of 1964, Mauritania voted for the Union Africaine et Malgache de Coopération Economique (UAMCE), of which Ould Daddah became the first president. By this time he was completely opposed to Houphouet-Boigny's African policy and refused to antagonise Guinea and Mali by giving his support to the Ivory Coast in its dispute with these two countries.

Finally, Ould Daddah withdrew from the Organisation Commune Africaine et Malgache (OCAM), the organisation which replaced UAMCE in July 1965. He had been reluctant to join it in the first place, and when it proved ready to extend membership to Congo-Léopoldville, at that time governed by an administration headed by Moïse Tshombe, Mauritania resigned its membership. In 1967, Mauritania sent representatives to Cairo to the small summit conference of revolutionary African countries, together with Algeria, the UAR, Guinea and Tanzania. Thus, in the space of six years, Mauritania had completely reconsidered and reoriented its foreign policy.[3]

Economic Interests

No doubt this change in foreign policy was a very logical evolution, in keeping with the religion and history of its large Arab majority. It was also the only realistic course to take if the recently

227

created state of Mauritania was to survive intact. Morocco has shown little sign of withdrawing from its former position. What will happen if and when Morocco claims Rio de Oro from Spain? With this possibility in mind, President Ould Daddah got in touch with the Spanish authorities, and in March 1966 the Spanish Foreign Minister visited Mauritania. If Rio de Oro achieves its freedom, it is equally plausible that Mauritania might lay claim to it, with the consent of both Algeria and the UAR. What does Spain think of all this? Would Spain ultimately deal with Morocco or with Mauritania? Will Algeria take this opportunity of settling its feud with Morocco? When Ould Daddah visited Algiers in March 1967, he agreed to keep the Algerian leaders informed and to consult them on the matter of the Spanish Sahara. It is known that Nouakchott and Algiers would agree to a UN-sponsored referendum and fall in with its outcome, but there is plenty of scope for a vigorous campaign before the referendum.

There are important interests involved in this whole area. For instance, the Miferma company, which has been set up to exploit the iron deposits of Fort Gouraud,* belongs 55·8 per cent to a French consortium (Société d'Engineering BRGM, Usinor, Denain-Anzin and financial associates), 15.2 per cent to an Italian (Finsider), 5 per cent to a German (Thyssen), 19 per cent to a British (BISC) oil company—and only 5 per cent to Mauritania. The development has necessitated the building of a railway 420 miles long from Fort Gouraud to the harbour of Port Etienne, at a cost of $160 million. Of this, $60 million has been loaned by the World Bank and $30 million by the French government. Another major industrial interest is the Mauritanian operating company to be formed to exploit the copper reserves of Akjoujt. This company will be dominated by Charter Consolidated, part of the great Anglo-American mining group, and other shareholders will be the Mauritanian government, the Bureau des Recherches Géologiques et Minières (BRGM), the French mining company

---

* In 1965, 5,965,000 tons were exported—a 20 per cent increase over 1964. In 1966, 7,157,000 tons were exported, another 20 per cent increase over 1965.

Penarroya and the Banque de Paris et des Pays Bas. Production is to start in 1970 with the extraction of the equivalent of 27,000 tons per year of saleable copper.[4] The Planet Oil and Mineral Corporation of the United States proposes to invest an initial $1·5 million in prospecting for hydrocarbons off the coast between Nouakchott and the border of the Spanish Sahara.[5] Industrial fishery operators, such as Guelfi, a French company, are setting up an industry which could process 100,000 tons of fish annually. To do so they will need to recruit perhaps a thousand Mauritanian fishermen—no easy task, as Mauritanians have not been traditionally a fishing people. Finally, it is possible that industrial investment will be made in the potential resources of Rio de Oro, such as phosphates and oil, and—less likely—in transport facilities for the Gara-Djebilet iron.

All in all, therefore, it seems that this small poverty-stricken African country might come to play an important role on the international stage. Admittedly, Mauritanian agriculture is virtually non-existent, but its Gross National Product increased by 9 per cent in 1965, its present per capita value being estimated at about $140. Ever since iron ore was first sold, the trade balance has been favourable (a 7,400 million CFA francs surplus in 1964, compared with a 3,400 million deficit in 1963),* and the budget has needed no subsidy from France to achieve a balance, thanks to the taxes and dues paid by the French company, Miferma. Mauritania is more fortunate than many other African countries since its resources are readily saleable—though, of course, they are vulnerable to fluctuations in the world prices for iron and copper. It is, therefore, in the interests of the great powers to guarantee peace and stability in this part of the world and to support the government of Mokhtar Ould Daddah.

The contradiction in Ould Daddah's policy is no more than superficial. Mauritania is apparently leaning towards the African 'revolutionaries' in order to remain unaligned and uninfluenced by any of its Black African neighbours. On the domestic front

* In 1965, a surplus of 8,300 million CFA francs, and, in 1966, a surplus of 12,400 million.

Ould Daddah has tried to allay the rivalry between the Moors and the black peoples of the river banks. Mauritania has abandoned its membership of OCAM, but has remained a member of the technical organisations of West Africa, the Union Douanière (customs union) and Union Monétaire (monetary union), and also of the great inter-African air company, Air Afrique. Much has been done to avoid violence and extreme feelings; there have been no further incidents during the 1966–67 school year, even though it has been decided to introduce the teaching of Arabic, by very slow degrees, to enable the black peoples from the Senegal river area to become accustomed to this unfamiliar language. A mixed commission has been set up to study the problems and consider the different interests and outlooks involved. Ould Daddah has repeatedly tried to point out in his speeches that it could be an advantage for a country to develop two parallel cultural traditions. Much to the satisfaction of the educated black Mauritanians, the key portfolio of Foreign Affairs was entrusted to one of their number, Wame Birane.[6] The young men who demonstrated and went on strike, causing the schools to be closed down for the rest of the year, are tired of such behaviour and are now busily making up for lost time. The national congress of the PPM in January 1968 confirmed this policy of sharing power with the black minority. Another key portfolio, the Finance Ministry, has been given to a black Mauritanian, Sidi Mohamed Dogana.

Much may reasonably be expected of Mauritania if it is no longer disturbed by feuding and political rivalry, if Ould Daddah remains in power and continues his present realistic political policy of striking a fair balance between the 'revolutionary' Arabic group and the moderate black African group and of encouraging the development of mineral resources. In the near future, however, the profits from the exploitation of mineral resources must, of course, be reinvested in agricultural development on the fertile strip on the banks of the Senegal river, to avoid an excessive lack of balance in the economy and to allow both parts of the population to profit from economic development. Here, as elsewhere, political stability is closely related to economic and social stability.

8. Mali

In their attempts to establish a nation, Mali's leaders would often appeal to past glories, for these—with a common religion and a common code of morality, specific to the Malian people—were all that they had on which to base their appeal to a national spirit, since the country was endowed with no natural frontiers and its peoples included no specific ethnic unit. Old maps of Africa included a large territory called Upper Senegal, delineated at random in 1904 and subsequently denuded of several regions: in 1911 an area in the west, later to become Niger; in 1919 an area in the south, which became Upper Volta. This arbitrary sub-division reflected a feeling of unease on the part of the colonial administration, for this country, then called Soudan, where powerful empires had once thrived, might prove difficult to handle if it were left too big a colony. The Mali of today covers an area of 465,000 square miles and a population approaching five million.

Mali's history stretches back to the great empire of Ghana which flourished between the eighth and eleventh centuries and whose fame reached as far as Europe. It was overthrown by the Malinke tribal group under the dynasty of Mansa Sundiata, who, in the twelfth and thirteenth centuries, built up a great kingdom, the kingdom of Mali, which incorporated part of the former Ghana. In the fifteenth and sixteenth centuries this empire, ruled by the Songhai who had replaced the Malinke, began to disintegrate. It was subjected to inroads and invasions both by Arabs and by pagans, some penetrating from the north, from Timbuktu, led by Moroccans, and others from the west, led by the Bambara. The powerful empire which had survived several changes of leadership during its past history was now exposed to the influence and the pressure of all the great tribal groups of modern West Africa—the Fulani, the Dogon, the Toucouleur.

Among the many contrasting influences, the product of its dramatic historical background, to which Mali is now subject, the Muslim element is the most prominent. Although it is a land-locked country, Mali has never been isolated. It had strong and effective links with the adjacent countries—Guinea, Senegal, Mauritania, Niger, Upper Volta—since most of the great tribal groups of West Africa spread across the arbitrary colonial borders. The colonial administration built roads to the south, towards the Gulf of Guinea,* and a railway from Niger to Dakar over 800 miles long, 460 miles of which was within the territory of the then Soudan. Other transport facilities were provided by the river Niger, which was navigable between January and July.

Soudan, which reassumed the old and glorious name of Mali after the split with Senegal, had little difficulty in establishing a national identity, for all the great empires and kingdoms of the past which had successively held sway over this part of Africa could be recognised as 'parent states of the modern system'.[1] 'This historically grounded sense of identity', which Professor Joseph Ki Zerbo has called Mali's 'tradition étatique', is reinforced by the continuity of certain types of social institutions. Specifically Islamic institutions—such as the hadj, the koranic school, the fast of Ramadan and the basic Islamic festivals, and the Sufi brotherhoods and their leaders, the marabouts—have come to form a recognised part of the national life, even for those who are not in any formal sense Muslims. Other institutions deeply rooted in Mali society are Sudanic rather than Islamic in character, particularly 'such occupationally specialised social groups as blacksmiths, fishermen, butchers and praise singers (*griots*), which are sometimes referred to as "castes" '.[2] These institutions date back as far as the fourteenth century and exist even today, in spite of the egalitarianism enforced by the modern Mali government, which is strenuously trying to abolish the inequalities of the traditional social structure.

---

* Bamako-Conakry: 620 miles; Bamako-Abidjan: 666 miles.

The Union Soudanaise and the Mali Federation

The Union Soudanaise, which over the years 1946 to 1958 established itself first as the dominant, and later as the only, political party of Soudan, took advantage of the strong traditions and memories of the past in asserting its position. A local section of the RDA, the party endorsed the new concepts of African unity and of a federation of African peoples, and it found a ready response among the local peoples. For a while it blindly followed the general policies of the RDA as they had been laid down in Bamako at the historic meeting of October 1946: to form an anti-colonial front that would gather together 'all peoples, all races, all political parties, all the workers' unions, all the religious and cultural associations of Black Africa'. Both in outlook and in structure, the Union Soudanaise resembled the Parti Démocratique Guinéen (PDG). The policies of the political bureau and the congress at the top were quickly spread throughout the country through a chain of regional committees and local sections. Like the PDG, the Union Soudanaise had an elaborate network of local committees in rural parts and district committees in towns, through which every party member could be promptly contacted, mustered and alerted for action. By the additional influence of women's and youth organisations—the Union des Femmes du Mali and the Jeunesse de l'Union Soudanaise—and of the trade union, the Union Nationale des Travailleurs, the grip of the party on the country was made complete. Both the women's association and the trade union were represented in the political bureau.

But however close its affinities with Guinea, Soudan shrank from emulating the dramatic vote of 'No' at the 1958 referendum, with its unpredictable and possibly dangerous consequences. It preferred to vote for a moderate 'Yes', much to the indignation of the fiery Abdoulaye Diallo, the leader of the Union Générale des Travailleurs de l'Afrique Noire (UGTAN) and Minister of Labour from 1957 to 1959. He angrily quitted his own country and went to Guinea, where Sékou Touré could not but welcome a supporter of his policy. Soudan, in spite of its revolutionary tendencies, had been impressed by the almost unanimous vote of 'Yes' of its French-speaking neighbours. The strongest incentives for the country to vote 'Yes' were prudence and solidarity among Africans, as was evinced in an editorial of *L'Essor*, the party newspaper, on September 27, 1958: 'We shall be able to establish African unity once and for all through the two great federations of AOF (French West Africa) and AEF (French Equatorial Africa), provided each leader forgets his personal ambitions and each territory its local idiosyncracies.' The Soudanese approach was closely akin to that of the Senegalese: the immediate aim was the establishment of primary federations.

On the other hand, the Union Soudanaise did not at that time have a sufficiently firm grip on the country (as did, for instance, the PDG in Guinea) to take a defiant stand and demand immediate independence. Only after the March 1959 elections did it emerge supreme over all the other parties, eliminating the Parti Soudanais Progressiste of Fily Dabo Sissoko and Hamadoun Dicko, which had been pre-eminent in colonial days and at the time of the Loi Cadre. After the elections, however, with all the eighty seats in the Legislative Assembly in its hands, the Union Soudanaise was able to carry out its policies unhindered. The party continued to favour a policy of federation, and thus a clash with Houphouet-Boigny was unavoidable, because of the policies he adopted after the referendum. His refusal to support any move that might have helped to re-establish the primary federation of West Africa of pre-colonial days caused the Soudanese leaders to break with the RDA and find common grounds of policy with their Senegalese neighbours. However, the dream of a great Mali Federation, gathering together all the countries of the former French West Africa, never materialised: Upper Volta, Niger and Dahomey expressed a nebulous interest, but finally wavered and backed out—not without encouragement from the French, who preferred the concept of an Entente centred on Abidjan. Only Senegal and Soudan were completely in earnest in their intention to federate: in March 1959, the Union Soudanaise merged with the Union Progressiste Sénégalaise (UPS) to become the Parti de la Fédération Africaine.

But, notwithstanding their enthusiasm, the Federation of Mali proved to be short-lived. The Bamako leaders later explained their difficulties by pointing out how divergent were the economic, political and social views of each. The Union Progressiste Séné-galaise had originally blossomed under the loving care of the colonial masters and, as a result, it was stigmatised by its critics in Soudan as a self-satisfied middle-class movement. Moreover it was divided into several small groups which found it very difficult to reach any over-riding party unity, whereas, by contrast, the Union Soudanaise was a unified revolutionary party that had fought against colonial rule and had been held in great disfavour by the colonial administration. It was held that neo-colonialist elements inside the UPS might infiltrate into the brother party and pollute its pure spirit of revolutionary anti-colonialism.

Another unavoidable truth was that both countries were led by very experienced, strong-minded men who would be most reluc-tant to relinquish part of their power—on the one hand, Léopold Sédar Senghor and Mamadou Dia, and on the other, Modibo Keita. Keita, a genuine descendant of the chiefs of the Mali Empire, one of the founding members of RDA, Secretary of State for Overseas Territories in a French cabinet of 1957, was in fact far closer in spirit to Sékou Touré. The two men shared many aspirations and viewpoints. Both held that the only acceptable solution to the Algerian problem was to give full power to the Front de Libération Nationale (FLN) to lead the country to com-plete independence, the solution demanded by the Arab League. Both maintained that a newly independent African state should adopt Socialist policies and that the necessarily difficult field of economic development would be best controlled, and best pro-tected from abuses and dishonesty, if it were completely centralised and directed by a state administration. They were impatient of any un-African pressures and eager to induce all African countries to unite and seek together purely African solutions, and were resolutely distant in their new relations with the former colonial power.

Keita had believed that such ideas would best be put into

practice in a primary federation with a truly federal government, and he had believed that Senegal as well as Soudan would be ready to forego part of their prerogatives. However, it seems that, rather unrealistically, he had imagined that it would be Soudan which called the tune, and he did not foresee the possibility of the emergence of personal rivalries. Who, for instance, was to have been President of the Soudan-Senegal Federation? The secession from Senegal came as a relief to the Soudanese people. They had come to realise that federation would be no way for Soudan to discover its true identity. And it was in their search for this identity that they laid emphasis on their country's former glories. 'Here in Mali, we have a country with a long tradition of administration, a long tradition of culture, a long tradition of social and cultural organisation.'[3] 'Now we are ourselves', Modibo Keita claimed, 'and I would go so far as to assert that secession from Senegal was an upheaval that stirred all the peoples of Soudan. It will provide the opportunity for the Soudanese Republic to reach its political, economic, social and cultural goals by truly Socialist methods and with essential concern for the welfare of our poorest elements.'[4]

Mali on its own

The secession was a source of gratification to the national pride of Mali, but it was to prove a severe handicap to economic development in the first years of independence. On the Dakar-Niger railway, Mali's only link with the coast, all traffic ceased. This placed a stranglehold on Mali's imports and exports. This serious problem was later partially solved by road transport down to Bobo Dioulasso in Upper Volta, from where the railway ran to Abidjan on the coast. With its trading outlets blocked on one side, Mali soon came to realise that it could not afford to quarrel with its neighbours of the Conseil de l'Entente and that it must necessarily establish friendly relations with them.

As a reaction to what they considered Senegalese neo-colonialism, the Malians stepped up the rate of their programme

for the nationalisation of all production. A Malian five-year plan
(1961–65) was quickly initiated. It gave the highest priority to
agricultural development, the only possible means of ensuring
economic independence, and of increasing exports. Another aim
was diversification of the economy. It made provision for the
setting up of small-scale processing industries to increase the
value of exports such as groundnuts, cotton and cattle, by
the construction of oil mills, ginning mills, textile factories and
modern slaughterhouses. Wherever possible, the indigenous
product was to replace the imported. A search for crude oil and
mineral resources was to be initiated. It was also intended that a
social policy should be established as a basic concern of the
regime, with education and health services developed with the
same intensity as the creation of the administrative structure.[5]

The five-year plan was to impinge on, and was to be effected by,
every sector of the nation. In the villages, rural co-operatives were
to be established to provide a system for marketing local produce,
to buy the necessary consumer goods and to make loans to farmers.
The scheme was named Groupement rural de production et de
secours mutuel (GRPSM). As a first step towards the collectivisation
of agriculture, each village was to be given land to cultivate by a
common effort. The villages were grouped into regions named
'zones d'expansion rurale', in each of which there was to be a
Centre coopératif d'éducation et de modernisation agricole
(co-operative centre for agricultural education and modernisation)
with its co-operative stores, classes for instruction in reading,
medical unit and agricultural machinery depot. At the national
level government controls covered every aspect of the development
programme. The most important was the Société Malienne
d'Importation et d'Exportation (SOMIEX). It enjoyed an absolute
monopoly over the purchase and export of the groundnut harvest,
which provided one-quarter of all Mali's exports, making it Mali's
most important source of wealth. It also was given complete control over the import of essential commodities such as sugar, tea,
flour, soap, salt, milk, petrol, cement and matches. However, these
same products continued to be traded and retailed by private

organisations, so that the success of SOMIEX was dependent on the good will and co-operation of that sector of private trade violently anathematised ever since independence. The state controlled and organised many other economic activities, including the distribution of books and newspapers (Librarie populaire du Mali), transport, banking and pharmaceutical goods.

Mali thought that only by such drastic measures could it shake off the grip of colonialism or at least lessen the hold of foreign business on its economy. The government tried to neutralise the influence of traders, both large and small, but their main enemies remained the big trading companies, which were expected to fade away rapidly once they no longer controlled imports and exports. Mali aimed at a truly Socialist society, not one dominated by the middle class. The first concern of every social group was to be the welfare of the people. Such measures were to ensure that the middle class of traders would never again flourish in Mali. However, so thorough a nationalisation of almost all the means of production and of the whole trading system meant that a large caste of government officials was established to control the very complex administrative structure. These civil servants, this red-tape aristocracy, self-satisfied and conscious of its rights, was to pose a different kind of problem.

Evolution in Mali

For all French-speaking African countries, the immediate concern of foreign policy after independence was to establish a new relationship with France, at least in its preliminary stages. Mali, though embarking on the difficult course of Socialism, declined to adopt the dramatic secession of Guinea. Modibo Keita repeatedly emphasised that Mali felt neither resentment nor bitterness: it merely wanted to work out its own destiny in its own way: 'We were too dependent on the former colonial power. Trade with France accounted for 80 per cent of our imports. Our balance of payments depended entirely on France. Credits were allocated to trade [more precisely to the "commerce de traite"] rather than used for capital investment.' Mali was making a dogged effort to become independent—perhaps more so than any other African country. 'The Africa which we long for must be built away from colonialist nations.' To rid itself of all the relics of colonial power was a primary requirement, in their view. All French military bases were to be evacuated: hence, in 1961–62, Malian troops took charge of the outposts of the Southern Sahara and thereby became entrusted with the delicate task of controlling the very unruly nomads.

The outlook of independent Mali also demanded an independent currency. This was officially created on July 1, 1962, but Mali insisted that it was not breaking away from the French franc zone. Even when the general purport was the same as in Conakry, the tone in Bamako would always remain courteous and restrained. Modibo Keita proved extremely shrewd and pliant in his relations with France: though he might inveigh against French policy in Algeria, for instance, he would always retain his good manners and self-control. Nevertheless, Mali spent seven tedious years of negotiation with France over questions of finance. Mali stubbornly maintained that there was no inconsistency in establishing a national currency and yet remaining within the franc zone and within the West African monetary union, and they wished their own franc to be guaranteed by the French franc, even if a certain ceiling was to be assigned. France strongly dissented from this view, arguing that excessive concessions to Mali might endanger France's entire financial policy in West Africa and bring about a division within the monetary union.

Mali tried hard not to lose face. It was determined not to sever all connections with France and the rest of the Western world. For seven years it remained an associate member of the EEC, though such sympathies were hardly in keeping with Socialist ideologies and with the common revolutionary platform of the Ghana-Guinea-Mali union established in 1960–61 and later enlarged into the Casablanca group. Guinea's indictment of the EEC as an instrument of neo-colonialism proved no deterrent to Mali's joining the Yaoundé convention, signed by the countries of the

Common Market on the one hand and by African states on the other.

Meanwhile the negotiations between France and Mali dragged on, sometimes official, as in June 1965 and January 1967, and sometimes unofficial, and at several venues. To resolve this prolonged disagreement became a matter of increasing urgency, for the daring economic experiment that Mali had launched was not proving a success, in spite of tremendous efforts on the part of the government. The Malian franc was rapidly losing value; the finances of the country were in a sad state; too much money had been spent on unproductive expenditure for prestige purposes, such as the building of a presidential palace and of a big hotel. Because of the growth of innumerable government departments with their teeming personnel, administrative costs had increased out of all measure and were growing much more quickly than was revenue. Prior to 1960, colonial Soudan traditionally exported food to its neighbours, being 5,000 million CFA francs in credit every year since the Second World War. Now the situation was completely reversed and the balance of trade showed a heavy deficit.

thousand million CFA francs

	1962	1963	1964	1965	1966	1967
Exports	2·5	2·6	4·1	3·9	3·2	6·5
Imports	11·3	8·4	9·0	10·6	8·9	16·2
Balance	− 8·8	− 5·8	− 4·9	− 6·7	− 5·7	− 9·7

The five-year plan was a failure. Its implementation was so delayed that at times it seemed hardly possible that anything could have been planned beforehand. As in other countries which had not adopted state control—such as Senegal, Cameroun, Congo–Brazzaville—experience was showing that the plan had been inadequately conceived and that it was no more than a series of ill-coördinated programmes arbitrarily pieced together.[6]

However, the Malians were not daunted by temporary failures.

In February 1967 they finally signed a financial agreement with France and agreed on a drastic devaluation of the Malian franc by about half. The Malian central bank has been kept in being, but the Malian franc, like the CFA franc, is guaranteed by the French Treasury. Malian banknotes are issued by agreement with the Banque Centrale des Etats d'Afrique de l'Ouest, so that they are quasi-convertible with those of the West African monetary union and other banks of the franc area.

The monetary situation in Mali will really be seen to be improved when this financial agreement takes full effect. First of all, however, Bamako must adopt severe measures of austerity to help balance the national budget. Malians are fully determined to get out of their financial difficulties with their neighbours and with France; they demonstrated the sincerity of their intentions both by devaluation and by sending their Finance Minister, Louis Nègre, as an observer to an OCAM meeting, pending the annual meeting of the World Bank and of the International Monetary Fund, held in September 1967 in Rio de Janeiro. Mali is most likely to re-enter the franc area before long—a happy consequence of its foreign policy which has maintained a most careful balance between opposite poles. Mali had opted for Socialism and was irresistibly drawn towards its fellow-travellers of the East, and yet it had resolved that these friendships should never impair its good relations with France, the EEC and the West. On the other hand, Mali refused to be constrained by economic considerations and reserved the right to shape its destiny on ideological principles. Keita certainly never wavered in his rigidly anti-colonialist and anti-imperialist policy. He gave his support to the Algerian Front de Libération National, to the Lumumba-Gizenga faction in Congo–Léopoldville and to the freedom movements in Angola and South Africa. He proved to be one of the most truly neutralist leaders, freely criticising whom he pleased, both in the East and the West, and paying visits to whomever he pleased.

In Bamako, in March 1964, there were street demonstrations against 'the criminal purposes of American imperialists in Vietnam and in the Congo'. On the other hand, Mali adopted a very

241

cautious attitude to the loans—'mere commercial deals'—which are the invariable consequence of visits from Chinese or Russian information missions. The sequence of eminent visitors to Mali evinced an intriguing eclecticism: Chou En-Lai in January 1964, then Jacob Malik, Vice-Minister of Foreign Affairs of the USSR, and Mennen Williams, the American Assistant Secretary of State for African Affairs. Mali was shrewd enough never to take sides in the feud between Communist China and the USSR, even though China seemed to be a particularly trusted ally: half the industrial developments of recent years were entrusted to Chinese experts— for instance, a textile plant in Ségou, a cigarette and match factory, a ceramics workshop and a broadcasting station. Agreements for co-operation were, of course, also concluded with Russia, which built two cement factories. By contrast, United States aid to Mali was comparatively small—far less important than, for instance, US aid to Guinea—and Mali is very little dependent on the USA for its imports. To round off this finely balanced commercial picture, Mali enjoyed good relations with the EEC countries, and therefore entered into commercial and technical agreements with West Germany, but refused to recognise East Germany.

There is a similar distinction between Mali and Guinea in the area of inter-African relationships. Whereas Guinea is markedly aligned towards one camp, Mali succeeded in establishing friendly relations throughout. Naturally enough, the days immediately following independence saw a phase of elation and unbridled enthusiasm when the Ghana-Guinea-Mali union was established (though it was nothing but a legal fiction and the theme of lively Ghanaian 'highlifes'). It was soon followed by a 'hard' stage, when the Ghana-Guinea-Mali union, together with several North African countries, grew into the Casablanca group. That, too, did not last long. Unfortunately for Mali, it is a land-locked country, a fact about which its revolutionary-minded friends could do nothing. One difficult outlet through Guinea was not sufficient and the very hypothetical concept of a trans-Saharan road, had it ever come to fruition, would have proved a long, expensive and completely unprofitable venture (though Keita and Ben Bella met at one time and toyed with the idea). Mali had perforce to fall in line with its neighbours, with whom, in any case, it had strong common ethnic and historical bonds beneath the apparently divergent ideologies. It very quickly patched up its differences with Upper Volta and Niger, which had blamed Mali for sheltering exiled elements of their political oppositions. In another direction, Mamadou Dia's fall afforded a fine opportunity to re-establish good relations with Senegal: both countries were very pleased when their common railway line was reopened in June 1963. Further, Keita was readily persuaded by Senghor that, with the help of the United Nations Development Programme, the large area of the Senegal basin should be developed and that an inter-state committee should be set up on which Senegal, Mauritania, Mali and Guinea would be represented. Mali responded more readily than Guinea as it was more directly concerned; present research studies are leading to the possibility of a multi-purpose dam, which might, depending on the availability of finance, be built on the river on Malian territory in Gouina and which would, amongst many other things, improve navigation on the river and thereby provide Mali with another means of communication.

Whereas Guinea vigorously protested about the inconsistency of belonging both to the Organisation of African Unity and to the Union Africaine et Malgache (later to become OCAM), Mali was discreet enough not to adopt Guinea's hostile attitude and to avoid alienating the countries which it meant to conciliate— Senegal, Niger, Upper Volta, Ivory Coast—by wounding criticism (see chapter 10, pages 290–6). Unlike its volatile friends, Mali never took it upon itself to act as a mentor to the moderate elements of Africa, and never took the line that its loyalty to the OAU and to revolutionary Africa, unquestioned as it was, should preclude it from establishing good relations elsewhere. Indeed, Keita travelled all over French-speaking Africa in an attempt to bridge the gap between the two groups. He exerted an indirect influence over the tentative rapprochement between the Conseil de l'Entente and Nkrumah. However, he soon came to realise that the moderates would remain profoundly suspicious of Mali until it aligned itself more positively with their camp. On the commercial front, the depreciated Malian currency and the country's lack of foreign exchange proved a hindrance to the establishment of satisfactory relations between Mali and the other members of the French-speaking group.

Internal Policy

The whole political life of Mali centred on one leader, Modibo Keita, who had the same hold on the Malian masses as has Sékou Touré on Guinea. Everyone looked up to the great wise man and praised his political shrewdness and self-restraint. Keita's prestige was certainly enhanced among his followers when he emerged as the African leader who brought to an end the dispute between Algeria and Morocco over their joint Saharan frontier near the iron mines of Gara-Djebilet. Both King Hassan and President Ben Bella agreed to fly to Mali and to refer their dispute to Keita as arbitrator: they accepted his strong advice to sign a cease-fire. Consequently, in the same year, Keita was awarded the Lenin Prize for Peace.

Under the authority of its greatly respected leader, the Union Soudanaise and its political bureau gained comprehensive control over the nation's life. The National Assembly carried little weight, merely enacting legislation without debating it. The goals of economic planning and Socialist policy received the highest priority, and since their implementation required the active co-operation of the entire people, an administrative network was set up to explain to the people the changes that were necessary and to spur them on to greater efforts. But these Socialist policies cut across the long-standing traditions of African life. Malian farmers have frequently resisted the collectivisation of the land and shown reluctance to take part in communal agricultural work. The party fought a stubborn battle against tradition, controlling the ceremonies associated with weddings and circumcisions and encouraging the farmers to save instead of spending lavishly on family celebrations and running into debt as they were wont to do. There was a streak of puritanism in the Malian brand of Socialism, and the regime prided itself on its moral and cultural reforms. Gambling was forbidden. The activities of children were closely controlled; they were encouraged to attend evening talks and games, and attendance at school was rigidly enforced. Party members went unflaggingly the rounds of the country to exhort, expound, discuss, and finally to listen to criticism, since the people were often averse to the drastic measures proposed and resentful of the hold the party was trying to gain on them.

At times during the early 1960s the government's policy led to violent repercussions, for instance among the Tuareg population of the desert fringe of north-east Mali. The nomads, traditionally unruly, spurned all orders from Bamako: they are a fair-skinned people and object to taking orders from a black official. The Tuareg in the Adrar des Iforas revolted when the government maladroitly ordered them to settle in villages. Troops were sent from Bamako to suppress the rebellion in the desert, and Algeria was asked to co-operate by preventing the rebels from fleeing across the Saharan frontiers. When Keita went to Algiers on a state visit in July 1964, he accused French officers in the French Saharan bases of conniving with the rebellious Tuareg and he declared himself convinced that an imperialist plot had been fomented against Mali, with infiltration into the Malian armed forces, attempted murders and sabotage, and the setting up of organised subversive commando groups. He said he would not hold the French government responsible, provided it was ready to investigate and to accept that certain elements within its army were working against the best interests of France. Ben Bella readily weighed in, fulminating against certain Malians 'unworthy of their country' (meaning, of course, the Tuareg), warning them that they should not expect any leniency from Algeria if they crossed its borders. In the event, the Algerian government did nothing, and order was restored in Mali only when the Tuareg found they could escape safely into the wilds of the Algerian Sahara.

Within the entrepreneurial classes, all the businessmen, tradesmen and shopkeepers could not view the Socialist policies of the government with equanimity and they expressed their anger and indignation in violent street demonstrations on July 20, 1962. In their efforts to gain the support of all classes of Mali society, the government had repeatedly reassured the trading classes that the regime was Socialist only in its organisation of the economic life of the country, that it was in no way Communist and that its sole aim was to give every Malian enough to eat, but town traders remained hostile and consequently receptive to the propaganda from the opposition, the Parti Soudanais Progressiste of Fily Dabo Sissoko and Hamadoun Dicko. The government reacted more violently than it should have done towards a mere traders' demonstration, for it knew who was encouraging them. The two opposition leaders were hunted, arrested, tried and condemned to death after a state trial in October. Socialist leaders in France, including Emile Roche, the President of the Conseil Economique et Social, felt it their duty to ask for a pardon for the condemned men, and the sentence was commuted to a life term with enforced labour. The government made great efforts to suppress all other opposition and to calm down the general excitement. In spite of the fine words of its declaration of leniency, anyone who disobeyed the stringent trade regulations was ruthlessly punished. No one was allowed to become rich, and austerity led to resentment of the rigid government control. The opposition tried once again to rear its head. A new opposition party, the Parti Progressiste et Démocratique, was formed under Mamadou Fain-Ke, and tried to run candidates at the 1964 elections, but they were foiled when the government decided there would be a one-list vote and the Union Soudanaise won 99·89 per cent of the votes. After the overwhelming victory, Fain-Ke was put under house arrest, together with a number of village chiefs who were reproached for being too lukewarm in their support of the government. The victory demonstrated to Keita that he held the country in a firm grip and so could proceed to enforce other necessary measures of austerity:

salaries were cut by 10 per cent, taxes heavily increased and many government departments reorganised.

Keita was striving to overhaul the finances of the country, to cut down the balance of payments deficit, and to meet the conditions of the International Monetary Fund for granting a long-term loan which would improve the financial position sufficiently for Mali to be able to re-open its negotiations with France. Unfortunately, France did not respond during the period 1964–65, for it had been seriously disturbed by the unexpected deaths of the two opposition leaders, Fily Dabo Sissoko and Hamadoun Dicko, who, according to the official account, were killed in an ambush of Tuareg rebels while they were being taken to a different prison.

Keita never flagged during these difficult years. He would visit the most remote villages to exhort the farmers to labour and be thrifty; in the towns he constantly inveighed against the shameful luxury of certain profiteers. He would emphasise Africa's need for stability, declaring that the disturbances occurring throughout French-speaking Africa were instigated from abroad and were a humiliation to the whole of Africa. He would not flatter his people but roused their enthusiam to encourage them to bear the hardships essential to national development. On January 1, 1965, he said: 'Mali will meet greater difficulties than in the past year and must expect to encounter growing opposition from private business, from smugglers and from traffickers who have been gathering strength.' He had just discovered that many responsible officials of SOMIEX had been guilty of fraud and embezzlement: fifty of them were arrested. In addition, the Diallo and Hausa traders were growing increasingly resentful. Trade was yet again reorganised and the authority of the government reinforced.

It was a measure of the real strength of the government that the prevailing discontent among townspeople and the suspicion among the highly conservative villagers did not crystallise into any serious opposition. The only danger for Keita came from his immediate assistants and followers, and in 1967, realising that the moderates and the progressives might find common ground in agreeing *against* him, thereby jeopardising the ambitious task he had undertaken, he dissolved the political bureau, replacing it by the Comité National de Défense de la Révolution (CNDR). He reasoned that he could well meet a similar fate to his friend Kwame Nkrumah, and in fact this emergency authority, established in 1966, was reanimated in 1967 and given supreme control over all party and state institutions. He tried to explain his decision by saying that the team in power was insufficiently cohesive and ready to compromise on the strict revolutionary principles of the party. Some political observers analysed his reactions as being a move to the left; it is true that he invited the semi-exiled Seydon Badian Kouyaté, well known as a supporter of Communist China, to rejoin the government, after he had been ignored in the cabinet reshuffle of September 1966. Furthermore, Keita repeatedly declared that the country must at all costs remain Socialist and revolutionary.

His decision was met with expressions of joy—his popularity was unimpaired. The people's resentment centred on the harsh, haughty and sometimes dishonest party officials. They could not tolerate the bourgeois opulence of some of the important officials who, despite the austerity, were rumoured to have free access to government funds. The crowds hailed the dismissals of some of them with great joy—for instance, Dossolo Traoré, Party Treasurer, and Idrissa Diarra, Political Secretary. Most probably Keita had foreseen the new economic difficulties which the financial agreement with France would entail—the very necessary devaluation would lead to reduced salaries and increased prices—and so resolved to get rid of the unpopular elements of his government to make his position yet stronger before he asked for further efforts from the nation. He realised that it was necessary for him to maintain strict control over civil servants and government officials, the sector of the Mali people which would feel most strongly restrictive budgets, for he had seen that elsewhere in Africa they constituted an impatient elite often responsible for crises and for engineering anti-government plots.

Keita expelled those of his party followers who proved unable to sustain their lofty ideals through seven dreary years and those too easily tempted by selfish bourgeois self-gratification. He never flagged, and never gave up fighting for social justice. One of his ambitions was to demonstrate to the world that corruption is not a necessary ingredient of an African government. In Mali, Socialism meant, above all, improved conditions of living for the masses and an idealistic, unselfish government. However, he also tried to keep a balance between a Socialist economic organisation and the requirements of geography. Co-operation with France was the immediate target. In a speech on National Day (September 22, 1967), he reiterated that Mali was striving to apply the financial and monetary agreements signed with France.*

* The text of this chapter was altered in proof as a result of the coup in Mali, in November 1968. For details of the coup, see chapter 11, page 375.

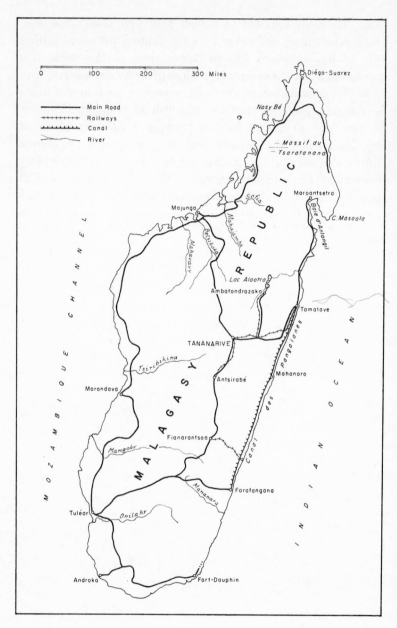

5. Madagascar

9. Madagascar

MADAGASCAR, the great island off the south-east coast of Africa, is in many ways unique among the African countries formerly under French colonial rule. It is regarded by every geography book as part of Africa though separated from it by the 200 mile-wide Mozambique Channel, and its fauna, flora, inhabitants and terrain are all quite distinct. The fifth biggest island in the world (228,000 square miles) seems virtually a continent in its own right, and indeed the geologists believe it is a relic of a continent that once included Australia and the peninsula of India. It is not surprising that Madagascar has developed in isolation from the main currents of French-speaking Africa. Viewed from Madagascar, the problems of continental Africa sometimes seem irrelevant. When, after interracial strife and bloodshed, the tiny island of Zanzibar united with Tanganyika to form the progressive revolutionary state of Tanzania under the rigid rule of Julius Nyerere, Madagascar maintained a careful watch on events; but when a country of French-speaking Equatorial or West Africa turns out its government, Madagascar takes little notice. However, it cannot afford to ignore events in South Africa or in the Portuguese colony of Mozambique.

Madagascar's 6 million inhabitants in an area of 228,000 square miles represent an average population density of just over 26 per square mile, but they are very unevenly distributed. Forty per cent occupy the central plateau, which ranges in height between 2,000 and 6,500 feet, and in which is to be found the capital, Tananarive, and the large city of Fianarantsoa; these form part of the highly-populated area with over 300 inhabitants per square mile. Most of the population of Madagascar is rural, living in small villages and hamlets scattered over the country; only 10 per cent live in the towns, which include, as well as the two inland towns already mentioned, the coastal communities of Tamatave,

Majunga, Tuléar and the military harbour and naval base of Diego-Suarez. The people of Madagascar are a strangely mixed population. The predominant racial type is Asiatic (Indonesian), and there are also a number of African racial groups, most of them to be found on the west coast. There are the Antesaka and Antandroy, coming from the south and south-east; the present Merina, descendants of an inter-breeding between the Hova (the former noblemen); and the Vazimba, the Betsileo, the Tsimihety and Bara, from the high plateaux. An ethnic map of Madagascar would be extremely intricate, for the Malagasy are constantly moving within the island,[1] and because the island, even though it is so isolated, has had a very turbulent history.

More than most of the countries of modern Africa, the Madagascar of today is deeply rooted in its past. Strictly confined as they were by geographical restrictions, the several racial groups fought each other over the centuries. Later, large kingdoms were established, with several tribes and clans gathered under one rule. Eventually, two major rival kingdoms emerged and were continually at war with each other—Sakalava (in the western-central part of Madagascar) and Merina (in the centre). The people of the north dominated and oppressed the weaker peoples of the west coast, and the tribes of the high plateaux sought to assert their authority over the peoples of all the lower-lying areas. In the eighteenth century, Merina thwarted the expansion of its rival and took its capital, the fine city of Majunga, so that at last, long before colonisation, the whole island was united under a powerful Merina monarchy, with the intelligent Hova as a powerful aristocracy. The memory of the great king, Amdrianompomimerina (1787–1810), is still vivid today, as is the traditional distrust shown by the coastal population for the arrogant tribes of the high plateaux. One of the shrewdest moves of the government that came to power with independence was to placate the resentment of the coastal population by giving them important responsibilities.

Portuguese sailors first discovered the island in 1500; then came the Dutch, the English and the French. In the nineteenth century,

English Protestant missions settled side by side with the French Catholic ones. Queen Ranavalova III preferred the former and her education at the London Missionary School of Tananarive led to disagreements with the French general, Galliéni, at the end of last century. Europeans who landed and tried to penetrate the country were harried mostly by Hova warriors, especially under Queen Ranavalova III. Many of the first nationalists under French colonisation were Hova, who, in the dynamic Malagasy newspapers (see chapter 2, page 60), would extol the glorious past of the Merina kingdom and assert the permanence of the Malagasy language and tradition. The Malagasy have often irritated other French-speaking Africans by referring to their great past with its strong traditions.

Madagascar can now boast of ten years of independence, free from major quarrels, acute political problems, tribal bitterness or violent clashes between regions. Perhaps, independent Madagascar has learned from its famous past history of the futility of national strife, or it may be that the sunny self-restrained character of the Malagasy has prevailed. They are, by and large, a very happy people, deeply religious but not fanatical. Catholics and Protestants live happily side by side. None the less they are firmly insistent on their political rights and on freedom from outside interference—characteristics which they displayed during the great rebellion of 1947. While in other African countries leaders are striving to educate their peoples towards the concept of common ideals and interests and to introduce them to the concept of the nation, in Madagascar the people are already well aware that they are unified within one great country.

The peaceful condition of Madagascar is also due in no small measure to the shrewd political leader of the Malagasy: Philibert Tsiranana, formerly representative for Madagascar at the French National Assembly and Vice-President of the Executive Council of Madagascar at the time of the Loi Cadre, has achieved much for a free peaceful Madagascar because he has consistently appealed to his compatriots' pride, good will and love of peace. Shortly after Independence Day—July 26, 1960—when Tsiranana had already been President of the Republic for over a year, he addressed the Malagasy people, asking them to bury all past resentments, and in particular entreating all former parliamentarians who had been exiled since the rebellion of 1947 to return with open and sympathetic minds and to join forces with him rather than oppose him. He asked them to accept independence as a fact and not resent the continuation of French influence over administration and business in Madagascar. This was a subtle stroke, aimed at enlisting the support of some if not all of the former rebels. The three former rebel leaders—Joseph Raseta, Joseph Ravoahangy and Jacques Rabemananjara—had all returned to their country; Tsiranana had personally appealed to the French government to commute their sentences of imprisonment and France had relented. After all, Madagascar had obtained the very independence for which 80,000 people had died only twelve years previously.

Yet foreign journalists and observers attending the Independence Day celebration could not help wondering what sort of a problem such famous rivals would represent for Tsiranana. He was a cautious moderate and his Parti Social Démocrate (PSD) was a former branch of French SFIO,* whereas the most famous of the leaders in exile, Rabemananjara, was a brilliant, sharp, enthusiastic left-wing intellectual, a devout Catholic and a poet (before 1960, he had been, together with Alioune Diop and Léopold Sédar Senghor, one of the promoters of *Présence Africaine*). It seemed unlikely that Rabemananjara would withdraw from the scene and fade away, or that, alternatively, he would join the government party. Would he form a new party?

When he arrived home, 'Rabe' remained loyal to his old party, the Parti de la Rénovation Malgache, which had given its support to the 1947 rebellion. At the legislative elections in September 1960, he stood as candidate for the party on the same list as the party leader, A. Bezaka, the mayor of Tamatave. Both were victorious, and they provided the nucleus of an opposition. The fiery young politician was greatly revered by his compatriots: his

* Tsiranana had been a friend and political protégé of the French Socialist leader from Marseilles, Gaston Defferre.

revolutionary past and his intellectual standing were well-known and respected. He was certainly of the calibre to oppose Tsiranana. But Rabemananjara's actions demonstrated his nobility of character: he accepted that political rivalries would serve only to hamper national development, and he agreed with the President that unity was the major concern. One year after the 1960 elections he decided that his own party would merge with the government party. Now Tsiranana had a great ally in place of a major rival. He had consistently advocated persuasion rather than the forcible assertion of authority and his principles were receiving their reward.

The President was far too wise and gentle, far too typically Malagasy, to impose a 'strong' constitution and establish a one-party system. He knew that he should pay due consideration to regional interests and should avoid damaging tribal pride, especially on the eastern coast. In that respect, it greatly helped that Tsiranana did not belong to the noble Hova, from the high plateaux, but stemmed from an ordinary north-western tribe—in fact, he was the son of a cowherd. The constitution he introduced was of a federal type, with an assembly and a senate, and was designed to take account of local interests.

There still remained several parties in Madagascar, always ready to criticise the President's policy. The Congrès de l'Indépendence de Madagascar (known as the AKFM), which had campaigned for a 'No' vote at the referendum in September 1958, had won an important number of votes but only three seats, as compared with the government party's 75 seats out of 107. It was the only opposition party of any significance, with very varied elements in its ranks: nationalists, Socialists and Communists. Naturally it attacked the government's conservative, pro-French, pro-West line. It advocated a wide scale nationalisation of the Malagasy economy, especially the mines and means of communication. The Rassemblement Chrétien de Madagascar had a moderate platform and many of the two million Catholic Malagasy as its members. It lacked strength and cohesion and its policies were too close to those of the government for it to be any danger. The

Monima (Mouvement National pour l'Indépendance de Madagascar) had separated from AKFM after 1958 in the hope of becoming a third force, together with the Christian party. The Fronts Populaire Malgache (FIPIM), led by Raseta, one of the nationalists exiled in France, recommended a policy of 'positive neutralism', meaning that the country should not be so closely bound to the Western world. The Communist Party had been outlawed in 1949 and illegally re-established in 1960. Its members were mostly very young people. In practice, it supported the AKFM.

The government party, PSD, had one million members and was extremely active and well organised, so that Tsiranana had no fear of this widely-diverse opposition. Like President Senghor in Senegal, he considered that all that was needed was to hold the country with the support of a strong and dominant party. After Rabemananjara's Parti de la Rénovation had come over to it, the government controlled 90 out of the 107 seats in Parliament. Rabemananjara was appointed Minister of Economics and his political ally, Ravoahangy, Minister of Health. When they aligned themselves with Tsiranana's party they had done so on one condition: that a common doctrine should be established, a Malagasy version of Socialism, and that some of their followers should become members of the executive committee of the party.

Thus the only serious opposition to be reckoned with was the AKFM, with its large proportion of Merina from the central province of Tananarive and from the high plateaux. Moreover, political hostility never degenerated into serious clashes and the opposition was content with expressing disapproval in vehement speeches and sharp reproofs in the press.

The PSD now sought to win over new members, by standing as a nation-wide party. The party had at first appealed to the west coast population, whereas the Parti de Rénovation had a majority from the east coast, and AKFM was rather a Merina-Hova party from the central area. Tsiranana's party laid increasing emphasis on overcoming political opposition by patient persuasion and conciliation. It won the legislative elections in August 1963 and also the municipal elections of December 1964 (where it won 598 seats out of 784). At the municipal elections, AKFM, with its strong hold on the centre of the country and Merina clientele, won a majority of seats in Tananarive town council for the simple reason that in the capital the ballot was proportional and not on the basis of a 'scrutin de liste majoritaire'. At the presidential elections in March 1965, Tsiranana was re-elected with 97·77 per cent of the votes. Finally, at legislative elections held in August 1965, the PSD, with 94 per cent of the votes, won 104 seats, and the AKFM, with 4 per cent of the votes, won 3 seats. The regime was unique in French-speaking Africa in having a President, but at the same time strongly emphasising the concept of a Federal Parliament, taking care of the political climate in each of the various localities.

The exceptional stability of government in Madagascar is further emphasised by the prolonged tenures of the major ministerial offices. Such fundamental stability would not be endangered by a two-party system, but this could arise only if the small opposition parties were prepared to join forces with the AKFM. This is unlikely however, since the emphasis on federation in the constitution has encouraged the development of local politics, and the smaller nationally-based parties are anxious to retain their limited but active provincial supporters. Moreover, the AKFM has never been well integrated. There are several independently-minded elements among its very progressive young members, but the leadership is firmly retained by the sedate Protestant minister Andriamanjato. It has never been a nation-wide party, nor has it tried to gain an audience in some of the regions.

When all factors are taken into account (the restriction of the opposition to certain localities, the geographic distribution of the constituencies, and the laws relating to franchise), it becomes clear that the ruling party is in fact the only national party, and, behind the rules of the democratic game, strictly respected by the government, there exists to all intents and purposes a one-party system. The President's congenial personality dominates Malagasy political life. He will plunge into lengthy extempore speeches; he will surprise his audience with telling slogans and racy anecdotes, whether he is addressing an audience of Malagasy peasants

257

or African heads of government. An excellent comedian, he has a direct appeal to any audience. He always sounds indomitably optimistic, in spite of the economic difficulties of his country. He has won people over because he was manifestly too much the common man to overawe them. This happy-go-lucky attitude may well be one of the secrets of his success. Colonial rule had lain somewhat heavily on Madagascar, even at its end. Consequently the new government set up after independence could not afford to be strict and authoritarian. When it was essential to rally together different provinces or different bodies of opinion, Tsiranana never tried to dominate or impose his will. He would joke and cajole, and people of all political colours and from all localities soon came to like him and to put their implicit trust in him.

In his dealings with France Tsiranana was equally flexible and subtle. Madagascar was the second country (after Federal Mali) to seek complete autonomy and to withdraw from the Community after France had 'granted' independence. On April 2, 1960, France and Madagascar reached full agreement. As the former colony's membership of the Community had no strictly constitutional foundation, it merely asked permission to leave. It was prepared to recognise General de Gaulle as the President of the Community, but that was as far as it would go, as it no longer played any part in his election. However, no former colony has remained more loyal and consistently faithful to General de Gaulle. Of its free will, but on the proud basis of an arrangement between equal states, Madagascar chose to remain a close friend of France. It decided to throw in its lot unreservedly with the Western world. It entertained warm neighbourly sentiments for the African continent, but, while maintaining a close interest in the events on the mainland, it took a detached view of them. It was 'likewise eager to arrive at close friendship with the free states of Western Europe'.[2]

Madagascar's political views were entirely its own. The country was aggressively anti-Communist and particularly anti-Chinese. Madagascar wanted to ally itself with Nationalist China, the 'outpost of the free world': 'France may recognise Red China; it may be in its interest, but it is not in ours.' 'There is a danger of political infiltration that France is well able to repel, but which a small, poor, underpopulated state like ours cannot.'³ A trade mission from Soviet Russia was received, but the immediate reaction to the Russians was one of caution: 'We do not know them well enough.'* Of course, from Tsiranana's point of view this policy had its dangers, for the only opposition party that carried any weight, the AKFM, was in contact with Marxist parties throughout the world and was harbouring well-known Communist elements in its midst at home. Tsiranana was clearly concerned about the countless missions and visits of Russians and Chinese all over East Africa. He feared that they were building up armed forces there.

Tsiranana insisted, for the same reason, that he would permit, and even entreat, the French to maintain their forces in the military base of Diego-Suarez. Only the French would be capable of defending Madagascar. Tsiranana's policy is the epitome of an 'aligned policy'. 'We have the courage to say that those who advertise themselves as "non-aligned" are, in fact, as much aligned as the others.' He was most alarmed when France, in 1964, decided to withdraw its troops. Moreover, from an economic point of view, it was a blow: the presence of French troops brought 3,000 million Malagasy francs (1 Malagasy franc = 1 CFA franc) to the Treasury and gave work to a number of Malagasy.

As was the case with Senegal, France remained by far the most important ally, but Madagascar was perfectly ready to maintain friendly relations with any non-Communist country. Naturally, Tsiranana's recognition of the Nationalist Chinese regime recommended him greatly to the United States and a trade agreement was rapidly signed between the two countries. Tsiranana's view that he stood in between Africa and Asia was reflected in the early establishment of contacts with Malaysia, Japan and Australia.

Tsiranana's foreign policy is another manifestation of his

* However, Tsiranana was too sly to keep a negative attitude for long and in 1966 a trade agreement was signed with Russia under the condition that there would be no political implication.

cautious conservatism. The so-called Malagasy Socialism is similar to the 'radical-socialisme' of French domestic politics. 'My Socialism is PSD, scientific and non-doctrinarian. I don't want any of those lazy nationalisations, which are only a way of stealing the neighbour's goods. We shall nationalise in a dynamic way by building factories wherever the private sector proves unable to. We are not rich enough to nationalise. For when you nationalise, you must have plenty of civil servants. Look at Algeria: they have nationalised so much that nothing is working there any more.'[4] It is rather lukewarm and lacking in vision and vigour. However, in its present form it is acceptable to many in Madagascar—both Catholic and Protestant, and in the high plateaux and in the coastal areas—who would not be attracted by more extreme doctrines. The national character of Madagascar is perhaps rather non-chalant and indifferent to everyday problems, which explains why the picture is not all rosy and why the economy is so slack.

In the economic field the government faces a most difficult task. Although the majority of Malagasy are engaged in it, agricultural production accounted for only 40 per cent of the GNP in 1960. The trade balance is adverse and shows no sign of improvement, as these figures (in thousand million Malagasy francs) reveal:

	1962	1963	1964	1965	1966	1967
Exports	23·3	20·3	22·6	22·6	24·1	25·7
Imports	30·0	31·5	33·5	34·2	34·9	35·9

Madagascar exports coffee, sugar, rice, sisal, vanilla (of which it is the largest producer in the world) and meat. Coffee exports fell from 7,400 million Malagasy francs in 1962 to 5,900 million in 1963, but the average annual figure, 1962–66, is estimated to be about 6,800 million. It is likely to reach an 8,000 million ceiling in the years to come. Exports of sugar fell by nearly half over the period 1963–65 (2,200 million Malagasy francs and 1,200 million respectively), because of reduced buying by France. Sales of vanilla have remained steady. Most alarming and complex of all is the rice situation. Rice is the basic staple food of the Malagasy population and, because production has not kept pace with the population boom over the past twelve years, exports of it have fallen. Much of the de luxe quality rice traditionally grown for the export market is now consumed within the country. Exports fell from 58,000 tons in 1958 to 28,000 tons in 1964, with a corresponding disastrous drop in export earnings.

A most ambitious five-year plan was launched for the period 1964–68. Although results are not yet available, the plan made provision for a crash programme of providing enough land to support 300,000 farmers. Rice production is to be increased to give a surplus of 125,000 tons for export in 1973, as well as to feed the expected population of 7,300,000 (6,100,000 in 1966).[5] Although such forecasts might seem somewhat unrealistic, rice imports increased from 33,000 tons in the first six months of 1964 to 66,000 tons for the same period in 1965.

The fall in food production has had a very adverse effect on the economy, for the country has not only to find food for its increasing population, but it has to buy essential materials and capital goods: fertilisers, machinery, vehicles, petrol, etc. The growing deficit is obviously a great source of worry for the government, for it is by no means easy to overcome. The pleasant varied landscape in Madagascar is deceptive: the land is generally poor. The highly intricate structure of land tenure presents a grave problem and the plots are too small to be efficient. There is a need for regional development programmes (such as the one on the banks of Lake Alaotra, north-east of Tananarive), to encourage and advise thousands of farming families with a view to greater efficiency under the leadership of the village headman. A better-organised system of agricultural credit would also assist development.

The government is trying to develop cattle breeding for the country has the potential to sustain much higher exports of meat. The fishing industry is another possible line of development. Efforts could be made to improve the beautiful Malagasy forests that, over the past century, have been damaged by bush fires— the result of sheer laziness; young trees are now being replanted, and the plan makes provision for the development of a national pulp and paper industry.

In 1968 it seemed that the production of rice was increasing and sales of coffee were growing. Exports (22,600 million Malagasy francs in 1965; 25,700 million in 1967) have risen more than imports and the deficit in the trade balance is slightly smaller. But the gross national product has hardly changed and is still disturbingly low, around $93–95 per capita in the period between 1962 and 1966.

It is most essential for Madagascar to reduce its trade gap and to increase its food production, but efforts in this direction have been discouraged by, for instance, the very low returns on investments, both public and private, in the production of rice.

On the whole this large and beautiful island has few resources. Unlike most French-speaking African countries, it has hardly any mineral resources, other than graphite and mica. However, Madagascar could develop the chrome deposits at Andriamena, where there are good prospects: 120,000 tons per year could be produced initially, rising to 200,000 tons per year. With its central high plateaux, it has great potential for hydro-electric development though, as yet, only part of this is being exploited: the total output today is no more than 80 million KW as compared with a potential 80,000 million KW. There is also the possibility of developing a bauxite mine to produce and export alumina, in the south at Mandare. The people of Madagascar are intelligent and they have access to plenty of external assistance. There is no real reason for the present economic stagnation. Perhaps the climate is too evenly warm, and life too easy. Great civilisations may once have flourished here, but for modern life more vigour and more sustained efforts are needed.

President Tsiranana has tried his best to bring the country to the point of economic take-off, but he is faced by an increase in population that negates what little economic progress is made. He has taken upon himself the burden of goading on his compatriots; but he might well weary for, though he is only 55, his health may have been impaired by those ten strenuous years. Who could replace him? Where is there to be found as shrewd and as determined a man? Among some of the former exiles, with their immense popularity and commendable self-restraint, such as Rabemananjara, or the strong, clever Minister of the Interior, André Resampa? Whoever it is may be more efficient in steering the course of the great island, but it is doubtful whether he will do it with as much good humour and patience as Philibert Tsiranana.

Part Three

Final Clarifications and Conclusions

10. Inter-African and International Relations

THIS RAPID survey of the evolution of the fifteen countries which make up French-speaking Africa has left two series of problems still to be dealt with—the role played by these countries in international affairs of both direct and indirect concern to the African continent; and the economic realities and current political trends of the area in the light of the military coups which have upset power in French-speaking Africa (to be discussed in the next chapter).

On gaining their independence, the countries of French-speaking Africa felt it essential that they play their part on the international stage as quickly as possible, and this led them to place an undue emphasis on diplomatic affairs. Even so, although the suddenness with which they acted resulted in considerable disorganisation in the establishment of their diplomatic service, the French-speaking African countries were, by and large, quite effective, since they were able to draw on substantial previous experience.

As early as 1946, African politicians, elected to the French Parliament either as MPs or Senators, were attending the debates on foreign policy: they had learnt how to get information, they had talked with French colleagues and with foreign diplomats, they had learned to weigh the evidence and form their own balanced judgments. Men like Touré, Senghor, Houphouet-Boigny, Tsiranana and Aubame were by no means novices in the international field when they became ministers, premiers or heads of state. It had been in France's obvious interest to prepare the way for them: this was clearly a means of continuing to exert influence over them, or at any rate of seeing that their minds worked in the same way as the French. Between 1958 and 1960, when they were still part of the Community, most of the African states passed through a 'pre-diplomatic' stage of evolution in

267

which they were already self-governing countries.[1] During this transitional stage, the Quai d'Orsay, though still responsible for the external relations of the new states, showed itself very willing to help them to set up their future diplomatic services.

With the help of diplomatic advisers sent by France to work side-by-side with them, the heads of state and political leaders were familiarised with international affairs. It was these men who in 1960 played a discreet back-stage role in setting up the mechanisms for the administration of foreign affairs. This was a vast task, and one vitally important to the African states, for, as soon as they gained their independence, they immediately became involved in international affairs. Further, African delegates were often included in delegations of the French Republic and the Community—that is how they were designated—to various international organisations. Thus, the French delegation to the General Assembly of the United Nations was led by Houphouet-Boigny, to the Trusteeship Council by Senghor, and to the UN Economic Commission for Africa by Gabriel Lisette. The two years of transition from autonomy to full independence gave the new states the opportunity to adapt themselves to the international scene without excessive confusion.

It was an intoxicating experience for the new states to find themselves on the international stage, able to express their views in the highest of councils as between power and power on a basis of equality. No longer did they need to lean on France. The isolation from the rest of the world which went with their membership of the Community was a thing of the past. They were free to treat with any country they chose—no longer only with France—and they took advantage of the new situation, while never forgetting the strong bonds still existing between the former mother country and themselves.

INTER-STATE RELATIONS

Before independence, France maintained a centralised co-ordinated control over the territories which constituted the

Federations of West Africa and Equatorial Africa: these territories were in contact with each other but only through the medium of the French administration. However, as soon as African political parties were authorised within the French Union, direct 'across the board' relationships developed, notably as a result of the activities of the RDA and its local sections within the two federations. Similarly, but of less importance, the Mouvement Socialiste Africain (MSA) became established in several African countries. From the outset, political action had been fully co-ordinated, and herein lies the key to the great success that the RDA achieved. As soon as the new states gained their independence they found themselves subject to external pressures which led them to set up their own individual one-party systems. Under these circumstances it is not surprising that novel relationships came to be established between states that had had no history of their own under colonial rule and discovered their true identity almost overnight.

Congo-Brazzaville had no reason to quarrel with any of its neighbours except, of course, Congo-Léopoldville (see below pages 282–4). But an unfortunate incident at a football match between Gabon and Congo in September 1962 led to a 'Gabonese hunt' in Brazzaville and Pointe Noire that ended with the expulsion of 2,700 Congolese from Gabon. It was an absurd episode that led to mediation by the Central African Republic between Léon M'Ba and Fulbert Youlou and a round table meeting of the Equatorial African states in Yaoundé.

The *Central African Republic* was equally troubled by the prolonged crisis in Congo-Léopoldville and, further, suffered from its proximity to the rebellious areas of Southern Sudan, which led to an influx of refugees and created a climate of tension that it could well have done without.

Chad found itself confronted with a yet more delicate problem. The Muslim opposition was sustained by the moral support of Cairo, and, from time to time, by practical support from Sudan, in the form of armed incursions into the eastern part of the country, notably in the province of Ouadaï, which were particularly embarrassing to Chad.

Cameroun always enjoyed the best of relations with its French-speaking neighbours. On the other hand it had difficulties with Nigeria as a result of the referendum held in the Southern and Northern parts of former British Cameroons. In addition, and independently of this, the rebel party, the UPC, obtained support and practical resources from the border areas between the two parts of Cameroun. Furthermore, Cameroun incurred the hostility of Ghana and of Guinea, where Félix Moumié, the leader of the UPC, had sought refuge. When the Nigerian civil war broke out, Cameroun, though on Biafra's frontier, sided with the Federal government, despite French policy and the recognition of Biafra by Gabon and the Ivory Coast.

Niger was at variance with Mali, which had sheltered the exiled rebel Djibo Bakary. It also quarrelled with Dahomey over the unfortunate little island of Lété in the middle of the river Niger. Throughout Nkrumah's reign, Ghana was Hamani Diori's bête noire. Djibo Bakary's followers were always welcomed in Ghana and received both moral and material support. By contrast, Niger enjoyed excellent relations with its neighbour Upper Volta.

As a consequence of the flow of Mossi migrant labour, *Upper Volta's* relations with Ghana were always especially close. In 1961, notwithstanding the Conseil de l'Entente, Maurice Yameogo approached Nkrumah, and a trade agreement and customs union were contemplated between the two countries; however, Upper Volta, pressed by its fellow-members of the Entente, did not pursue the matter. On the contrary, Ghana was accused by Upper Volta of wanting to annex part of its territory. This dispute was resolved in 1965 by the Organisation of African Unity, and in June 1966, after the fall of Nkrumah, the problem of the disputed border was settled on the basis of the old agreement of 1893 between France and the United Kingdom.

Togo had no cause for disagreement with its neighbour Dahomey, but the Ewe controversy led to a bitter dispute with Ghana that has not yet been concluded. This entire problem is a typical example of a problem created and perpetuated by the actions of the former colonial powers.

The *Ivory Coast* must necessarily keep on the best of terms with Upper Volta as the large migrations of Mossi labour make the two countries closely interdependent. But it soon fell out with Guinea, and, apart from a few intermissions, the two countries have remained bitter enemies. The root of the quarrel lay in the fact that Guinea had challenged the whole of French-speaking Africa by taking a stand against neo-colonialism, whereas the Ivory Coast was a shining example of successful and beneficial economic co-operation with the former colonial power. The Ivory Coast, moreover, was giving shelter to a growing group of exiled Guineans, embittered by the economic failure of their country. In February 1967, Guinea held an Ivory Coast trawler off the coast of Guinea under the pretext that its crew were planning to kidnap Kwame Nkrumah. This was followed by the arrest and detention of several Guineans in Abidjan (including Louis-Lansana Beavogui, the Minister for Foreign Affairs) who were merely stopping over at Abidjan airport during a regular flight. The incident demonstrates that the two countries have never tried seriously to resolve their differences, and reveals peculiar ideas on the rules of diplomacy. It took several months for the dispute to be settled by the two countries.

Guinea also nursed resentment against Senegal, which harboured numerous Guinean exiles. Guinea gave its support to the anti-Portuguese insurrection in Portuguese Guinea, all the more readily since a small 'maquis' unit of the outlawed Senegalese opposition party, the PAI, was operating in the Senegalese border area of Casamance. So long as Nkrumah remained in power, Mali and Ghana were Guinea's only friends in the region.

Senegal has had its differences with Mali, but relations between them are now good. Currently it has no major problem with Mauritania, except perhaps for Senegal's tendency to support the black peoples of the river area against the Arab majority.

Mauritania's serious disagreements with its neighbour Morocco have already been discussed (see chapter 7) and, in spite of its gradual dissociation from Black Africa, Mauritania has not yet resolved these difficulties: Morocco still persists with its claims.

Mali has been shrewd enough to maintain good relations with all its neighbours, after an initial period of difficulty with them. It avoided causing offence even to Algeria, in spite of some disturbances among the nomads, and signed an agreement with Mauritania over their common frontier following a meeting in February 1965 in Kayes between Modibo Keita and Mokhtar Ould Daddah.

Finally *Madagascar*, being an island, had no border problems to contend with.

The colonial powers had bequeathed the most irrational frontiers that took virtually no account of ethnic, geographical or historical considerations and yet, greatly to their credit, the young African states accepted, in the main, the existing boundaries. A more important cause of dissent arose when domestic political differences led exiled political minority movements to seek asylum in neighbouring states, where, in some cases (notably in Ghana and Guinea), they were warmly welcomed. These exiled opposition groups soon became the cause of rupture in French-speaking Africa; this was exacerbated by their differing attitude to the Congo crisis, and eventually French-speaking Africa split into two distinct groups.

The Groups

The African states sought such a realignment, partly as a defence measure against the opposition elements in exile, supported as these were by powers outside Black Africa; and also because they had come to realise that they should all stand together—more especially since most of them remained members of the French franc area. Historical considerations encouraged them to continue the inter-relationships established in the days of colonialism. They had now come to realise how far the Loi Cadre of 1956 had led them astray in allowing each little territory its own local national assembly and government. Of course, the opinions of the political leaders of Africa differed, but a federation or confederation, or any kind of regional regrouping of territories, would at the very least have restrained the proliferation of administrative and technical services, of local universities, of embassies, of all the costly paraphernalia of independence which bore so heavily on the economy of each country. What savings the treasuries of the African states could have effected if only the balkanisation of the two colonial federations had been restrained!

Hence, with the precedent of the former Community before them, the French-speaking African states again sought and demanded the setting up of some communal organisation between them, even after the failure of the 'renewed' Community. Guinea, also, after it had broken with France and become isolated, was anxious to align itself with friendly states; it joined up once again with Ghana, setting up the Ghana-Guinea Union in 1959 (which Mali later joined in 1961), though this was never more than an administrative fiction.

The former French African colonies (apart from Soudan—now Mali—and Guinea) linked themselves together by gradual stages, starting at the regional level, as instanced by the Union Douanière Equatoriale and the Conseil de l'Entente. In October 1960 a conference was held at Abidjan at which eleven states were represented. Madagascar was absent, as it had not yet decided to abandon its policy of insularity. However, it took part in the Brazzaville Conference in December 1960, which led to the establishment of the 'Brazzaville group' and the decision to explore the prospects for economic collaboration. The Dakar Conference, which was held between January 30 and February 4, 1961, led to the setting up of the Organisation Africaine et Malgache de Coopération Economique (OAMCE). Its legal existence was established in March 1961 at Yaoundé, which became the headquarters of the new organisation. Finally, the Tananarive Conference in September 1961 established an administrative structure through the Union Africaine et Malgache (UAM) and the Union Africaine et Malgache de Défense. This consolidated the political policy of the group, particularly regarding foreign affairs.

Meanwhile, the Casablanca group was also taking shape. It was oriented much more specifically towards political matters. It

273

extended beyond the limits of Black Africa in the strict sense, and its aims were specifically Pan-African. It differed from the UAM in that economic considerations were subordinate to the political. The countries that sent representatives to Casablanca from January 4 to 7, 1961 (Ghana, Guinea, Mali, UAR, Morocco, Algerian GPRA and Libya), agreed with Morocco on the Mauritanian affair, and were ready to support the provisional Algerian government in exile and Patrice Lumumba in the Congo. The Casablanca Charter provided for the establishment of an African consultative assembly, an African high command and several standing committees: first political; and, at a later stage, economic and cultural.

Rather than attempt an analysis of the attitudes and motivations of these two groups, which has been undertaken in several works dealing with African unity and Pan-Africanism,[2] an account will be given here of the differences between them. The question of Mauritania has already been mentioned—admittedly very briefly —in chapter 7, but it was above all over the Algerian and Congolese questions that the two groups came into direct opposition.

The Algerian Crisis*

The Algerian affair was a source of great embarrassment to the African leaders. The Algerian cause—a claim to autonomy and independence, and to recognition of their rights, their liberty and the integrity of their territory—was the same as that of the Black Africans. Yet the same France that in 1955–56 had shown itself most ready to relinquish its hold on the African 'Territoires d'Outre-Mer', resolved firmly to retain its control of Algeria. The Loi Cadre for Black Africa of Gaston Defferre coincided with the 'hard', 'Socialist' stage of French policy in Algeria introduced by

* There were several debates at the UN on Algeria and it was included on the agenda of the General Assembly, in spite of French opposition, in September 1955. Basing themselves on Article 2, Paragraph 7, of the UN Charter, the French delegation considered the question as *ultra vires* and refused to attend the debates.

Guy Mollet. At this time the leaders of Africa, in their role as MPS and Senators in France, were taking part in debates on the Algerian problem. Houphouet-Boigny and Modibo Keita were members of several French cabinets between 1956 and 1958. The French delegations to the United Nations included Africans: from 1958 onward they attended the meetings of specialist institutions such as the FAO, WHO and ILO as observers or as associate members, and in this way came into contact with delegates from those Afro-Asian countries which enjoyed full membership. The Algerian problem was thus brought squarely before them and they clearly had to come to a decision on it. How did they react?

Clearly the Algerian affair had fewer repercussions and roused fewer strong feelings in Black Africa than in France—at least, in the early stages, and this in spite of the fact that African troops, Guineans and Senegalese among others, were in action with the French army, exactly as they had been in Indochina. The leaders of African opinion were readily bemused and converted to the views expressed by French propaganda; the French must remain in Algeria, a French territory, in the name of liberalism and of the struggle for a free world. However, the reactions of the European circles to the events of May 13, 1958 (see pages 15–16) were a different matter. De Gaulle's return to power, his determination to grant the Black African countries, first, internal autonomy, and then full independence, encouraged Africans to take a detailed interest in their own affairs and to leave the Algerian problem to Paris to look after. During the years 1958–60, anyone in Parisian business and military circles who was convinced that the Algerians had a right to independence did well to keep his views to himself if he did not want to be branded as an extreme radical, a traitor or a Communist. On the other hand the African elite—the leaders, the political parties, the trade unions—were soon to be compelled by the force of events to align themselves with one side or the other.

In Guinea (and also in Mali after its split with Senegal) the choice seemed obvious and simple: the war must cease; Algeria must become independent; France should recognise the GPRA at once. Should France not wish to negotiate with the GPRA, the United Nations should compel it to do so by organising a referendum, as in Togo and Cameroun. Guinea aligned itself unreservedly with countries such as Ghana, UAR, Tunisia and Morocco which took a hard anti-imperialist line. Immediately on gaining independence, Guinea recognised the GPRA, and withdrew its troops who had been fighting with the French in Algeria. Its view was typical of all the members of the Casablanca group.

Madagascar saw the problem equally clearly, but its conclusion was quite the reverse of Guinea's. On no account would it interfere in French internal affairs: Article 2, Paragraph 7, of the United Nations Charter would be strictly adhered to. The Malagasy attitude was an extreme manifestation of what was 'neo-colonialism' to the Brazzaville group.

The remaining countries of the Community were confronted with a particularly delicate situation in the years 1958–60. It is significant that at the All-African Peoples' Conference held at Accra in December 1958, which was attended by party and union leaders from all Africa, the representatives of the French-speaking group did their utmost to avoid any resolution that might cause offence to France, particularly references to the war in Algeria and indictments of French imperialism. They tried to emphasise concepts such as independence and African unity rather than mount any direct attack on France.[3] At the same time the speeches of the African leaders showed that, thanks to the inside knowledge of French political opinion they had gained from the meetings of the Executive Council of the Community, they did not doubt that France would ultimately grant Algeria its independence. The terrorist attacks of the OAS in Algeria, and the attempts on de Gaulle's life, reinforced their support for France, because they realised that a stable French government was essential not only to the well-being of France itself and for an end to the Algerian war, but was also an essential pre-requisite of their own stability.

All the member-states of the Community (apart from Madagascar, for reasons which have already been explained) met at Abidjan from October 24 to 26, 1960, to discuss the Algerian problem.* This meeting was undoubtedly a rejoinder to that held in August 1959 in Monrovia, at which the members of the Casablanca group joined four non-aligned countries—Ethiopia, Liberia, Sudan and Tunisia—to discuss the Algerian war. They had received a delegation from the GPRA, thereby recognising the legality of the Algerian government in exile. The Abidjan conference was a necessary measure, for a United Nations session was about to open, the first at which fourteen French-speaking African countries were to appear in force as full members, and it was necessary for their leaders to be fully informed on the matter and prepare public opinion in their own countries to accept their own views on the causes and consequences of the war. In spite of Madagascar's absence, the meeting was a success. It recommended that the French-speaking African countries should present a unanimous viewpoint at the UN and should be represented by only a few speakers—a course which was adopted at the 15th session of the UN in 1960.

Soon after the Abidjan meeting, Mamadou Dia and Hamani Diori went to Tunis to meet President Bourguiba of Tunisia and Ferhat Abbas, President of the GPRA; and Léopold Senghor and Houphouet-Boigny went to Paris to meet General de Gaulle. The object of these meetings was to see the way the wind was blowing; and, while not proposing themselves as mediators, the African leaders offered to assist any negotiations between France and Algeria in the absence of intervention from the United Nations.

While offers of this kind stemming from the French-speaking African countries did not have much real effect, they were not without some significance. They showed the French government quite clearly that French-speaking Africa had reached 'the point of no return'; they had admitted the GPRA without formally recognising it; they had expressed their concern over France's ambiguous attitude to the war (secret missions, but at the same time intensification of hostilities—though the latter, it is true, was largely initiated by the army). They were coming to realise that the liberal policies from which they themselves had benefited were

* Two other questions were on the agenda: Congo and Mauritania.

not being applied to others. They wished for peace and for the recognition of the right of Algeria to independence, and they called on France to fall in with their views. This, then, was the spirit they brought to the United Nations.

It is unnecessary to go over all the details of the development of the Algerian affair at the United Nations; the positions taken by the African delegates, in the light of the considerations outlined above, are our chief concern. The most important sessions of the General Assembly were that of 1960 and, to a lesser degree, that of 1961. From an African point of view the earlier sessions of 1958 and 1959 were of less interest.

The 1960 session began in complete confusion over the intentions of the French government, which did not attend. The discussion soon became very heated as the views of the Afro-Asian bloc clashed with the more moderate attitude of the French-speaking African countries. This was the least cheerful aspect of the exchanges in Commission 1 (the political commission) where Mongi Slim of Tunisia and Ismaël Touré (the brother of Sékou Touré) came into violent conflict with the spokesman of the French-speaking African countries, Gabriel d'Arboussier, Senegal's Minister of Justice. In fact their differences were an argument between deaf men. The Afro-Asian group could not understand why every African state excepting Guinea and Mali stressed their friendship with France and thereby 'betrayed the cause of Algeria'. Nevertheless, the delegation to Ferhat Abbas, even though it had not culminated in an explicit public declaration of the African leaders' position, had showed that French-speaking Africa wished the GPRA well. As Senghor explained in the preface to an official pamphlet of the Senegalese government, published just after the UN session,[4] the moderate African states were unable to agree with the GPRA's demand for a referendum to be conducted by the United Nations.

A resolution was put forward which asserted Algeria's right to self-determination and independence, but at the same time proposing, in Paragraph 4 of the resolution, that a referendum be organised under the supervision of the United Nations. The voting was as follows: *For:* 47, including Guinea, Ghana, Liberia, Mali, Morocco, Nigeria, Togo and Tunisia; *Against:* 20; *Abstentions:* 28, including all other countries of Black Africa (and Congo-Léopoldville).[5] All the French-speaking states acceded to that part of the resolution which affirmed Algeria's right to independence, but refused to subscribe to Paragraph 4 when it was made the subject of a separate ballot: *For:* 38, including Ghana, Guinea, Liberia, Mali, Morocco, Nigeria, Togo and Tunisia: *Against:* 33, including Senegal, Central African Republic, Congo–Brazzaville, Gabon, Ivory Coast and Niger; *Abstentions:* 23, including Upper Volta, Cameroun, Chad, Madagascar, and Dahomey.

Voting was not consistent. They would perhaps have done better to follow Senegal's lead, but instead they vacillated, either for fear of committing themselves or for want of clear instructions. Madagascar's attitude is not surprising—if it were to remain faithful to the line it adopted after the Abidjan conference, it had to abstain from every poll.

One thing that is clear from these proceedings is that the African delegations recognised an independent Algeria before France did so. To quote Mamadou Dia, speaking in 1960 in New York, 'we are all in favour of an independent republic of Algeria obeying the rule of the majority and respecting the rights of the minority'— that is, of the European population. It is certainly true that the African governments avoided hurting de Gaulle's susceptibilities and did not adopt an overtly anti-French position. On December 19, 1960, following the UN assembly, the French-speaking states meeting at Brazzaville reasserted their unwillingness to adopt the facile and unconstructive solution 'of relying on the UN organising and controlling the referendum'. They paid tribute to de Gaulle and affirmed their faith in the concept of decolonisation, maintaining that the only hope of bringing the war to an end was through direct negotiations and 'the honest and democratic application of the principle of self-determination, as had been solemnly proclaimed by General de Gaulle'.

In 1961 negotiations between France and the GPRA seemed to

be making good progress, particularly after de Gaulle's recognition, in his speech of September 5, that the Sahara was an integral part of Algeria. Consequently, the tone at the 16th session of the United Nations was less antagonistic, and augured well for an early end to the fighting. This time the spokesman for French-speaking Africa was Arsène Usher of the Ivory Coast, who loudly praised de Gaulle as 'a man true to his words, a man of sincerity and good faith, the man of Brazzaville', and this viewpoint was endorsed by Houphouet-Boigny at the end of the session. He reaffirmed African support for the French policy of direct negotiation without the participation of the United Nations, saying: 'Because we sincerely love all our Algerian brothers, those who are fighting and those who are not taking part in the fighting, because we understand them, because we also love the people of France, we consider that we have no right to be content with facile positions which are but cowardly solace; on the contrary we believe that we must continue without flagging to exhort both sides, especially France, to do everything possible to achieve Algerian self-determination in 1961 at the latest.'

The Crisis in Congo-Léopoldville

Though they did not participate in the debates of the Security Council in July 1960—those following the mutiny of the Congolese Force Publique, the violence in the Lower Congo and the desperate, useless flight of the Belgian population—it was nevertheless inevitable that the countries of French-speaking Africa should become involved in the long drawn out Congolese crisis. At first, however, it was only the independent states which reacted to the Congolese affair, for in mid-1960 the renewed Community was still in process of evolution and its members had not yet become fully independent. Ghana, Guinea, Ethiopia, Liberia, Nigeria, Morocco and Tunisia all sent contingents which went to constitute the famous 'blue helmet' force of the United Nations, and strove to prevent the spread of anarchy and chaos across the entire former Belgian colony, especially after the secession of Katanga on

July 11, 1960, and the subsequent secession of Kasai, another mining state rich in diamonds, where the Congolese leader Kalonji had set up a puppet kingdom.

Guinea followed in the footsteps of Ghana which had thrown itself headlong into the battle to the defence of Patrice Lumumba, the leader of the Mouvement Nationaliste du Congo (MNC). Lumumba had met Kwame Nkrumah and Sékou Touré at the All-African People's Conference at Accra in December 1958. They were attracted to Lumumba: his revolutionary fervour was clear to all, he bubbled over with energy and enthusiasm, he was bent upon leading his country to complete independence without any distraction from any local peculiarities which would militate against his concept of federalism, he would not countenance the separatist policies followed in the Lower Congo and in Katanga. It is necessary to recall here that Patrice Lumumba had come to power as the result of a compromise. His party, the MNC, which stood for a unitarian state, had won the elections over several parties including the party of Joseph Kasavubu, who wanted a federal Congo. In order to retain some of their authority beyond independence, the Belgians had supported the unitarian party and suggested, as a compromise, that Kasavuba should become head of state with Lumumba as Premier. Lumumba's determination to subdue all the reactionary economic interests in the Congo was particularly attractive to Nkrumah and Sékou Touré, and they looked on him as a true brother. Nkrumah went as far as contemplating the incorporation of the Congo, once it had gained independence, into the Ghana-Guinea Union.[6]

Ghana's view was that the Congolese affair should provide a demonstration of the solidarity of African states in their support of a brother state. Nkrumah saw this as an ideal opportunity for him to put his Pan-African principles into practice. It was he who took all the initiative in encouraging active African participation in the UN operation in the Congo and he was faithfully followed by Sékou Touré, who to the end remained 'the most Lumumbist of Lumumbists' in the cause of a united and revolutionary Africa. A quotation from Frantz Fanon, included in an article in a special issue of *Le Mois en Afrique* in April 1966 on Congo-Léopoldville, epitomises the Casablanca doctrine: 'Let us not forget: it is our own fate which is at stake in the Congo'[7]—that is to say, the fate of Ghana, Guinea, Mali, UAR and the still colonial Algeria. To Fanon the evolution of Congo-Léopoldville was intimately related to that of all revolutionary Africa. But the situation and the subsequent course of events were so absurd that revolutionary Africa was helpless to protect Lumumba—in spite of, or because of, the 'blue helmets'; in spite of, or because of, the United Nations, which was clearly unable to prevent General Mobutu's first coup d'état which replaced the government team by a group of intelligent, ambitious, but highly inexperienced young intellectuals, the Collège des Commissaires.

In fact the die was already cast when Lumumba organised the Pan-African Conference of August 1960. Its purpose was not to achieve African unity, but to consolidate Lumumba's position in the face of the United Nations. Lumumba was trying every trick he knew, and was threatening to invoke the aid of the Soviet Union in fighting the secession of Katanga. All the independent states of Africa, including all the French-speaking countries, were invited to this conference. Only Cameroun, Togo, Ghana, Guinea, Morocco and Tunisia accepted the invitation; Sékou Touré and Nkrumah themselves did not attend. Guinea alone declared itself ready to send Lumumba some military assistance against Katanga.[8] Patrice Lumumba was already isolated and lost.

In many ways Congo–Brazzaville's attitude typified that of moderate Africa as compared with that of revolutionary Africa. As early as 1957–60, when the first steps were being taken towards the decolonisation of the Belgian Congo, Congo–Brazzaville had lent its support to Joseph Kasavubu, the leader of the Association des Bas Congo (Abako). The ethnic groups on either side of the river were closely related. Fulbert Youlou regarded Kasavubu as a cousin and had welcomed him and his family when the first differences arose between Abako and the Belgian colonial administration. During the years 1958–60 Youlou regularly sent Christian Jayle, his political counsellor and Minister of Information, to

Léopoldville, to impress upon Kasavubu that prudence and moderation were essential in his dealings with Belgium. But Youlou was not acting in good faith. He had no wish for the Belgian Congo to become independent before his own country. On the contrary: for a time he had his own thoughts of territorial aggrandisement and contemplated the re-establishment of the old Kingdom of the Lower Congo of the sixteenth century. It is, indeed, not inconceivable that Youlou and Kasavubu contemplated the idea of a confederation of the Lower Congo and the Middle Congo—i.e., the North and South banks of the river. Between them, these two regions contained the greatest potential for the development of electrical power in the whole of Africa, with the projects for the industrial complexes of Inga in the Belgian Congo and of Kouilou in the former French Congo. But these were pious hopes. The news of a compromise between Kasavubu's Abako and Lumumba's MNC came as a severe blow to Youlou and stirred him to irrational hatred of Communism. Thereafter he became the champion of the reactionary, anti-Communist, anti-revolutionary sentiment which characterised the evolution of Congo–Brazzaville during the years 1958–61.

During the political strife in Léopoldville during July and August, Youlou made available his own national station, Radio Congo (and not Radio Brazzaville, a French station, as was alleged), to spokesmen of Kasavubu, who denounced the hysterical proclamations of Lumumba and his lieutenant Gizenga, the influence of Russia and Czechoslovakia and 'the dangerous pseudo-revolutionary Marxist clique which had gathered around Lumumba and his henchman'.

With Kasavubu proving incapable of leading the country, and notwithstanding Lumumba's steady drift towards isolation, Congo–Brazzaville soon abandoned its brethren on the other river bank and directed its affections towards Katanga and Moise Tshombe. This sudden change might have been discreetly suggested to Fulbert Youlou by his advisers (particularly Delarue, a French right-winger), who suggested that Youlou align himself with Tshombe, maintaining that he, more than any other African

politician, was fighting for 'a free world and Catholicism'.*
Besides, Katanga was rich and Youlou and his advisers thought
they might reap a material reward for supporting the leader of
the Katangese secession. In particular, Youlou hoped that, in
return for his support, Katanga might finance the Kouilou dam
project.

The attitude of Congo–Brazzaville was not adopted by all the
countries of moderate French-speaking Africa. They were more
cautious and circumspect. Apart from Congo-Brazzaville, which
had the problem of the Congo on its doorstep, the countries of the
Community had no need to commit themselves. In July 1960,
none of them was a member of the Security Council, and only
Cameroun was a member of the United Nations. It was not until
the 15th session, in November 1960, that they took up an official
position on the matter.

At the time, the Community was organised in such a way that
France still dealt with external political affairs, and the French
government had advised prudence and caution, at least in the early
months of the affair. France first took the side of Belgium when it
was accused by the Soviet Union of having sabotaged Congolese
independence and fomented a 'colonialist plot' by encouraging the
Katanga rebellion. 'A ridiculous charge', declared the French
representative at the United Nations, Armand Bérard, and he was
supported by the United States and the United Kingdom. In
accordance with Article 2, Paragraph 7, of the Charter, France
refused to interfere with the domestic problems of the Congo,
assuming that the United Nations was incapable of resolving the
Congolese problem and that only the Congolese themselves could
and should resolve their own problems. This was the darkest,

* It is appropriate to mention here that, after the Katangese secession,
Tshombe was also surrounded by French 'ultras' who had left their
country in disgust over political developments in France and Algeria:
men like Colonel Trinquier and, later, Major Faulques. Tshombe's
mercenaries included many French soldiers, a number of them fugitives
from Algeria and former members of the OAS, who had committed acts of
terrorism in France and Algeria and were guilty of subversion against the
French state.

most strained period of the difficult relations between de Gaulle and the United Nations ('la période du "Machin" '), when France found itself voting with the Soviet Union against the resolution of September 20, 1960, which asked member states to pay a special contribution to the UN Fund for the Congo. France was, in fact, denying the right of the United Nations to take action—a position explained by France's own situation in relation to the war in Algeria.

The Brazzaville group was naturally influenced by the French policy, but, apart from Congo–Brazzaville, they did not react strongly. They deplored the events in Léopoldville, were gratified that troubles of that kind had not arisen with themselves and congratulated themselves over the wise policy of decolonisation adopted by France. They refused to attend the Pan-African Conference at Léopoldville. They deplored Lumumba's extravagant utterances and his megalomania. They feared that his overtures to the Soviet Union would lead to international problems that Africa would come to regret. Men of experience like Houphouet-Boigny and Senghor could not fail to be seriously worried by the unfolding of events and the deterioration of the political situation.

The first official action taken by the states of the Community was at the Abidjan meeting of October 1960, which has already been mentioned in connection with the Algerian problem. The question of the Congo appeared on the agenda, but only as a relatively unimportant matter: the main topics of discussion were the recognition of independent Mauritania and the question of peace in Algeria. They still remained uncommitted over the Congo, still making some show of neutrality and vacillating—perhaps because the delegation from Congo–Brazzaville included a representative from Katanga.

By contrast they took a more courageous stand at the Brazzaville Conference, at which Kasavubu, Tshombe and Kalonji were present as observers. A solution strictly African in character was advocated, an improved version of the earlier French proposals—that the conflicting political factions of Congo–Léopoldville should meet and by themselves arrive at a solution, without interference from any other power or from the United Nations.

> The undersigned States and Madagascar salute the effort under-taken by UNO to save the Congo (Léopoldville) from chaos and anarchy. . . . Unfortunately the rival blocs have tried and are still trying to recolonise the Congo (Léopoldville) either directly or indirectly through the intermediary of certain Asiatic and African states. . . . The real independence of the Congo (Léopoldville) needs, without doubt, UNO continuing to bring its technical assistance, but UNO is not required to [act as a] substitute for the Congolese authorities. Above all, what is required in the Congo (Léopoldville) is that no other state intervenes in its domestic affairs through the intermediary of soldiers or diplomats. The practical solution of the Congolese problem can only be found at a Round Table Conference, which would group together the representatives of every party without exception.[9]

This implied recognition of the legality of Kasavubu's govern-ment; even if this legality were in doubt, the government was certainly carrying out its current business. Previously, in Novem-ber 1960, the UN debate on the recognition of the Kasavubu delegation sent to the United Nations had turned on identically the same point and the moderate African bloc had then strongly supported the Abako leader. This support from the moderates, who included a large part of the French-speaking group, was most welcome and timely for Kasavubu, who was greatly agitated by news of the establishment in Stanleyville of a revolutionary government set up in the name of the imprisoned Patrice Lumumba by his lieutenant Gizenga. Congo–Léopoldville was more than ever torn asunder and in the throes of crisis.

As a result of the recommendations of the Brazzaville Confer-ence, a round table conference met in Tananarive in March 1961. All the Congolese leaders were to have attended, but in the mean-time Patrice Lumumba had been murdered, in early 1961, and Gizenga boycotted it. Nothing very startling emerged from the conference, but it was a success for Tshombe, who became 'interlocuteur valable', and who was to head the Congolese government in 1964–65, after Adoula had held the office for a period. The moderates of French-speaking Africa, now known as the states of the OCAM (see below, page 293), sought to encourage Congo–Léopoldville to join them, hoping that association with them would give it the opportunity, at last, of embarking on a phase of normal, undisturbed evolution. They were encouraged in this approach by France's rather equivocal attitude. One may wonder whether the French attitude had not been motivated by the fear of a 'big' Congo which would have competed politically and economically with the countries of the Community. This may well be the reason why Michel Debré, the French Premier, sent an *unofficial* representative to Elisabethville in April 1961 to assure the Katanga government that it could rely on the *unofficial* support of France. This representative, Bistos, assured the African states of France's readiness to recognise Katanga.[10] There proved to be no sequel to these approaches, which probably did no more than to establish a tenuous liaison which went to explain the subsequent receptions given by de Gaulle to Tshombe in his role of head of government in Congo–Léopoldville. France and the French-speaking African states who had encouraged the Congo to join the OCAM were ready to entrust Tshombe with the task—with the help of Belgian and international capitalism—of 'putting the house of the Congo in order': of maintaining peace and order, and at long last of promoting the economic development of his country.

By contrast, revolutionary Africa, as it had already shown in 1964 over the question of welcoming the leader of the Congolese delegation to the OAU, refused to recognise 'the murderer of Patrice Lumumba' (as they named Tshombe) in any capacity.

A development at this stage which merits mention is the change in the attitude of Congo–Brazzaville after the fall of Fulbert Youlou. It became first anti-Tshombe, then pro-Lumumba, or rather pro-Mulele, the spiritual heir of Lumumba, who had set up an expatriate government in Brazzaville after Gizenga's government had been ousted from Stanleyville by the United

Nations forces and the Congolese national army. Instructed by Chinese officers in camps in Gamboma and Impfondo in the north of Congo–Brazzaville, small commando units were established which crossed the river and engaged in acts of terrorism in the areas of Kwilu and of Lake Leopold II in Congo–Léopoldville.[11] These commandos at one stage were able to hold their own against the Congolese national army, though only for a short time. It then seemed likely that Congo–Brazzaville would join the Casablanca group, but in the event it became reconciled with Congo–Léopoldville, recognising General Mobutu's final military coup in December 1965 and becoming reconciled to considering Congo–Léopoldville's union with the Union Douanière des Etats d'Afrique Centrale (UDEAC). By this time it was true to say that international opinion was becoming very weary of the Congolese affair, and a widespread sense of disenchantment accounts for the inconsistencies in the political lines of the African states. How could it be otherwise? Few were those who appreciated the situation when the confidant of Lumumba, Sergeant Mobutu, now a general, participated in his arrest; when a few years later the same general was heard extolling his memory; when revolutionary Africa, though violently opposed to Mobutu, hardly raised a voice in protest when he seized power, since they thought their only common enemy to be Moise Tshombe. The last military coup in the Congo left everybody cold—including French-speaking Africa.

African Unity

In spite of widely diverging views over many basic issues, the African states have always displayed a great determination to understand each other and to join their forces in a common effort. An example of this is the Commission of Technical Co-operation in Africa south of the Sahara (CCTA), which sought to establish technical co-operation among all the countries of Black Africa Several specialised bodies were set up (as well as a secretariat-general) which covered the following topics: rural economy and

288

soils, and labour problems; phyto-sanitary problems; pedology; animal health; trypanosomiasis; geology and climatology; and cartography. Conferences, technological meetings, and a wide-ranging network of specialised panels maintained by the Scientific Council for Africa effected an interchange of information of great value to the engineers, scientists, technicians, economists, and agronomists working in Africa for the African states. The scientific and technical programme of the CCTA was a remarkable achievement which merits a permanent record for the benefit of future historians and scientists of Africa. But the doubtful origins of the CCTA—it dates back to colonial times—have certainly discouraged many from undertaking this task. These origins make the political role played by this organisation of particular interest, for, paradoxically enough, it represented the first tentative steps towards African unity.

The CCTA was set up in 1954 by the colonial powers—France, Belgium, the United Kingdom and Portugal—and South Africa and the Federation of Rhodesia and Nyasaland. Its headquarters were in London. In 1957, Ghana and Liberia joined; in 1958, Guinea; in 1960, Cameroun and all the French-speaking countries, including the Congo–Léopoldville; and in 1961–62, the East African countries. Apart from Togo and Ethiopia, all the sub-Saharan countries became members. At the end of 1957, under the influence of a new secretary-general, the CCTA began to decolonise itself: its headquarters were transferred from London to Lagos and African staff were recruited to senior posts. Delegates from Black Africa could visit South Africa and Luanda in Angola in complete freedom. The standing committees and the technological conferences of the CCTA provided a forum at which delegates of any colour and any political leaning could meet, and French-and English-speaking Africans could exchange their views. Over the years 1958–63 the forward-looking policy of the CCTA led to the gradual erosion of white dominance, until finally the African countries were in the majority. Clear warnings were then given to Portugal and South Africa: Ghana temporarily withdrew its membership in protest against their presence. It rejoined in

289

January 1963 at the time of the annual conference, held at Dar-es-Salaam, at which three recommendations which had been made the previous year, at Abidjan, were adopted: (i) Portugal was expelled—a decision of particular significance since this was the first time that such action was taken against the country at an international conference—South Africa having previously withdrawn on its own initiative; (ii) the activities of the Commission would no longer be restricted to the area south of the Sahara; (iii) the colonial powers—France, the United Kingdom and Belgium—were henceforth to have the status of associate members. It is particularly noteworthy that the CCTA had realised, in the scientific and technological spheres, the very unity so dear to African eyes. It is equally significant that Africans of every kind—French- and English-speaking, moderates and revolutionaries—came to a mutual understanding within the CCTA. From 1960 onwards the CCTA enjoyed the whole-hearted support of countries with as widely diverging views as the Ivory Coast and Guinea. However, the CCTA as originally conceived was not to survive: it was perpetuated with a new constitution as the Committee for Scientific and Technical Research of the OAU, the new political organisation of the countries of Africa. This owed its existence to the efforts of many African heads of state from 1960 onward to bridge the gaps which already existed between them—or at any rate to make sure that they did not widen still further. The CCTA had served a valuable purpose as a 'melting-pot', but the political level at which it could operate was not very advanced, and it was essential to look beyond it and set up African political organisations at the highest levels.

The first necessary step towards this end was to arrive at a reconciliation of the views of the political leaders of English- and French-speaking Africa which would provide the basis for a unified African policy at the United Nations. The first attempt in this direction was a conference held in Monrovia from May 8 to 12, 1961. It was meant as a counterpoise to the Casablanca group. Its main themes were: (i) complete equality between all African and Malagasy states; (ii) condemnation of any country offering asylum to subversive groups in exile; (iii) the concept of African unity not as the political integration of the sovereign states of Africa, but rather as an identity of aims and actions among them. Thus the Monrovia group was in effect an enlarged version of the Brazzaville group.

The next necessary step was to bring an end to dissensions among African delegates at the United Nations over Mauritania, Algeria and the Congo, and here Nigeria and Ethiopia played especially active roles. Although the conference held in Lagos in January 1962 was in some measure a failure (the Casablanca group refused to participate in any of the debates because the GPRA had not been invited), it nevertheless represented a long step forward since it studied a draft charter which contemplated an inter-African political organisation and which laid down the outlines of the means of economic and financial co-operation, of overcoming problems of language, and of co-ordinated effort in education.

The Casablanca group advocated the setting up of only one major organisation with subsidiary bodies, such as the CCTA in its new form, but was opposed to any regionally-based organisations such as the UAM and the OAMCE. In brief, revolutionary Africa wanted its own 'Bandung', an ambition achieved with the Addis Ababa conference of May 22–26, 1963. The achievements of this conference were truly spectacular: in spite of their different outlooks, the divisions between them and their quarrels, thirty African heads of state came together and adopted the charter which set up the Organisation of African and Malagasy Unity. This meeting was nothing less than euphoric. It is true that Nkrumah failed to carry his idea of a 'supranational Africa', the conference preferring to adopt a slower pace and to accept a more flexible approach to a united Africa, aiming at an African equivalent of de Gaulle's 'Europe des Patries'. The conference unanimously adopted resolutions supporting the black revolutionary movements in Southern Rhodesia, attacking the Portuguese in Mozambique and Angola, and aiming at the expulsion of South Africa from all international organisations, especially the FAO and the ILO.

The very fact that there was room for discussion between the advocates of a 'supranational Africa' and the advocates of 'l'Afrique des Patries' was in itself a warning. The OAU is the outcome of a compromise between 'revolutionary' and 'moderate' Africa, and constitutes the defeat of the ideologies of Casablanca. The OAU was a 'conservative' body from its inception, which explains its internal anomalies and its failures. For instance, the Brazzaville group found itself confronted with a dilemma at the very beginning of the OAU—should it, or should it not, continue to maintain UAM and its subordinate organisations? Sékou Touré maintained that to subscribe to the Addis Ababa charter meant the dissolution of each and every regional organisation; the survival of the UAM would be an insult to the OAU. In fact, the UAM and the OAMCE were dissolved, in a spirit of conciliation, shortly after the Addis Ababa conference, being replaced by the Union Africaine et Malgache de Coopération Economique (UAMCE); but such a compromise solution did not satisfy the moderates of French-speaking Africa, least of all the Conseil de l'Entente. Their attitude hardened over the years 1963–66 when they saw the OAU subjected to a series of setbacks. No unified action was taken to help Congo-Léopoldville, which continued to sink into chaos and anarchy. No joint political action was taken to boycott the products of South Africa and Portugal; and, indeed, several African countries continued to trade with them as they had previously. The handling of the Southern Rhodesian affair was characterised by complete indecision and disunity: some African states broke off relations with Britain and others did not. The decolonisation committee achieved nothing; the idea of sending African troops to Angola and Mozambique remained a dead letter. Finally, on the economic and scientific fronts, the OAU lacked the means to implement its policy of unification. The only achievement in this direction was the establishment of an African Development Bank, but its scope was limited.

After the failure of the great Afro-Asian conference at Algiers in November 1965, all the brave hopes of Africa faded. All the fine-sounding resolutions proved to be little more than mere words.

Houphouet-Boigny, who had anticipated this outcome even before the Addis Ababa charter was signed, urged the re-adoption of the aims of the UAM and the establishment of a body with similar aims, the Organisation Commune Africaine et Malgache (OCAM). In this he was strongly supported by France, which naturally favoured the continuation of some mechanism for co-operation between the states of the former Community. Houphouet-Boigny's proposals received considerable stimulus from the spate of political incidents and coups which occurred in 1963 and 1964. These have been discussed in Part II and are, in brief: Sylvanus Olympio's murder in Togo in January 1963; Fulbert Youlou's downfall in August 1963; Hubert Maga's downfall in October 1963; the attempted coup in Gabon in February 1964; unrest in Chad in September 1963; a series of plots against the Ivory Coast government in 1963 and 1964; frontier incidents in Niger in September 1964.

France was greatly disturbed by these developments. It had already stuck out its neck by intervening in Gabon and wished to avoid doing so again if it could possibly be avoided: on the contrary, France now proposed to abandon its existing military bases in Africa. Therefore it was all the more essential for it to ensure the continued well-being of its economic and commercial interests. Some stable and permanent administrative arrangement was necessary, which would rise above the rivalries and squabbles of the African states and would bind together French-speaking Africa and make it stronger and more effective. Such a scheme did not seem beyond the bounds of possibility. The UAM and the OAMCE had been effective while they existed and the Conseil de l'Entente and Customs Unions for West Africa and Equatorial Africa were still in being. Above all, the French-speaking countries had one thing in common of the greatest importance to them —their economies were all linked by common membership of the French franc area.

The concept of the OCAM was first discussed and approved at Nouakchott in February 1965, and it was formally enacted at Abidjan in May. Its policies were based on two broad principles: non-intervention in the internal affairs of other nations, and

293

support for the legal government of Congo-Léopoldville.[12] Its
immediate objectives can be set out under five headings: (i) to
provide a moderate group, and a modifying influence, within the
OAU; (ii) to break Nkrumah, whom they considered responsible for
many of the current evils of Africa, accusing him, in particular, of providing a base for many of the subversive movements within Africa
(notably against Togo) and of engineering the attempted murder
of Hamani Diori;* (iii) to restore peace to Congo-Léopoldville
(Tshombe, being the head of the government at the time when
OCAM was set up, was invited to join it); (iv) to exert a moderating
influence on some of the more extreme African revolutionary
outlooks and to convert their devotees to the 'moderate' viewpoint
(they hoped that Mali, in particular, might be won over to the
franc area if its negotiations with France proved successful); (v)
finally to attract other, non-French-speaking, African countries to
join the OCAM, even if by doing so they undermined the raison
d'être of the OAU. To put it in another way, Houphouet-Boigny
wanted to set up a new Monrovia group. But his efforts were
frustrated, first by the refusal of Sir Abubakar Tafawa Balewa to
become a member, for fear of disrupting the unity of the OAU, and
then by the drama of events in Nigeria.

As yet there is insufficient data on which to base a balanced
judgment of the OCAM, but certain conclusions can already be
drawn. The new regimes which have been in power since 1963
have reasserted their loyalty to France and to the French-
speaking community. The military coup in Ghana was greeted
with joy, not only because it overthrew Nkrumah but also because
it was a severe blow to Pan-African, Pan-Arabic, revolutionary
and non-aligned Africa. The Nigeria crisis and the still unsolved

* According to *Moniteur Africain* of August 16, 1967, the Ministry of
Information of the new government of Ghana has published a pamphlet
devoted to former President Nkrumah and his seditious acts. One of the
appendices of this document is written by Nkrumah himself and is called
"The Togolese Revolution". It mentions a plan formulated by him with
a view to overthrowing, about the end of 1963, by force and violence the
Togolese government. Togo was to be conquered and to become the base
for controlling all the other states of the Entente.

problems have been object lessons in support of the policies of the OCAM; and the chronic budgetary problems of the African countries have provided practical economic arguments in favour of regionally-based collaboration.

Even so, three countries have displayed some reservations over the policies agreed at Nouakchott. Mauritania refused to take part in the Abidjan meeting, rejecting Houphouet-Boigny's overtures and in particular refusing to be associated with Tshombe. At this time it was moving towards Cairo and Algiers, whose policy of 'encircling' Morocco was having its effect. On July 8, 1965, Mauritania withdrew from the OCAM, though it remained a member of the franc area and of the Union Douanière des Etats de l'Afrique de l'Ouest (UDEAO). Cameroun was made uneasy by the increasingly important part played by the Ivory Coast and Houphouet-Boigny. Moreover, President Ahidjo feared that too intimate an alignment with the African moderates might discredit the 'progressive' spirit of his colleagues in their exchanges with the very progressive Bamileke. At one stage Ahidjo contemplated joining the 'neutralist' camp, but different counsels prevailed—in part his fidelity to his long-standing friends; in part the economic advantages of remaining within the OCAM. Congo–Brazzaville refused to attend the meetings in Nouakchott and Abidjan because of its antipathy towards Tshombe's regime. Later, however, it became reconciled to General Mobutu and decided not to leave the OCAM.

Senegal's position was always a delicate one. Although a strong supporter of the OCAM, Senegal could not ignore the fact that its three neighbours—Mali, Guinea and Mauritania—had all decided not to join. Senghor's views were profoundly influenced by Houphouet-Boigny's actions, but he did not necessarily align himself with the Ivory Coast's policies. Senegal followed its own diplomatic policies which aimed at putting into practice two ideas close to Senghor's heart: a regional West African group, and the concept of 'Francophonie'.

The establishment of a regional West African group to include, as a first stage, the states adjacent to the Senegal river (which would thus include the three non-member states of the OCAM), and later to extend to include all West Africa was one of Senghor's dreams. Senegal was concerned above all with securing the development of the river valley with the help of the United Nations (the UN Development Programme and, if possible, the World Bank), an undertaking that would cost several million dollars for a paper study alone. The inter-state committee set up for this purpose provided the basis for a rapprochement between Senegal and Mali and Guinea. As already mentioned in the chapter on Mali, recent economic difficulties which beset Guinea in 1966 led it to withdraw, but it resumed its participation in November 1967.

The concept of 'Francophonie', of a globally-based cultural, economic, financial and political association of all French-speaking peoples in Africa, in Europe and beyond Europe as well, thereby extending far beyond the confines of the OCAM, was the second of Senghor's dreams, and another instance of the similarity of outlook between him and de Gaulle. This concept of a French 'commonwealth' struck a responsive chord in Tunisia, where Bourguiba's views have always had much in common with Senghor's. But Algeria and Morocco received it with great caution, even with direct hostility. Although Paris did not commit itself, Senghor's plan must surely have appealed to de Gaulle, in view of the opinions that he voiced during his visit to Canada in 1967. In fact, at the time of writing, there has been no concrete sequel to Senghor's proposition, unless one can count the proposal for the setting up of an inter-parliamentary group of all French-speaking countries. Certainly nothing that can be called truly constructive has arisen.

The OCAM remains the rallying point of all the French-speaking moderates in Africa. In a sense, it represents a step backward, for Africa has returned to the system of political groupings of 1960. They have recently come into conflict once more over the Israel affair, with an Afro-Asian group siding with the Arabs and the Communists and the moderates following the West. The affair has its own particular significance since, for the first time, it put

France, doubtless only temporarily, on the opposite side to most of the Francophile African states.

The Israel Question

Israel is very popular with most countries of Black Africa. It is a developing country that won its independence by its own efforts against the Arab and Eastern world, and partly, too, against the Western world. It set out to develop its resources with vigour and courage under conditions every bit as difficult as those found in the desert regions of Africa. The Israeli achievement provided a splendid example for Africa. To quote an African scholar: 'In the United States I can study the history of economic development; in Israel I can see economic development in action.'[13] Finally, Israel is a young country, not to be suspected of colonialism or of paternalism, which is animated by a real ideology which inspires its kibbutzim and its moshavim and which is an ideal and an example to the African states. Moreover, the Israelis have overcome the psychological complexes of racially-oriented thought and they have left behind them the humiliations of their forebears in the ghettos of Central Europe. The Africans have had their own struggles with racialism and these struggles have strengthened their bonds of sympathy with the Israelis. Africans have also had their own problems with the Arabs and remember invasions during their pre-colonial history. They remember how they were taken to the northern parts of Africa as slaves. They therefore felt something like fear when they realised the 'imperialistic' nature of Nasser's demands, using as he did the inter-African conference as a forum for promoting his ideas. The problems which had confronted the young state of Israel were the same as those facing all the African states: administrative reform, setting up from scratch a new constitution and a new national economy, diversification in the agricultural and industrial areas, training a skilled labour force. The Africans and the Israelis adopted similar solutions: collectively-owned land, youth camps, communally-based developments, the concept that human resources are a valuable asset.

Religious differences have been completely transcended: cordial relations were established between Jewish Israelis and African Christians, Muslims and nationalists. Bilateral agreements and agreements for economic co-operation were signed between Israel and a whole range of African states: with Mali (1960), Ivory Coast (1961 and 1962), Upper Volta (1961 and 1962), Togo (1961), Madagascar (1961), Dahomey (1961 and 1962), Niger (1962), Gabon (1962), Central African Republic (1962), Congo–Brazzaville (1962) and Cameroun (1962 and 1963).[14] Exchanges of missions between African countries and Israel were progressively stepped up over the years 1960–64. Scholarships were given to young Africans to study in Israel and some went as far as learning Hebrew to overcome the language barrier. Israel sent a number of experts to tropical Africa, especially in the fields of agriculture, irrigation, rural engineering and education. The Israeli President, the Premier and the Minister of Foreign Affairs paid state visits to a number of countries and a hearty welcome, in return, was given to African leaders when they came to visit Israel.

'Several of the recently emancipated countries have clearly realised that true sovereignty in this world must necessarily rest upon technical and economic power. Such is the case of Israel, whose creative dynamism has established a national character which has impressed itself on the Middle East, where its friends are but few.' Thus spoke Mamadou Dia at the time he was Premier of Senegal.[15] Many of the French-speaking African states were eager to follow the pattern set by Israel in agriculture, training and rural development. At a less exalted level, many became convinced that by following Israel's example many of their hopes would be realised and positive achievements would result. They believed they had found in Israel a country that had found the answers to all their problems. However, thinking of this kind overlooked several considerations. Israel had been and still was the recipient of heavy reparations for the wartime atrocities of the Nazis, as well as of donations from Jews throughout the world. It is a small country with an unusually devoted and well-trained nucleus of a working population. It had every incentive to fight to the death for its survival, as its very physical existence was challenged by the Arab world. This provided the strongest stimulus to toil, to struggle and to win through—a stimulus which was lacking in Black Africa.

Israel had several reasons for responding to the admiration of the non-Arab 'Third World'. The Israelis felt they owed a duty to the underprivileged nations to impart to them the fruits of their experience and knowledge, particularly since Israel itself was an underdeveloped country—or, at least, a country in the throes of development. Its geographical position stimulated it to such an undertaking. Situated at the hinge of the Mediterranean basin, Israel is a projection of Europe into Africa and Asia.[16] There were also strong elements of self-interest in Israel's association with Africa. It was obviously greatly to Israel's advantage to end its isolation in the Middle East and to enlist some support from outside; above all, support which would in future have votes in the United Nations. In any future crisis Africa, and particularly French-speaking Africa, could be a very valuable source of support. Furthermore, to end its isolation, Israel needed to develop external trading contacts.

The successful outcome of the relationship between French-speaking Africa and Israel is to be ascribed to two causes additional to those quoted above. Africa took its line from Paris, and from its foundation Israel had been viewed with great favour by France, particularly during the Algerian war—as witness, the Suez affair of 1956. About 1962–64, however, the links between France and Israel weakened as a result of changes in France's overall foreign policy. De Gaulle now wanted to bring the Algerian affair to a satisfactory conclusion, and to establish a normal relationship with the Arab world—to the disadvantage of Israel. The African world was reluctant to follow France in this tortuous political course, partly because of Africa's long-standing distrust of the Arab world, which dated back to the days of the slave trade. The reluctance of the Arab world to recognise Mauritania had roused the old feelings of antagonism and indirectly operated to the favour of Afro-Israeli relations. Moreover, 'revolutionary' Africa is pro-Arab—another reason for the French-speaking OCAM group to support Israel. As a generalisation, however, this is not entirely correct. The leaders of Ghana (Nkrumah, urged on by his adviser George Padmore) and Mali professed a great admiration for Israel and sent large numbers of young Ghanaians and Malians to join in the life of kibbutzim and moshavim. This did not deter 'revolutionary' Africa, particularly at the Casablanca conference of 1961, from formally condemning the 'imperialism' and 'neo-colonialism' of Israel. By contrast, at the conferences of non-aligned countries in Belgrade in September 1961 and in Addis Ababa in May 1963, nothing was said in condemnation of Israel.

The crisis of June–July 1967 clearly demonstrated the continuing deep attachment of most of French-speaking Africa to Israel, especially when it came to voting in the United Nations on the resolutions relating to the Arab-Israeli war. There were two resolutions, one of the 'non-aligned' countries insisting upon an *'immediate'* withdrawal of Israeli troops from all occupied territory, and a second, the more moderate motion (the so-called Latin-American motion), *requesting* Israel's withdrawal, expressing the hope for coexistence in the Middle East based on good neighbourly relations and reaffirming that Jerusalem should be given the status of an international city. The following French-speaking African countries voted for the first resolution: Cameroun, Congo-Brazzaville, Gabon, Guinea, Mali, Mauritania, Senegal. Madagascar and Togo voted against it, and the Central African Republic, Chad, Dahomey, Ivory Coast and Niger abstained. The following voted for the second resolution: Cameroun, Central African Republic, Gabon, Dahomey, Ivory Coast, Madagascar, Chad, Togo. Congo-Brazzaville, Guinea, Mali, Mauritania and Senegal opposed it, and Niger abstained.

As neither resolution obtained a two-thirds majority, both were rejected. But before the actual vote—during debates, discussions and informal back-stage exchanges—heavy pressure was brought to bear upon the African countries from several directions. France adopted the role of Pontius Pilate, siding neither with the Arab world nor with Israel. France was afraid that it would lose its good reputation in the Arab world, so dearly won since the Algerian war, and yet maintained that nothing should be done to jeopardise the survival of the young state of Israel. It found itself siding with the Soviet Union in voting in favour of the first and strictest resolution, and, just like the Soviet delegation, sought to win French-speaking Africa's support for it. The French tried to exploit their loyalty to the former 'mother country'; the Russians appealed to their 'sense of compassion' for the Arabs. Had their hopes been realised and all the OCAM countries voted for the first resolution, it would have comfortably gained the two-thirds majority needed for its adoption.[17]

The voting shows clearly that the African countries adopted widely divergent positions. Guinea, Mali and Mauritania voted for the more extreme motion of the 'non-aligned' countries and against the motion of the moderates. They had no hesitation in supporting the Arab group. By so doing Mauritania clearly demonstrated that it had formed new allegiances since its break with the OCAM. It is Senegal's voting which is surprising. Was it still ready to follow France's line unhesitatingly? Not entirely, for it voted against the Latin American motion, while France abstained. Was it a matter of internal politics—not to incur the criticism of the increasingly active radical elements at home by supporting the 'imperialist and colonialist bloc'? Was its vote intended as a criticism of the United States, which—had it not been preoccupied elsewhere—could have thrown in its weight to bring the conflict to an end, and which, in the eyes of some, was responsible for its having arisen? Did Senghor want to demonstrate his independence of France and of Houphouet-Boigny, the spokesman of the OCAM? Was he afraid of alienating Guinea, Mali and Mauritania and so undermining the good relations he had gradually established with them as prospective members of a possible organisation of the states bordering on the river Senegal? Or was Senghor trying to placate the Muslim Arabic-speaking elements in his own country, who provided most of his political support, and to keep on friendly terms with the United Arab Republic and Algeria, where he had been so warmly received in February 1967, and where, it seems, he decided to 'rub out the lines of demarcation' between North Africa and the countries south of the Sahara?

Madagascar, followed by Togo, adopted an unambiguous position in voting for the second resolution and against the first. Rakotomalala, the permanent representative of Madagascar, advocated negotiations between the two opponents and warned against the perpetuation of the precarious status quo. He declared bluntly that at least some of the OCAM countries were determined not to be influenced either by Soviet or by Gaullist diplomacy.[18]

Most of the other OCAM countries did not let themselves be influenced, either, but they abstained to emphasise their disapproval of the first resolution and thereby reaffirmed their loyalty to Israel. The Minister of Foreign Affairs of the Ivory Coast, Arsène Usher, speaking on behalf of all the countries of the OCAM, proposed a compromise recommending the withdrawal of the Israeli troops and suggesting that a special status be given 'to the Sacred Precincts in Jerusalem that they might be open to all and protected from desecration by act of war'. He expressed his grave doubts as to whether the General Assembly would do anything beyond making recommendations to the Security Council[19] —and in this he proved to be absolutely right. As a result the French delegation, which had been given explicit instructions to expound the French attitude to French-speaking Africa, could not persuade them to follow its line. One African statesman was quoted as having declared: 'General de Gaulle's policy in the Middle East is irrelevant to the actual situation. It is motivated by his hatred for the USA, which quite by chance won a great victory there. In these circumstances we will not follow de Gaulle. This is a splendid opportunity for us to show that we are not mere satellites—as some have alleged.'[20]

However, generally, African diplomacy—apart from that of Guinea, Mali and at times Togo—has danced to the tune piped by France. This went for Algeria as much as anyone. In acting in this way, the African countries were expressing their loyalty and friendship to France and were also acting in accordance with their own interests. During the early years of the Congo crisis the African countries took careful notice of French policy before determining their own course, but the Congo was an African problem, and they felt themselves to be fully competent to deal directly with those involved. The Israeli affair, which was of indirect interest in that it influenced the relations of the French-speaking African countries with the Arab world, marked a clear-cut divorce of African diplomacy from French policy; they no longer had any pretence to a common viewpoint. The highly equivocal French policies even had the effect of dividing the members of the OCAM among themselves, because the discussions were so complicated and uncertain.

However, even if French-speaking Africa has become less 'Gaullist' after the Israel affair, plenty of bonds still exist between the African countries and France. What is important is that the events in Israel once again divided the African world within itself—the Congo provided one of the earliest precedents for this—and it was divided not into purely African groups but within a world-wide political framework. The political groupings in Africa, and their influence on the prospects for African unity, can be analysed objectively only in their relation to the greater divisions in the world.

FRENCH-SPEAKING AFRICA AND RELATIONS BETWEEN EAST AND WEST

The politicians and trade-unionists of Africa first met the problems of the 'Cold War' in the Palais Bourbon in France, the headquarters of the National Assembly; in Brussels, at the headquarters of the 'free' and 'Christian' international trade unions; and in Prague, at the central offices of the World Federation of Trade Unions.

Up to 1946, successive generations of French Communists had virtually ignored Africa and the Africans. The visit to Paris in 1946 of leaders of the RDA, their affiliation to the French Communist

Party, and the participation in the second RDA congress at Abidjan in 1949 of militant French Communist leaders such as Waldeck Rochet and Raymond Barbé, led to the exchange of views, friendship, and the enthusiastic adoption of a common policy—the struggle against imperialism and colonialism. Afterwards, the RDA severed all its links with the Communist Party and became one of the most fierce enemies of Communism in Africa. Despite the unions' affiliations to the World Federation of Trade Unions and the contacts with French Communism, no African Communist Party was ever created and the African CGT—the Marxist trade union federation—never attained any importance. Only the Parti Africaine de l'Indépendance (PAI) of Mahjmout Diop in Senegal can be considered a Communist Party, in that it reflected the views held by its head; parties such as Sékou Touré's PDG and Félix Moumié's UPC in Cameroun display no more than a kind of 'national Communism'.

In fact Africans were not easily influenced by Marxist ideology. The colonial administrators of former days had carried out instructions from Paris to create a climate which was antipathetic to Communist agitation, and the Christian missions, both Catholic and Protestant, played an important part in conditioning young Africans to reject the atheistic creeds of Communism and Marxism. During this period, too, France was engaged in several colonial wars in which the French army, which included many coloured colonial troops, was seen as defending the free world against the inroads of Communism. Moreover, the Marxist outline did not exist in Africa: there was no proletariat, no true wealthy African bourgeoisie, not even the notion of property.

Before 1958 only a few African politicians and students had seriously considered the division between East and West. With the independence of Guinea, and, much more so, of Congo-Léopold-ville, many more Africans were confronted with the choice between East and West. In its complete isolation in 1958–59, Guinea had nowhere to turn except to the Soviet Union and the popular democracies of Eastern Europe. But what was it in the interests of the other African countries to do? To look to the East, to look to the West, or to treat with both while still retaining a preferred position in relation to France? Or would they do best to turn their backs on the 'Red' camp and to align themselves with the West?

Most of French-speaking Africa rejected Marxism and Communism. In Senegal, for example (as has already been discussed in chapter 6), Senghor does not entirely reject Marxism, but has adapted it to fit in with his own humanist ideals. He maintains that African Socialism need not be Communist in character—as, indeed, he must, in view of his profoundly religious audience. In Guinea, by contrast, Sékou Touré adopts Marxism and Leninism in so far as they provide him with slogans, principles and incentives to further action; but he rejects the basic principle of the class struggle as entirely inapplicable where the concept of the community is so deep-rooted and society is divided into ethnic groups, fraternities and associations of every kind. In Sékou Touré's own words, Africa is fundamentally 'communaucratic'. 'Certain aspects of the doctrine of Marxism had their uses in providing a rational basis for the African trade union movement. We have adopted all those aspects of Marxism that are relevant in an African context. We have had no wish to adopt this science as an end in itself, but as with every science, we took it to serve our own society while preserving our society's originality, its own characteristics, and its human wealth.'[21] This attitude accounts in part for the vacillating policy which Sékou Touré followed, looking alternately towards America and Russia; at one stage expelling the Soviet Ambassador, Solod, while not committing himself to an anti-Soviet policy. But is Sékou Touré well advised to reject the concept of the class struggle? Has not independence led in every African state to the creation of an elite, a bourgeoisie, or rather a petty bourgeoisie—which enjoys the privilege of dissociating itself from the 'have-nots', the 'proletariat' of the towns and of the bush? It is an instructive study to observe the difference in the attitude of Mali. There, Black African society is not regarded as a classless society: class differences exist, and imply not a diversification of interests but mainly an opposition of interests.[22]

305

The rest of French-speaking Africa behaved similarly, rejecting both Communism and the materialist capitalistic attitude of the United States. They never took the 'good fellowship' and bonhomie of the Americans very seriously. They accepted their aid and their dollars but they spurned their ideologies. They were never confronted with a choice between the political systems of Socialism and capitalism; they had only to decide between the different economic structures that would follow from acceptance of aid from either bloc.[23] The Ivory Coast settled for free enterprise, which encourages foreign investment and financial concessions. Capitalists are welcome to the country and free enterprise is encouraged. By contrast, Guinea has decided that the entire economic machine shall be driven from the centre—by the government—and all private enterprise is discountenanced; but these principles have not deterred Guinea from concluding preferential agreements with capitalist organisations such as Pechiney, FRIA and Harvey Aluminium.

Africa is much more practically minded than is generally believed. Its leaders are prone to high-flown ramblings in public, but this is only a façade. They are quickly coming to realise that it is the realities of day-to-day life that are really important, and hence the lack of warmth in their relations with the Soviet Union and China.

Russian diplomacy in Africa from 1958 to 1962 was badly conceived. The Soviet Union misinterpreted the wider significance of Guinea's vote of 'No' and Guinea's subsequent haste to accept help from Eastern Europe. It was wrongly concluded that all of French-speaking Africa would follow Guinea in breaking completely away from France, and that, with the help of the Soviet Union and the rest of the Communist bloc, the way would then be clear for all the young African states to adopt Socialism. They divided the African countries into the following simple classification—the revolutionary Socialist states: Guinea, Mali and Ghana; the 'positive neutralists': the UAR and Morocco, but no state in Black Africa; those with whom they entertained economic relations: Ethiopia, Sudan, Liberia, Somalia, Libya, Uganda, Tanzania (generally speaking, on a very limited scale); those already on the path to capitalism: Togo and Senegal; and finally, the reactionaries: the Ivory Coast, Mauritania, Gabon, Congo–Brazzaville.[24] Such an attempted classification was clumsy, and was still less useful when various countries changed their political viewpoint. Thus, for instance, Mauritania, having since joined the Arab group, would be included in the first of the above categories, and yet it still tolerates the presence of foreign entrepreneurs exploiting its mineral resources. Russia's diplomatic misfortunes culminated in the expulsion of its ambassador, Solod, from Guinea, on the grounds that he had interfered in the students' strike of November 1961 (which had led to a clash between Sékou Touré and the teachers' trade union), that he was excessively arrogant in his dealings, and that he had pressed too strongly Soviet intervention in the life of Guinea. The Russians' hopes were never realised in Guinea, in spite of their important assistance in the form of goods, technologists and advisers. They arrived in Africa with the preconceived idea that colonialism had achieved nothing, and that the Africans were backward people ready to accept whatever was offered. African students in Russia encountered some very strange reactions (did they live in trees and exist entirely on bananas?) and some quite genuine racial clashes took place in the popular democracies which did nothing to help relations between the Soviet Union and Africa.[25]

Fortunately a more realistic attitude prevailed after Khrushchev's downfall. The Soviet Union came to realise that it was for the Africans themselves to expunge the relics of colonialism, and neo-colonialism, in their own way. This point of view led them to make contact with the more moderate of the African states as well. Cameroun entered into diplomatic relations with Russia in March 1964. A Soviet ambassador was appointed to Chad in June 1965. The Central African Republic signed an agreement for scientific co-operation with Russia in August 1964 and a cultural agreement in March 1965. Senegal received a Russian ambassador as early as 1963, and in 1965 completed an important agreement over fisheries. Niger signed a trade agreement in June 1964, Togo a cultural agreement in 1965. Finally, even Madagascar, without going so far as to enter into formal diplomatic relations with Russia, signed a trade agreement in 1966. Congo–Brazzaville was the second OCAM country, after Senegal, to enter into diplomatic relations with Russia, in March 1964—in spite of its former strongly anti-Communist views. A Soviet embassy was established in Mauritania in 1965. Several countries have also entered into similar relations with the allies of the Soviet Union. At present, ten commercial agreements[26] are in force between the Soviet Union and French-speaking Africa (including the 'revolutionary', pro-Arab countries), but the UAR accounts for 64 per cent of all Russian-African trade, compared with tropical Africa's 28 per cent. The official figures given by the Russian Ministry of Foreign Trade seem ridiculously small.[27]

		million roubles*
Congo–Brazzaville	exports	2·4
Guinea	exports	8·7
	imports	3·2
Ivory Coast	exports	0·3
	imports	4·6
Mali	exports	8·8
	imports	2·3
Senegal	exports	0·1
	imports	0·5
Togo	exports	0·7
	imports	0·6

* 1 dollar = 0·9 rouble.

The problem of establishing relations with China immediately raises the question of what is meant by China—Chiang Kai-shek's Nationalist China or Mao Tse-tung's Chinese People's Republic? The choice was the origin of yet another division among African countries. The UN debates on the Chinese question between 1960 and 1966 show that a strong majority of the African countries favoured the Nationalist regime—particularly Gabon, the Ivory Coast, Madagascar, Niger, Togo and the Upper Volta. These countries were consistent in their violent opposition to the activities of Communist China in Africa. Niger and the Ivory Coast were especially strong and persistent in their denunciations of the infiltrations and subversive activities of Communist China in Africa, which they held to be encouraged by Ghana. They maintained (and, notwithstanding Nkrumah's fall, still maintain) that the presence of Chinese Communists in Africa constituted a grave threat. The attempt on Hamani Diori's life at the Tabasqui in Niger (see chapter 4, page 158) was said to have been the act of a Sawaba militant who had been trained in Nanking. These countries were unanimous in rejecting the replacement at the United Nations of the Nationalist China representatives by a delegation from Peking. Cameroun, which concurred with the line taken by its friends Gabon, Madagascar, and the members of the Conseil de l'Entente, had better reasons than most for its antagonism, for Communist China had always given strong material and moral support to the illegal UPC followers of Félix Moumié and Um Nyobe. Nothing came of a Communist Chinese goodwill mission which visited Cameroun in 1964 in an attempt to improve relations; and, to this day, guerrilla forces continue active in the Bamileke region. Chad took a less positive line, and did not commit itself by actually voting in the United Nations on Chinese representation, but so far has declined any contact with Peking. The relations between these countries and Nationalist China are excellent: cultural and other agreements for co-operation have been completed, and the visits of experts in rice growing and fishing have often proved very welcome and useful.

Guinea and Mali, on the other hand, adopted the reverse view of the People's Republic as soon as they became independent. They voted for the admission of Communist China to the United Nations every time the question arose. Guinea managed to reconcile friendly relations with Peking and substantial aid from America. Mali was less successful in this, for the US State Department has been inclined to turn away from Mali as a result of its prolonged flirtation with Communist China.[28]

Senegal has adopted an ambiguous position regarding the two

Chinas. The Senegalese government voted in favour of granting
de jure recognition to Peking in 1960, but, at the same time, maintaining that it was unjust to expel a country of 12 million inhabitants from the United Nations, voted for Nationalist China's
remaining a member, though surrendering its permanent seat on
the Security Council to Peking. In pursuit of this equivocal policy,
Senegal broke off relations with Nationalist China and recognised
Peking. The Nationalist Vice-Minister for Foreign Affairs was
most courteously welcomed in Dakar a few months afterwards, but
nevertheless Senegal voted for the admission of Peking to the
United Nations in 1966. At the present time neither Communist
nor Nationalist China has diplomatic relations with Senegal.

The Central African Republic's attitude to the Chinese question
has gone through three stages. In the first stage, relations were
established with Nationalist China, which sent experts in rice-
growing in Bangui in 1963; in May 1964 an agreement for co-
operation was concluded. In the second stage, in September of the
same year, Dacko swung over to the left, recognising Communist
China and negotiating a loan of 1 billion CFA francs. Then, in
December 1965, the army took over, one of the ostensible reasons
for the coup being the supposed danger from the presence of the
Communist Chinese. Their diplomatic mission, thirty strong, was
promptly expelled. In 1966 the Central African Republic voted
for Nationalist China at the United Nations.

Dahomey's attitude also fluctuated as a result of internal political
changes. In November 1964 Dahomey recognised Communist
China and in April 1965 requested Nationalist China's representative to leave. But after the coup of December 1965 Soglo decided
on a drastic revision of his predecessor's policy and resumed
relations with Nationalist China.

Congo–Brazzaville provides the most extreme example of a
volte face following a change in domestic politics. At one time it
was the most conservative of all the French-speaking African
countries, a trusted ally of Tshombe and a focal point in Africa for
Nationalist China's diplomacy. Then, after the downfall of
Youlou, the new administration recognised Communist China in

February 1964 and broke off relations with Nationalist China in June of that year. Peking then came forward with an interest-free loan of 1,235 million CFA francs, followed in June 1965 by an agreement to provide technical and economic aid amounting to 5 billion CFA francs. Chinese officers have been despatched to Congo–Brazzaville as advisers to the army, primarily to train rebel forces from Congo-Léopoldville for action across the frontier. In 1966 at the United Nations Congo–Brazzaville supported the membership of Communist China, but more recently relations have become cooler and the Congolese government is beginning to look towards Cuba for advice.

Mauritania, in its new role of a radical, progressive, pro-Arab country, had no option in 1965 but to break with the Nationalists and turn to the Communists.

So long as African governments continue unstable and subject to sudden overthrow, it will be very difficult to predict their future policy. Only time can tell. In concluding this short survey of Sino-African relations, three points must be emphasised. First, when it recognised Communist China in 1964, France did not carry its African supporters with it. There are several possible reasons for this: the influence of and pressure from the United States on the African moderates; France, in contrast to Africa, had nothing to fear from China; and perhaps simply the independence of African diplomacy from the Quai d'Orsay. Secondly, in spite of some local success achieved because its experts were readily adaptable and were not preoccupied with racial matters, Communist China's overall approach in Africa was no less misguided than was Russia's. An editorial in *Le Monde* of January 6, 1966, very justly said: 'China doubly deceived itself in believing that, as dual objectives of its foreign policy, it could organise a majority of the under-developed countries behind it in an anti-imperialist, anti-American front, and that the same countries could be persuaded to side with it in its dispute with the USSR: thus siding with it on two separate political fronts. Between 1961 and 1965 China achieved several substantial diplomatic successes in Africa, but after the sequence of coups d'état, including those in Ghana and

Congo-Léopoldville, Africans have become increasingly distrustful of Communist China.'

Thirdly, it soon became clear that the multiplicity of Communist China's embassies and its many experts were sent to Africa not to help the Africans, but as a weapon of propaganda for the cause of anti-imperialism. The promises of development finance were sometimes—as in the case of the Central African Republic—not honoured.[29] Further, China frequently interfered, or was accused of interfering, in the domestic affairs of the African states. French-speaking Africa took very unkindly to interference: they wanted to lead their own lives. All they wanted was technical assistance and material help; they had no wish to become involved in the Sino-Soviet dispute. On the contrary, this quarrel was a matter of grave disturbance to them as a serious threat to future world peace, and every shade of African opinion, from Guinea at one extreme to the Ivory Coast at the other, wished equally fervently to remain aloof from it. If one pressed the question, it would probably transpire that, while the over-riding reaction of Africa was one of indifference, there was, if anything, some slight tendency to favour the Soviet Union. Another factor militated against the Chinese—the violent explosions of the 'cultural revolution' there. French-speaking African states were grateful for the stern efforts the Soviet Union appeared at that time to be making to avoid a third World War and to arrive at peaceful coexistence with the West. Russian cultural and commercial missions to Africa took good care not to appear as rivals to the sources of French aid, and as a result the moderate, so-called 'neo-colonialist', countries of Africa began to view the Soviet Union in a less unfavourable light.

Can one finally conclude that French-speaking Africa is 'non-aligned'? Certainly, it has not positively committed itself to either of the blocs which have dominated the world for the past twenty years. The African states have followed a deliberate policy of vacillation, now swinging to the East, now to the West, now looking to both sides simultaneously, but never committing themselves irrevocably either way. Mamadou Dia, when Premier of Senegal, summed up this attitude in a speech at the United Nations in New York on December 8, 1960: 'On the battlefield of the Cold War, the two great blocs are playing for higher and higher stakes. The Third World might bid still higher and seek to exploit this rivalry. It could try to maintain a balanced position between the two sides and so preserve a façade of independence.' This may be all right for big countries, but, according to Dia, the smaller ones cannot afford that kind of risk. The Third World must take up a clearly defined position with respect to East and West, the United States and the Soviet Union. Neither camp has the whole truth on its side: they must both accept the existence of the other and embark on constructive exchanges. It is simple common sense, adds Mamadou Dia, that we shall get nowhere unless we decide on what the world of tomorrow is to be: the United Nations must rise above the rivalries of the Cold War and stimulate exchanges between the two camps. This language, if idealistic in the extreme, has nevertheless overtones of particular significance for the two groups into which present-day Africa is divided. Dia declared that the African contingent at the United Nations might 'endeavour to present a sincere testimony of what can happen to a continent which aims at settling itself and at promoting inter-state co-operation nurtured within its own bosom, based on a Socialism which respects the spiritual values of the individual'. Fine talk of this kind would be highly commendable if it were more than mere words, but it is clear that Africa has proved quite unable to remain uncommitted. It has demonstrated its incapability of speaking with a unanimous voice in every one of the great debates of the United Nations of the 1960s—Algeria, Congo, Israel, China. Non-alignment means not taking sides, 'deciding freely according to one's own aims and ideals and the goals at which one's people are aiming. Neutralism, non-alignment, non-commitment, all stem from the desire to safeguard one's liberty and independence.'[30] But is such an attitude possible for the African states?

At the Belgrade Conference of non-aligned countries in December 1961, Black Africa was thinly represented: no one from French-speaking Africa except Guinea, Mali and—strangely enough—Congo-Léopoldville (because of the temporary Adoula-Gizenga alliance). The countries of the former Community viewed the policy of non-alignment with great suspicion, all the more, they maintained, as it was being prompted by influences external to Africa. Non-alignment, as conceived by Marshal Tito, by President Nasser, by President Sékou Touré or by Fidel Castro, had nothing in common with the hopes of the peoples of Africa, who could never be conditioned to accepting ideologies and attitudes alien to them. It was their wish that the two great blocs should live in peaceful coexistence, but they regarded the brand of non-alignment practised by Guinea, Ghana and Mali as 'dishonest', for beneath its façade it concealed a preference for the East and a turning away from the West.

In fact, the moderates of the Brazzaville group, the OCAM countries, had already come to a decision, subject to the various shades of opinion which have been mentioned above, as for instance in the cases of Senegal and Cameroun. Thus Houphouet-Boigny, in *Fraternité* of March 24, 1961, declared: 'It is our wish that Africa should become a bigger Switzerland, whose neutrality is warranted by all. But we are not children and we are well aware that the world is divided into two camps and that both have designs on Africa. The first African states to achieve independence joined the Afro-Asian bloc—the Bandung group that opted for "positive neutralism". We have come to realise that behind Bandung lies China and the world of Communism.'[31] Later, the Africa of the OCAM moved towards alignment with the Western world, as was clearly indicated by the voting of its members at the United Nations on the Congo, and particularly on China and on Israel.

Recent developments in international relations have undoubtedly lent further support to the stand taken by French-speaking Africa in resisting the 'non-alignment' of the Bandung group, which failed to live up to the standards it imposed on itself in a crucial test, that of remaining uncommitted in the Sino-Soviet dispute. The myth of Bandung vanished in Algiers in November 1965, by which time it was obviously lacking what had been in 1955 'le ferment et le ciment du mouvement'[32]—the struggle against Western colonialism.

But have these great international problems any real significance in the world of today? The Cold War is no longer a major problem. We are witnessing a rapprochement between the Soviet Union and the United States—in spite of the Vietnam War—as a result of Chinese successes in the worlds of diplomacy and atomic weapon development. Hence the USSR–US agreement on the non-proliferation of nuclear weapons. The atomic race and the outbreaks of violence in China—these are the real dangers of the modern world, dangers which Africa cannot ignore.

African nationalism arose as a political rebellion against colonialism. Pan-Africanism expressed the wish of Africans to prove their continental solidarity, their independence and their equality with other continents. African Socialism—an expression constantly on the lips of African leaders—is an expression of the cause of under-privileged Africa.[33] Neutralism and non-alignment now appear as meaningless concepts since a new division has appeared. In a world of two major powers and China, with splits within each of the major camps, the division is between the 'haves' and the 'have nots'; the rich (and the rather less rich) nations and the poor (and the rather less poor). It is within this new division of the world that Africa, and particularly French-speaking Africa, supported by France and the European Common Market, will have a voice to be listened to. Africa will establish its own personality, not by electing to join one or the other of the power blocs, but by defining its own role within the broad ambit of international politics which will take account of this new division in the world. Perhaps it is the OCAM countries, alone of Africa, which, with the support of France and the EEC, have the experience and the wish to establish themselves within this framework.

This may be pure wishful thinking. The French-speaking African states seem to have the basis and the structures to face the 'haves', provided they do not fall apart and, as will be discussed in the last chapter of this book, provided they do not become too involved in 'military follies'. Yet the OCAM is limited in its membership.

It does not include Mauritania or Guinea or Mali. But is it not possible that relations may improve between these countries and the other French-speaking states and that some sort of co-operation may be established? (On the other hand, Congo–Kinshasa is a member of the OCAM.) The future is hard to predict. The idea of regional organisations such as the OCAM is a good one if it helps co-ordinate the work of sub-regional bodies which are carrying out their activities autonomously, such as the Union Douanière et Economique de l'Afrique Centrale (UDEAC), the Union Douanière de l'Ouest Africain (UDOA), the Conseil de l'Entente or the newly established Organisation des Pays Riverains du Fleuve Sénégal, although, in this latter organisation, Senegal is the sole OCAM member. These are encouraging and interesting ventures. A committee for the development of all the neighbouring countries of the Niger basin may also be most interesting if it is eventually established. The Chad Basin committee is also worth noting, especially since it implies co-operation between French-speaking states and an English-speaking state.

Such 'sub-regionalisation' is appropriate provided it does not create or lead to discontent and hence division. In this instance the union between Congo–Kinshasa, Chad and the Central African Republic, without Gabon, Congo–Brazzaville and Cameroun, is, in many ways, most depressing. It may disrupt the UDEAC which, in spite of certain constraints, is a coherent body that makes sense, as well as the UDOA, the customs union for West Africa. But the UDEAC was more ambitious in its objectives since it aimed at an economic union between the former French West African countries and Cameroun, as indicated in chapter III. Of course, the traditional inter-trade trends have not changed much. Congo–Brazzaville continues to sell a large amount of its industrial products to the other states of the UDEAC, while this is not so for the Central African Republic, Gabon, Chad or even Cameroun. Goods sold by Congo–Brazzaville in 1966 to its UDEAC partners were valued at about 3,425 million CFA francs against 646 million by Cameroun, 546 million by CAR, 110 million by Gabon and 12 million by Chad.[34] This situation is of great concern to Chad, which considers itself as not gaining much from its association with the other members of the UDEAC. On the one hand, Cameroun and Gabon feel that they—as the 'rich' countries of the UDEAC—are contributing too much to the 'solidarity fund' which is of benefit mainly to the 'continental' states. On the other hand, what new advantages would Chad and the Central African Republic gain from an association with Congo–Kinshasa? Their major bottleneck is transport. Chad, for example, has more to gain by improving its relations and trade routes with Cameroun. The Trans-Camerounais railway may change the present situation completely in this respect. Therefore the UDEAC, despite its day-to-day difficulties, should be maintained, for it could be a real success in the long run. It might be a good proposition for Congo–Kinshasa to join the UDEAC, although it is easy to understand the fears of the present members—notably Gabon, Cameroun and Congo–Brazzaville—of becoming over-ruled by this large country should it progress and develop.

In any case, the UDEAC, the UDOA and the OCAM would seem to be 'interlocuteurs valables' between the European Common Market and French-speaking Africa. For, as we shall see in the final chapter of this book, the structures of the 'franc zone' and of the EEC are really determining to a great extent—in addition to the specific efforts of each country, supported by multilateral and bilateral aid—the development of the 'have nots' of French-speaking Africa.

11. Economic and Political Realities

ECONOMIC DEVELOPMENTS IN THE NEW STATES

MUCH OF THE STRUCTURE of traditional Africa survived into the colonial period and beyond it to the days of decolonisation: moreover, it will not readily be completely superseded, even with the introduction of an African financial and commodity market structure. On the contrary, the emergence in some areas of a new middle class enjoying political and administrative power has served only to reinforce the anomalies that were already obvious in the period of colonisation. The middle ages survive to rub shoulders with modern life. As has already been discussed (page 45), the wage-earners of the towns came to play an increasingly important part in controlling their countries through their trade unions and their political parties. The imbalance between town and country (as illustrated in Table 1) is a fundamental factor in French-speaking Africa. Apart from the overriding consideration of the growth of the cities since independence, as a result of the constant increase in the numbers of administrators, there is also un-evenness in the development of different regions. Taking Cameroun as an example, we see first a difference between West Cameroun—formerly British—and East Cameroun—formerly French. The population of the West is one-quarter that of the East; its proportion of the country's exports and road system is one-sixth and of its wage earners two-sevenths; only 29 per cent of those of school-age in the West receive education, compared with 64 per cent in the East. Further, there is a sharp contrast between the Northern and Southern regions of East Cameroun, which is characteristic of all the coastal countries whose economies depend on cash-crops. The difference in East Cameroun is striking: the Southern region includes two-thirds of the population, 95 per cent of all industry and 90 per cent of all wage-earners. A similar difference appears

318

between the two main towns. The harbour town of Douala contains 40 per cent of all modern industry compared with 24 per cent in Yaoundé, the federal capital.[1] We can therefore expect the Gross Domestic Product per capita to be much higher in urban areas.

Table 1: Gross Domestic Product per capita in the Countries of French-Speaking Africa (period 1961–65)

	Total population (*1965*)	Urban population (*1961–63*)	GDP per capita, in $US, *1961–63* whole country	rural area	urban area
Congo–Brazzaville	840,000	264,000	168	72	371
Gabon	463,000	65,000	330	135	1,632
Chad	3,307,000	162,000	63	34	617
Central African Rep.	1,352,000	192,000	106	49	437
Cameroun	5,229,000	737,000	121	60	466
Ivory Coast	3,835,000	440,000	223	102	1,041
Dahomey	2,365,000	330,000	71	43	227
Niger	3,328,000	210,000	80	51	471
Upper Volta	4,858,000	495,000	49	33	178
Togo	1,638,000	330,000	87	55	207
Senegal	3,490,000	779,000	198	80	567
Guinea	3,500,000	—	70 (1959)	—	—
Mauritania	1,080,000	85,000	115	61	611
Mali	4,576,000	430,000	68	40	318
Madagascar	6,420,000	1,356,000	105	45	300

Table 1 is also of interest in demonstrating the economic anomalies inherent in the present geographical distribution of the African states. In chapter 10, the view was put forward that the countries of OCAM are a coherent body from the political viewpoint, in spite of temporary differences; however, on the economic level there are great inequalities, and it is mainly to compensate for this uneven distribution of wealth and resources among its members that the OCAM was established after the OAMCE and the UAM. The differences between the Federations of French West

Africa and French Equatorial Africa, the relative importance of Brazzaville and Dakar as capitals of these federations and the greater economic and financial part played by Libreville and Abidjan were stressed in chapter 2, as were the differences between the countries of the coast and of the savannah. In the brief surveys of each country attention was focused on the complicated economic circumstances of the land-locked countries of the savannah, which led to the establishment of special 'solidarity' funds, within the framework of the UDEAC and of the Conseil de l'Entente, to provide a counterpoise to these economic anomalies.

Agricultural Revolution vs. Industrial Revolution

One might infer from the steady rise in the Gross Domestic Product of French-speaking Africa over the period 1958–65 (cf. Table 2) that its economic circumstances are encouraging: but the reality is otherwise. The stage of agricultural revolution attained in Europe by the mid-eighteenth century has not yet been reached in Africa. Paul Bairoch, in his *Diagnostic de l'évolution économique du Tiers Monde, 1900–1966*, published in 1967, gave an approximate assessment of agricultural productivity in Africa, though reliable statistics are lacking and calculations in this field are most arduous. According to Bairoch, the weighted averages of the indices of agricultural productivity (i.e. the net agricultural output per active male working in agriculture) tended to decrease for African countries over the period from 1934 to 1964:

1934–38	*1946–50*	*1953–57*	*1960–64*
7·08	7·26	5·19	4·71

In France in 1810, on the threshhold of the Industrial Revolution, the index of agricultural productivity was 7,[2] and in the half century before that date, agricultural productivity had increased by about 40 per cent. Among the developed countries generally, the techniques of agriculture advanced irregularly in the sixteenth and seventeenth centuries, and it is estimated that prior to this development their index of agricultural productivity was about 5 —a figure, it is to be noted, slightly greater than that of the African countries of the present day.

The average productivity of developing countries throughout

Table 2: Gross Domestic Product in French-Speaking Africa

	1958	*1965*	Percentage of increase *1958–65*
	(billions CFA francs)		%
Mauritania	14	41	+ 193
Ivory Coast	113	248	+ 119
Gabon	26	50	+ 92
Eastern Cameroun	93	176	+ 89
Niger	46	77	+ 67
Central African Rep.	29	44	+ 52
Madagascar	123	182	+ 48
Chad	40	58	+ 45
Senegal	134	187	+ 40
Upper Volta	43	60	+ 40
Dahomey	34	47	+ 38
Congo–Brazzaville	24	33	+ 38
Mali	63	80	+ 27

Source: French National Assembly, Commodities and Trade Committee, *Discussions of Aid Budget,* 1968.

the world is about half that of fully developed countries at the time when they embarked on the stage of industrialisation. Its present level is the same as was theirs *before* they undertook their Agricultural Revolution. Nevertheless, it appears that many African countries, as well as many developing countries elsewhere, seem determined to 'skip' this stage, which was an essential preliminary to the industrialisation of those countries which are by now developed. It is well nigh impossible for a country to 'take-off'—though they hardly seem to realise it—by industrialising for the sake of industrialisation, without first deciding how, by whom, with whom, with what, and for whom this industrial development will be promoted. The classic example of Britain seems to be ignored by many African economists or planners. There the Industrial Revolution did not hinder agricultural development but rather provided an incentive for it. The countries of Western Europe were unable to industrialise without a corresponding major increase in agricultural production to meet the heavy demands of those who left the agricultural sector of the economy. When Britain reorganised its agriculture and embarked on a phase of rapid industrialisation, it was led towards a policy of colonial expansion to obtain access to those agricultural commodities it could not produce at home, as well as the raw materials necessary for industrialisation. Exports of Britain's manufactured goods met the cost of its imports of food. France did not follow the exact pattern, as its economy was more diversified, but it, too, aimed at a balance between agricultural and industrial expansion.

The countries of Africa took the opposite course—or, rather, they were constrained to do so. The only parts of their agricultural or mineral resources that were exploited were those of interest to the highly developed countries. In a few major towns and harbours, a small number of modern process industries were established,* and this policy eventually led to some measure of 'take-off' of the national economies. Production of coffee, cocoa, palm

---

* See the numerous examples of agricultural, mineral and industrial development in the chapters on Senegal, Ivory Coast, Gabon, Cameroun, etc.

oil and groundnuts was stimulated, but nothing was done to promote food crops: it was assumed that subsistence agriculture would meet the requirements of the population. The per capita output of food decreased in Black Africa by 0·4 per cent per year over the years 1952–55 and 1962–65—a most alarming development if one bears in mind that 85 to 90 per cent of the population subsist on agriculture and cattle-breeding.

Senegal may be cited as an example. Here the traditional organisation of agriculture has proved adaptable to the production of crops for export, chiefly groundnuts. It has been estimated that out of every $3 (US) of revenue from exports in 1966, $2 were immediately redeployed to food imports. Under these circumstances, where can Senegal look for a source of income to pay for imports of capital goods?

On the basis of United Nations statistics, Bairoch has pointed out, firstly, that non-food crops have increased more rapidly than food crops.

Food output	*Index* (1953–57 = 100)
1934–38	69
1949–53	89
1953–57	100
1961–65	122

Total agricultural output	*Index* (1953–57 = 100)
1934–38	67
1949–53	88
1953–57	100
1961–65	125

Secondly, that the increase in population has been so fast that it immediately absorbed any increase in production; indeed, production per capita has in fact decreased. The index numbers of agricultural output per head would now be 97 compared with 122 for food output; and 103 for total agricultural output compared with 125. The data given in the chapters of Part II indicate heavy imports of food by most countries of French-speaking Africa: mainly sugar, dairy products (in the case of countries on the coast), wheat and rice. Over the period 1958 to 1965 Senegal's rice imports were tripled. For the new social classes of both the towns and the villages (farm-hands, small and large land-owners, migrant labourers, skilled labourers, students from the technical schools, civil servants and employees of the private sector) have developed new attitudes and acquired new tastes. The old staple African diet —manioc, fonio and millet—has been replaced by other cereals, such as wheat and rice. Naturally, this leads to a disturbance in the balance of trade of African countries. Moreover, basic food imports must be augmented by luxury foods—soft drinks, wine, beer and spirits. The imports of beverages into the countries of French-speaking Africa other than Guinea in 1964 are shown in Table 3.

A comparison between imports of this kind and imports of capital goods to aid production is even more telling. In 1964, the total imports of certain classes of goods for the whole of French-speaking Africa (except Guinea) were as follows (in thousand million CFA francs):[3]

Fertilisers	1,517·8
Agricultural equipment and implements	1,200·0
Tractors	3,741·5
Machinery, tools	2,478·1
Spirits	7,294·2
Private cars	5,592·6
Petrol (for private cars)	3,561·6
Perfumes, cosmetics	1,269·1

These figures are telling and point up a number of unusual aspects of the true economic situation. In some instances, such as the Ivory Coast, excellent investment projects exist that will promote the production of traditional export goods such as coffee, cocoa, palm-oil and rubber. New plantations are being established: on-site processing is actively encouraged; a start is being made towards industrialisation, with assembly lines producing light equipment and machinery normally manufactured in Europe, and

Table 3: Imports of Beverages, French-Speaking Africa

	Imports of beverages, million CFA francs	% of total imports of food	Imports of wine million CFA francs	Imports of beer million CFA francs	Other alcoholic beverages million CFA francs
Senegal	698·6	4·4	292·0	93·6	–
Mali	64·5	3·9	–	–	–
Mauritania	46·1	14·5	9·4	18·9	–
Ivory Coast	1,597·5	15·5	1,067·3	78·6	–
Upper Volta	–	–	–	–	–
Niger	214·4	19·9	62·3	96·8	–
Dahomey	289·7	19·0	84·9	15·8	–
Congo	868·7	29·0	414·5	256·8	–
Gabon	901·8	37·3	299·6	403·5	–
Central African Republic	309·6	29·3	159·9	34·7	–
Chad	401·6	29·8	129·8	152·1	–
Cameroun	920·9	25·1	343·7	320·9	–
Togo	282·7	17·1	95·0	113·9	–
Madagascar	1,233·8	29·7	709·1	255·1	–
Total	7,829·9		3,667·5	1,840·7	1,786

Source: Revue Partisans, special issue, No. 29–30, May–June 1966, p. 17.
The dash (–) indicates figures not available.

a new wage-earning urban population has come into being.* On the other hand, the traditional farmers of the bush are left to their own devices and no effort is made to increase their food production, since they are considered as unprofitable—which means they would not bring large profits to foreign firms. Thus, the overall economic structure is no different from the colonial pattern: the same firms buy local products in order to export them and sell imported manufactured goods (which may, perhaps, be of a higher standard than in former days). But whereas previously the whole system centred on a subsistence economy and relied on a local population directly responsible to the colonial administration, today this subsistence pattern is fast disappearing in the face of increasing demands from the African peoples; they have altered their feeding habits with improved living conditions and, quite often, with the recent urbanisation of their lives. The industrial revolution has not yet come to pass, and the agricultural revolution has not yet been fully accomplished. The only substantial advance during the few years since independence is in the methods of development and exploitation; no longer are Europeans the only ones to profit from the riches of Africa.

The major economic problem facing the young African states is to eliminate the balance of payments deficit relating to food as quickly as possible, and certainly over the next twenty to forty years. It might be a valuable exercise to compare the present cost of imported foodstuffs with what they might cost if they were produced at home. Such an investigation might indicate that in the case of those countries with low agricultural production, barren soil and very low rainfall, it would always pay to import part of their necessary foodstuffs and to meet the expense from more profitable exports. Thus Gabon—with its exports of timber, crude oil, uranium and manganese, and in the near future its iron ore—has

* Its proportion of the whole of the active population varies greatly: Madagascar and Cameroun, 7 per cent; Ivory Coast, 10 per cent; Senegal, 8 per cent; Congo-Brazzaville, 17 per cent; Guinea, 4 per cent; Central African Republic, 11 per cent; Gabon, 18 per cent; Mauritania, 5 per cent; Upper Volta, Dahomey, Mali, Chad, Niger and Togo, 3 per cent.

no incentive to improve its domestic agricultural production, for which both natural resources and labour are lacking: it can afford to feed on imports. The same holds true for Mauritania, par excellence a mining country, which would do far better to concentrate on the development of its mines, and eventually of its fisheries, and to abandon the greater part of its aims in the field of agriculture. (A few small agricultural projects can be launched on the banks of the Senegal river, but neighbouring Senegal will benefit from them at least as much as will Mauritania.) Niger too could concentrate on the development of mining and industry, especially its uranium resources.

The ten years that have elapsed since independence have produced a clearer picture of the very real financial problems and economic difficulties which confront the young developing countries, but it is open to question whether they have clearly appreciated that the major obstacle to development is the deterioration in the food situation. The rural populations have become increasingly conscious of their own plight, of the restrictions on their means and resources, but many political and administrative leaders, who are fully appraised of the basic facts, are more than ready to stick their heads in the sand and to rely on foreign aid, for want of any other simple solution.

Foreign Aid to French-Speaking Africa

The tremendous support given by France to its former colonial overseas territories between 1946 and 1958 has already been emphasised (see chapter 2, page 70 *et seq*). The African countries soon grew accustomed to these vast investments from the metropole, so that the choice between immediate independence and the attainment of full independence by degrees resolved itself into choosing between the more difficult and the easier economic and financial path. When the African countries arrived at independence, the majority immediately entered into agreements for co-operation with France. These agreements were two-sided: France conceded its political and administrative privileges in favour of the new African countries and committed itself to continuing economic, financial and technical aid; African governments, for their part, acknowledged that they were administratively still weak and immature and that they needed foreign investment, and, as a *quid pro quo*, they pledged themselves to protect French interests in Africa. In short, African countries became politically independent, but gained little or no economic independence, well knowing that any alternative would involve them in serious difficulties and sacrifices. This financial and economic dependence takes several aspects, the most important being economic and financial aid.

From the outset, the administrative and technological structure of the African countries was in the hands of the French 'co-operation officers'. Except in the case of a few countries, it was a Frenchman who was the 'man on the spot', who alone could deal with technical or administrative problems. These French technical advisers were usually honest and conscientious men who saw themselves as servants of the countries in which they were working. In Africa south of the Sahara they numbered 13,386, as compared with 9,324 Britons, 2,784 Belgians and 3,784 Americans in similar employment.[4] Furthermore, every level of African education was greatly dependent on 10,000 French teachers (by 1964, a little over 9,000), and on a number of young teachers whose military service took the form of teaching in overseas countries.[5] For example, the administrative structure of the Ivory Coast is a replica of that of France and is supported chiefly by Frenchmen. It has been decided that not until the early 1970s can all the 'key posts' of the administration be taken over by Ivorians; the administration itself will not be completely Africanised until the late 1970s.

The commercial and industrial life of the French-speaking African countries still depends on a few large French firms, mentioned at the end of chapter 1. In recent years their number has in fact increased, since many French companies have set up branches in Africa, particularly in the more prosperous countries such as Cameroun, Gabon, Ivory Coast and Senegal. Often the firms proved more radical in outlook than the national administrations themselves, with a policy of incorporating Africans into their directorates as soon as they could. Many firms were reorganised to make the state on whose territory they were operating a substantial, perhaps even a majority, shareholder, with representation on the board. On occasion, even the chairman might be an African. Similarly, local branches of French banks were reorganised to become national institutions, with the parent bank enjoying only a minority participation.

Many international holdings (French, Italian, American, British, German) have become interested in the development of Africa and play an important role in its mining industry (in Gabon, Mauritania and Guinea for instance). Following the assimilation of the French-speaking African countries into the European Economic Community as associate members, Italian and German interests established a foothold in Africa, with the result that the economic allegiance of Africa is becoming reoriented from exclusive affinity with France to the Common Market generally. (A similar development is taking place in English-speaking Africa also, where, indeed, the trend began even before independence.) This evolution of French-speaking Africa is, of course, quite consistent with the orthodox doctrine of Gaullism—provided always that France maintains its leadership of the Common Market (see chapter 1, p. 37).

Another manifestation of the close relationship between France and its former colonies is that, after independence, they all, apart from Guinea (and, for a time, Mali) agreed to remain members of the franc area in view of the very real economic advantages. The franc area was created as a defence measure in 1939, with the decision to impose exchange control on the French franc for any resident of France or of the so-called French 'Empire', and these regulations continued in force after the war. By analogy with the franc area, a parallel currency was then established in French Africa, known as the CFA (colonies françaises d'Afrique) franc. Thereafter the control regulations were gradually relaxed until exchange control was abrogated by the law of December 28,

1966. This franc area within French-speaking Africa—now called the Communauté Financière Africaine—is based upon several institutions. As well as the Banque de France, there are the Banque Centrale des Etats de l'Afrique Equatoriale et du Cameroun (BCEAEC), closely linked to the Union Douanière et Economique de l'Afrique Centrale (UDEAC) the Banque Centrale des Etats de l'Afrique de l'Ouest (BCEAO), closely linked to the Union Monétaire Ouest-Africaine (UMOA); the Institut d'Emission Malgache; and the Institut d'Emission Franco-Malien. A third of the members of the board of directors of BCEAO and half the members of the board of directors of BCEAEC and of the Institut d'Emission Malgache are French government representatives —which demonstrates the strength of the grip France has maintained on the monetary policy of its former colonies in Africa. Of course, in its own interest as well as in the interest of its former overseas territories, France must ensure monetary stability; by shouldering responsibility for monetary decisions, it endeavours to support the African monetary system and to prevent inflation and imbalance in external finances.

When France decided to devalue in 1958, there was an immediate repercussion on the CFA franc and the Malagasy franc. By contrast, no devaluation of the CFA or of the Malagasy franc can occur without the consent of France and of all interested states. In several instances, the devaluation of local currencies was contemplated in view of the large deficits in the balance of trade. But the economic situation of the states concerned was such that devaluation would have had very little effect. Moreover, these states are able to make use of the franc area, which was set up expressly to counteract the effect of any deficit. The French Treasury has opened an operational account for each central bank into which each bank transfers its entire holding of CFA francs which are automatically converted into French francs. The Bank of France guarantees that the currencies of the African states will be automatically converted into French francs, at a fixed exchange rate, and that they will extend to them unlimited credit, even if their operational accounts show a deficit. As a *quid pro quo*, the

African central banks must deposit all their foreign currency reserves at the Bank of France in the form of French francs (which ensures the French Treasury of a far from negligible amount of foreign currencies). In the long run, it is to the advantage of the African states to depend, as they do, on the French Treasury: they can ignore any difficulties with their balance of payments, and can remain totally unconcerned at any deficit in their trade balance. They rest secure in the knowledge that any deficit they incur will eventually be met.

Thus, the franc area means much more than mere monetary collaboration: it is an entire system of economic and financial assistance.[6] It makes provision for the entirely free transfer of capital, which is a great asset for French private interests, as incomes can be transferred and capital removed whenever they are disposed to do so—the ultimate protection in the case of any serious political difficulty. Such total freedom provides the incentive for private capital to take risks in investment in the economy of the African countries; fresh injections of capital into African economies must make for brisker trade.

However, the essential link between France and its former overseas territories is in the aid actually granted to them. The main channels (other than the provision of funds for technical assistance, notably the cost of French teachers sent to Africa and of scholarships for African students in France) are the Fonds d'Aide et de Coopération (FAC) and its paying agent, the Caisse Centrale de Coopération Economique. French aid dispensed through the FAC is mainly in the form of grants. Since 1962, it has also been disbursing long-term loans, with a very low rate of interest: such loans represent 8 per cent of all funds provided since 1962.

The aid from the FAC takes two forms. First, broadly-based operations undertaken by the French government and its bodies, or by inter-state organisations, at the request of the African states, dealing with general technical surveys and studies, research into agriculture or mining, cultural or social activities and school building. Second, the development programmes of the countries. Tables 4 to 6 show the relative importance of the credits

331

reserved for these two categories of operations, from 1959 to December 31, 1966. Table 4 indicates the year-by-year value of the credits disbursed by the FAC since its establishment. The main beneficiaries are, of course, the thirteen states of Black Africa of the franc area (including Mali) and Madagascar. Some support has also been given to Congo–Kinshasa, Ethiopia, Burundi and Rwanda. The years 1959–60 and 1962–63 saw a sharp increase in credits, followed by a decrease in 1964; in 1965 and 1966 aid has been maintained at just over 500 million French francs (rather more then $ (US) 100 million). Tables 5 and 6 are more detailed, but they refer only to the development programmes of the states. Table 5 gives the distribution of credits for each country and for each year between 1959 and 1966. Table 6 also shows the distribution of credits for each state, but indicates this time the operations involved for the whole period from 1959 to the end of 1966. In each table all reference to operations in Congo–Kinshasa, Ethiopia, Burundi and Rwanda have been eliminated, which accounts for the slight discrepancies between these tables and Table 4. It is noteworthy that credits have fluctuated widely since 1959 and that the average amount disbursed on development programmes is about 330 million French francs a year (about $ (US) 70 million). The major beneficiaries are Madagascar (by far the greatest), Cameroun, Ivory Coast, Dahomey, Senegal, Niger and Mauritania. The tables also show that two-thirds of all sums granted have been devoted to development projects, production and the infrastructure.

The Caisse Centrale also acts as 'delegate payer' (payeur délégué) of the European Development Fund (EDF). Payments under that heading, on the French account, amounted to 430 million francs in 1966 as compared with 425 millions in 1965— which means an additional 85 million in account units (i.e., dollars) to French bilateral aid. This therefore represents a very substantial augmentation of French aid to Black Africa and to Madagascar. The concept of the EDF is interesting for several reasons. It originated from French initiative which dated back to before the independence of the African territories. At the Common

Table 4: Credits Disbursed by the Fonds d'Aide et de Coopération, 1959–66

(figures in thousand francs)

	1959	1960	1961	1962	1963	1964	1965	1966	Total
Operations of general interest	46,556	170,497	124,827	192,376	305,025	262,441	195,264	202,540	1,499,526
Participation in development programmes of the African states	307,002	355,566	333,460	296,793	383,189	333,756	315,479	321,906	2,647,151
Total	353,558	526,063	458,287	489,169	688,214	596,197	510,743	524,446	4,146,677

Source: Caisse Centrale de Coopération Economique, *Rapport d'Activités, 1966*, Paris 1967.

Table 5: Credits allocated by the Board of Management of the FAC for Development Programmes in French-Speaking Africa and Madagascar, from its origin up to December 31, 1966: Distribution by State and by Year

(figures in thousand francs)

	1959	1960	1961	1962	1963	1964	1965	1966	Total
Senegal	12,784	26,961	23,771	27,535	22,482	43,467	12,022	23,073	192,095
Mali	22,646	34,515	14,600	22,020	1,601	5,441	463	3,230	104,516
Ex-Federation of Mali	9,442	11,394	6,332	—	—	—	—	—	14,504
Mauritania	4,530	27,218	71,235	13,743	14,405	14,280	19,619	9,876	174,906
Ivory Coast	19,580	35,481	20,621	39,306	51,034	21,737	48,223	32,131	268,113
Upper Volta	20,218	23,142	19,783	19,018	19,626	17,056	21,186	24,020	164,049
Dahomey	88,050	15,119	23,247	11,644	35,599	19,703	16,447	23,505	233,314
Niger	10,132	26,047	2,400	27,206	33,849	30,684	22,773	31,834	184,925
Gabon	9,604	18,967	19,722	19,197	16,380	9,951	16,843	17,279	127,943
Congo	12,836	23,445	15,980	10,276	24,051	16,305	2,430	7,111	112,434
Central African Rep.	7,102	24,749	15,906	4,840	13,641	34,510	8,987	16,153	125,888
Chad	10,386	25,710	11,314	12,102	31,628	23,080	29,544	16,286	160,050
Madagascar	35,464	58,250	46,461	52,001	62,919	44,167	54,361	46,317	399,940
Cameroun	37,882	1,341	41,797	37,256	39,248	31,694	44,109	43,478	276,805
Togo	6,346	3,227	12,955	649	15,503	14,736	4,638	19,372	77,426
Total	307,002	336,366	349,124	297,793	481,944	316,711	292,645	322,665	2,616,908

Source: Caisse Centrale de Coopération Economique, *Rapport d'Activités, 1966*, Paris 1967.

Table 6: Credits allocated by the Board of Management of the FAC for Development Programmes in French-Speaking Africa and Madagascar, from its origin up to December 31, 1966: Distribution by State and by Type of Operation.

(figures in thousand francs)

Country	Contributions	General expenses	Development and production	Infrastructure	Capital goods for social services	Total	In the form of advances
Senegal	2,508	19,065	74,740	38,114	57,668	192,095	29,530
Mali	—	5,022	82,974	7,257	9,263	104,516	12,600
Ex-Federation of Mali	—	6,318	—	6,560	1,626	14,504	—
Mauritania	57,974	14,274	33,379	61,722	7,557	174,906	7,800
Ivory Coast	—	36,516	74,400	45,969	111,228	268,113	10,940
Upper Volta	—	25,069	76,561	25,717	36,702	164,049	760
Dahomey	—	8,469	51,355	152,314	21,175	233,313	—
Niger	—	22,681	74,950	59,539	28,356	184,926	5,400
Gabon	300	12,624	29,134	63,292	22,593	127,943	300
Congo	—	15,280	40,347	35,493	21,314	112,434	4,700
Central African Rep.	26	8,214	54,610	36,736	26,302	125,888	2,960
Chad	—	19,536	54,743	47,242	38,529	160,050	4,040
Madagascar	—	39,736	161,501	110,453	88,250	399,940	8,091
Cameroun	—	27,674	54,343	122,461	72,327	276,805	—
Togo	—	3,883	21,392	40,946	11,205	77,426	900
Total	60,808	263,761	884,429	853,815	554,095	2,616,908	88,021

Source: Caisse Centrale de Coopération Economique, *Rapport d'Activités, 1966*, Paris 1967.

Market meeting in Venice in May 1956, France persuaded its partners to establish this fund, which was to supplement the aid already granted directly to overseas territories which were still the responsibility of member countries of the EEC. France's partners were at first somewhat reluctant; they felt the French territories would be more favoured as they were more numerous. Moreover, in its early days, the idea of such a fund smacked of colonialism: its operation would ensure that the colonial powers would continue to exert influence on their former overseas possessions. The projects financed in these territories by the fund were to be prepared and submitted to the Brussels authorities by the metropolitan powers. Later, a special clause was to associate all the overseas departments and territories which were still dependent on member states to the European Economic Community established by the Rome Treaty on March 25, 1957. A fund of $ (US) 581 million was established as from January 1, 1958, for a five-year term. One of the intentions of France was that it should not shoulder this entire burden alone, and, indeed, West Germany bore an equal share, as is indicated by the following figures: West Germany and France, $ (US) 200 million each; Belgium and the Netherlands, 70 million each; Italy, 40 million; Luxemburg, 1·25 million. These funds were to be distributed to overseas territories according to the following proportions: territories having special relations with France, $ (US) 525 million; territories having special relations with the Netherlands, 35 million; territories having special relations with Belgium, 30 million; the territory (Somalia) having a special relation with Italy, 5 million. For various reasons —difficulties over the detailing and initiation of projects, lack of responsible officers, delay in the organisation of the fund—the EDF had not completed its operations by the end of 1962 as had been originally planned: by that time, only $ (US) 512 million of the 581 million initially allocated had been committed.

In the meantime, the territories of Africa had gained their independence and expressed their wish to negotiate for associate membership of the Common Market on a basis of equality with the founder members. France could hardly refrain from supporting its former territories in their negotiations, for after independence, even more than in 1956, France considered it was no longer its exclusive responsibility to look after their economic and social development and their welfare. The problem was no longer to satisfy the immediate needs of the African states, but to select from the projects submitted to France those which, in its sole discretion, it deemed most promising. Hence the sequel to the attainment of independence by the African states in 1960 was that the FAC depended still more than previously on the EDF; for

> underdevelopment in the African and Malagasy states [has] become an international issue. France has maintained relationships of close friendship with them; it is linked to them by a common language, culture and civilisation, and lends them very active support in the fields of technical and financial cooperation. By so doing, it does no more than fulfil its moral obligation to maintain solidarity. But it could wish that other nations as rich as itself would shoulder a similar burden, so that the problems which it once tackled single-handed might now be the responsibility of collectively-based support.[7]

The key problem of the stabilisation of world prices proved to be the most difficult part of the subsequent negotiations: indeed it was a major stumbling block. France's earlier solution was a very simple one—merely to set up 'stabilisation' funds out of which the former colonies received uneconomically large payments for their tropical produce, so that they had nothing to fear from fluctuations in the world markets. France had provided a preferential market for African and Malagasy commodities, and long discussions were needed to readjust the situation with respect to the six EEC members, since the Netherlands and Germany could not give total preference to the products of French-speaking Africa, 'tied' as they were by their traditional customers in Latin America, Asia and the Middle East. It was impossible, moreover, to continue indefinitely the overpayments for the commodities from Africa, and France had to undertake to discontinue this system. The French-speaking African countries

337

asked for some compensation in the form of a subsidy that would annul their loss once France stopped 'overpaying'. The new association agreement was signed in Yaoundé on July 20, 1963, and came into force on June 1, 1964. The second EDF began its operations at the same date, for a fresh period of five years (1964–69), without, however, abrogating the provisions of the first EDF which was still in full spate. The Yaoundé agreement made provision for the establishment of a 'zone of free circulation of commodities', which granted the associated states free access to the Common Market, and opened up the associated states as markets for EEC products. New institutions were established on a basis of parity: the Association Council was composed on the one hand of members of the Council of Ministers of the EEC and on the other of representatives of the associated states; the Association Committee, the permanent organ of the Association Council, was constituted on a similar basis of equality. The Parliamentary Conference of the Association was the counterpart of the European Parliament; and finally there was an Arbitration Court of the Association.

The second EDF is superior to the first, but it is also more diversified. Its credits total $ (US) 800 million, out of which $70 million are loans from the European Investment Bank at normal rates. Of the remaining $730 million,* $680 million are to be grants and $50 million are to be special loans at a 2 per cent interest over forty years and a ten year period of grace. But the original feature of the second EDF is the manner in which the $730 million is distributed: $500 million is earmarked for economic and social investment and for purposes of general technical co-operation (studies, research, vocational and occupational training, training of cadres) while $230 million is destined for aid to production and diversification. The assistance to production is intended to facilitate the establishment of a more efficient marketing system, to bring down prices to the level of the world market

---

* Divided as follows: West Germany, $246·5 million; France, $246·5 million; Italy, $100 million; Belgium, $69 million; Netherlands, $66 million; Luxemburg, $2 million.

(by support of prices and by improvements in the organisation of agriculture). The assistance to diversification is intended to enable the associated states to achieve a more balanced economy, both by the promotion of new crops and, wherever possible, by setting up new process industries. Most of the credits for these ends are granted to French-speaking countries: several states receive production and diversification aids (Senegal \$46·7 million; Mali \$5·6 million; Niger \$6·5 million; Ivory Coast \$46·7 million; Congo–Brazzaville \$6·4 million; Madagascar \$31·6 million) while three receive diversification aid only (Mauritania \$5 million; Upper Volta \$6 million; Gabon \$4 million). Four other states, non-members of the franc area, receive the other \$32 million. Thus it is the French-speaking countries that are most concerned with the institutions established by the Yaoundé agreement. They are well aware of the coolness towards the agreement shown by countries such as Germany and the Netherlands which would prefer to see interest-bearing loans take the place of many of the outright grants—though the EDF administrators stress it is unwise to make loans to countries that are unlikely to be able to repay them. Germany, whose contributions are equal to those of France, gets back 6 per cent of its contributions to the EDF through contracts granted to German firms; but French firms, which have long been established in the associated states, still succed in capturing 70 per cent of all the contracts awarded.

African Grievances

The African states are not altogether satisfied with the situation. First, they maintain that the European countries have not abided by the clauses of the Yaoundé agreement. They prepared a case which summarises the key problems of African and Malagasy states,[8] which figured on the agenda of the meeting in Algiers of the seventy-seven states of the Third World, and at the United Nations Conference for Trade and Development, held in New Delhi. The countries of the OCAM have sought to show that European markets were not opened up to commodities from

French-speaking Africa and Madagascar. It appears from documents published by the EEC that the annual rate of growth for exports from Latin and Central America to Europe has been 8·1 per cent, for exports from Asiatic countries 5·7 per cent, as compared with only 3 per cent for exports from the OCAM countries. The most striking example is the boom in the imports of bananas from Latin America, whose value increased by 64 per cent as compared with a mere 11 per cent rise in the value of bananas imported from Africa. The OCAM complains especially strongly against West Germany, France's main partner in the EDF, whose markets, after Yaoundé, should have been opened more widely to African exports, but where the consumption of bananas, while increasing by 30 per cent over the period 1962–65 (from 467,000 tons to 607,000 tons), showed no variation in the traditional pattern of trade. The African countries maintain that German importers could easily have honoured their existing contracts with Latin America, while turning to Africa to meet the very timely increase in German domestic consumption. But this they did not do: Germany failed to fulfil its undertakings to its African partners.

Table 7: German Imports for 1965 of OCAM Commodities in $ (US) (c.i.f. prices).

	Total imports	Imports from OCAM	Percentage
Fresh pineapple	2,265,000	47,000	1·78
Groundnuts	14,518,000	64,000	0·44
Bananas	81,193,000	1,000	0
Timber	113,896,000	55,434,000	48·67
Cocoa (in beans)	74,656,000	27,423,000	36·73
Green coffee	285,409,000	10,362,000	3·63
Rubber	84,386,000	1,734,000	2·05
Cotton	177,223,000	918,000	0·51
Cabbage palms	21,972,000	1,104,000	5·02

Source: Moniteur Africain, June 7, 1967.

Table 7 demonstrates that, for other commodities, too, German imports from the OCAM are often little more than a cypher.

The second complaint is that the price of African commodities

Table 8: Price of Traditional Tropical Commodities Purchased by the
EEC.

	1958 (price in $/ton)	*1965* (price in $/ton)	Percentage decrease
Bananas (Ivory Coast)	131·82	87·39	34
Cocoa (Cameroun)	842·84	381·71	55
Coffee (Central Afr. Rep.)	807·17	645·97	20
Cotton (Dahomey)	654·24	497·28	24
Vanilla (Madagascar)	16,772·00	10,141·97	23
Groundnuts (Niger)	181·93	143·45	22

Source: Moniteur Africain, June 7, 1967.

displays a steady decrease, as is shown by Table 8. The fall in these
prices would have been even more important if the French market
had not continued to extend preference to African goods. A
comparison of the indexes for food prices over the years 1958–66
show an increase from 100 to 113 among the industrialised countries as contrasted with a fall in the developing countries from 100
to 88. Moreover, producers' prices have been falling steadily in the
same period—and herein lies the reason for the discrepancies
between the standards of urban and rural Africa already mentioned. In the Ivory Coast, a country comparatively rich by Black
African standards, where 87 per cent of the coffee and 95 per cent
of the cocoa is produced on small holdings rather than on large
plantations, agricultural prices have varied in the following
manner.

Crop year	Coffee Price $ per kg.	Cocoa Price $ per kg.
1958–59	0·47	0·36
1959–60	0·42	0·38
1960–61	0·38	0·38/0·32
1961–62	0·32	0·28
1962–63	0·32	0·28
1963–64	0·32/0·36	0·28
1964–65	0·36	0·28
1965–66	0·30	0·22

The third point—a consequence of the first two—is the constant deterioration in the terms of trade, that is to say the relation between the value per unit of exports and the value per unit of imports. Some have spoken of a 'plunder of the Third World'.[9] Payments per ton of imports by the industrialised countries increased by 8 per cent over the period 1950–62; but their income from exports to the Third World increased by 19 per cent over the same period. This state of affairs is a result of the failure of trade in primary goods to hold its own with that of manufactured goods. The index ratio between primary and manufactured goods has fallen successively from 122 in 1950 to 100 in 1958, 98 in 1959 and 92 in 1965. Among manufactured goods generally, it is capital goods that have shown the sharpest increase. Imports have also been markedly influenced by the 80 per cent increase in freight rates over the period 1957–65. Thus, the sale price of a ton of coffee from the Ivory Coast would buy 24 tons of cement in 1957 but only 18 tons in 1965, and a ton of cocoa from the same source would buy 20 tons in 1958 and 14 tons in 1965. One ton of Camerounese cocoa was in 1965 the equivalent of 800 metres of unbleached material, as compared with 2,700 metres in 1960. It has been estimated that this deterioration in the terms of trade has led to a loss to the Third World in 1962 of $ (US) 11,000 million or 130 per cent of the total financial aid received in that year. The OCAM cites the Ivory Coast as having lost over $ (US) 200 million between 1960 and 1965 on three main commodities alone: $120 million on coffee, $73 million on cocoa and about $12 million on bananas. The total aid that it received from all sources in the same years was only $60 million.

These being the circumstances, the OCAM is now raising the cry: 'Fair trade is better than aid'. Its specialists argue that the United States helped Europe to restore its tottering economy in the years 1945–56 by the Marshall Plan and the Economic Co-operation Administration for obvious political reasons, and did not lose much in the bargain. Now that Europe itself is strong and powerful, especially in the framework of the EEC, it must show itself to be even more generous than in the past—for the survival of the

OCAM countries 'as free and stable economico-political units' will depend on the generosity of their European partners. OCAM's present demands are that the price of commodities be stabilised at a fair price and that the articles of the Association of African and Malagasy States to the EEC be literally applied.

Of course, the grievances of the OCAM group are closely similar to the general complaints of the seventy-seven countries from the Third World against the thriving and industrialised countries. The Algiers Charter of the seventy-seven stands as an historic landmark, for it is more than a mere summary of grievances; it is a 'declaration of the rights of developing countries', and these countries have already shown that on certain general matters, at any rate, they can present a united front.[10] The spokesman of the African group at Algiers, Senegal's Doudou Thiam, described the Algiers Charter as an indication of the prevailing desire of all countries of the Third World to co-operate with the richer, more highly industrialised nations, but he said that it is also a solemn refutation of the old colonial pact, according to which the former colonial countries were allowed to produce only raw materials and had to import the manufactured goods. This outdated pact, he said, must be replaced by new rights—the right to develop. 'The problem of development', he declared, 'and of the aid required from industrialised powers, cannot be any longer a matter of ethics, can no longer smack of patronising charity. It must instead become a legal duty.'

France may be expected to prove most sympathetic to these trends in policy, which very largely echo its own official viewpoint which has been expressed in great detail in the so-called Jean-neney Report.[11] This Report strongly denies that French policy in Africa was ever motivated by economic considerations and asserts that the advantages it sought were of a loftier kind: it tried to keep the friendship of many an African state, which might 'in unfore-told circumstances, respond with diplomatic or military support';[12] and France could expect to derive indirect economic advantages and to enrich itself culturally. It is to France's advantage to provide modern industrial capital equipment—it could in the

343

future lead to the receipt of valuable orders. By helping the countries of the Third World, France encourages the expansion of its own firms and spreads the fame of its technicians. On the other hand, France has tried to make other countries aware of the French way of life and methods of thinking, and to broadcast French culture. Finally, in the long run, such co-operation is expected to accelerate the development of the recipients whose peoples will become welcome partners of France: 'their new prosperity will have an impact upon our older prosperity. A process of mutual development will gradually establish itself, and whereas now it is effective and valuable only inside the Atlantic framework, it will later spread and develop in other continents.'[13]

Needless to say the greater part of aid from the public sector of France is still directed towards the African countries of the franc area, though after de Gaulle's visit to some countries of the Third World there have been slight increases in French aid in other directions. French co-operation programmes for the whole of Africa (including North Africa, i.e. chiefly Algeria) were estimated to represent 73 per cent of the total aid from France in 1965, as compared with 88 per cent in 1960. In 1962, the OECD estimated that aid from members of the so-called Development Aid Committee amounted to $(US) 13·6 per capita in Africa north of the Sahara, and $4·4 per capita in Africa south of the Sahara, as compared with $4·1 in South America, $5 in the Middle East, $1·9 in South Asia, and $3·3 in the Far East.[14] Bairoch's figures are even more eloquent: $10·9 per inhabitant in the franc area in Africa south of the Sahara, and $28·1 per inhabitant for Algeria.[15]

It must be remembered, however, that Tables 5 and 6 have shown that French overseas aid is no longer increasing. To deal with overseas aid generally is beyond the scope of this book, but it may be noted that the United Nations has asked that, during the present decade, one per cent of the national income of the donor country be allocated to capital aid, whether public or private. The corresponding percentage for the previous period (1956–61) had been higher, averaging 1·10 per cent; by 1966 it had fallen to a mere

0·88 per cent (Table 9).[16] France still heads the countries of the Development Aid Committee, but public outlay has fallen off markedly while private input has remained roughly the same. The Development Aid Committee's comment on these figures is that 'consideration of last year's developments among the developing countries provides little basis for agreement with the optimists'. Such a disillusioned conclusion stems not only from an observation of the decrease in aid, but also from the instability recently apparent in many countries of the Third World, notably in Africa.

POLITICAL REFLECTIONS

Of the fifteen heads of state of French-speaking Africa, eight have remained in power since the first days of independence of 1960 to the end of 1968: Léopold Sédar Senghor, Mokhtar Ould Daddah, Sékou Touré, Hamani Diori, Félix Houphouet-Boigny, François Tombalbaye, Ahmadou Ahidjo and Philibert Tsiranana. Six countries have experienced a coup d'état: in the case of Congo–Brazzaville, engineered by a political opposition; and in the others—Central African Republic, Dahomey, Upper Volta, Togo and Mali—by the army. French-speaking Africa, unsupported as it is by any stable economic framework, is threatened by grave political dangers. Though it is as yet too early to view the history of the young independent Africa in true perspective and to give a truly dispassionate and objective judgment, it is possible to analyse the principal threats to political stability.

As already discussed in earlier chapters, authoritarianism has everywhere become more stringent and more dominant, particularly since 1960–61. Political parties and trade unions have become less effective; only those prepared to reach some kind of accommodation with the new governments were allowed to survive. More was heard of the African unions on the international scene than at home, where little notice was taken of their representations. As regards the political parties, only those in power had any hope of surviving. With the coming of independence the tendency

345

Table 9: The Net Flow of Financial Resources as a Percentage of National Income 1962–66.

	TOTAL OFFICIAL FLOW, NET					TOTAL PRIVATE FLOW, NET					TOTAL OFFICIAL AND PRIVATE FLOW, NET				
	1962	1963	1964	1965	1966	1962	1963	1964	1965	1966	1962	1963	1964	1965	1966
Australia	0·53	0·63	0·62	0·68	0·67	—	0·04	0·12	0·13	0·04	—	0·68	0·73	0·80	0·71
Austria	0·25	0·04	0·22	0·48	0·49	0·31	0·06	0·10	0·19	0·17	0·56	0·10	0·33	0·68	0·66
Belgium	0·77	0·81	0·66	0·84	0·64	0·47	0·86	0·75	0·89	0·67	1·24	1·67	1·42	1·73	1·31
Canada	0·19	0·32	0·39	0·35	0·52	0·19	0·11	0·04	0·12	0·14	0·38	0·43	0·43	0·47	0·66
Denmark	0·12	0·16	0·15	0·16	0·30	0·12	0·01	0·30	0·03	—0·02	0·24	0·17	0·44	0·19	0·28
France	1·76	1·39	1·24	1·06	0·95	0·76	0·68	0·82	0·80	0·75	2·51	2·06	2·07	1·87	1·70
Germany	0·69	0·60	0·53	0·55	0·54	0·27	0·23	0·36	0·30	0·27	0·96	0·83	0·89	0·85	0·81
Italy	0·33	0·28	0·13	0·20	0·24	0·84	0·56	0·44	0·39	1·04	1·17	0·84	0·57	0·59	1·28
Japan	0·19	0·27	0·19	0·36	0·37	0·43	0·24	0·29	0·36	0·32	0·62	0·51	0·48	0·73	0·69
Netherlands	0·59	0·32	0·35	0·44	0·55	0·45	0·81	0·49	1·08	0·93	1·04	1·12	1·18	1·53	1·49
Norway	0·17	0·47	0·35	0·22	0·23	—	0·02	0·12	0·49	0·07	0·17	0·50	0·48	0·71	0·29
Portugal	1·63	1·90	2·11	0·65	0·70	—	—	—	0·29	0·44	—	—	—	0·94	1·14
Sweden	0·16	0·18	0·23	0·25	0·34	0·16	0·24	0·24	0·23	0·31	0·32	0·42	0·48	0·47	0·64
UK	0·64	0·60	0·66	0·61	0·60	0·50	0·45	0·57	0·65	(0·56)	1·15	1·04	1·23	1·26	(1·16)
USA	0·77	0·76	0·66	0·64	0·60	0·18	0·18	0·25	0·33	(0·16)	0·94	0·94	0·92	0·98	(0·76)
Total DAC countries	0·72	0·69	0·61	0·60	0·57	0·30	0·27	0·34	0·39	0·31	1·02	0·96	0·95	1·00	0·88

for the executive authorities to arrogate all political power to themselves became more pronounced.[17] Very often the office of elected vice-president was eliminated from the constitution. Exceptions were few: for instance in Congo–Brazzaville, where a vice-president was necessary to win over the northern opposition; in Cameroun, where the differing viewpoints of the two halves of the Federation had to be reflected in the executive power; and in Dahomey, where the office of vice-president provided a mechanism for disrupting the unity of the opposition. The role of the national assemblies was reduced to little more than voting the means by which presidential policies might be enacted—by legislation and by financial authorisations. Some measure of control was open to them, but in no case was an Assembly allowed to call in question the political authority of the chief executive. This left little room for an opposition. They became not parliaments, but little more than ratifying bodies ('chambres d'enregistrement'). One party and one party alone assumed complete power;[18] sometimes, admittedly, because it was the only one in existence, as was the case with the Parti Démocratique de Côte d'Ivoire (PDCI) and the Union Soudanaise in Mali; sometimes because it commanded an overwhelming majority in the Assembly, as with the Parti Démocratique de Guinée (PDG); sometimes because all the dominant figures of the country gathered around one leader, like the Mauritanian chiefs around Mokhtar Ould Daddah, or the professional and intellectual elite in Niger around Hamani Diori— both of whom were influential and strong personalities who strongly disagreed with those political parties which sought a radical reorganisation of African society. The 'parties of the masses', with their overwhelming majorities, like the PDG or the Union Soudanaise, became organised in a pyramidal structure with local sections in the villages of the bush or in the urban districts and with local, provincial and national committees; and with the support of youth groups. One fact clearly stands out: the single party system can be seen as an overriding necessity originating in a complex chain of events stretching back to the origins of the new states.

The Trade Unions

The trade unionists, who had worked side by side with the politicians in the long struggle for independence, suddenly appeared as a 'pack of trouble-makers'. Even so they represented only a small section of the population, among the proletariat and sub-proletariat of the towns. The number of salaried workers was very small, and so, correspondingly, was the number of union members. In French Equatorial Africa in 1955, there were 154,754 salaried workers out of a total active population of 1,166,250; in French West Africa in 1955–7, 377,500 salaried workers out of a total active population of 4,666,000.[19] These figures are to be compared with the official International Labour Organisation estimates of 68,550 union cards in French West Africa and 9,450 in French Equatorial Africa.[20] The trade union leaders seldom came from the uneducated proletariat, but were usually junior civil servants, bank clerks or employees of private firms, and it was at this level that contact was maintained between the party leaders and the unions—though in fact it was the rank and file of the unions who had often provided the stimulus for the political evolution of modern Africa and had been a force to be reckoned with in the fight against colonialism. Naturally enough, the union leaders themselves aspired to positions of political authority; and, equally, once victory had been achieved, the unions wished for their own share of the newly-won power. There are many former trade unionists among the political leaders of Africa: heads of state like Maurice Yameogo, David Dacko, François Tombalbaye and Sékou Touré, or ministers like Camille Gris in the Ivory Coast, Abdoulaye Diallo, first in the Soudan and later in Guinea, Joseph Ouedraogo in Upper Volta, Kikounga N'Got and Tchichellé in Congo–Brazzaville. But the interests of the nationalist politician clashed with the somewhat narrower interests of the trade union leader. The leaders of independence came to be as wary of trade unionism as the colonial administration and big business had been. In former French Equatorial Africa, the number of wage-earners was estimated in 1964 to be 352,000, most of them in Cameroun with 160,000 (7 per cent of the active population); whereas in Congo–Brazzaville they numbered 70,000 (17 per cent). In West Africa (excluding Guinea) they numbered 405,960 in 1964, most of them being in the Ivory Coast (171,000, or 10 per cent of the total active population), and in Senegal (140,000, 8 per cent); in most other countries the proportion was as low as 3 per cent. Guinea had 65,000 wage-earners (4 per cent of the total active population) and Madagascar 187,000 (7 per cent of the active population).

Tribal Politics and External Threats

One of the most galling inheritances from colonial times was the partitioning of Africa, often at random, into large and small territories, with complete disregard for ecological considerations. Tribes and ethnic groups with common traditions, languages and cultural backgrounds were cut in two—for instance the Ewe on each side of the Togo–Ghana border; the Yoruba in both Dahomey and Western Nigeria; the Lari around the Stanley Pool in Congo–Brazzaville and in Congo–Léopoldville (now Kinshasa). On the other hand, rival tribes were thrown together and compelled to arrive at a reluctant and unstable entente, as had been the case in pre-colonial days. The discontent which followed such arbitrary partitioning encouraged the formation of many rival political parties: for instance, in Congo–Brazzaville, the Mouvement Socialiste Africain (MSA) representing the northern M'Bochi and the Union Démocratique de Défense des Intérêts Africains (UDDIA) representing the Lari in the Stanley Pool area; in Gabon, the deep division between northern and southern Fangs led to the formation of separate parties, the Union Démocratique de la Société Gabonaise (UDSG) and the Bloc Démocratique Gabonais (BGD); in Dahomey, Hubert Maga's Rassemblement Démocratique Dahoméen (RDD) supported by most of the north and by a few from the south, Apithy's Parti Nationaliste Dahoméen (PND), supported by the south-east and

349

the south-west, and Ahomadegbé's Union Démocratique Daho-méenne (UDD), which was dominant in the centre of the country. The innumerable parties which arose in the final days of the colonial era flourished on traditional tribal enmities, and their existence spelt unrest, and possibly a real threat, to the parties which came to power after independence.

Whether real or imaginary, fears of external intervention were in many cases the strongest influence leading to a one-party system. These fears arose from many different sources. In some cases, countries had allied themselves with one of the large groups of rival states; these rivalries produced activities which led to constant accusations of 'interfering in the domestic affairs of their neighbours'. Such accusations were first levelled at the unions, particularly at the Union Générale des Travailleurs d'Afrique Noire (UGTAN) which supported Sékou Touré and sought to spread its influence in the Ivory Coast and Senegal. A more enduring factor was the role of outlawed political parties and exiled leaders; for instance, Djibo Bakary, formerly mayor of Niamey, and before that, Vice-President of Niger—thus the predecessor in office of Hamani Diori, later President of Niger. Bakary became the leader of the Sawaba movement (Movement for Liberty) and, from exile, he directed the tiny resistance groups in his native land. Until his death, many abortive coups and plots throughout French-speaking Africa were attributed to Félix Moumié, the leader of the rebel groups formed from the former Union des Populations Camerounaises (UPC).

The political leaders came to feel the need for an increasingly tight grip on the political situation. It was an easy matter for governments to point to the articles of their constitutions, which were modelled on Article 16 of the French constitution, as a justi-fication for imprisoning political suspects, censoring the press, restricting the rights of the individual and strengthening the powers of the police. In fact, however, the power of the executive derived less from interpretation of the written constitutions than from the fact that a powerful, highly organised party was in power, whatever its status might be in strictly constitutional terms.[21] In

1963–64 the opposition parties had few prospects ahead of them; those that chose to lie low and lead a clandestine life had neither money nor support, and only those parties on the government side were able to take an active part in the political and administrative life of the country. This was the kind of situation that prepared the ground for the military coups that were to engulf so many African states.

The African Middle Class

In his message to the nation of January 10, 1962, Sékou Touré said that '*the* party' had become identified with the revolutionary reconstruction of society. But in spite of all he said there had been no revolution in Africa in 1960; no basic reorganisation of the way of life or the social structure on the attainment of independence. True enough, there was, as we have already seen, something of an egalitarian revolution, with the colonial subjects taking the place of their masters and trying to take over all their assets and possessions. But the new leaders found themselves confronted with a tragic situation which they had not expected, but which was an unavoidable sequel to colonialism. The men who came to power had been educated by the Westernising colonisers, had adopted their ways, their habits, their outlook, had become so assimilated into a Western culture, in spite of the purely intellectual attraction of 'negritude', that they were completely cut off from the masses of the vast world of rural Africa. For the man in the street, or the man in the bush, they were very often just a new kind of ruler replacing the old. African politicians could shout themselves hoarse proclaiming that the class struggle was alien to Africa; but in fact independence created new classes of 'haves' and 'have nots'. It was a black bourgeoisie that came to power. It was this bourgeoisie, composed of an educated elite, which was to give confidence to the 'donor' countries, obtain from them important technical, economic and financial help, be most active in debating those international problems which concern Africa, and proclaim loudly that Africa should *unite*; but at the same time it was soon to be destroyed by

351

power. The so-called egalitarian revolution was one way by which this bourgeoisie was made ineffective. The discrepancies between the conditions in the urban and rural areas that were described earlier in this chapter bear evidence to this sad fact, as does the large unproductive expenditure we have observed, and the squandering of large sums on unnecessary administrative organisations.

The criticisms commonly levelled by the leaders of Africa themselves—for instance, the leaders of the Central African Republic, Senegal, Upper Volta and Mali—are the corruption of the civil services, fraudulent conversion of public funds, and the absence of a sense of communal responsibility among the people. Although this latter could very properly be applied to the administrations themselves, it is quite wrong to use it as a justification for compelling by force—even at gunpoint—the poor peasants and nomads to pay their taxes. A whole chapter on taxation in Africa would not suffice to uncover all the details of the activity of governments in this field. Other obvious corruptions are the disproportionately high salaries of MPs, ministers, ambassadors and higher civil servants. The figures tell an eloquent story.

Out of a total current expenditure in Senegal in 1964–65 of 35,000 million CFA francs, 47·2 per cent was disbursed on salaries. The Senegalese Plan and Finances Commission pointed out that the country was spending twice as much on salaries as on operating and maintenance costs. In fact, current expenditure exceeded revenues. This came as no surprise, for Senegal had inherited the whole burden of the federal administration established at the time of the AOF. A similar situation existed in Brazzaville, where on January 1, 1964, 11,000 were employed in the administration: in four years, expenditure on civil servants had increased by 88·8 per cent. In the Ivory Coast, expenditure on the civil service amounts to 58 per cent of the total budget, and civil servants, including the army, number 29,000. If we deduct 6,000 in the army and an equal number of teachers, and also a few of the lower-graded state employees, there remain about 15,000 civil servants—less than 0·5 per cent of the total population—consuming 58 per cent of the total national budget.[22] Similar examples could be found in Dahomey, Madagascar or Togo.

The decolonisation of Africa gave birth to a new administrative upper middle class and to an embittered bureaucracy of minor state employees, jealous of the advantages of their new 'patrons'. It also led to the creation of national armies. Thus, with the military on the one hand and the 'red tape' middle class on the other, Africa over the years 1958–61 created those very bodies which were later to foment political unrest. Moreover, whenever any kind of insurrection occurs, it is the army, the only coherent and organised body remaining, which either steps into power or lends its support to whatever power rises up.

The African Army, its Origins and Motivations

Before considering the recent military coups of the new Africa, it is essential to explain the origins and the development of the African national armies of today.[23] Circumstances are very different in Black Africa from those in Asia or in the Middle East, where a tradition of militarism has long been established. In South-East Asia, locally-based military forces had been established with the active support of the British colonial power; after they had been neutralised, they were often nevertheless asked to help and used to maintain order and to protect the interests of the Crown. The Arab armies of the Middle East, for their part, were a legacy of the Turkish Empire. Black Africa, on the other hand, had practically no military tradition in colonial days. Its conquest by the colonial powers had been comparatively easy, and, apart from special emergencies, such as the two World Wars, small military contingents had proved fully adequate to deal with the few small local clashes which occurred. There was little violence and the military force was seldom invoked. Thus the modern armies of Africa are essentially post-colonial organisations. They were never established to fight for liberation against the colonial power, as, for instance, was the army of Algeria, which stemmed from the Front de Libération National.

353

The British, in accordance with their traditional policy of engendering 'self-government', set up at an early stage mature military and police forces commanded by African officers and NCOs. France, by contrast, incorporated African elements within its own forces—a reproduction in the military sphere of the policy of assimilation applied on the political front. It was even more of a success, in fact, than the assimilation policy practised on a territorial level, for it is well known that in the army a man easily loses his identity, is obliged to defer to the rules, regulations and ethos of the unit and to identify himself with the communal uniforms, emblems and demeanour of the soldier. Such a mould had, of course, been cast according to European standards. The African and Malagasy soldiers enlisted in the army lost their individuality just as readily as did their French comrades. But the effect was far greater on the Africans, for they were completely cut from their traditional tribal milieu and thrown into a new one, just as traditional but quite alien from anything they had known. The compensation for so demoralising a loss of identity was the security they gained for themselves and their families, who either followed them and rapidly assimilated Western manners, or stayed at home and thrived on their share of the soldiers' pay.

After the Second World War, in which a significant number of colonial troops had been involved, France tried to train African and Malagasy officers and NCOs by methods similar to those practised in France. The French military colleges (Coetquidan, for example) were opened to citizens of all French overseas territories, who were to enjoy a status identical with that of French citizens. A new military college, Efortom, was founded, specially adapted to the needs of trainees from Africa. It was to provide crash-courses for those African and Malagasy NCOs who had gained practical military experience without having had the opportunity of formal officer training. Every year 25 to 30 'sous-lieutenants' are prepared for lieutenants' appointments in the regular army—this programme continues to the present day. In colonial days there had also been special military schools for children which gave them a general education and some background technical knowledge

354

which fitted them for the military life at the end of their course. In 1950, in the French overseas territories, there were the following African and Malagasy army personnel: one colonel, 3 majors and 50 lieutenants or sous-lieutenants; by 1960, there were 4 colonels, 6 majors, 31 captains, 157 lieutenants or sous-lieutenants, as well as 800 army children ('enfants de troupe') receiving education. All these officers were fully trained, and were to become the leaders of the young African armies.[24] However, imbued in them was a very particular outlook which turned their aspirations to power outside a strictly military milieu: Lieutenant-Colonel Sangoulé Lamizana became President of Upper Volta; Colonel Bokassa became President of the Central African Republic; until 1967 Lieutenant-Colonel Soglo was President of Dahomey; and Lieutenant-Colonel, now General, Eyadema is President of Togo. All of them, except Eyadema, are former officers of the French army, sharing the same beliefs and aspirations as French officers. In 1958, Bokassa was a lieutenant in the French army before becoming an officer in the CAR army. Lamizana had ended his career in the French army as a major. Soglo had enlisted at 21, had fought in the 1939–40 campaign as a sergeant-major, had landed in the south of France in 1944 as a sous-lieutenant; he was still a French citizen in 1961 and adopted Dahomean citizenship only when he was appointed a colonel. Eyadema was the only one who had spent a long period in the ranks. Between 1953 and 1961 he rose steadily from private to sergeant-major, and was commissioned only after Olympio's death.

All these soldiers, who later graduated into political leaders, had fought in the Indochina campaign. They had been very close to the French officers who believed they were waging war in Indochina, and later in Algeria, to fend off Communism and protect French interests overseas. Such viewpoints, in no way shared by all their compatriots, should have remained very alien to an African. But 'la discipline fait la force principale des armées' ('discipline is the main strength of armies'); they had been taught to obey, to respect and defer to their seniors; and so they obeyed orders and did their duty as officers. Eyadema was in a slightly different position, but the present Togolese leader also happened to have taken part in the Algerian campaign. And the heads of states are not the only examples: in Togo, Colonel Dadjo, the present leader of the Comité Togolais de Réconciliation Nationale, fought with the Free French Forces in 1941, and was appointed captain after three years in Indochina, and the number of his French decorations and medals won in military campaigns and with the French Resistance commands respect. Soglo's successor as President of the Republic of Dahomey, Lieutenant-Colonel Alley, is a former pupil of the army's school for children in Bingerville (Ivory Coast), a former private in the Fifth Regiment of 'tirailleurs sénégalais' in Dakar, and saw service first in Indochina in 1950 to 1953 and then in Algeria from 1956 to 1961, before his return to Dahomey as a sous-lieutenant.

Thousands of African officers, NCOs and private soldiers were to be abruptly transferred from the unified French army to several national armies. According to provisions of the short-lived Franco-African Community, established in 1958, the army was to remain under a unified control, but when the Community broke up and the states gained their independence, France 'bequeathed to the new African and Malagasy nations part of its own troops'.[25] The details of the transfers of troops involved were the subjects of formal agreements. Most states (other than Guinea and Mali) also entered into defence agreements with France. French bases, while being maintained by African personnel, nevertheless still belonged to the French army; a somewhat complex situation, but one not unprofitable to the young African nations, for the cost of maintaining these bases brought important revenues to the African treasuries, and later their withdrawal was to prove a severe financial loss —in some cases catastrophic—as has been pointed out in Part II. Moreover, the former African and Malagasy soldiers who were paid pensions brought to their countries invisible credits of no small importance.

Table 10 indicates the countries with which France has concluded defence agreements and where it maintains troops (chiefly

Madagascar, Senegal, Ivory Coast, Chad and the Central African Republic). It seems striking enough to mention the combined navy and air force exercise in Ivory Coast called 'Alligator III' which, in September 1967, gathered 8,000 men on the French side (two thousand having, in fact, participated in the operations) and 1,500 men on the Ivorian side. These manoeuvres had political as well as military objectives. The Ivory Coast government wanted to prove the loyalty of the army, to show it was much more concerned with protecting the country against any possible external aggression than in seeking to overthrow the government. It was also an opportunity for the Ivory Coast army to have further contact with the French army, to which many Ivorian soldiers and officers used to belong. 'Alligator III' was for the French an interesting exercise, the forces involved proving to be inadequate, with equipment that was too heavy and too slow. The manoeuvres were under the command of General Kergavarat, the French Commander-in-Chief in Central Africa, and General Thomas d'Aquin Ouattana, the Chief of Staff of the Ivory Coast army.

Table 10 shows the characteristic African contrast between the smallness of the armed forces and the enormous military expenses in the former overseas French territories. The armies of the new countries were never very large, but recent events have shown that, in Africa, ninety paratroopers are capable of overthrowing a government. It is notable how severe a financial burden these national armies can prove: 20 per cent of the ordinary budget in Mauritania and Cameroun, more than 20 per cent in Mali, well over 10 per cent in Senegal, Madagascar, Niger, Dahomey, Togo, etc. These figures do not include the important gendarmerie forces* that often provide a counterpoise to the influence of the army, as in the Ivory Coast. There are also special forces or

* Cameroun, 3,000 men strong; Central African Republic, 500, with a 'republican guard' of 700 men; Chad, 550; Congo–Brazzaville, 1,400; Dahomey, 1,200; Gabon, 600; Ivory Coast, 1,500; Madagascar, 3,100; Mali, 1,000; Mauritania, included in the total figure for the whole army; Niger, 1,300 (including 1,000 in the 'national guard'); Senegal, 1,500; Togo, 1,000; Upper Volta, 1,500 (including 1,000 in the 'national guard').

Table 10: Armed Forces of French-Speaking African States

Country	Population	Total armed forces	Defence estimates (million CFA francs)	Total budget 1965 (million CFA francs)	Remarks
Congo–Brazzaville	840,000	1,800	925	10,462	Bilateral defence agreement with France. Also large Chinese military mission active in Brazzaville. Cuban assistance perhaps much more active than the Chinese, until 1968 coup.
Gabon	463,000	750	625	8,236	Bilateral defence agreement with France.
Central African Republic	1,322,000	600	575	7,244	Bilateral defence agreement with France. Small French garrison at Bouar.
Chad	3,307,000	900	1,426	10,500	Bilateral defence agreement with France. Small French base in Fort Lamy.
Cameroun	5,229,000	3,500	3,900	19,959	All French troops have left the country. No defence treaty but technical assistance agreement under which France has provided funds and handed over military equipment.

Ivory Coast	3,835,000	4,000	2,175	31,875	Bilateral defence agreement with France and a regional defence agreement with France, Niger and Dahomey. French military air base at Port Bouet, a suburb of Abidjan.
Upper Volta	4,858,000	1,500	700	4,974	No defence treaty with France nor any French bases. Only technical co-operation agreement which provides for French military assistance.
Niger	3,328,000	1,200	900	8,386	Bilateral defence agreement with France and regional defence agreement with France, Dahomey and Ivory Coast.
Dahomey	2,365,000	1,800	995	8,268	Same as for Niger. Last French troops left in March 1965.
Togo	1,638,000	1,450	672	4,974	Bilateral defence and aid agreement with France, signed after the military coup which overthrew President Olympio.
Senegal	3,490,000	5,500	5,200	45,948	Bilateral defence treaty with France. Centre of a 'zone d'outre-mer'.

Table 10—*cont. over page.*

Table 10—contd.

Country	Population	Total armed forces	Defence estimates (million CFA francs)	Total budget 1965 (million CFA francs)	Remarks
Mauritania	1,050,000	1,000	1,000	5,581	Bilateral and technical assistance agreement with France.
Mali	4,576,000	3,500	2,175 (Mali francs)	10,025 (Mali francs)	All French troops left Mali in 1961; there is no defence treaty with France. Military equipment received from Soviet Union and Eastern Europe (before 1968 coup).
Guinea	3,500,000	5,000	1,450 (Guinean francs)	18,000 (Guinean francs)	Military equipment supplied by both Czechoslovakia and the Soviet Union.
Madagascar	6,420,000	4,000	2,500 (Malagasy francs)	25,500 (Malagasy francs)	Bilateral defence agreement with France. Centre of a 'zone d'outre-mer'. 2,500 French troops stationed at port of Diego-Suarez.

Source: Table prepared on the basis of information provided by David Wood, The Armed Forces of African States, Institute for Strategic Studies, Adelphi Papers, No. 2 April 1966.

peoples' militia—as in the Ivory Coast, in Guinea and in Congo–Brazzaville—or very costly 'services civiques de la jeunesse'—a kind of Boys' Brigade (as in Congo–Brazzaville)—that could provide support for the regime in an emergency though their primary intention is to provide some kind of purpose for school-leavers who have not yet found a job: to strengthen their sense of patriotism.

Why should armies as such be necessary if such large quasi-military organisations exist? Partly because it was unthinkable that a new state should celebrate independence without at once establishing an army and a diplomatic corps: the former in order to ensure that the latter will be respected. These two requisites are obvious if one accepts the principle of the great French hero—the revered idol and the inspiration of so many African soldiers and politicians—General de Gaulle. The army is a necessary instrument of power and a symbol of national pride and unity.[26] Revolutionary France asserted itself on the battlefield of Valmy by triumphing over a coalition of all the tyrants of Europe with an army of the people, to the battlecry of 'Vive la Nation'. Who could imagine a free country without an army? Besides being a guarantor of the interests of the nation, a real purpose of the army of a newly-created nation was to promote and stimulate a feeling of patriotism. The problem was to turn overnight a group of officers and NCOs—belonging to the French army, sharing the ideals and prejudices of the French—into the commanders of a tiny, almost non-existent army of an African country. The military leaders bent to this task with great enthusiasm and efficiency, for they at once realised the part that they would play in building up the morale of the new nations by instilling discipline and a sense of unity, inspiring a sense of patriotism and a sense of moral values among the young—knocking into shape the most vigorous part of the nation, as it were.*

The governments were equally quick to appreciate what a

* 41 per cent of the total population of Upper Volta, 53 per cent of Niger, 45 per cent of Dahomey, is below 15 years of age; 56 per cent of Togo is below 20.

valuable asset the army could prove to be. All the existing army schools were maintained in being. With the administrative experience they had acquired in the French army, with the professional training that many had received, officers and men could promote the economic and social development of their country and their participation was often required, in the first years, in public works programmes. The importance of the army steadily increased. It soon became an instrument of domestic politics, acting both as a bulwark of political stability and an incentive for economic development. It is little wonder that it soon refused to limit its activities to external affairs (defence of the territory, protection of the frontiers, control and repression of all subversive coups), and demanded to play a part in the national life. There was a danger that it might duplicate the activities of other bodies, especially the gendarmerie, whose prime responsibility was to enforce order on the home front. The army is a new institution, and, moreover, is a privileged one, as it was in colonial days, but it was shrewd enough to lie quiet for a time, to remain 'la grande muette' (as the French army prided itself on being): it refused to take sides or to align with or against the regimes established in 1958, and warily shunned the more conservative circles of African society. Meanwhile the government paid much deference to the army and did what it could to increase its prestige: officers of good reputation who had attained high rank in the French army were further promoted. Political leaders look on their armed forces as on indispensable friends, the only mainstay of their young regimes, who alone could extend help to them in times of emergency.

In spite of the reluctance, however, the leaders of the armies were compelled to commit themselves. Their reluctance is easily explained by their unpreparedness, their lack of interest in political matters, and their disdain for the microcosmic military world in which they now found themselves after having belonged to one of the great armies of the world. To many of them the change must have seemed a 'come-down'. They were soon to encounter political decisions of which they disapproved, as for instance when they were told to recruit only from ethnic groups supporting the government. In the coastal countries, the armies were encouraged to seek recruits from the coastal areas, whereas in colonial days the French had always sought to recruit the tall, hardy Northerners of the inland areas. The new African armies soon came to include an inflammatory mixture of officers, NCOs and some older soldiers who had enjoyed the privilege of membership of the former great colonial army and had a nostalgic longing for its traditions and spirit, as distinct from most of the other ranks and the younger officers who had enlisted after independence. Yet, in spite of certain inevitable clashes in their midst, the African armies retained a certain cohesion, which was made evident when they had to move into action. For the army was in fact compelled to act on several occasions. It is possible to distinguish three different characteristic situations.

In the first situation, the army provides support for a tottering political regime. For instance, in Senegal the army chose to support Senghor rather than Mamadou Dia. In Cameroun it carried out its role in defeating the guerillas of the UPC with the help of important elements of the French army; and it is still inspecting and carefully controlling the dangerous Bamileke areas in order to prevent any resurgence of maquis activity. The army in Chad suppressed the border incidents (see pp. 118-19). It continues to play the role it was assigned in the old European tradition: it protects and supports power, on behalf of the nation, so that power is indebted to its army.

In the second situation, part of the army rises against the established power but fails in its coup. Such was the case in Gabon—though it was only a partial failure, for were it not for the intervention of French paratroopers under the provisions of the defence agreement signed with France, it would have succeeded in putting the opponents of Léon M'Ba into power. In the Ivory Coast, the army never contemplated overthrowing the government; but it was the gendarmerie, not the army, that repressed subversive activity, and the government maintained that the army's outlook had been too 'lukewarm' during the 'plots' of 1963; it ruled that the armed forces should be reduced and sent to the frontier areas to guard against a possible invasion from Guinea (see page 141). In Niger, mutineers were ruthlessly punished, and the army on the whole remained loyal.

In the third situation, exemplified in Togo, Dahomey, Central African Republic and Upper Volta, the army seized power and assumed a political role. In Congo–Brazzaville, it acted behind the scenes and fomented the agitation that paved the way for Youlou's downfall. Events moved too quickly for France to intervene as it had in Gabon, notwithstanding similar defence agreements. The fallen governments were replaced by new cabinets, controlled by the army, who were shrewd enough to reassert, *at once*, their loyalty to France and to ratify the economic, financial and military agreements. De Gaulle's government cannot extend support to any African government that cannot stay in power, as was the case with Youlou's. It could only forewarn the new regimes that, should instability and anarchy prevail, French aid might be discontinued. There had been such uproar after the French intervention in Gabon that France could not afford to act similarly again, for fear of being stigmatised by the whole world as shamelessly neo-colonialist. Only a few African regimes—Senghor's in Senegal, Houphouet-Boigny's in the Ivory Coast, Ahidjo's in Cameroun, Tombalbaye's in Chad—could use their close personal links with France and its leader, and ask for help in case of emergency. According to official data given by the French Ministry of Information, French troops intervened ten times in Africa from 1960 to 1964 (Gabon and Cameroun included): three times in Mauritania in 1961, once in Congo–Brazzaville in 1960 (where, however, it did no more than cordon off certain African urban quarters when they became overheated following clashes with the Matsuanist sect), in Niger in December 1963, and 'several times' in Chad.

All the rebellions against governments had two factors in common. They were essentially urban operations, usually limited to the capital town; this is very characteristic of the discontent among urban and semi-urban populations and of the utter indifference to political matters of the people of the bush: the 98 or 99 per cent votes for Youlou, Yameogo and others were either fictional or artificially inflated. The other common factor is that wherever a coup took place, no neighbouring state made any move to come to the assistance of the overthrown regime. Even when Olympio was assassinated in Togo, the mild reaction which spread over Africa soon abated. The inter-state agreements over defence or mutual assistance, such as those between the Entente states, were no more than a dead letter. Houphouet-Boigny did not feel himself under any obligation to fly to the rescue of his former colleagues and friends, Maurice Yameogo or Hubert Maga, when they were deep in trouble. Such a total disregard for the downfall of the once mighty shows how easy it was, and still is, for a small group of determined and well-armed opponents to engineer the overthrow of any African government, by attacking key-points and seizing control of the police and of the broadcasting stations. The smallness of African armies was no limitation on their ability to act swiftly and efficiently. Wherever they were confronted by a breakdown in a government, by riots, demands from the trade unions, unrest in the capitals or main towns (for instance Cotonou, Porto Novo and Ouagadougou), they responded to those who raised the cry: 'We want the Army.' They reacted ostensibly in favour of those who stood for obedience, discipline, honesty and austerity, and ejected those political leaders who were accused of being unscrupulous and of squandering the slender resources of the country. Such were the motives of Soglo and Lamizana and Bokassa, but, once in power, they soon came to realise that the situation could be improved only under a permanent ruler. Soglo rapidly learned the problems which beset a civilian government, for the political parties at once resumed their quarrelling and the three political leaders—and especially the two most militant, Apithy and Ahomadegbé—could never reach any agreement. Therefore, Soglo came to believe that he alone could govern the country. It was proving impossible for the army to provide protection for the ruling power and to avoid stepping in to play an active role in the conflict of party politics and differing tribal interests. A similar situation arose in Togo, where, after the military coup against Olympio, the civilian government found itself under the protection of the army. Here, again, the army assumed control over the entire machinery of government.

Speaking to the newspaper *Le Figaro* on May 12, 1966, Colonel Lamizana declared:

> We had been taught two things by the French army: discipline, and how to save the state's finances. This lesson we have not forgotten in five years. When we stepped in, we found the coffers of the state empty. First we cut down the ministers' salaries and got rid of all abuses. Civil servants had their rent, gas and electricity bills paid by unauthorised state allowances.* We have set everything in order, closed down certain embassies and a television station that was in no way educational and transmitted to only a hundred private TV sets. . . . The army is very close to the local population. We refuse to be a political party. And we could never undertake to rebuild the nation if we stooped down to such quarrels. We ignore, for the time being, the parties who are trying to re-establish themselves. Ours is a temporary mission. But it must last some time for fear the country should relapse into its past errors.

General de Gaulle might well have spoken almost identically. He might not have referred so pointedly to the army, but would have emphasised as forcibly that his *mission* was to reunite the country and prevent it from falling back into its past turmoils. However sincere his principles, Colonel Lamizana was anticipating that it was he who was to remain at the head of the government—and the other colonels had the same thought at the back of their minds. All of them except Soglo proved correct.

Anatomy of the Army Coups

In Upper Volta, the military forces halted the trade union

---

* All were habits of the white colonial masters, and had been kept by African rulers as necessary status-symbols, in the name of the 'egalitarian revolution'.

demonstration and restored order by eliminating Yameogo 'in his own interests', for his own protection. When the first President of Upper Volta fell, foreign governments that had hitherto backed him were surprised and disturbed. However, the new military government proved stable and reliable, and Lieutenant-Colonel Lamizana made a good impression at once by declaring that private interests were perfectly safe under his protection. Yet the situation was far from simple and the former President's attempted suicide was an indication of his desperate frame of mind as well as of a deteriorating political atmosphere. The country's difficult economic and financial situation could not change overnight and the new 'strong' government had no choice but to ratify the existing austerity measures decreed by the former head of state, and even increase taxation. Moreover, once the trade unions had called on the army for help, opposition parties who up to then had been lying low rose up from their oblivion and sought to re-establish their former positions.* Fortunately for the new government and for peace and order in Upper Volta, they were unable to unite to establish a common front that might have replaced the military after a period of transition. However, in September 1966, violent riots broke out in Yameogo's constituency, between some of his former followers and Joseph Ki-Zerbo's Mouvement de Libération Nationale. Such serious incidents, together with the utter inability of the former parties to define a common platform, readily persuaded the military government that it was advisable to remain in control, and in December 1966 Lamizana announced that, for the four years to come, the army would hold the reins of power, that all political activity would be suspended and that trade union activity would be tolerated provided it did not disturb public order.

In the Central African Republic, the army deliberately rebelled,

* The Mouvement de Libération Nationale, a semi-clandestine party, that had asked its political followers to vote 'No' at the referendum; the Union Démocratique Voltaïque, President Yameogo's former party; the Parti du Regroupement Africain of his great political rival, Nazi Boni; and the Groupement d'Action Populaire, a largely Muslim party.

because they were deeply shocked by the prevailing social injustices. David Dacko had been well aware of the existing social inequalities, but he lacked the strength to carry out his policy. When the army seized power, it decided to 'abolish' the middle class and yet at the same time to rid the country of all Chinese experts (see pages 112–14). At first Colonel Bokassa thought he was doing no more than pave the way for Dacko's return, by cleaning up political life and the financial situation and applying the social reforms that Dacko had projected. But soon the petty intrigues and plots of all the small political parties persuaded Bokassa that he should not relinquish power. The economic situation had had no time in which to improve; the number of unemployed had increased; the frontiers with Congo–Kinshasa and with Sudan remained dangerous; the general atmosphere was tense; discontent was rife and there were reports of a 'Front de Libération National de la République Centrafricaine' that had sentenced Dacko's successor to death. Bokassa and his governmental team were at loggerheads. A newcomer on the scene was rumoured to be Bokassa's possible successor, if another military coup were to succeed: he was Lieutenant-Colonel Alexandre Banza, Minister of State in charge of Finance and National Economy. Though these were no more than rumours, nevertheless, at the request of the CAR government, a regiment of French paratroopers was sent to Bangui shortly before November 11, 1967, in accordance with the defence agreements signed beween the two countries.[27]

In Togo, after the coup that overthrew Grunitzky and brought Colonel Eyadema into power as the new President of the Republic, there was no major incident, and Franco-Togolese relations were not impaired on the replacement of Grunitzky, a nominee of France, by officers who immediately before had served in the French army. Eyadema, who became a general in December 1967, acted in the authentic Gaullist tradition when he declared himself prepared to organise a referendum to ascertain whether the nation agreed with his policy; his followers were entrusted with preparing the election campaign. Being a Northerner himself, he has not much to fear from the traditional Northern indifference (in coastal countries), except if the case arose that an even shrewder Northerner tried to get the better of him; he is less secure in the south where the intelligentsia might find an able leader of a new opposition in Antoine Meatchi, formerly Vice-President of the Republic.

Dahomey had been dissipating its energies in a political tangle: inter-tribal rivalries, and clashes between strong political personalities. We have seen how Soglo interfered to arbitrate on the situation, and remained after he had lost all illusions on the possibility of re-establishing a civilian government. In 1966–67, the young technicians of the governmental team were working side by side with the soldiers, with commendable efficiency, but, ultimately, Dahomey was brought to the brink of a new crisis by the pressure of the suppressed political parties, by Northern intrigues (Maga's constituencies) and by Soglo's vacillations and scruples. The dynamic, enthusiastic young ministers, like Christian Vieyra or Moise Mensah, chose to quit; those who remained loyal to Soglo were older, wiser, more level-headed men like Zinsou, who held the portfolio of Foreign Affairs, and Bertin Borna, one of Maga's former ministers who resumed his role of Minister of Finance.

Shortly after his return 'not empty-handed' from a two-week visit to Paris—the first military head of state of Black Africa to have been formally invited by de Gaulle—Soglo was casually overthrown by sixty paratroopers on December 18, 1967. The pretext—if there was any—was the disapprobation by the trade unions, both in public and private, of the overlong enforcement of austerity measures. The coup had been wholly engineered and prepared by a young officer, Maurice Kouandete, just back from a specialised course at the Ecole de Guerre in Paris. Was it a reaction of the younger soldiers against the older ones? A clash between generations, the former considering the latter too conservative and over-scrupulous? Is it a mere military reaction of sophisticated young officers against their seniors who had risen from the rank and file? Is there perhaps an undercurrent of tribal feeling—

369

which would be an alarming indication of regression—since the revolutionary committee of fifteen members established by Kouandete tends to emphasise the north in its constitution, whereas Soglo came from Abomey, a town in the middle of the country? Such a rebellion shows a deep cleft inside the army: fundamental differences over the methods of military government, its points of weakness and its authoritarian methods. Soglo and his Vice-President, Lieutenant-Colonel Alley, often found it difficult to agree, but the latter was an honest man, loyal to his superior. He was asked by the 'Young Turks' to become President of the Republic, an unexpected move since they could have held what they had seized, had they not been immediately confronted by a most confusing situation. Soglo had sought refuge at the French Embassy and was refusing to resign; Zinsou was bent on giving up his former portfolio; and the young rebels were at first almost ignored by France, which had signed an economic and financial agreement with Dahomey and was now growing alarmed at the continuing instability of the Dahomean executive over the previous seven years (four presidents of the Republic since 1960). Their neighbours of the Entente were equally suspicious. Meanwhile the team in power had no authority to respond to and to reject the demands that trade unions had been formulating under the Soglo regime. Thus the revolutionary committee and members of the temporary government felt they should select a new President of the Republic and agreed on Lieutenant-Colonel Alley, whose loyalty to his former commander, in spite of their diverging opinions, had won the respect of his compatriots and enhanced his prestige in the country. However, Alley made a solemn undertaking to restore civilian rule. Presidential elections, held on May 7, 1968, were boycotted by 74 per cent of the registered voters, and no candidate emerged with a clear majority. Consequently, on June 28, Alley and his military council appointed Dr Emile Zinsou, a former ambassador to France and former Foreign Minister. It was, as *Le Monde* commented on July 10, a 'situation both tragic and paradoxical', particularly with the presence of three ex-presidents, Maga, Apithy and Ahomadegbé, in Lomé in neighbouring Togo. Zinsou's appointment gave rise to opposition among trade unionists, and led to the creation of a so-called 'National Front for Democracy'. Yet on July 28 a large majority ratified, through a referendum, the army's appointee. Dahomey could not have chosen better: Zinsou is the most respected politician of his country.

In Congo–Brazzaville the army had stayed neutral at the time of Youlou's overthrow in August 1963. The developments which took place then were political in nature, as the country rather unexpectedly re-oriented its sympathies from the 'moderates' to the so-called 'revolutionary' African states. After three years as Prime Minister, Pascal Lissouba offered his resignation on April 28, 1966, 'to resume his university career': it was an outcome of the background struggle going on between the moderate and the more radical Socialists.[28] He was replaced by the secretary of the party, Amboise Noumazalaye, previously Director of Economic Affairs and reputed to be a true pro-Chinese Marxist. Soon afterwards, on June 27, 1966, while the President was away in Tananarive at an OCAM conference, the paratrooper Captain Ngouabi, with several fellow officers and soldiers, attempted a mutiny on the Gabonese pattern. They sought to overthrow the government, and also to express their disapproval of the Cuban military instructors brought in to train the youth groups and the militia, but the Cuban instructors roused the militia and were able to quell the attempted coup.

The situation in Congo–Brazzaville by the end of 1966 was most intricate. The policy of non-alignment was getting nowhere, for the government was not prepared to commit itself in either direction. It turned down proffered help from the United States, and then from the Soviet Union, preferring Chinese experts; later a policy of association with Cuba was adopted, then a minor flirtation with North Vietnam.* Aid from the EDF and the FAC was continued, but experts from France and other foreign countries found their conditions of work very trying. The army had grown

* Several hundred technicians and military instructors are still in the Congo.

suspicious of the regime and had become an opposition to be reckoned with. It maintained a typically conservative outlook and blamed the government for attaching disproportionate importance to the civilian militia. But Ngouabi was a Northerner, and, as had been the case in many African countries, ethnic solidarity appeared as one of the underlying elements of the mutiny. The fear of new tribal uprisings in his favour persuaded the government not to dismiss the rebel Ngouabi from the service and his followers were soon set free. It seemed that the Congolese leaders were watching their step, well aware that any minor incident could bring their downfall, whether it was a fresh outbreak of tribal unrest or the sharply-expressed disaffection of any large social group in face of the scant achievements of the regime. It is significant that in April 1967 President Massemba-Debat pronounced himself against nationalisation, in the face of a motion passed by the one Congolese trade union organisation, and that in January 1968 he decided it was safer to govern alone, dismissing his Prime Minister to demonstrate that he opposed 'any radical Socialisation of the regime'. These steps were taken long after Yvon Bourges, French Secretary of State for Foreign Affairs (in charge of Co-operation), and formerly High Commissioner in Brazzaville, had paid an official visit to Brazzaville in order to relieve the slight strain in Franco–Congolese relations. The government's course through the earlier half of 1968 seemed to be to tack and veer between dangers as they loomed up. Then, in August–September 1968, Massemba-Debat was overthrown; the 1963 constitution was annulled and a National Council of the Revolution was established, with Mariem Ngouabi, who had been promoted to command of the army, as its chairman. He was later nominated President, with Alfred Raoul as Prime Minister.

The pattern of these military coups displays two recurring themes. First, they are never revolutionary in nature: no-one intends to modify the basic structure of the country. Their only purpose is to suppress the ruling regime and its corresponding political party. They play the part of ministerial crises, since the governments in power cannot be called to account or defeated in the so-called national assemblies. They are never the prelude to a spate of massacre and violence, as have been, for instance, the successive coups in Nigeria. Second, the motives of all these military actions are financial and economic. The army deems that the government is mismanaging the country and misusing public money and decides that it is its duty to put a stop to such misdeeds. This is a typical phenomenon of recent years in French-speaking Africa.

Such sudden coups d'état on a tiny scale, without any bloodshed, demonstrate the extreme brittleness of all African institutions, including the one-party system. The parties have had no real impact on the country; the 'social pyramid' of MESAN in the Central African Republic was an idol with feet of clay. The events of December 17, 1967, in Dahomey were even more worrying: the army seemed to be itself disunited and susceptible to pressures from political parties or ethnic groups. Whereas it, at one time, claimed to be the only stable element in a fragile African society in the making, it has proved in the event to be every bit as frail. If this holds true for Dahomey, why couldn't the infection spread elsewhere, to Bangui or Ouagadougou, for instance? Anywhere else 'Young Turks' may rise, and rebel, refusing to accept the yoke of supposedly incompetent elders and using as arguments the inevitably fragile economy and the inevitable dissatisfaction of town wage-earners.

Recent events in the rest of French-speaking Africa—especially in Guinea and Mali—should be mentioned briefly.

At the Eighth Congress of the Parti Démocratique de Guinée, held in September 1967, wisdom and a spirit of compromise seem to have prevailed. The opposition within the PDG and the political bureau, represented by Ismaël Touré, Fodeba Keita and Diallo Safoulaye, has won over the other leaders and induced them to adopt a more realistic outlook to extricate Guinea from its present isolation and to stimulate its economic development. A moderating influence was brought to bear on the pro-Chinese left wing, and its leader, Magassouba Moriba, the Minister of National Education, was compelled to resort to self-criticism in the course of the congress. As the army and police in Guinea tend towards a moderate viewpoint, Guinea may now be on safer ground. As a result of the general elections held on January 1, 1968, Sékou Touré, the only candidate, was re-elected as President of the Republic and a new government covering the major sectors of the economy and society of Guinea has been established, with Diallo Safoulaye and Ismaël Touré as prominent members of it. This means that Sékou Touré has not been brought to task for having at one stage given way to the left wing of the party. The future will tell whether this is merely another clever move of a shrewd and powerful leader or whether a true compromise has been struck between Touré and the more moderate group within his party, for the sake of political stability and the continuity of power.

The future of Guinea in the years to come will depend on several factors: whether American aid (withdrawn completely for 1967–68) will be re-established; whether the agreement signed with American and Canadian companies for the exploitation of the Boké bauxite deposit works successfully (see page 188); how far Russian economic, technical, scientific and cultural co-operation will be extended and increased;* how much relations with its more prosperous neighbours, Senegal, and especially the Ivory Coast, improve in spite of their deep divergences of opinion; and, finally, what sequel will follow from Sékou Touré's appeal to France on November 1, 1967, 'to re-establish relations for the sake and welfare of our two respective countries'. Senghor was intending to plead for Guinea in Abidjan and in Paris. Mauritania and Mali were both supporting his request, for they were the two countries who stood to benefit from a more active co-operation with Guinea, 'in order to promote the activities of the Inter-State Committee for developing the Senegal River Basin'. The Ivory Coast will continue to stand apart from Guinea as long as it remains isolated from the bulk of other French-speaking countries—that is, as

---

* Immediately after the PDG congress, two missions were sent to the USA and the USSR, the former led by Ismaël Touré and the latter by Diallo Safoulaye.

long as its long-standing quarrel with France remains unresolved
—for the resumption of diplomatic relations is of itself only an
empty gesture. General de Gaulle very warily brought up the
subject during a party in November 1967, given in honour of
Soglo. France is still watching to see which way things will turn
out: will the impetuous, but now far more sedate, leader of
Guinea be 'pardoned' at last?

Much to everyone's surprise, a military coup overthrew Modibo
Keita on November 19, 1968. The Malian people, who had seemed
to favour him, made no move in his support; the party, and the
apparently faithful and relatively strong militia, did not react. A
young and unknown group of officers, led by Lieutenant Moussa
Traoré, accomplished the bloodless coup, and established a
temporary semi-military government to run Mali until democratic
elections could be held. Captain Yoro Diakité replaced Keita as
head of state, Traoré preferring to play the role of 'éminence
grise'. Two of Keita's ministers, Jean-Marie Kone and Louis
Nègre, remain in the government, as Minister of Foreign Affairs
and Minister of Finance respectively.

There remain seven French-speaking countries where the
regimes have remained almost unchanged, in spite of temporary
difficulties, mainly because of the moral prestige of an outstanding
leader, wise and shrewd, who carried enough weight to impose his
own political line upon his party, his army and the masses. Yet
which of them can boast he is free from danger and that his regime
is truly stable, considering recent events in countries where a fall
of the ruling regime would have seemed hardly credible, but where
it has now been clearly demonstrated that a tiny group of determined men could be almost certain to succeed in overthrowing the
government? In such conditions, reading into the future appears a
tricky game. Several of those seven countries can rely on the
unstinted support of France, sometimes for sentimental reasons
and sometimes for more weighty economic ones: for instance,
Madagascar would fall into the first category; Gabon (for its
uranium, manganese, etc.), Niger (also for its uranium) and

375

Mauritania* into the second. The Ivory Coast is known to have sound economic foundations and Houphouet-Boigny has a very strong hold on his people—even more so than Senghor, who may encounter difficulties with younger men, eager to assume the reins of government and to transform the Senegalese social structure. However, Senghor was re-elected as President of Senegal in February 1968, receiving about 95 per cent of the votes cast, and he has strengthened his authority through a technical reshuffling of his government. The UPS also achieved a clear-cut victory. The government of Chad, too, is relatively stable, despite the efforts of the opposition and of the Front de Libération du Tchad (FROLINAT).

The key to political stability in the whole of the Third World is steady economic progress that might gradually relieve poverty and at the same time build up a real feeling of national unity, in order to erase as quickly as is feasible—though not too abruptly—all the outward signs of internal dissension and/or tribalism. Whether one likes it or not, whether indeed it should be regarded as the greatest achievement of 'neo-colonialism', in today's French-speaking Africa the Ivory Coast is undoubtedly the most commendable example, all the more as it has no obvious and easily accessible mineral resources. Cameroun might well be selected as the next most successful country of French-speaking Africa; it has reached a position of balance thanks to a soundly diversified economy. Both can serve as an encouragement to all the others—provided their elites do not dissipate the present achievements in wasteful competition for power. Gabon, too, may be cited as an example of achievement since independence, largely as a result of its vast mineral and forestry resources.

However, an intensification of economic and financial assistance from the rest of the world remains an essential requirement for progress, not only to the more favoured African countries but also to the poorer. And, despite some trends which give cause for

---

* Incidentally, Moktar Ould Daddah, the President of Mauritania, is trying to persuade his West African colleagues to form a West African Economic Community to comprise both French- and English-speaking states.

optimism, there remain some terrible doubts about the prospects for Africa. Suppose French-speaking Africa fails to follow—or cannot follow—the lead of the Ivory Coast and Cameroun. Suppose Africa's future should unfold as an endless succession of crises of the kind we have seen in Dahomey, which would soon dissipate the goodwill and exhaust the patience of the countries providing aid to Africa, and encourage them to adopt a European-based insularity.

French bilateral aid to Africa and Madagascar may eventually slacken: past efforts and support are not likely to be as great in the future. African countries and Madagascar may be forced to seek financial assistance from other sources, either bilateral or multilateral. Nevertheless, African policy will remain a 'domaine réservé' (reserved subject) of the Elysée Palace as long as de Gaulle remains head of state of France. He is proud of his decolonisation measures which did not lead to any Congolese or Nigerian disaster. He wishes to keep 'his' states out of any substantial disputes. Yet he becomes most upset and perturbed by these military disturbances, and quickly loses his illusions if he sees too many African states falling into 'pronunciamentos'. As an example of de Gaulle's attitude, it is interesting to note his reactions towards the claims of French Somaliland in 1967. They recall his reactions towards Guinea in 1958. His warnings were the same.

In September 1958, French Somaliland, known as 'Côte Française des Somalis', had agreed to keep its overseas territory status and hence had not become autonomous as had most of the other territories of French-speaking Africa. Many reasons explain the French Somalis' vote during the 1958 referendum: its limited resources, the size of the territory and the French influence, its geographical situation (surrounded by two states, both claiming rights over French Somaliland, not only for strictly political reasons as in the case of Somalia, but also for economic reasons as in the case of Ethiopia, for the railway between Addis Ababa and Djibouti is of utmost importance for the economy of the country). However, when de Gaulle, en route to Cambodia, paid a brief

377

visit to Djibouti, he was welcomed by riots and posters claiming independence. He found himself in the same situation as a few years before in Conakry and Dakar. In fact, the situation was even more tense and hostile. The weaker face of colonial administration became apparent when 500 paratroopers from France were called for and the town divided into sections in order to restore law and order. However, de Gaulle did not lose his head, but reacted as he did in 1958 in Conakry. 'If they want independence they can have it, but they must not expect any help from France. If, on the other hand, after a referendum, they agree to keep their ties with France, we shall do our best to improve the living conditions of the Afar and Issa [the two predominant ethnic groups of the territory], as well as the Somali.' (The Issa and the Somali were, incidentally, more in favour of breaking off relations with France.) Those who wanted to maintain close association with France obtained the majority of votes at the March 1967 referendum, thus avoiding an international crisis, as both Somalia and Ethiopia would have claimed French Somaliland had it become independent.

Today, French Somaliland is called the 'French Territory of the Afars and Issas'—for how long? In this short-lived crisis, the French administration and de Gaulle, who was as ill-informed as he had been in 1958 in Conakry, were beaten by events. The crisis shows that the French government is holding to its policy of giving support and assistance to the countries and territories which 'deserve' it.

In French-speaking Africa, regional groups like the UDEAC, the Conseil de l'Entente, the UMOA or the UDOA, and finally the OCAM, will play, as they already do, a most commendable part, for they stimulate co-operation and encourage the countries to intensify their still very tentative exchanges. They provide a counterpoise to the existing divisions between countries and free the very poor countries, especially those of the savannah belt, from their isolation by association with the coastal countries. However, on a political level, they are, and in the future will still be, faced by serious difficulties, mainly due to the political disturbances in some of the member countries. In the recent Dahomean crisis, however, they

have, for the first time, shown that they are not completely helpless. We have noted that the army seized power in some countries
because it proved to be the only organised force in existence. But
will the armies show sufficient wisdom and restraint not to cling
to power unnecessarily, and to rest content with playing merely an
intermediary role and preparing the way for a new and able
generation free of tribal prejudice?

This changing of the guard is one of the most acute problems in
Africa today. The first generation of African nationalists who
fought for decolonisation and independence are now growing old,
often wearied by the burden of the power they have exerted over
the last decade. The time is now ripe for change, but who will
replace them? In some countries, the next team is likely to be
prepared to succeed to power—for instance, Resampa or
Rabemananjara in Madagascar, and Philippe Yacé in the Ivory
Coast. In others, there seems no obvious successor among the
immediate followers—many African leaders are very isolated.
Undoubtedly, successors will arise. But what will be their action, their
impact? If they believe that 'Africa has had a poor start', will they
not be tempted to accelerate its evolution and completely reorganise the existing political structures, in the hope that, by
Socialising the means of production, they might bring about more
rapidly the social revolution for which they are yearning? The
examples of Guinea and Mali—particularly the former—serve as a
warning that the Socialist solution is no universal panacea in
developing countries, and that, unless they act with considerable
finesse, they may remain isolated from the outside world and find
that the bodies who took on the responsibility for developing their
means of production have abandoned them overnight and left
them stranded.

While there is good reason for believing that 'Socialisation' is
near to the needs and concerns of the people, revolutionary
enthusiasm may well mislead the younger generations. Moreover
a 'radicalisation' of power, such as Guinea has attempted, leads
to great difficulties and frustrations. How can Socialism, based on
non-African models, be established without a strong and genuine

379

proletariat, and with a rural population so isolated within its traditional environment? On the other hand, if the new generation believes that it matters little whether Africa's start is correctly or incorrectly based, that what matters is that it *should* start, with its own meagre resources, limited means and cumbersome inheritance from the past—tribal traditions, colonial habits, inequalities, climatic handicaps, endemic diseases—then they might bring Africa forward. In the process, moreover, they might succeed in introducing a radical bent—that is, to eliminate the anomalies of present-day Africa and its shameful social inequalities. Everybody wants to build an African Socialism, but how can such a Socialism be built when corruption and financial mismanagement prevail?

In this respect, the May 1968 so-called 'Revolution' in France may also have profound repercussions in French-speaking Africa. At the end of May and in early June, there were strikes in Dakar and against the Miferma company in Mauritania; in both cases, they were severely repressed. More important, perhaps, were the students' 'mouvements de contestation' at Dakar University, which were inspired by the same movements as in France and which may lead to further trouble, not only in Dakar but also in other student strongholds such as Abidjan and Douala. Although it is too early to make accurate predictions, it must be remembered that in most French-speaking African countries 40–50 per cent of the population is under 18 years of age (in some cases, that percentage is under 15). These are the people who will make tomorrow's Africa, who will vote, contest, demand. Moreover, many thousands of African students live in France and are influenced by the forceful revolutionary student movements; the lessons of their French comrades will not be forgotten. The French troubles have also reminded African governments of the extent of their dependence on France. When the French government decided to re-establish (temporarily) exchange controls in June 1968, the African governments were forced to follow suit (even if it was to their advantage), and the measures taken in December 1968 to protect the French franc have also had their effect on French-speaking Africa. It may be that over the next few years the African governments will try to loosen themselves as much as possible from French influence.

The destiny of French-speaking Africa, its hope of comparative stability and economic take-off, will depend essentially on how far it can make steady progress, despite its lack of resources, its high rate of population increase, the deficits in its budgets and trade balances, and its dependence on foreign aid. This book has been concerned with showing how far French-speaking Africa has succeeded, since independence, in bettering its lot. In many cases, admittedly, progress has been comparatively limited, since Africa set out effectively from scratch, but in every case it spells hope for the future.

Notes and References

1. GENERAL DE GAULLE AND AFRICA

1. In this connection see a passage from de Gaulle's press conference of April 11, 1961, quoted in André Passeron, *De Gaulle Parle, 1958–1962*, Paris 1962, p. 290.
2. Charles de Gaulle, *Mémoires de Guerre*, Vol. 1, Paris 1959.
3. Georges Cattaui, *Charles de Gaulle, l'homme et son destin*, Paris 1960, pp. 20–1.
4. Ibid.
5. Ibid.
6. Ibid.
7. De Gaulle, op. cit., Vol. 11, pp. 126–82.
8. Ibid., pp. 225–8.
9. Ibid., p. 226.
10. Ibid.
11. Emile Dehon, *Une nouvelle politique coloniale de la France*, Paris 1945.
12. Ibid., preface by General Leclerc.
13. Paul-Marie de la Gorce, *De Gaulle entre deux mondes*, Paris 1964, p. 434.
14. G. Chaffard, *Carnets secrets de la décolonisation*, Paris 1965, chapter on Governor Latrille.
15. De Gaulle, op. cit., Vol. III, p. 302.
16. *Année politique 1958*, Paris 1959; Chaffard, op. cit.
17. Chaffard, op. cit.
18. Ibid.
19. Passeron, op. cit., p. 450.
20. Speech to the representative assembly of Madagascar, quoted in Passeron, op. cit., p. 453.
21. Address at the Félix Eboué Stadium in Brazzaville, ibid., p. 456.
22. Address in Dakar, ibid., p. 461.
23. Ibid.
24. Address to the Representative Assembly in Tananarive, ibid., p. 455.
25. *Année politique 1958*, op. cit.
26. Ibid.
27. See Fernand Gigon, *Guinée, Etat pilote*, Paris 1959.
28. Sékou Touré, *Experience guinéene et unité africaine*, Paris 1961, pp. 81 and 85; text of his speech of August 25, 1958.
29. Ibid., p. 79.
30. See *Année politique 1959* and *1960*, Paris 1960 and 1961.
31. Passeron, op. cit., pp. 465–7.
32. Ibid., p. 471.

382

33. Ibid., p. 466.
34. Alfred Grosser, *La politique extérieure de la Vème République*, Paris 1965, p. 49.
35. Article by Serge Mallet in "Le Deuxième âge du Gaullisme", a special issue of *Esprit*, No. 318, June 1963.

2. THE BIRTH OF THE NEW AFRICAN STATES

1. See Georges Balandier, *Sociologie actuelle de l'Afrique Noire*, Paris 1955.
2. See P. Barnès, *Classe moyenne et communisme en Afrique*, Brussels 1960.
3. Albert Memmi, *Portrait du colonisateur et du colonisé*, Paris 1957, pp. 160–5.
4. Henri Brunschwig, *L'avènement de l'Afrique Noire*, Paris 1953, p. 189.
5. Ibid., pp. 190–1.
6. Aimé Césaire, *Cahiers d'un retour au pays natal*.
7. *Le Monde*, October 11, 1956.
8. See Arslan Humbaraci, *Algeria: A Revolution that Failed*, London and New York 1966.
9. Elie Kedouri, "Nationalism and Politics", in Vera Micheles Dean and Harry Haroutunian, *West and Non-West: An Anthology*, New York 1963.
10. Mamadou Dia, *Nations Africaines et Solidarité Mondiale*, Paris 1960.
11. Frantz Fanon, *The Wretched of the Earth*, London and New York 1965.
12. Thomas Hodgkin, *Nationalism in Colonial Africa*, London 1956; *African Political Parties*, London 1961; with Ruth Schachter, *French-Speaking West Africa in Transition*, New York 1961.
13. *La Documentation Française—Travaux et Recherches*, No. 17, "Situation de la Presse dans les Etats de l'Union Africaine et Malgache, en Guinée, au Mali et au Togo", Paris 1963. This gives interesting information and statistics on both the pre-independence and independent periods.
14. Mamadou Dia, op. cit.
15. Leo Hamon, "Introduction à l'étude des partis politiques de l'Afrique française", in *Revue juridique et politique d'outre-mer*, April–June 1959, October–December 1960, July–September 1961.
16. *Fraternité*, December 11, 1959, quoted by Hamon, op. cit., p. 30.
17. Paul Moussa, *Les chances économiques de la communauté franco-africaine*, Paris 1957, pp. 124–35.
18. See Secrétariat Général du Gouvernement, *La Documentation française: Notes et Etudes documentaires*, Nos. 2994 and 2995, "Les constitutions des Républiques africains et malgache d'expression française", Paris 1963.
19. D. G. Lavroff and G. Peiser, *Les constitutions africaines*, Paris 1961.

20. Jean Buchman, *Le problème des structures politiques en Afrique noire indépendante*, Université Lovanium, Kinshasa, July 1961.
21. Charles de Gaulle, *Les Mémoires de Guerre*, Vol. III, Paris 1959, p. 280.
22. See Secrétariat Général du Gouvernement, No. 2994, op. cit., pp. 9 and 11; Pierre Lampué, "Les constitutions des Etats africains d'expression française", in *Revue juridique et politique d'outre-mer*, October–December 1961.

3. EQUATORIAL AFRICA

1. *Le Monde*, August 15 and 16, 1965.
2. Banque Centrale des Etats de l'Afrique Equatoriale et du Cameroun, *Rapport, d'activités, 1965–1966*.
3. Philippe Decraene, "Le Tchad au bout du monde", *Le Monde*, March 28 and 29, 1967.
4. David E. Gardiner, *Cameroun: United Nations Challenge to French Policy*, London and New York 1963, gives a succinct and accurate account.
5. See article by Philippe Decraene in *Le Monde*, May 31, 1967.
6. Economist Intelligence Unit, *Economic Review of Former French Tropical Africa*, June 30, 1966. See also *Moniteur Africain*, June 28, 1967, according to which very promising signs of oil had been discovered in Western Cameroun in the Bakossi peninsula (Rio del Rey, Guedes).

4. THE ENTENTE STATES

1. Pierre Lampué, "Les groupements d'états africains", in *Revue juridique et politique d'outre-mer*, January–March 1964.
2. Ibid.
3. See Aristide Zolberg, *One Party Government in the Ivory Coast*, Princeton 1964.
4. "La bourgeoisie noire qui s'installe au pouvoir", a leading article in *France-Observateur*, September 3, 1959.
5. Derived from the Economist Intelligence Unit *Annual Supplement, 1964–1966*, and the United Nations *Monthly Bulletin of Statistics*.
6. *Revue des Marchés Tropicaux et Méditerranéens*, October 8, 1966.
7. *Le Moniteur Africain*, June 21, 1967.
8. Ibid., May 17, 1967.
9. *Le Monde*, May 13, 1967.
10. There is a very interesting literature and documentation on the Upper Volta migrant labour: Jean Rouch, *Les Songay*, Presses Universitaires de France, Paris 1954; Jean Rouch, *Migrations au Ghana*, Paris 1956; and a series of articles in the *Revue de l'Institut interafricain du travail* of the Commission de Coopération technique

en Afrique, Vols. VI (1959), VII (1960), VIII (1961) Nos. 1 and 3, and IX (1962) No. 1.
11. *Le Monde*, September 15, 1965.
12. *Le Moniteur Africain*, May 10, 1967.
13. *West Africa*, January 1, 1966, p. 3.
14. See R. Cornevin, *Histoire du Togo*, Paris 1959.
15. *Le Monde*, November 22, 1966.

5. GUINEA

1. Economist Intelligence Unit, March 1968.
2. *Financial Times*, August 27, 1965.
3. See B. Ameillon, *La Guinée, Bilan d'une indépendence*, Paris 1964.
4. *Le Monde*, November 20, 1966.
5. Ibid., October 9, 1966.

6. SENEGAL

1. See *Jeune Afrique*, October 1966, a special issue in honour of President Senghor's sixtieth birthday (including an interview with him). One is struck by the great warmth of his personal message.
2. See William J. Foltz, *From French West Africa to the Mali Federation*, New Haven 1965.
3. See Secrétariat Générale du Gouvernement, *La Documentation française: Notes et Etudes documentaires*, No. 2994, "Les constitutions des Républiques africains et malgache d'expression française", Paris 1963; Pierre Lampué, "Les constitutions des Etats africains d'expression française", in *Revue juridique et politique d'outre-mer*, October–December 1961; D. G. Lavroff, *La République du Sénégal*, Paris 1966.
4. See L. S. Senghor, *Congrès Constitutif du Parti de la Fédération Africaine*, Paris 1959; Mamadou Dia, *Nations Africaines et Solidarité Mondiale*, Paris 1960, p. 90.
5. See Dmitri-Georges Lavroff, *La République du Sénégal*, Paris 1966.
6. See L. V. Thomas, *Le Socialisme et l'Afrique*, Paris 1966.
7. Cf. *Moniteur Africain*, August 2, 1967.
8. *Jeune Afrique* interview with Senghor, op. cit.

7. MAURITANIA

1. Economist Intelligence Unit, *Economic Review of Former French Tropical Africa*, March 31, 1967.
2. *Le Monde*, February 19, 1966.
3. "La Mauritanie: au delà des amitiés Traditionnelles", *Le Mois en Afrique*, No. 16, April 1967.
4. Economist Intelligence Unit, *Economic Review of Former French Tropical Africa*, December 30, 1966.

385

5. Ibid.
6. *Le Monde*, October 28, 1966.

8. MALI

1. See chapter by Thomas Hodgkin and Ruth Schachter Morgenthau, in James S. Coleman and Carl G. Rosberg Jr., *Political Parties and National Integration in Tropical Africa*, Berkeley and Los Angeles 1964.
2. Ibid., p. 376.
3. Ibid., quoting Modibo Keita, *Le Mali en marche*, p. 9.
4. Modibo Keita, *Le Mali continue*.
5. See Samir Amin, *Le Mali, la Guinée et le Ghana: trois expériences africaines de développement*, Paris 1965.
6. Ibid.

9. MADAGASCAR

1. See Hubert Deschamps, *Migrations intérieures à Madagascar*, Berger-Levrault, Paris 1960.
2. See article by Tsiranana in *Jeune Afrique*, November 28, 1966, special issue on Madagascar.
3. Ibid.
4. Ibid.
5. Economist Intelligence Unit, *Economic Review of Former French Tropical Africa*, October 7, 1965.

10. INTER-AFRICAN AND INTERNATIONAL RELATIONS

1. See Jean Louis Quermonne, "Les engagements internationaux des nouveaux etats", in J. B. Duroselle and J. Meyriat, eds., *Les nouveaux Etats dans les relations internationales*, Paris 1962.
2. E.g., Colin Legum, *Pan-Africanism: A Short Political Guide*, rev. edn., London and New York 1965; Philippe Decraene, *Le Pan-africanisme*, Presses Universitaire, Paris 1959; I. William Zartman, *International Relations in the New Africa*, Englewood Cliffs 1966; Arnold Rivkin, *The African Presence in World Affairs*, New York 1963.
3. Thomas Hovet, Jr, *Africa in the United Nations*, Evanston 1963.
4. *La Paix en Algérie par la négociation: la position du Sénégal à l'ONU dans le débat algérien*, official publication of Senegalese government, with a preface by L. S. Senghor, Dakar 1961.
5. *Minutes of the UN General Assembly*, 15th Session, Article 71 of the agenda, Commission I, December 5–15, 1960.
6. Colin Legum, *Congo Disaster*, London 1961.
7. Roger Yves Verbeck, "Le Congo–Léopoldville et l'ancienne Afrique française", in *Le Mois en Afrique*, April 1966.
8. Claude Leclerq, *L'ONU et l'affaire du Congo*, Paris 1964.

9. Legum *Pan-Africanism*, op. cit., p. 198.
10. Jean Ziegler, *La contre-révolution en Afrique*, Paris 1963.
11. Le Centre de Recherche et d'Information Socio-politique (CRISP), *Les cahiers de Gamboma: instructions politiques et militaires aux partisans* (with an introduction by B. Verhaegen), Brussels 1965.
12. *Foreign Report*, May 13, 1965, "France's African Conservatives".
13. Quoted in Jean Halperin, "La politique d'Israel", in J. B. Duroselle and J. Meyriat, eds., *Politiques nationales envers les Jeunes Etats*, Paris 1964.
14. Ibid.
15. Mamadou Dia, *Nations Africaines et Solidarité Mondiale*, Paris 1960.
16. Halperin, op. cit.
17. *Le Monde*, July 4, 1967.
18. Ibid., July 5, 1967.
19. Ibid., July 30, 1967.
20. Ibid., July 2, 1967.
21. Sékou Touré, *L'experience guinéenne et l'unité africaine*, Paris 1961, p. 402.
22. Madera Keita, "La prééminence de l'appareil politique sur l'appareil administratif", in *Présence Africaine* ("Parti unique en Afrique"), No. 30, February–March 1960.
23. Rivkin, op. cit.
24. Zbigniew Brzezinski, *Africa and the Communist World*, Stanford 1963.
25. See Robert Levgold, "Lignes de force de la diplomatic soviétique en Afrique", and Gilbert Comte, "Le marxisme et l'Afrique", both in *Le Mois en Afrique*, No. 15, March 1967.
26. B. Rounov and G. Rubinstein, "Relations économiques soviet-africaines", in ibid.
27. Ibid.
28. See "Difficultés communistes en Afrique Noire", *Le Mois en Afrique*, No. 6, June 1966.
29. *Le Monde*, March 4, 1966.
30. Doudou Thiam (Senegalese Minister of Foreign Affairs), *La politique étrangère des Etats Africains*, Paris 1963.
31. Quoted in Léo Hamon, "Non-engagement et neutralisme des nouveaux Etats", in Duroselle and Meyriat, *Les nouveaux Etats . . .*, op. cit.
32. *Le Monde*, Editorial, November 3, 1965.
33. See W. H. Friedland and C. G. Rosberg, Jr, *African Socialism*, Stanford 1964.
34. *Le Monde*, April 9, 1968.

11. ECONOMIC AND POLITICAL REALITIES

1. Osendé Afana, *L'Economie de l'Ouest Africain: Perspectives de Développement*, Paris 1966.

2. Paul Bairoch, *Diagnostic de l'évolution économique du Tiers Monde, 1900–1966*, Paris 1967, p. 55.
3. See *Revue Partisans*, special issue No. 29–30, May–June 1966, p. 18.
4. See the Statement of M. J. P. Dannaud, Director of Coopération culturelle et technique, published in *Le Monde*, January 19, 1967.
5. Ibid.
6. See F. Bloch-Lainé, J. Chassepot, J. Delbas, etc., *La Zone Franc*, Paris 1956; Ministère d'Etat chargé de la réforme administrative, *Politique de coopération avec les pays en vois de développement (Rapport Jeanneney)*, Paris 1964; "La Zone franc et l'Afrique", *Le Mois en Afrique*, No. 16, April 1967.
7. Ministère de la Coopération, *Cinq ans de fonds d'aide et de coopération, 1959–1964*, Paris 1964.
8. See *Moniteur Africain*, June 7, 1967; and material issued by the Information Centre of Niger, Paris, on the OCAM leaders' viewpoint on the commercialisation of tropical commodities (June 1967), and particularly the memorandum drafted by President Hamani Diori in his capacity as active president of the OCAM, transmitted to the EEC in November 1966.
9. See Pierre Jalée, *Le pillage du Tiers Monde*, Paris 1965; and Bairoch, op. cit.
10. "La Charte d'Alger des pays en voie de développement", in *El Moudjahid*, October 26, 1967.
11. *Rapport Jeanneney*, op. cit., p. 18.
12. Ibid.
13. Ibid.
14. Goran Ohlin, *Réévaluation des politiques d'aide à l'étranger*, OECD, Centre de développement, Paris 1966.
15. Bairoch, op. cit.
16. OECD. *Réévaluation des politiques d'aide à l'étranger*, Paris 1966.
17. L. Dubois, "Le régime présidentiel dans les nouvelles constitutions des Etats africains d'expression française", in *Penant Revue de droit des pays de l'Afrique*, April–May 1962.
18. See Martin L. Kilson, "Authoritarian and Single-Party Tendencies in African Politics", in *World Politics*, Vol. xv, No. 2, January 1963, pp. 262–94.
19. P. F. Gonidec, "L'évolution du syndicalisme en Afrique noire", in *Quarterly Review of Labour Problems in Africa*, bulletin of the Inter-African Labour Institute of the CCTA, May 1963, Vol. x, No. 2, p. 102.
20. ILO, *Africa Labour Survey*, Geneva 1958, p. 266.
21. Pierre Lampué, "Les constitutions des Etats africains d'expression française", in *Revue juridique et politique d'outre-mer*, October–December 1961.
22. Quoted in *Revue Partisans*, special issue No. 29–30, May–June 1966.
23. See William Gutteridge, *Armed Forces in New States*, London 1962;

Morris Janowitz, *The Military in the Political Development of New Nations*, Chicago 1964; H. Daalder, *The Role of the Military in the Emerging Countries*, Paris n.d.

24. See Leo Hamon, *Entretiens de Dijon: le rôle extra-militaire de l'armée dans le Tiers Monde*, Paris 1966.
25. Ibid.
26. W. J. Foltz, "Psychanalyse des armées sub-sahariennes", in *Le Mois en Afrique*, No. 14, special issue named "Les Armées Africaines", February 1967.
27. *Le Monde*, November 17, 1967.
28. *Le Monde*, August 16, 1966.

Select Bibliography

1. REPORTS

Banque Centrale des Etats de l'Afrique de l'Ouest, *Rapport d'activités 1964; Rapport d'activités 1965; Rapport d'activités 1966*

Banque Centrale des Etats de l'Afrique Equatoriale et du Cameroun, *Rapport d'activités 1963–1964; Rapport d'activités 1964–1965; Rapport d'activités 1965–1966*

Caisse Centrale de Coopération Economique, *Rapport Général 1966*

Communauté Economique Européenne, *L'intervention de la CEE dans les pays associés*, by Jacques Ferrandi, Brussels 1962

Commission de Coopération technique en Afrique, *Colloque sur la Jeunesse sans emploi*, Publication 69, Lagos and London 1962

FAO, *Africa Survey: Report on the possibilities of African rural development in relation to economic and social growth*, Rome 1962

OECD, *Geographical Distribution of Financial Flows to Less Developed Countries, 1960–1964*, Paris 1966; *Geographical Distribution of Financial Flows to Less Developed Countries, 1965*, Paris 1967; *Efforts et politiques d'aide au développement, examen 1965*, Paris 1965; *Efforts et politiques d'aide au développement, examen 1966*, Paris 1966; *Efforts et politiques d'aide au développement, examen 1967*, Paris 1967; *Réévaluation des politiques d'aide à l'étranger*, by Goran Ohlin, Paris 1966

ILO, *Africa Labour Survey*, Geneva 1958

Ministère de la Coopération, *Cinq ans de fonds d'aide et de coopération, 1959–1964*, Paris 1964

Ministère d'Etat chargé de la réforme administrative, *La politique de coopération avec les pays en voie de développement* (the report is called '*Jeanneney Report*' with one volume of appendices), La Documentation Française, Paris 1964

Secrétariat Général du Gouvernement, *La Documentation française: Notes et Etudes documentaires*, No. 2530, "Commentaires sur la constitution du 4 octobre 1958 accompagnés du texte intégral de la Constitution", Paris 1959; Nos. 2994 and 2995, "Les Constitutions des Républiques africaines et malgache d'expression française", 2 Vols., Paris 1963; No. 3018, "La législation du travail dans les Etats africains et malgache d'expression française", Paris 1963; No. 2687, "La République islamique de Mauritanie", Paris 1960; No. 2732, "La République du Congo", Paris 1960; No. 2737, "La République Malgache", Paris 1960; No. 2739, "La République du Mali", Paris 1961; No. 2740, "La République du Cameroun", Paris 1961; No. 2754, "La République du Sénégal", Paris 1961; No. 2795, "La République Gabonaise", Paris 1961; No. 3202, "La République de

Guinée", Paris 1965; *La Documentation Française: Travaux et recherches*, No. 17, "Situation de la presse dans les Etats de l'union africaine et malgache, en Guinée, au Mali et au Togo", Paris 1963
United Nations Organisation General Assembly Plenary official records, *General Statements, 16th Session*, December 1961, items 90 and 92 on China; *General Statements, 17th Session*, October 1962, item 92 on China
United Nations Organisation General Assembly, official records, *First Committee, 13th Session*, item 63, The Question of Algeria, September 16 to December 13, 1958; *First Committee, 14th Session*, item 59, The Question of Algeria, November 30 to December 7, 1959; *First Committee, 15th Session*, item 71, The Question of Algeria, December 5 to 15, 1960; *First Committee, 16th Session*, item 80, The Question of Algeria, December 14 to 19, 1961

2. REFERENCE BOOKS, JOURNALS, PERIODICALS, NEWSPAPERS

Année Politique, 1958, Armand Colin, Paris 1959; and the volumes for the years 1959 to 1963, published by Armand Colin in Paris in succeeding years
Année Africaine, 1963, Pédone, Paris 1965; and the volumes for 1964 and 1965, published by Pédone in Paris in 1966 and 1967 respectively
L'Année politique africaine, 1966, Société africaine d'édition, Dakar 1966; *L'Année politique africaine, 1967*, Société africaine d'édition, Dakar 1967
Chronologie politique africaine, Fondation Nationale des Sciences politiques, Centre d'Etudes des Relations internationales, Paris, January–February 1961 to November–December 1966
International Financial Statistics, International Monetary Fund, Washington, February 1968
Etude Monographique de trente et un pays africains, 4 Vols., Union Africaine et Malgache de Coopération économique, Compagnie générale d'Etudes et de recherches pour l'Afrique, Paris 1964
Inventory of Economic Studies concerning Africa South of the Sahara, Joint project No. 4 of the Commission for Technical Co-operation in Africa, Lagos 1962–63

The following periodicals, journals and newspapers have been consulted regularly, supplying a constant flow of news, information and comment:

Le Monde (daily, Paris); *The Times* (daily, London); *The Economist* (weekly, London); *Jeune Afrique* (weekly, Paris); *The Economist Intelligence Unit—Former French Tropical Africa* (quarterly, London); *Le Moniteur Africain* (weekly, Dakar); *Revue des Marchés Tropicaux et Méditerranéens* (weekly, Paris); *Le Mois en Afrique: revue française d'études politiques africaines* (monthly, Dakar-Paris); *Africa 1964–1965–1966*, edited by Richard Kershaw (London); *Quarterly Review of Labour Problems in Africa*, bulletin of the Inter-African Labour Institute

of the Commission for Technical Co-operation in Africa, Brazzaville
1960–64; *Revue Partisans*—special issue "L'Afrique dans l'Epreuve",
No. 29–30, May–June 1966, Maspéro, Paris

3. GENERAL WORKS

Almond, G. A. and Coleman, J. S., *The Politics of the Developing Areas*,
Princeton University Press, Princeton 1960

Anguile, A. G. and David, J. E., *L'Afrique sans frontières*, Paul Bory,
Monaco 1965

Apter, David E., *Political Religion in the New Nations*, and *Ideology and
Discontent*, two duplicated papers, Institute of International Studies,
University of California, Berkeley

d'Arboussier, Gabriel, *L'Afrique vers l'Unité*, Saint Paul, Ivry 1961

Ardant, G., *Le Monde en Friche*, Presses Universitaires, Paris 1959

Balandier, Georges, *Sociologie actuelle de l'Afrique Noire*, Presses
Universitaires, Paris 1955; trans. into English as *The Sociology of Black
Africa*, Deutsch, London 1969; Praeger, New York 1969; *Afrique
Ambigüe*, Plon, Paris 1957

Brunschwig, Henri, *L'avènement de l'Afrique Noire*, Armand Colin,
Paris 1963

Clair, Andrée, *Le Niger, pays à découvrir*, Hachette, Paris 1965

Cornevin, R., *Histoire du Togo*, Berger-Levrault, Paris 1959

Davidson, Basil, *The African Awakening*, Cape, London 1955; *Which
Way Africa?*, Penguin, London 1964

Delavignette, Robert, *L'Afrique Noire française et son destin*, Gallimard,
Paris 1962

Deschamps, Hubert, *Peuples et nations d'outre-mer*, Dalloz, Paris 1954

Deutsch, Karl W. and Foltz, William, *Nation Building*, Atherton Press,
New York 1963

Dumont, René, *L'Afrique noire est mal partie*, Le Seuil, Paris 1962; trans.
into English as *False Start in Africa*, Deutsch, London 1967; Praeger,
New York 1967

Duveau, Georges, *Les instituteurs "Le Temps qui court"*, Le Seuil, Paris
1957

Fanon, Frantz, *Les Damnés de la Terre*, Maspero, Paris 1961; trans. into
English as *The Wretched of the Earth*, Grove, New York 1965; Mac-
Gibbon and Kee, London 1965; *Pour la Révolution Africaine*, Maspero,
Paris 1964

Filese, Teobaldo, *Communismo e Nazionalismo in Africa*, Istituto Italiano
per l'Africa, Rome 1958

Friedland, W. H. and Rosberg, C. G., Jr., *African Socialism*, Stanford
University Press, Stanford 1964

Graft-Johnson, *African Glory*, Praeger, New York 1954

Hodgkin, Thomas, *Nationalism in Colonial Africa*, Frederick Muller,
London 1956

Lacouture, Jean, *Cinq hommes et la France*, Le Seuil, Paris 1961; and
Baumier, Jean, *Le Poids du Tiers Monde*, Arthaud, Paris 1962
Lavroff, Dmitri-Georges, *La République du Sénégal*, Librairie Générale
de droit et de jurisprudence, Paris 1966
Lystad, Robert A., *The African World; A Survey of Social Research*,
Pall Mall, London 1965; Praeger, New York 1965
Mollien, Gaspard Théodore, *L'Afrique occidentale en 1818 vue par un
explorateur français*, Calmann Lévy, Paris 1967
Neres, Philip, *French-Speaking Africa*, Institute of Race Relations,
Oxford University Press, London and New York 1962
Rencontres internationales de Bouaké, *Tradition et modernisme en Afrique
Noire*, Le Seuil, Paris 1965
Richard-Molard, Jacques, *Problèmes humains en Afrique occidentale*,
Présence Africaine, Paris 1958; *Afrique occidentale française*, Berger-
Levrault, Paris 1956
Segal, Ronald, *Political Africa: A Who's Who of Personalities and Parties*,
Stevens, London 1961; Praeger, New York 1961; *African Profiles*,
Penguin, London 1962
Suret-Canale, Jacques, *Afrique Noire*, Vol. I: *Géographie, civilisations,
histoires*, Editions Sociales, Paris 1961; Vol. II: *L'ère coloniale 1900–
1945*, Editions Sociales, Paris 1964
Thomas, L. V., *Le Socialisme et l'Afrique*, 2 Vols., Le Livre Africain,
Paris 1966
Turnbull, Colin, *L'Africain désemparé*, Le Seuil, Paris 1965
Zieglé, Henri, *Afrique Equatoriale Française*, Berger-Levrault, Paris
1952
Ziegler, Jean, *Sociologie de la Nouvelle Afrique*, NRF Idées, Paris 1964

4. CHARLES DE GAULLE AND GAULLISM

Cattaui, Georges, *Charles de Gaulle, l'homme et son destin*, Fayard,
Paris 1960
Chetrit, Timsit, *La "retraite au désert" ou la pensée du Général de Gaulle
de 1946 à 1958*, mémoire de l'Institut d'Etudes Politiques de Paris,
Paris 1962
De Gaulle, Charles, *Les Mémoires de Guerre*, Vol. I: *L'appel 1940–1942;*
Vol. II: *L'Unité 1942–1944;* Vol. III: *Le Salut 1944–1946;* Editions de
Poche, Plon, Paris 1959
Dehon, Emile, *Une nouvelle politique coloniale de la France*, Flammarion,
Paris 1945
Esprit, special issue, No. 318, June 1963, "Le Deuxième âge du
Gaullisme", by Serge Mallet, S. Hoffman etc.
Gorse, Paul Marie de la, *De Gaulle entre deux mondes: Une vie et une
époque*, Fayard, Paris 1964
Grosser, Alfred, *La politique extérieure de la Vème République*, Le Seuil,
Paris 1965
Lacouture, Jean, *De Gaulle (le temps qui court)*, Le Seuil, Paris 1965

Mallet, Serge, *Le Gaullisme et la Gauche*, Le Seuil, Paris 1965
Macridis, Roy C., *De Gaulle: Implacable Ally*, with a foreword by Maurice Duverger, Harper and Row, New York and London 1966
Passeron, André, *De Gaulle Parle des institutions, de l'Algérie, de l'Armée, des Affaires Etrangères, de la Communauté, de l'Economie et des questions sociales, 1958–1962*, Plon, Paris 1962; *De Gaulle Parle, 1962–1966*, Fayard, Paris 1966
Viansson-Ponté, Pierre, *Les Gaullistes*, Le Seuil, Paris 1963
Werth, Alexander, *De Gaulle: A Political Biography*, Penguin, London 1965

5. COLONISATION AND DECOLONISATION

Africanus, *L'Afrique noire devant l'indépendance*, Plon, Paris 1958
Ameillon, B., *La Guinée, Bilan d'une indépendance*, Maspero, Paris 1964
Becker, J. and Sticken, John, *Nationalism and Socialism in Africa*, Iowa State University Press, Ames 1964
Belime, Emile, *Gardons l'Afrique*, Paris 1955
Buchman, Jean, *L'Afrique Noire indépendante*, Librairie Générale de droit et de jurisprudence, Paris 1962
Chaffard, G., *Carnet secrets de la décolonisation*, Calmann Lévy, Paris 1965
Cowan, L. Gray, *The Dilemmas of African Independence*, Walker, New York 1964
Crowder, Michael, *Independence as a Goal in French West African Politics, 1944–1960*, roneotyped manuscript, August 1964
Deschamps, Hubert, *La Communauté française, Evolution politique et juridique*, Institut d'Etudes Politiques, Paris 1961
Giglio, Carlo, *Colonizzazione e decolonizzazione*, Cremona 1964
Gigon, Fernand, *Guinée, Etat pilote*, Plon, Paris 1959
Grimal, Henri, *La décolonisation, 1919–1963*, Armand Colin, Paris 1965
Guerin, D., *Au service des décolonisés, 1930–1953*, Présence Africaine, Paris 1954
Guena, Yves, *Historique de la Communauté*, Fayard, Paris 1962
Harris, Richard, *Independence and After: Revolution in Under-Developed Countries*, Institute of Race Relations, Oxford University Press, London and New York 1962
Hodgkin, T. and Schachter, Ruth, *French Speaking West Africa in Transition*, International Conciliation, Carnegie Endowment for International Peace, New York 1961
Husson, Claude, *Socialisme et décolonisation*, Mémoire de l'Institut d'Etudes Politiques de Paris, 1959
Italiaander, Rolf, *The New Leaders in Africa*, Prentice Hall, Englewood Cliffs 1961
Judd, Peter, *African Independence*, Laurel, New York 1963
La Gravière, *Métropoles et colonies*, Mémoire Institut d'Etudes Politiques, Paris 1955

Lafon, Monique, *Recueil de texte le Parti communiste français dans la lutte contre le colonialisme*, Editions Sociales, Paris 1962

Lavergne, R., *Une révolution dans la politique coloniale de la France*, Paris 1948

Memmi, Albert, *Portrait du colonisateur et du colonisé*, Buchet-Chastel, Paris 1957

Milcent, Ernest, *L'AOF entre en scène*, Edition du Témoignage chrétien, Paris 1958

Pepy, Daniel, *Les Etats africains et leurs problèmes*, Cours pour l'Institut d'Etudes Politiques de l'Université de Paris, 1964–65

Post, Ken, *The New States of West Africa*, Penguin, London 1964

Roland, Oliver, *The Dawn of African History*, Oxford University Press, London and New York 1961

Rous, Jean, *Chronique de la décolonisation*, Présence Africaine, Paris 1965

Sartre, J. P., *Situation V, Colonialisme et anti-colonialisme*, Gallimard, Paris 1964

Touré, Sékou, *La Guinée et l'émancipation africaine*, Présence Africaine, Paris 1959; *Expérience guinéenne et unité africaine*, Présence Africaine, Paris 1961

6. INSTITUTIONS

Aurillac, Michel, "Les institutions sénégalaises", in *Revue juridique et politique*, January–March 1964

Blanchet, A., *L'itinéraire des partis africains depuis Bamako*, Plon, Paris 1958

Boyon, Jacques, "Pouvoir et autorité en Afrique Noire", in *Revue française de sciences politiques*, Vol. XIII, No. 4, December 1963

Buchman, Jean, *Le problème des structures politiques en Afrique noire indépendante*, Université Lovanium IRES, Notes et Documents No. 20/SPI, Kinshasa, July 1961 (roneotyped)

Bulletin de la Commission internationale des juristes, October 1962: "L'Opposition en Afrique tropicale"

Coleman, James S. and Rosberg, Carl G., Jr., *Political Parties and National Integration in Tropical Africa*, University of California Press, Berkeley 1964

Cornevin, R., "Evolution des chefferies dans l'Afrique Noire", in *Penant revue de droit des pays de l'Afrique*, September–October 1961

Centre de Recherche et d'Information Socio-Politiques (CRISP), *Les cahiers de Gambona, instructions politiques et militaires des partisans congolais (1964–1965)*, Brussels 1965

Currie, D. P., *Federalism and New Nations of Africa*, Chicago University Press, Chicago 1964

Daalder, H., *The Role of the Military in the Emerging Countries*, collection Institut d'Etudes Politiques de Paris, no publisher, no date

Diop, Mahjmout, *Contribution à l'étude des problèmes politiques en Afrique Noire*, Présence Africaine, Paris 1958

Dubouis, L., "Le régime présidentiel dans les nouvelles constitutions des Etats africains d'expression française", in *Penant revue de droit des pays de l'Afrique*, April–May 1962

Foltz, William J., *From French West Africa to the Mali Federation*, Yale University Press, New Haven 1965

Fortes, Meyer and Evans Pritchard, E. E., *Systèmes politiques africains*, Presses Universitaires, Paris 1964

Gonidec, P. E., *Constitutions des Etats de la Communauté*, Sirey, Paris 1959

Grosser, Alfred, "Le parti unique africain", in *Preuves*, July 1962

Guillemin, P., "La structure des premiers gouvernements locaux en Afrique Noire", in *Revue Française de Sciences politiques*, September 1959

Gutteridge, William, *Armed Forces in the New States*, Institute of Race Relations, Oxford University Press, London and New York 1962

Hamon, Léo, "Introduction à l'étude des partis politiques de l'Afrique française" in *Revue juridique et politique d'outre-mer*, April–June 1959, October–December 1960, July–September 1961; *Entretiens de Dijon: le rôle extra-militaire de l'armée dans le Tiers-Monde*, Presses Universitaires, Paris 1966

Herskovits, M. J., *The Human Factor in Changing Africa*, Knopf, New York 1962

Hodgkin, Thomas, *African Political Parties*, Penguin, London 1961

Hunter, Guy, *The New Societies of Tropical Africa*, Oxford University Press, London 1962; Praeger, New York 1964

Janowitz, Morris, *The Military in the Political Development of New Nations*, University of Chicago Press, Chicago and London 1964

Jennings, Sir Ivor, *Democracy in Africa*, Cambridge University Press, London 1963

Jouhaud, Yves, "La nouvelle constitution de la République du Congo", and "La nouvelle constitution de la République du Dahomey", in *Revue juridique et politique*, January–March 1964

Kilson, Martin L., "Authoritarian and Single-Party Tendencies in African Politics", in *World Politics*, Vol. xv, No. 2, January 1963

Keita, Madera, "La prééminence de l'appareil politique sur l'appareil administratif", in *Présence Africaine*, No. 30, February–March 1960

Laqueur, Walter, "Communism and Nationalism in Tropical Africa", in *Foreign Affairs*, July 1961, p. 610

Le Cornec, Jacques, *Histoire politique du Tchad de 1900 à 1962*, Librairie générale de droit et de jurisprudence: Bibliothèque constitutionnelle et de science politique, Vol. iv, Paris 1963

Lewis, W. Arthur, *La chose publique en Afrique occidentale*, Futuribles, Paris 1966

Ly, Abdoulaye, *Mercenaires Noirs*, Présence Africaine, Paris 1957

Lampué, Pierre, "Les constitutions des Etats africains d'expression française", in *Revue juridique et politique d'outre-mer*, October–

December 1961; "Les groupements d'états africains", in *Revue juridique et politique d'outre-mer*, January–March 1964

Lavroff, D. G. and Peiser, G., *Les constitutions africaines*, Pedone, Paris 1961

Milcent, Ernest, "Forces et idées forces en Afrique occidentale", in *Afrique Documents*, May 1960

Schachter, Ruth, "Single party systems in West Africa", in *The American Political Science Review*, Vol. LV, No. 2, June 1961

Spiro, Herbert J., "New Constitutional Forms in Africa", in *World Politics*, Vol. XIII, October 1961

Senghor, L. S., *Congrès Constitutif du Parti de la Fédération Africaine*, Présence Africaine, Paris 1959

Seurin, Jean Louis, "La démocratie en Afrique noire", in *Revue de l'Action Populaire*, Paris, June 1960, p. 691

Sy Seydou Madani, *Recherches sur l'exercice du pouvoir politique en Afrique Noire (Côte d'Ivoire, Guinée, Mali)*, Pedone, Paris 1965

Tixier, Gilbert, "Les Etats du Conseil de l'Entente", in *Penant revue de droit des pays de l'Afrique*, No. 686, April–May 1961

"Union des Républiques d'Afrique Centrale", in *Revue Europe Outre-mer*, No. 366, July 11, 1960

Wood, David, *The Armed Forces of African States*, Institute for Strategic Studies, Adelphi Papers, No. 27, April 1966

Zolberg, Aristide, "L'école africaine de la démocratie", in *Preuves*, December 1962; *One Party Government in the Ivory Coast*, Princeton University Press, Princeton 1964

7. ECONOMIC AND SOCIAL STRUCTURES

Afana, Osendé, *L'Economie de l'Ouest Africain: Perspectives de Développement*, Maspero, Paris 1966

Amin, Samir, *Le Mali, la Guinée et le Ghana: trois expériences africaines de développement*, Presses Universitaires, Le Tiers Monde, Paris 1965

Bairoch, Paul, *Diagnostic de l'évolution économique du Tiers Monde, 1900–1966*, Gauthier-Villars, Paris 1967

Barbé, Raymond, *Les classes sociales en Afrique Noire*, Economie et politique, Paris 1964

Barnès, P., *Classe moyenne et communisme en Afrique*, Les Cahiers Africains, No. 3, Editions Créations de Presse, Brussels 1960

Berg, Elliot J., "The Economic Basis of Political Choice in French West Africa", in *The American Political Science Review*, Vol. LIV, No. 2, June 1960

Bloch-Lainé, F., Chassepot, J., Delbas, J., etc., *La Zone Franc*, Presses Universitaires, Paris 1956

Bovy, *Le Mouvement syndical ouest-africain*, CEDESA, Brussels 1965

Cahiers pédagogiques No. 49, *Enseignement et civilisation en Afrique Noire*, Paris, September 1964

Centre de documentation et de diffusion des industries, des mines et de l'énergie outre-mer, *L'homme africain face à ses responsabilités techniques*, Paris 1964

Chauleur, Pierre, "Les plans de modernisation de l'Afrique noire et de Madagascar", in *Revue juridique et politique*, January–March 1964

Chardonnet, Jean, *L'industrialisation de l'Afrique*, Droz, Paris 1956

Compagnie Française d'Afrique Occidentale, *Rapports des Assemblées générales, 1947–1948; 1957–1958; 1960–1961; 1964–1965*

Compagnie Lyonnaise de Madagascar, *Rapports des Assemblées Générales, 1949–1950; 1957–1958; 1960–1961; 1963–1964*

Conflits de génération, Bibliothèque de Prospective, Presses Universitaires, Paris 1963, Chapter 1: "Les conflits de génération en Afrique au Sud du Sahara"

Davies, Ioan, *African Trade Unions*, Penguin, London 1966

Debono, René, "De la zone franc à une nouvelle zone dans le cadre de la CEE?", in *Développements et civilisations*, No. 32, December 1967

Decoster, S. and Gloris, P., *Ascension sociale et enseignement dans les Etats et dans les territoires de l'Afrique moyenne*, Brussels 1963

Diop, Cheik Anta, *Les fondements culturels, techniques et industriels d'un futur état fédéral*, Présence Africaine, Paris 1960

La Fédération syndicale mondiale et l'Afrique, Fédération Syndicale Mondiale, La Ferté Bernard 1961

Fonds d'investissement pour le développement économique et social, *1948–1958—A Decade of Progress*, Paris 1959

Hardy, Georges, *Une enquête morale: L'enseignement en A.O.F.*, Paris 1917

Husson, G., *Les investissements privés au Gabon*, Mémoire de l'Institut d'Etudes Politiques de Paris, Paris 1964

Institut d'Etude du Développement Economique et Social, *Investissements publics, 1946–1960*, Paris 1964

Jalée, Pierre, *Le pillage du Tiers Monde*, Maspero, Paris 1965

Kamarck, Andrew M., *The Economics of African Development*, Praeger, New York 1967; Pall Mall, London 1967

Kilson, Martin C., "Social Forces in West African Political Development", in *Journal of Human Relations*, special issue, Spring–Summer 1960, Wilberforce, Ohio

Kitchen, Helen, *The Educated African*, Praeger, New York 1962

Lacharrière, Guy de, *Commerce extérieur et sous-développement*, Presses Universitaires, Paris 1964

Lapierre, René, *Investissements publics et privés en AEF*, Mémoire de l'Institut d'Etudes Politiques de Paris, Paris 1960

Lewis, L. J., *Education and Political Independence in Africa*, Nelson, London 1962

Masson, Paul, *L'aide bilatérale*, Presses Universitaires, Etudes de Tiers Monde, Paris 1967

Meynaud, Jean and Salah-Bey, Anisse, *Le syndicalisme africain*, Payot, Paris 1963; trans. into English as *Trade Unionism in Africa*, Methuen, London 1968

Moussa, Paul, *Les chances économiques de la communauté franco-africaine*, Armand Colin (Cahiers de la fondation nationale des sciences politiques), Paris 1957; *Les Nations prolétaires*, Presses Universitaires, Paris 1959

November, András, *L'Evolution du mouvement syndical en Afrique occidentale*, Mouton, Paris 1965

Paulme, Denise, *Femmes d'Afrique Noire*, Mouton, Paris 1960

Pechiney, *Rapports des Assemblées Générales, 1955–1956; 1958–1959; 1960–1961; 1962–1963; 1964–1965*

Perroux, François, *L'Economie des Jeunes Nations*, Presses Universitaires, Paris 1962

Charles Peyrissac, *Rapports des Assemblées Générales: 1957–1958; 1959–1960; 1963–1964*

Société commerciale de l'Ouest Africain, *Rapports des assemblées générales: 1957–1958; 1960–1961; 1963–1964; 1964–1965*

Société des pétroles d'Afrique équatoriale, *Rapports des assemblées générales: 1957–1958; 1960–1961; 1962–1963; 1964–1965*

Touré, Sékou, *Congrès Général de l'Union Générale des Travailleurs de l'Afrique Noire*, Présence Africaine, Paris 1959

UNESCO, *Bulletin international des Sciences Sociales*, Vol. VIII, No. 3, "Les Elites africaines", 1956

Vinay, Bernard, "Les conditions d'un marché commun africain existent-elles?", in *Penant revue de droit des pays d'Afrique*, April–May–June 1965 and July–August–September 1965

8. International Affairs

Alwan, Mohamed, *Algeria Before the United Nations*, Robert Speller, New York 1959

Brzezinski, Zbigniew, *Africa and the Communist World*, Hoover Institute on War, Revolution and Peace, Stanford University Press, Stanford 1963

Conte, Arthur, *Bandoung, tournant de l'histoire*, Laffont, Paris 1965

Dean, Vera Micheles and Harootunian, Harry, *West and Non-West: an Anthology*, Holt, Rinehart and Winston, New York 1963

Decraene, Philippe, *Le Panafricanisme*, Presses Universitaires, Paris 1959

Dia, Mamadou, *Nations Africaines et Solidarité Mondiale*, Presses Universitaires, Paris 1960; trans. into English as *African Nations and World Solidarity*, Praeger, New York 1962

Dinant, Georges, *L'ONU face à la crise congolaise*, Brussels 1961

Duroselle, J. B. and Meyriat, J., *Les nouveaux Etats dans les relations internationales*, Armand Colin (Cahiers de la Fondation Nationale des Sciences politiques), Paris 1962; *Politiques nationales envers les Jeunes Etats*, Armand Colin (Cahiers de la Fondation Nationale des Sciences politiques), Paris 1964

Gardiner, David E., *Cameroun: United Nations Challenge to French Policy*, Institute of Race Relations, Oxford University Press, London and New York 1963

Hovet, Thomas, Jr., *Africa in the United Nations*, Northwestern University Press, Evanston 1963

Humbaraci, Arslan, *Algeria: a Revolution that Failed*, Pall Mall, London 1966; Praeger, New York 1966

Leclercq, Claude, *L'ONU et l'Affaire du Congo*, Payot, Paris 1964

Legum, Colin, *Congo Disaster*, Penguin, London 1960; *Pan-Africanism, A Short Political Guide*, revised edition, Pall Mall, London 1965; Praeger, New York 1965

La Paix en Algérie par la négociation: la position du Sénégal à l'ONU dans le débat algérien, official publication of the Senegalese government, with a preface by L. S. Senghor, Dakar 1961

Martin, L. W., *Neutralism and Non-Alignment*, Praeger, New York and London 1962

Morison, David, *The USSR and Africa 1945–1963*, Institute of Race Relations, Oxford University Press, London and New York 1964

O'Brien, William, *The New Nations in International Law and Diplomacy*, Institute of World Polity, Georgetown University, Washington DC 1965; Stevens, London 1965

Queuille, Pierre, *L'Histoire de l'Afro-Asiatisme*, Payot, Paris 1965

Rivkin, Arnold, *The African Presence in World Affairs*, Free Press of Glencoe, New York 1963

Rouch, Jane, *En Cage avec Lumumba*, Editions du Temps, Paris 1961

Thiam, Doudou, *La politique étrangère des Etats Africains*, Presses Universitaires, Paris 1963

Zartman, I. William, *International Relations in the New Africa*, Prentice Hall, Englewood Cliffs 1966

Ziegler, Jean, *La Contre-révolution en Afrique*, Payot, Paris 1963

Index

Note: For Congo-Brazzaville (former French Congo), the abbreviation Congo-B. is used; for Congo-Kinshasa (former Belgian Congo, later known as Congo-Léopoldville), the abbreviation Congo-K. is used.

401